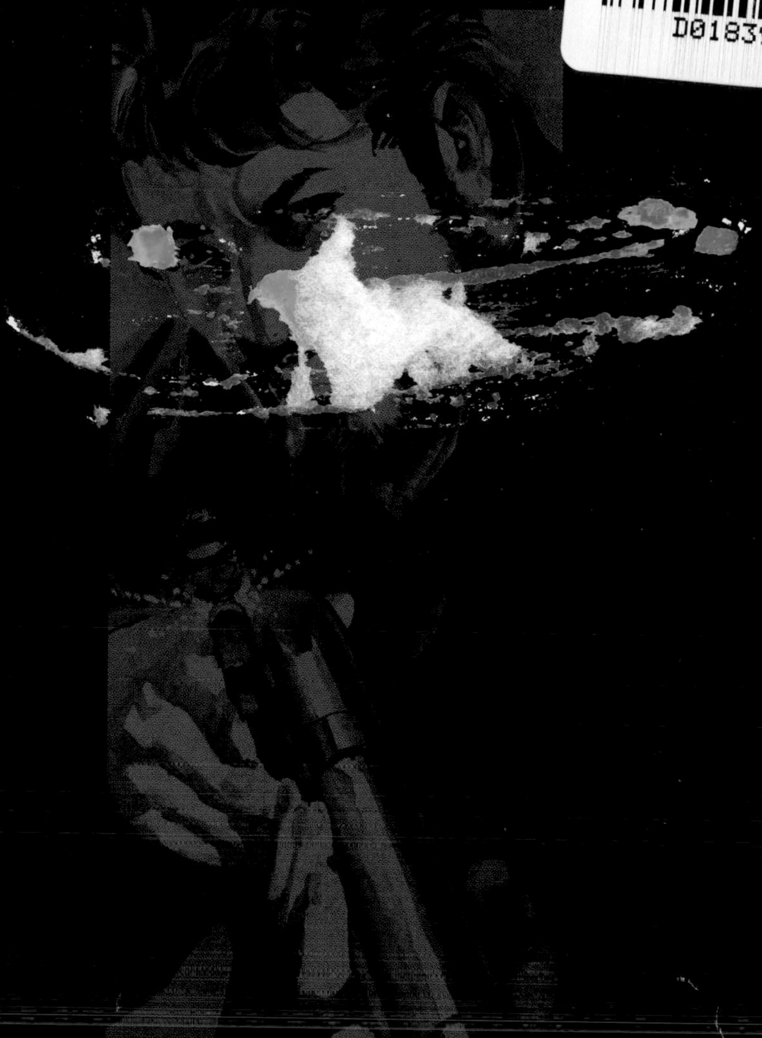

NIKOLAI DANTE

HERO OF THE REVOLUTION

NIKOLAI DANTE CREATED BY ROBBIE MORRISON AND SIMON FRASER

NIKOLAI DANTE

HERO OF THE REVOLUTION

ROBBIE MORRISON
Writer

JOHN BURNS ★ SIMON FRASER
Artists

SIMON FRASER
Cover Artist

Creative Director and CEO: Jason Kingsley
Chief Technical Officer: Chris Kingsley
2000 AD Editor in Chief: Matt Smith
Graphic Novels Editor: Keith Richardson
Graphic Design: Simon Parr & Luke Preece
Reprographics: Kathryn Symes
PR: Michael Molcher
Original Commissioning Editor: Matt Smith

Published by Rebellion, Riverside House, Osney Mead, Oxford OX2 0ES, UK
www.rebellion.co.uk

ISBN: 978-1-907992-22-3
Printed in Malta by Gutenberg Press
Manufactured in the EU by LPPS Ltd., Wellingborough NN8 3PJ, UK.
First Printing: July 2011
10 9 8 7 6 5 4 3 2 1

Printed on FSC Accredited Paper

A CIP catalogue record for this book is available from the British Library.

For information on other *2000 AD* graphic novels, or if you have any comments on this book, please email books@2000ADonline.com

To find out more about *2000 AD*, visit www.2000ADonline.com

DATA DOWNLOAD

Name: Nikolai Dante: the Hero of Rudinshtein.

Status: Rogue, brigand and adventurer.

Location: After the last Revolution, many of the old Soviet states and nations lay in ruins. But from the ashes the Mafiya Clans rose, remaking themselves as aristocratic dynasties. Vladimir the Conqueror emerged as leader of the most powerful house, the Makarovs, and appointed himself Tsar of All the Russias. This brave new world mixes aliens and anachronisms, with bio weapons and shapeshifters as common as Imperial concubines and noble duels. Nothing is ever as it seems.

Backstory: Nikolai Dante was the bastard offspring of infamous female pirate Katarina Dante and Dmitri Romanov, the vicious patriarch of the Romanov Dynasty. After a decade of fending for himself as a thief and adventurer, Dante bonded with a Romanov Weapons Crest. This gave him special abilities (see Weaponry) and he joined the ranks of the Romanovs.

The streetwise swashbuckler was given his own province to command, Rudinshtein, poorest of the Romanov territories. Dante turned this to his advantage by rescuing his citizens from brutal invaders. This earned him the title Hero of Rudinshtein — the first Romanov ruler to be celebrated by his subjects.
Soundbite: "I'm too cool to kill!"

Weaponry: Dante's Weapons Crest is a highly sophisticated battle computer, which enables him to extend cyberorganic 'swords' from his hands and enhances his natural healing abilities. The Crest is also dutybound to educate its host in the ways of the aristocracy and mould him into a potential ruler of the universe.

The Huntsman 5000 is an alien firearm coded to Dante's geneprint. Ammunition is created internally and replenished automatically. When targeted and fired, shells instantaneously adapt into the most effective means of terminating the enemy — whoever or whatever they may be...

Status Report: After witnessing Vladimir the Conqueror's destruction of Manhattan, Dante attempts to assassinate the ruthless Tsar, but is stopped by the Lord Protector who is revealed to be Konstantin Romanov, the evil half brother Nikolai thought he had killed!

Jena Makarov decides to switch sides and rescues Dante from the imperial dungeons. The reunited lovers set about raising a revolutionary army, so that they can finally oppose the Tsar and free the empire from his tyrannical grip...

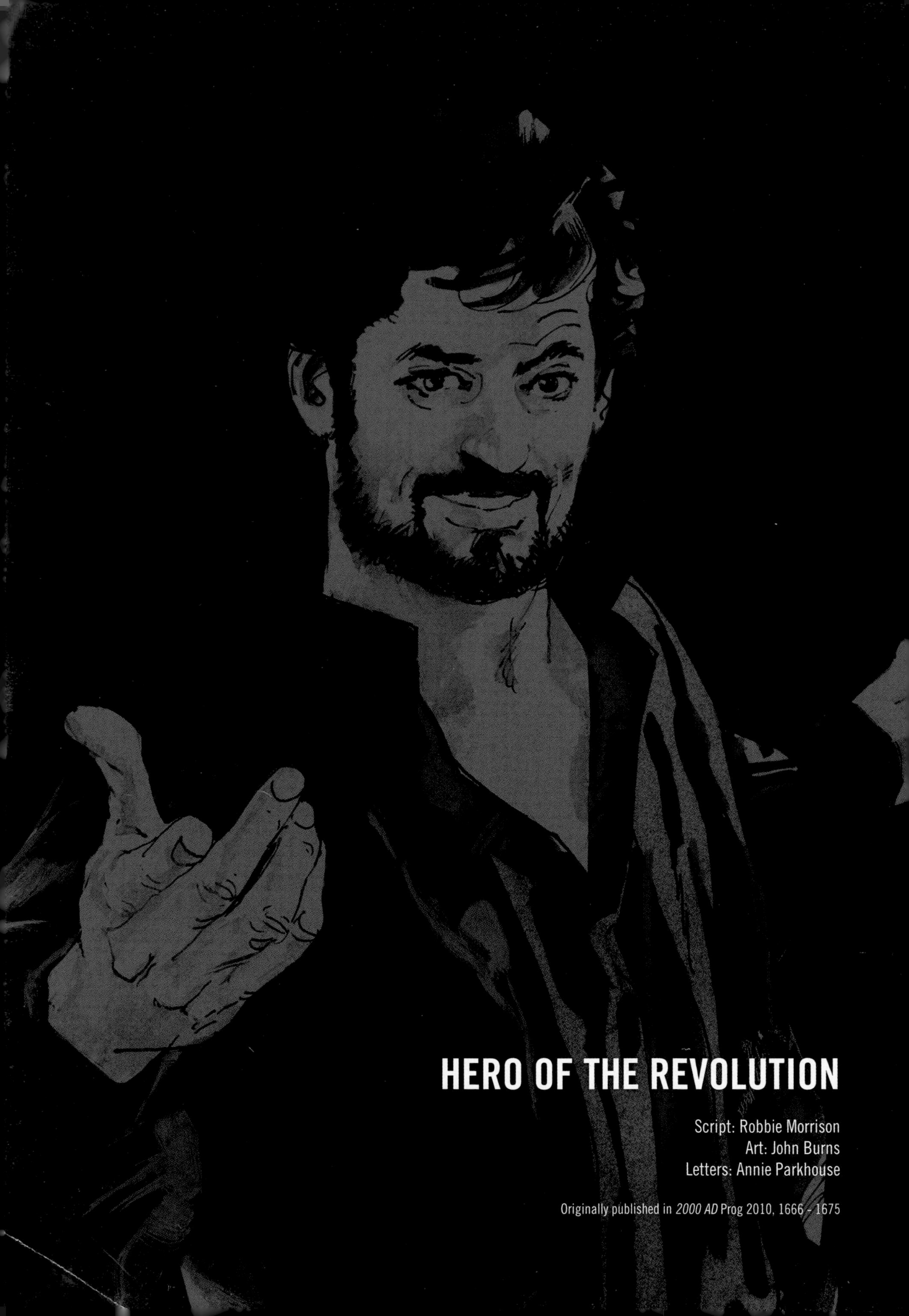

HERO OF THE REVOLUTION

Script: Robbie Morrison
Art: John Burns
Letters: Annie Parkhouse

Originally published in *2000 AD* Prog 2010, 1666 - 1675

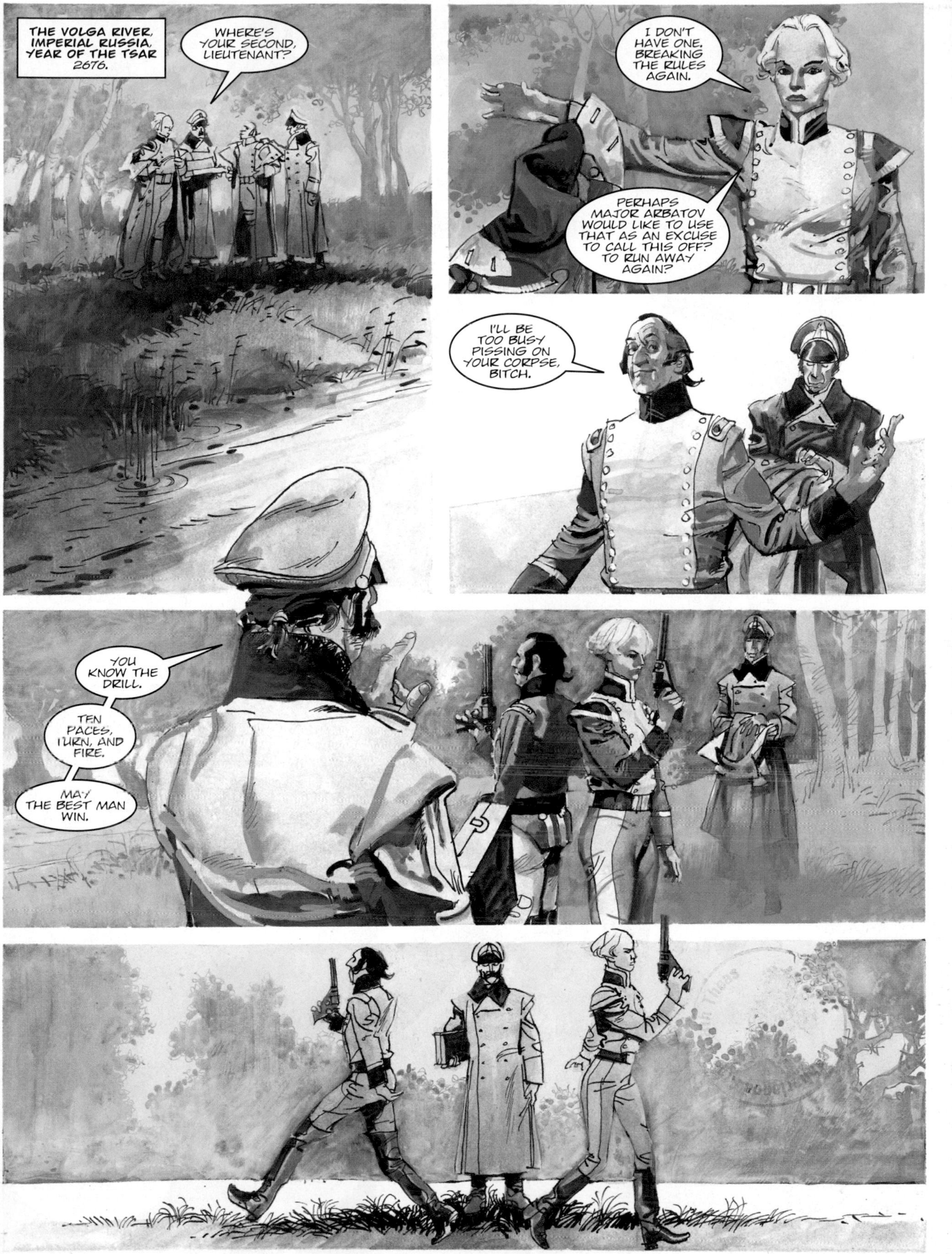
THE VOLGA RIVER, IMPERIAL RUSSIA, YEAR OF THE TSAR 2676.
WHERE'S YOUR SECOND, LIEUTENANT?
I DON'T HAVE ONE. BREAKING THE RULES AGAIN.
PERHAPS MAJOR ARBATOV WOULD LIKE TO USE THAT AS AN EXCUSE TO CALL THIS OFF? TO RUN AWAY AGAIN?
I'LL BE TOO BUSY PISSING ON YOUR CORPSE, BITCH.
YOU KNOW THE DRILL.
TEN PACES, TURN, AND FIRE.
MAY THE BEST MAN WIN.

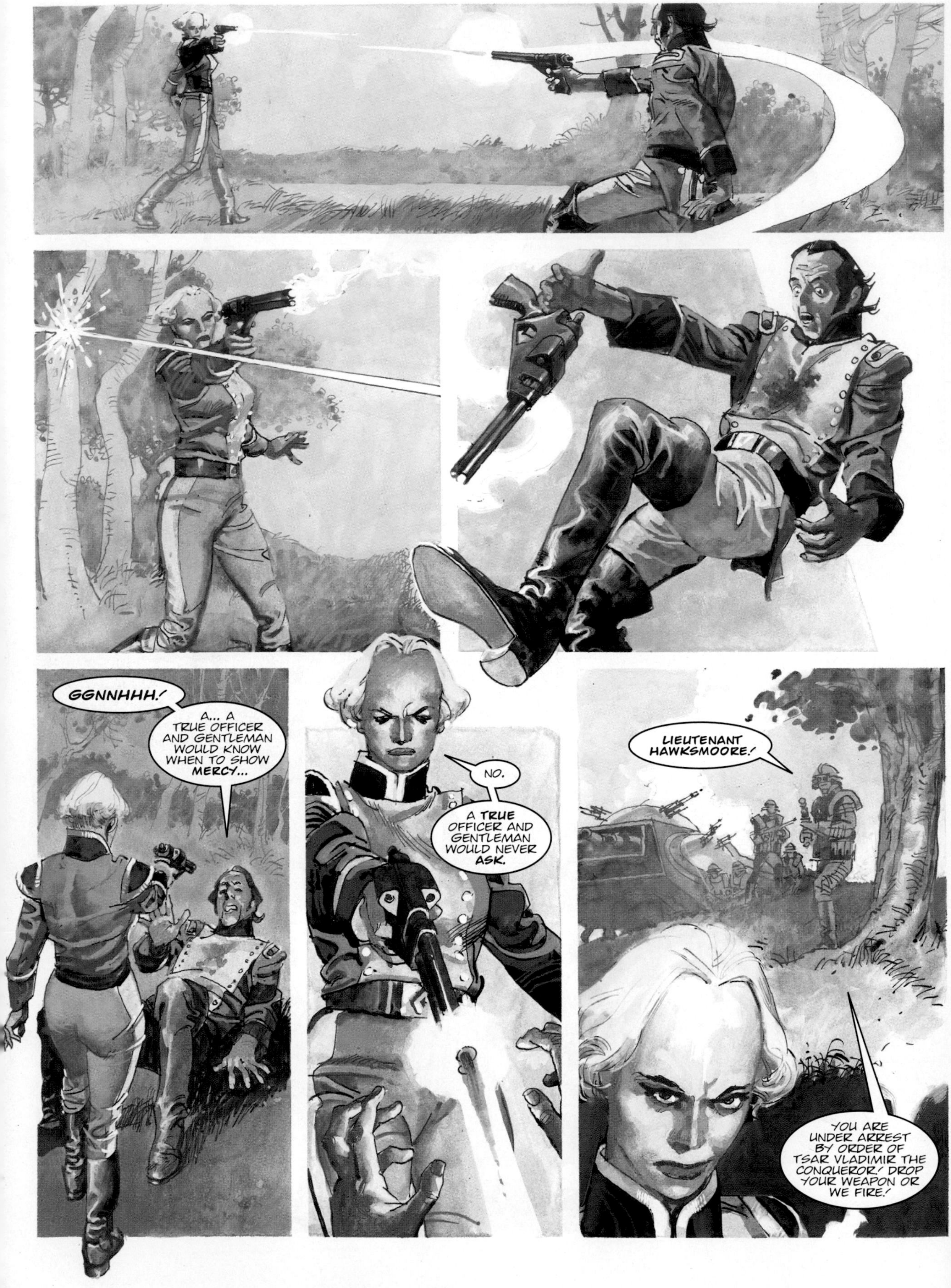
GGNNHHH!
A... A TRUE OFFICER AND GENTLEMAN WOULD KNOW WHEN TO SHOW MERCY...
NO.
A TRUE OFFICER AND GENTLEMAN WOULD NEVER ASK.
LIEUTENANT HAWKSMOORE!
YOU ARE UNDER ARREST BY ORDER OF TSAR VLADIMIR THE CONQUEROR! DROP YOUR WEAPON OR WE FIRE!

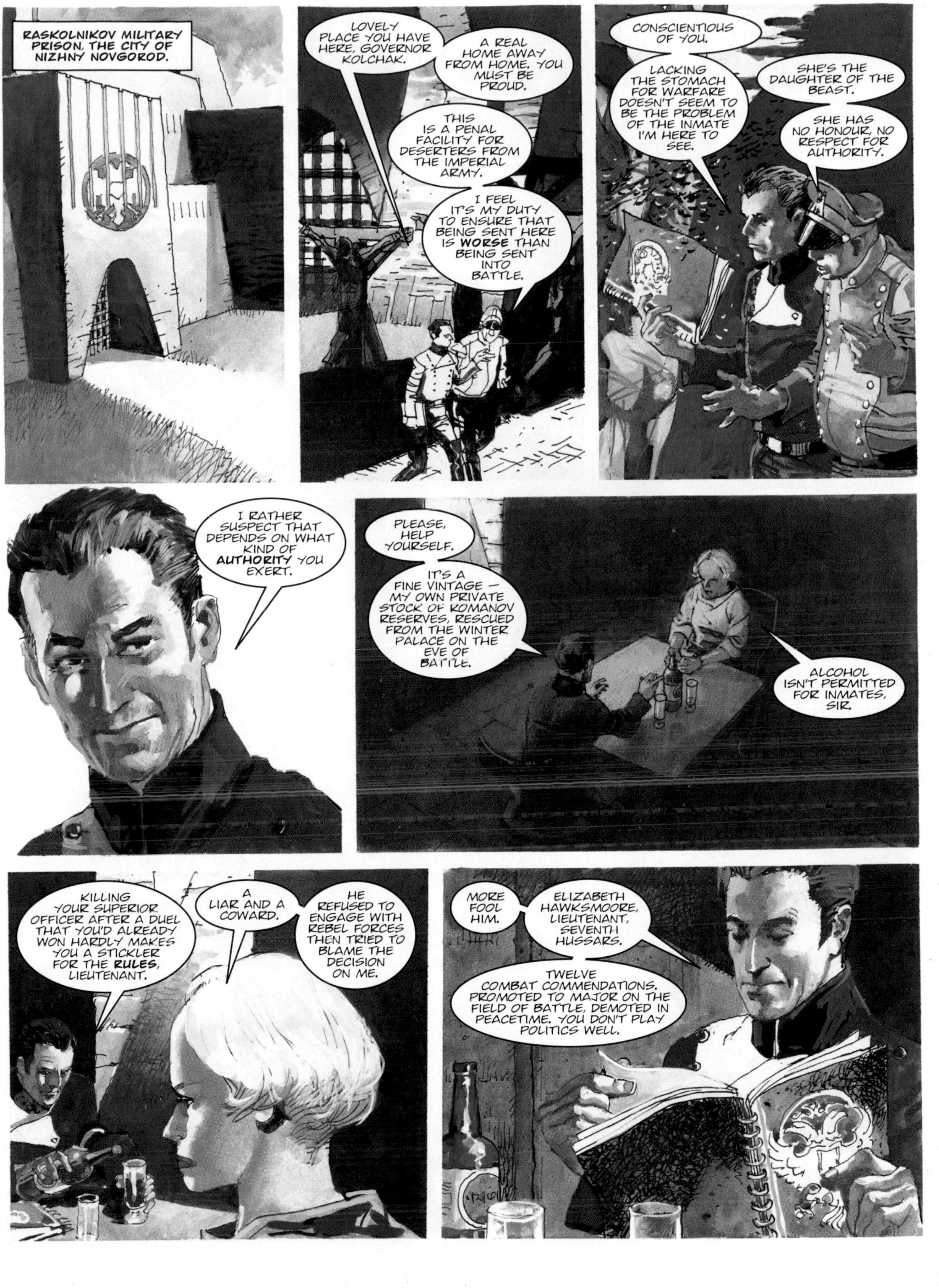
RASKOLNIKOV MILITARY PRISON, THE CITY OF NIZHNY NOVGOROD.
LOVELY PLACE YOU HAVE HERE, GOVERNOR KOLCHAK.
A REAL HOME AWAY FROM HOME. YOU MUST BE PROUD.
THIS IS A PENAL FACILITY FOR DESERTERS FROM THE IMPERIAL ARMY.
I FEEL IT'S MY DUTY TO ENSURE THAT BEING SENT HERE IS WORSE THAN BEING SENT INTO BATTLE.
CONSCIENTIOUS OF YOU.
LACKING THE STOMACH FOR WARFARE DOESN'T SEEM TO BE THE PROBLEM OF THE INMATE I'M HERE TO SEE.
SHE'S THE DAUGHTER OF THE BEAST.
SHE HAS NO HONOUR, NO RESPECT FOR AUTHORITY.
I RATHER SUSPECT THAT DEPENDS ON WHAT KIND OF AUTHORITY YOU EXERT.
PLEASE, HELP YOURSELF.
IT'S A FINE VINTAGE — MY OWN PRIVATE STOCK OF KOMANOV RESERVES, RESCUED FROM THE WINTER PALACE ON THE EVE OF BATTLE.
ALCOHOL ISN'T PERMITTED FOR INMATES, SIR.
KILLING YOUR SUPERIOR OFFICER AFTER A DUEL THAT YOU'D ALREADY WON HARDLY MAKES YOU A STICKLER FOR THE RULES, LIEUTENANT.
A LIAR AND A COWARD.
HE REFUSED TO ENGAGE WITH REBEL FORCES THEN TRIED TO BLAME THE DECISION ON ME.
MORE FOOL HIM.
ELIZABETH HAWKSMOORE, LIEUTENANT, SEVENTH HUSSARS.
TWELVE COMBAT COMMENDATIONS. PROMOTED TO MAJOR ON THE FIELD OF BATTLE, DEMOTED IN PEACETIME. YOU DON'T PLAY POLITICS WELL.

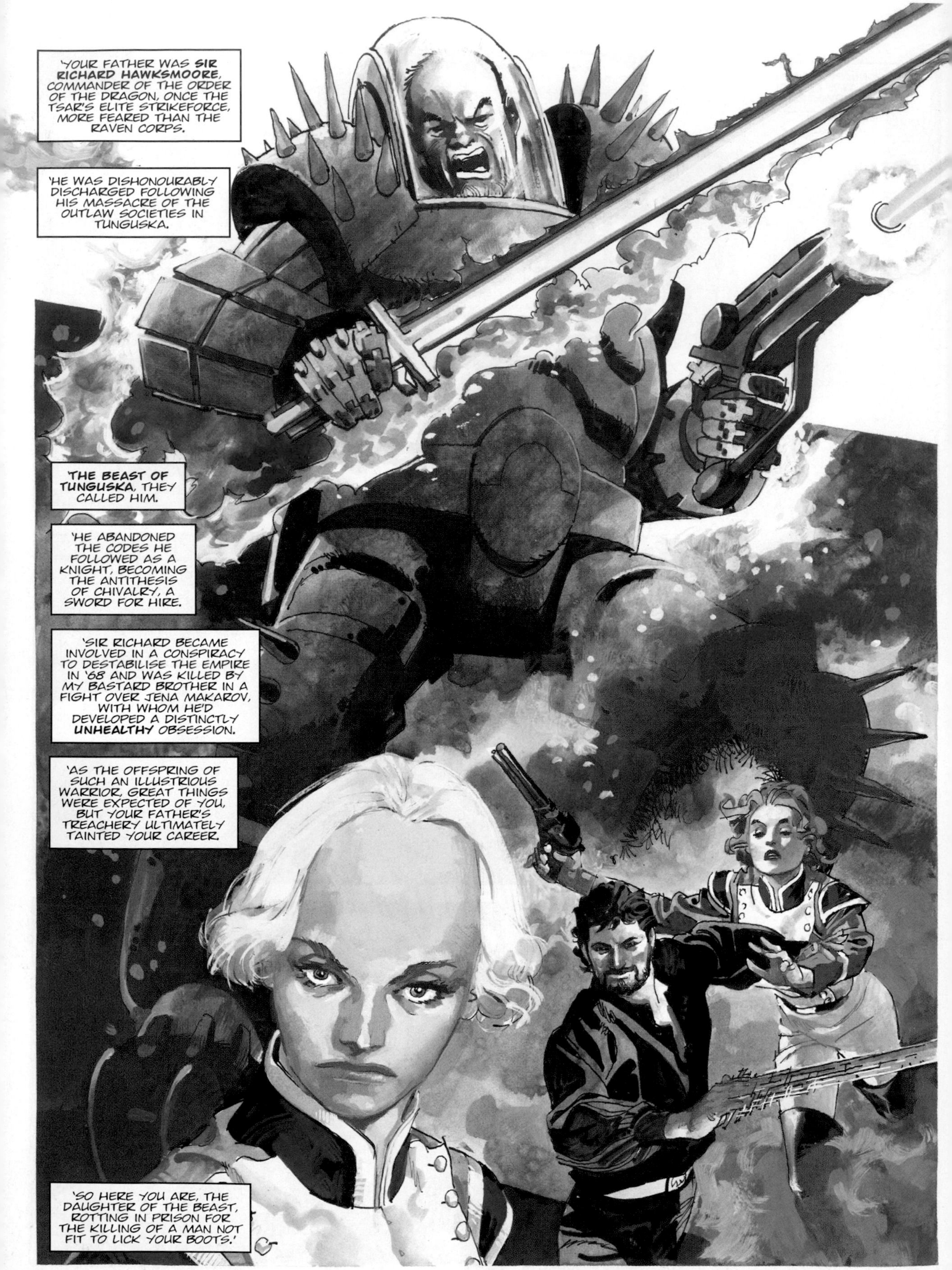
'YOUR FATHER WAS SIR RICHARD HAWKSMOORE, COMMANDER OF THE ORDER OF THE DRAGON, ONCE THE TSAR'S ELITE STRIKEFORCE, MORE FEARED THAN THE RAVEN CORPS.
'HE WAS DISHONOURABLY DISCHARGED FOLLOWING HIS MASSACRE OF THE OUTLAW SOCIETIES IN TUNGUSKA.
'THE BEAST OF TUNGUSKA, THEY CALLED HIM.
'HE ABANDONED THE CODES HE FOLLOWED AS A KNIGHT, BECOMING THE ANTITHESIS OF CHIVALRY, A SWORD FOR HIRE.
'SIR RICHARD BECAME INVOLVED IN A CONSPIRACY TO DESTABILISE THE EMPIRE IN '68 AND WAS KILLED BY MY BASTARD BROTHER IN A FIGHT OVER JENA MAKAROV, WITH WHOM HE'D DEVELOPED A DISTINCTLY UNHEALTHY OBSESSION.
'AS THE OFFSPRING OF SUCH AN ILLUSTRIOUS WARRIOR, GREAT THINGS WERE EXPECTED OF YOU, BUT YOUR FATHER'S TREACHERY ULTIMATELY TAINTED YOUR CAREER.
'SO HERE YOU ARE, THE DAUGHTER OF THE BEAST, ROTTING IN PRISON FOR THE KILLING OF A MAN NOT FIT TO LICK YOUR BOOTS.'

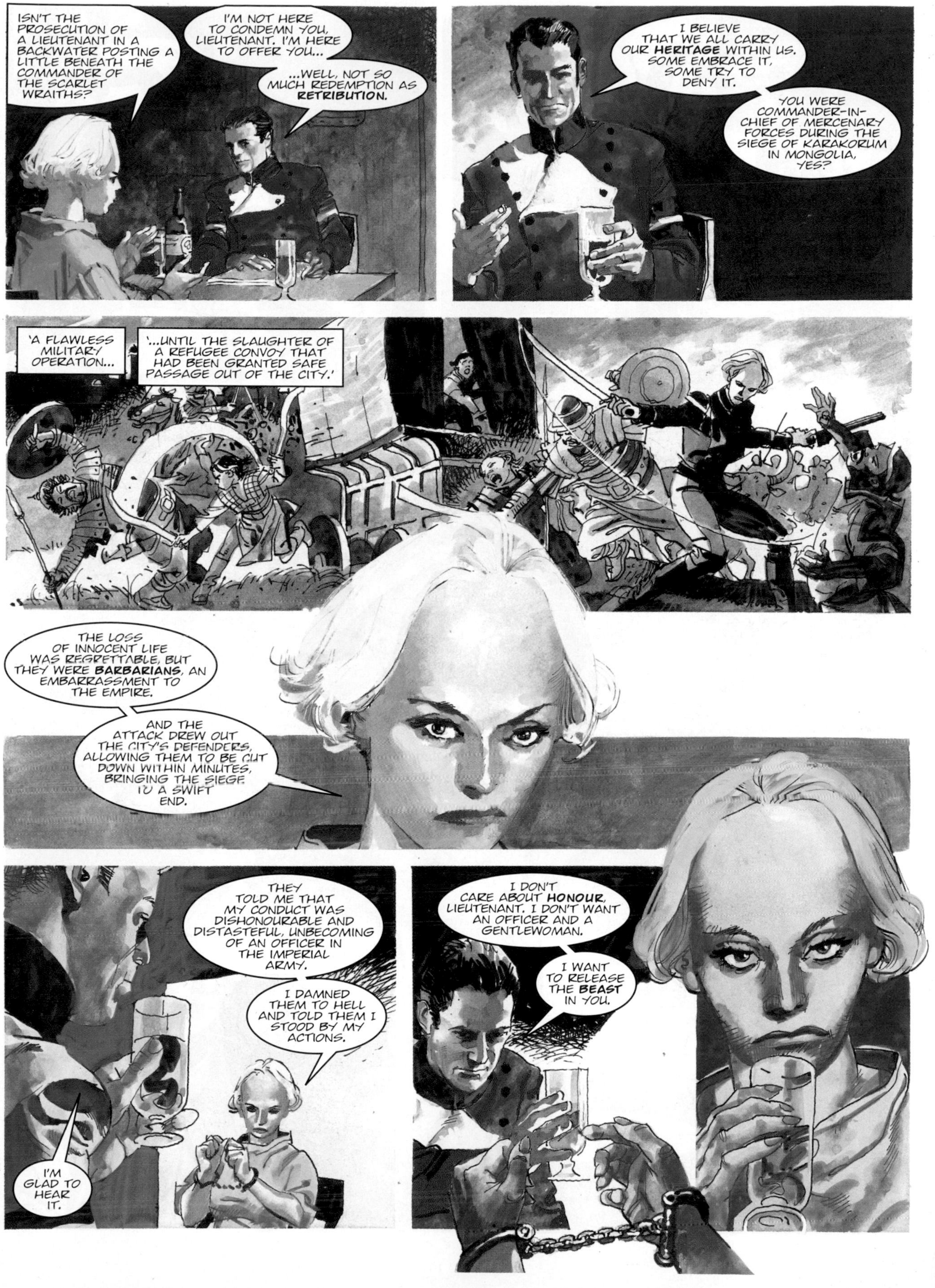

ISN'T THE PROSECUTION OF A LIEUTENANT IN A BACKWATER POSTING A LITTLE BENEATH THE COMMANDER OF THE SCARLET WRAITHS?
I'M NOT HERE TO CONDEMN YOU, LIEUTENANT. I'M HERE TO OFFER YOU...
...WELL, NOT SO MUCH REDEMPTION AS **RETRIBUTION.**
I BELIEVE THAT WE ALL CARRY OUR **HERITAGE** WITHIN US. SOME EMBRACE IT, SOME TRY TO DENY IT.
YOU WERE COMMANDER-IN-CHIEF OF MERCENARY FORCES DURING THE SIEGE OF KARAKORUM IN MONGOLIA, YES?
'A FLAWLESS MILITARY OPERATION...
'...UNTIL THE SLAUGHTER OF A REFUGEE CONVOY THAT HAD BEEN GRANTED SAFE PASSAGE OUT OF THE CITY.'
THE LOSS OF INNOCENT LIFE WAS REGRETTABLE, BUT THEY WERE **BARBARIANS**, AN EMBARRASSMENT TO THE EMPIRE.
AND THE ATTACK DREW OUT THE CITY'S DEFENDERS, ALLOWING THEM TO BE CUT DOWN WITHIN MINUTES, BRINGING THE SIEGE TO A SWIFT END.
THEY TOLD ME THAT MY CONDUCT WAS DISHONOURABLE AND DISTASTEFUL, UNBECOMING OF AN OFFICER IN THE IMPERIAL ARMY.
I DAMNED THEM TO HELL AND TOLD THEM I STOOD BY MY ACTIONS.
I'M GLAD TO HEAR IT.
I DON'T CARE ABOUT **HONOUR**, LIEUTENANT. I DON'T WANT AN OFFICER AND A GENTLEWOMAN.
I WANT TO RELEASE THE **BEAST** IN YOU.

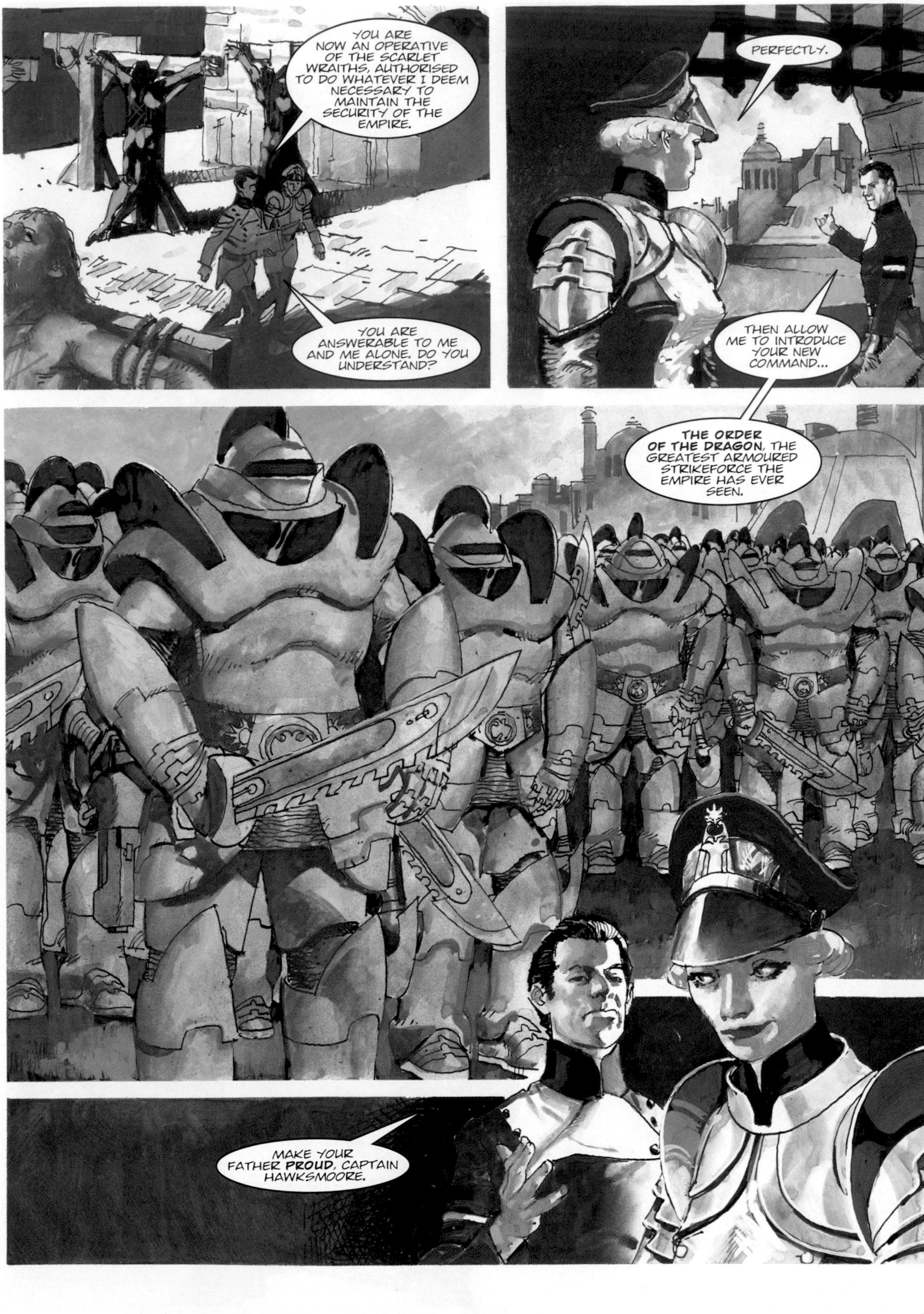
YOU ARE NOW AN OPERATIVE OF THE SCARLET WRAITHS, AUTHORISED TO DO WHATEVER I DEEM NECESSARY TO MAINTAIN THE SECURITY OF THE EMPIRE.
YOU ARE ANSWERABLE TO ME AND ME ALONE. DO YOU UNDERSTAND?
PERFECTLY.
THEN ALLOW ME TO INTRODUCE YOUR NEW COMMAND...
THE ORDER OF THE DRAGON, THE GREATEST ARMOURED STRIKEFORCE THE EMPIRE HAS EVER SEEN.
MAKE YOUR FATHER PROUD, CAPTAIN HAWKSMOORE.

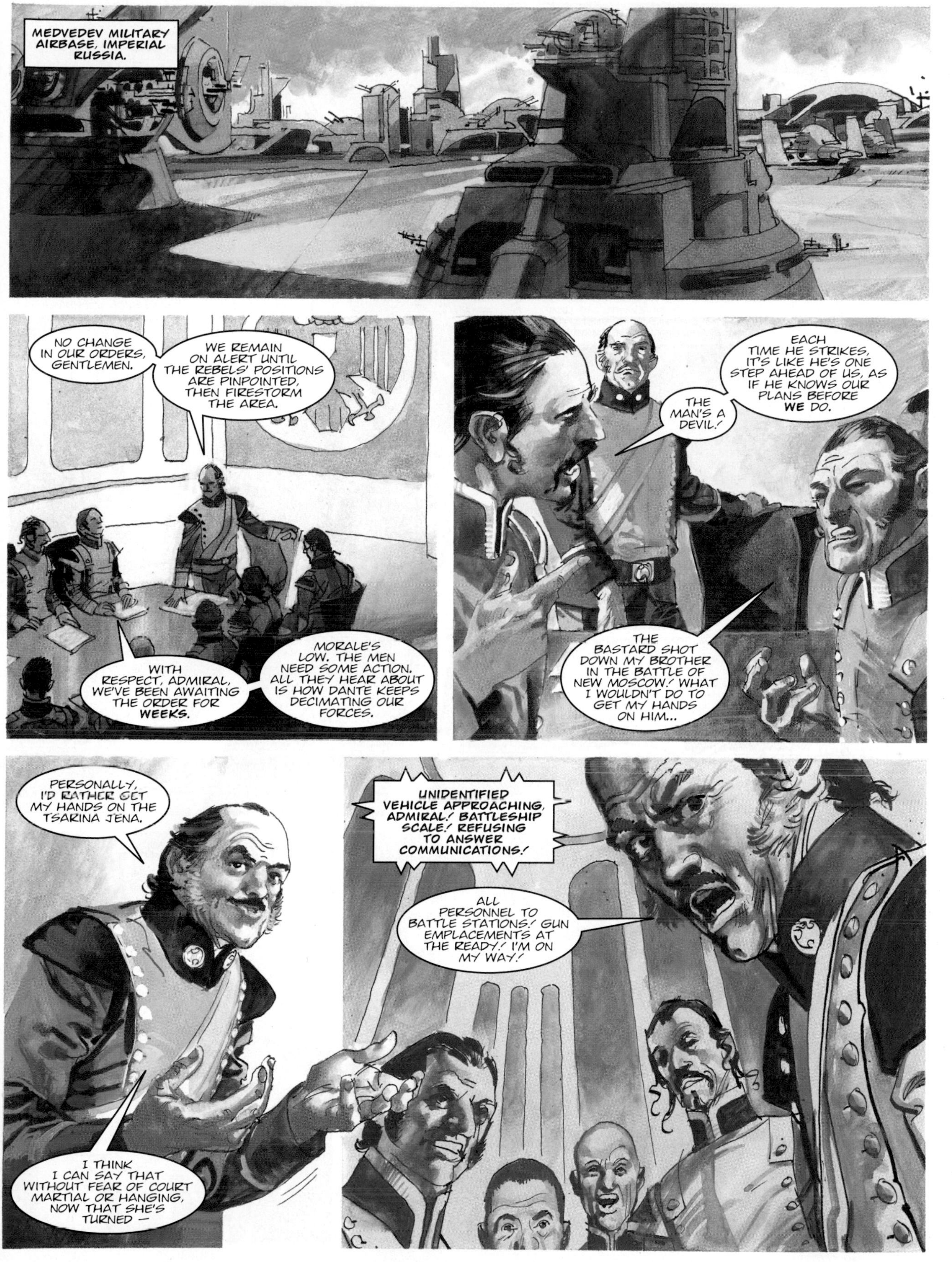
MEDVEDEV MILITARY AIRBASE, IMPERIAL RUSSIA.
NO CHANGE IN OUR ORDERS, GENTLEMEN.
WE REMAIN ON ALERT UNTIL THE REBELS' POSITIONS ARE PINPOINTED, THEN FIRESTORM THE AREA.
WITH RESPECT, ADMIRAL, WE'VE BEEN AWAITING THE ORDER FOR **WEEKS**.
MORALE'S LOW. THE MEN NEED SOME ACTION. ALL THEY HEAR ABOUT IS HOW DANTE KEEPS DECIMATING OUR FORCES.
THE MAN'S A DEVIL!
EACH TIME HE STRIKES, IT'S LIKE HE'S ONE STEP AHEAD OF US, AS IF HE KNOWS OUR PLANS BEFORE **WE** DO.
THE BASTARD SHOT DOWN MY BROTHER IN THE BATTLE OF NEW MOSCOW! WHAT I WOULDN'T DO TO GET MY HANDS ON HIM...
PERSONALLY, I'D RATHER GET MY HANDS ON THE TSARINA JENA.
I THINK I CAN SAY THAT WITHOUT FEAR OF COURT MARTIAL OR HANGING, NOW THAT SHE'S TURNED —
UNIDENTIFIED VEHICLE APPROACHING, ADMIRAL! BATTLESHIP SCALE! REFUSING TO ANSWER COMMUNICATIONS!
ALL PERSONNEL TO BATTLE STATIONS! GUN EMPLACEMENTS AT THE READY! I'M ON MY WAY!

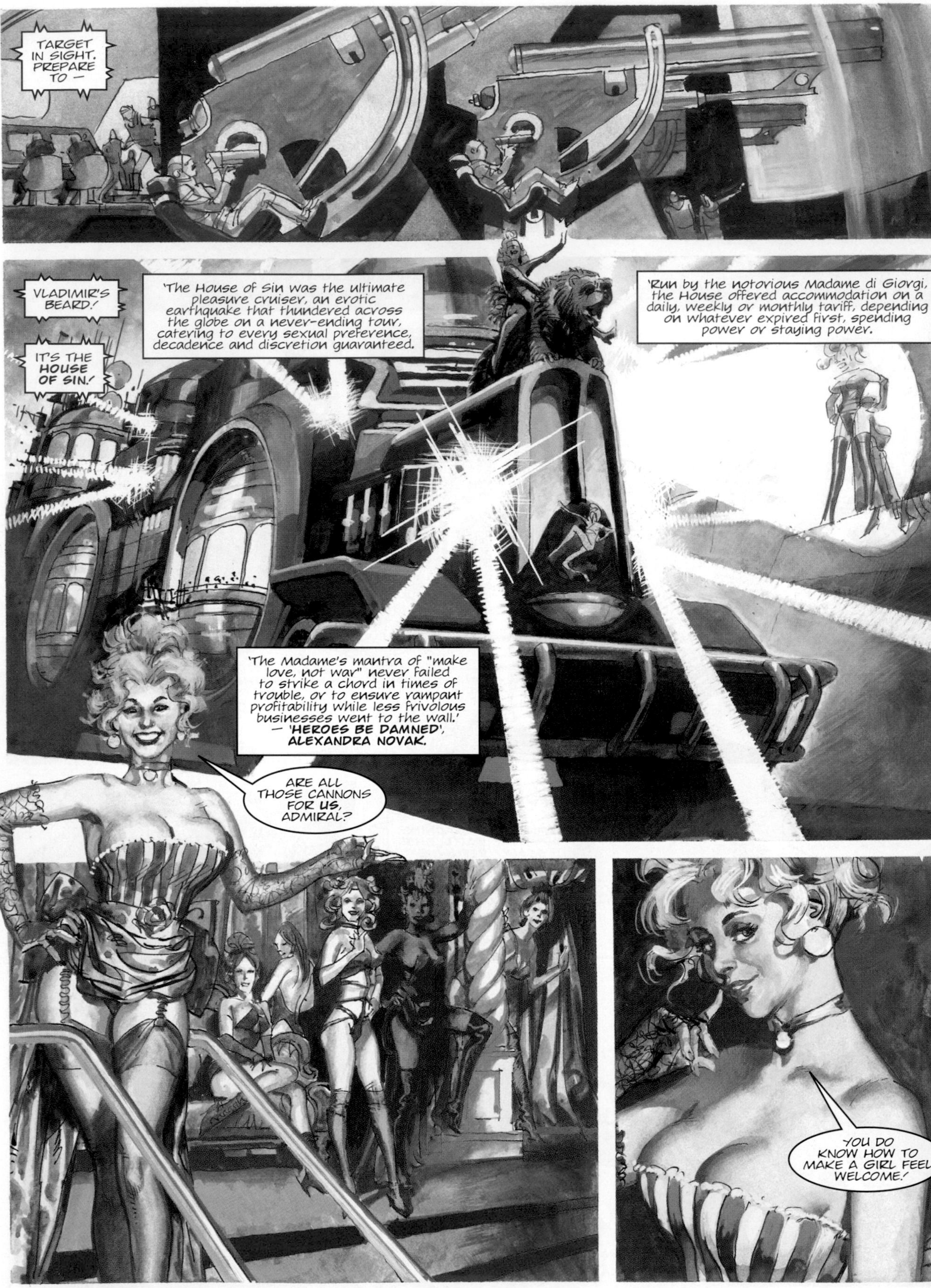

TARGET IN SIGHT. PREPARE TO —
VLADIMIR'S BEARD!
IT'S THE HOUSE OF SIN!
'The House of Sin was the ultimate pleasure cruiser, an erotic earthquake that thundered across the globe on a never-ending tour, catering to every sexual preference, decadence and discretion guaranteed.
'Run by the notorious Madame di Giorgi, the House offered accommodation on a daily, weekly or monthly tariff, depending on whatever expired first, spending power or staying power.
'The Madame's mantra of "make love, not war" never failed to strike a chord in times of trouble, or to ensure rampant profitability while less frivolous businesses went to the wall.' — 'HEROES BE DAMNED', ALEXANDRA NOVAK.
ARE ALL THOSE CANNONS FOR US, ADMIRAL?
YOU DO KNOW HOW TO MAKE A GIRL FEEL WELCOME!

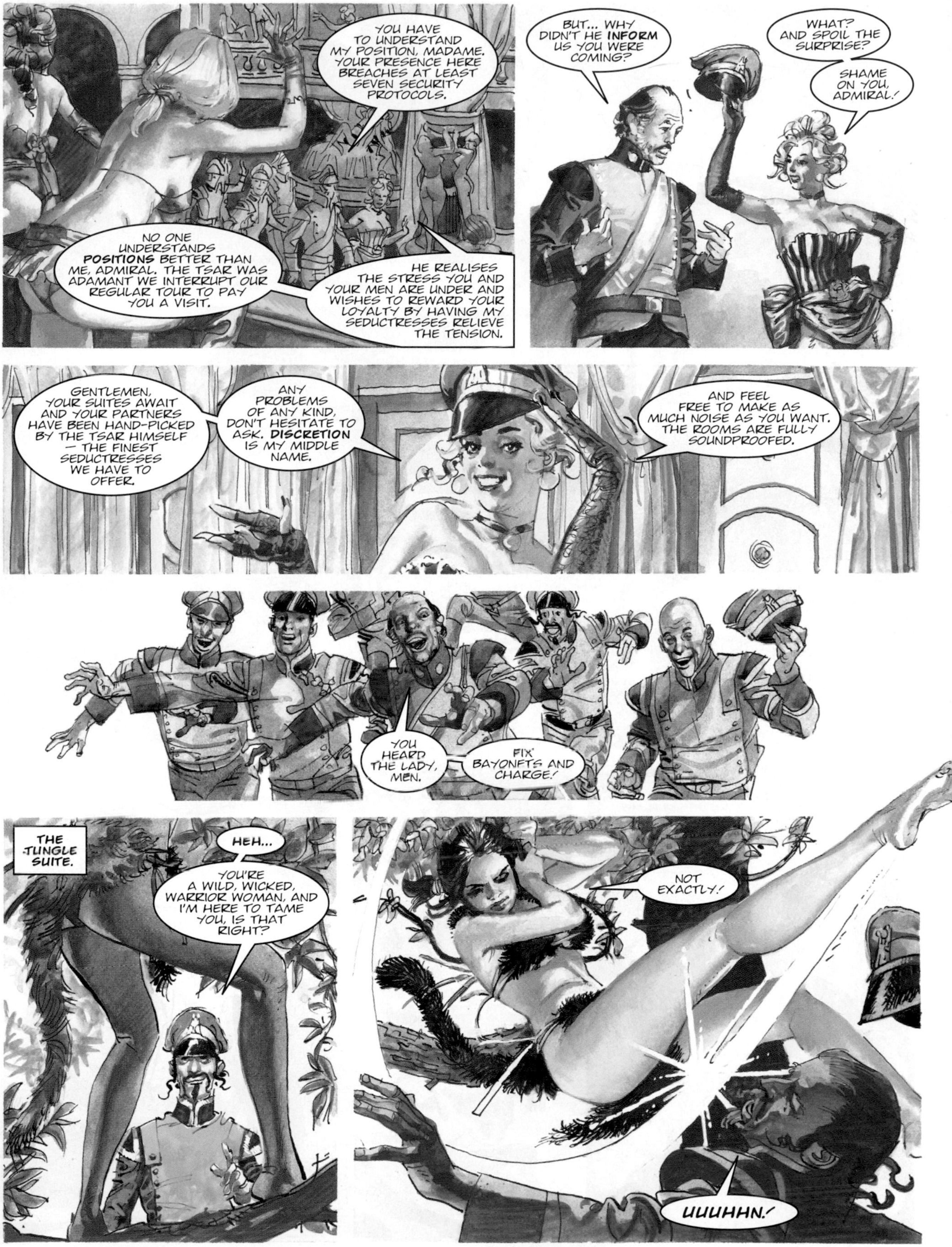
YOU HAVE TO UNDERSTAND MY POSITION, MADAME. YOUR PRESENCE HERE BREACHES AT LEAST SEVEN SECURITY PROTOCOLS.
NO ONE UNDERSTANDS POSITIONS BETTER THAN ME, ADMIRAL. THE TSAR WAS ADAMANT WE INTERRUPT OUR REGULAR TOUR TO PAY YOU A VISIT.
HE REALISES THE STRESS YOU AND YOUR MEN ARE UNDER AND WISHES TO REWARD YOUR LOYALTY BY HAVING MY SEDUCTRESSES RELIEVE THE TENSION.
BUT... WHY DIDN'T HE INFORM US YOU WERE COMING?
WHAT? AND SPOIL THE SURPRISE?
SHAME ON YOU, ADMIRAL!
GENTLEMEN, YOUR SUITES AWAIT AND YOUR PARTNERS HAVE BEEN HAND-PICKED BY THE TSAR HIMSELF — THE FINEST SEDUCTRESSES WE HAVE TO OFFER.
ANY PROBLEMS OF ANY KIND, DON'T HESITATE TO ASK. DISCRETION IS MY MIDDLE NAME.
AND FEEL FREE TO MAKE AS MUCH NOISE AS YOU WANT. THE ROOMS ARE FULLY SOUNDPROOFED.
YOU HEARD THE LADY, MEN.
FIX BAYONETS AND CHARGE!
THE JUNGLE SUITE.
HEH...
YOU'RE A WILD, WICKED, WARRIOR WOMAN, AND I'M HERE TO TAME YOU, IS THAT RIGHT?
NOT EXACTLY!
UUUHHN!

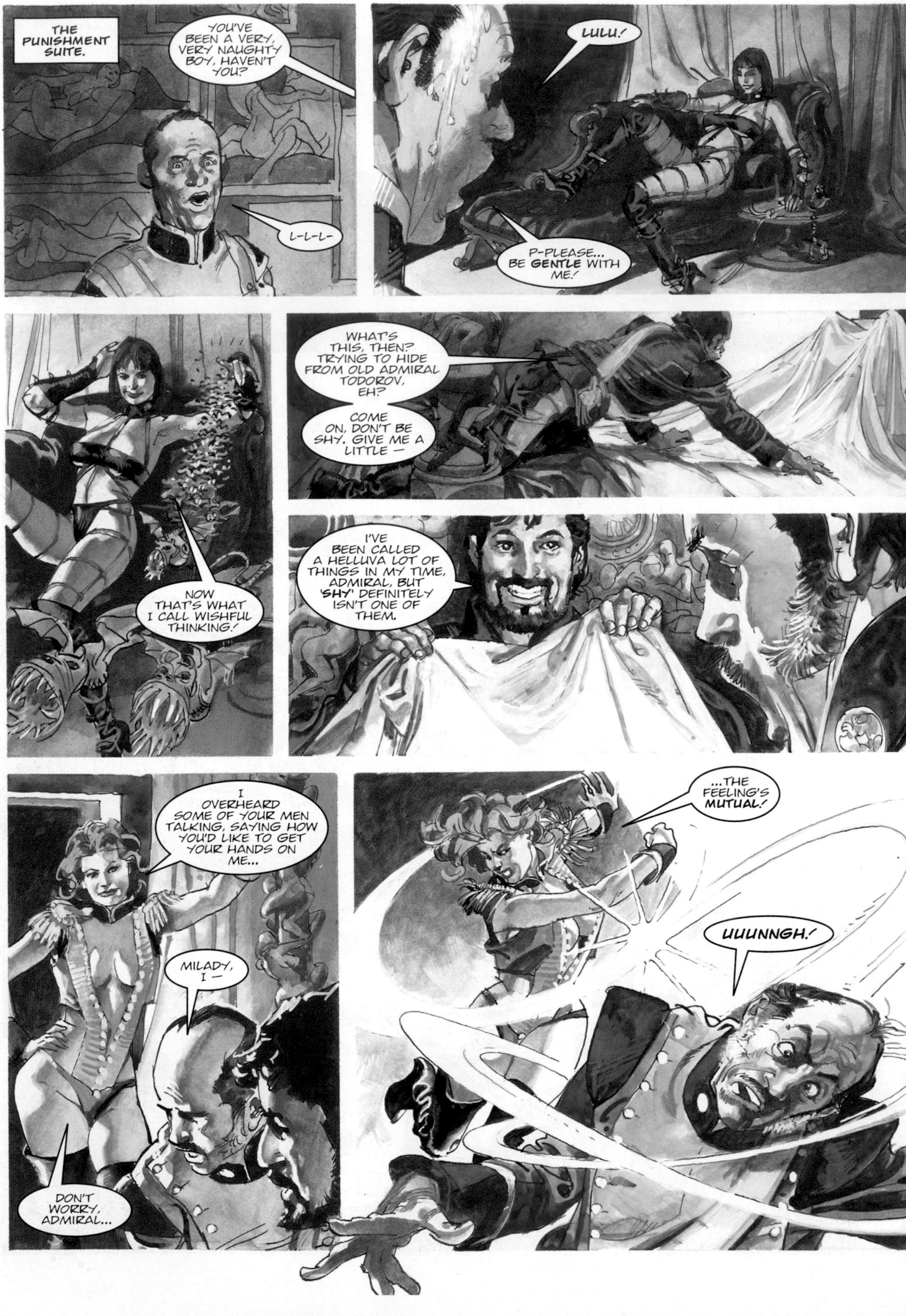

THE PUNISHMENT SUITE.
YOU'VE BEEN A VERY, VERY NAUGHTY BOY, HAVEN'T YOU?
L-L-L-
LULU!
P-PLEASE... BE GENTLE WITH ME!
NOW THAT'S WHAT I CALL WISHFUL THINKING!
WHAT'S THIS, THEN? TRYING TO HIDE FROM OLD ADMIRAL TODOROV, EH?
COME ON, DON'T BE SHY. GIVE ME A LITTLE —
I'VE BEEN CALLED A HELLUVA LOT OF THINGS IN MY TIME, ADMIRAL, BUT 'SHY' DEFINITELY ISN'T ONE OF THEM.
I OVERHEARD SOME OF YOUR MEN TALKING, SAYING HOW YOU'D LIKE TO GET YOUR HANDS ON ME...
MILADY, I —
DON'T WORRY, ADMIRAL...
...THE FEELING'S MUTUAL!
UUUNNGH!

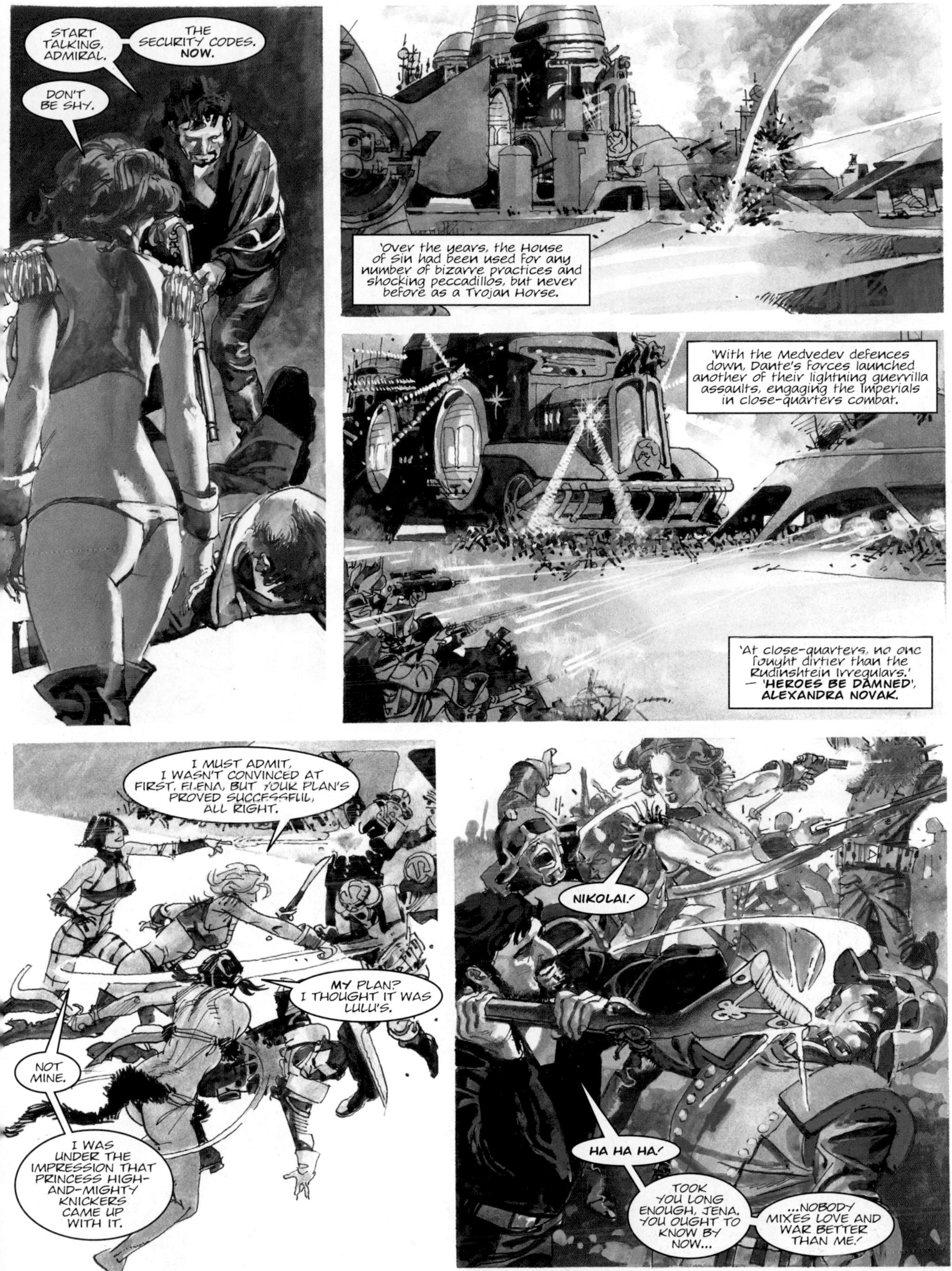
START TALKING, ADMIRAL.
THE SECURITY CODES. NOW.
DON'T BE SHY.
'Over the years, the House of Sin had been used for any number of bizarre practices and shocking peccadillos, but never before as a Trojan Horse.
'With the Medvedev defences down, Dante's forces launched another of their lightning guerrilla assaults, engaging the Imperials in close-quarters combat.
'At close-quarters, no one fought dirtier than the Rudinshtein Irregulars.' — 'HEROES BE DAMNED', ALEXANDRA NOVAK.
I MUST ADMIT, I WASN'T CONVINCED AT FIRST, ELENA, BUT YOUR PLAN'S PROVED SUCCESSFUL, ALL RIGHT.
MY PLAN? I THOUGHT IT WAS LULU'S.
NOT MINE.
I WAS UNDER THE IMPRESSION THAT PRINCESS HIGH-AND-MIGHTY KNICKERS CAME UP WITH IT.
NIKOLAI!
HA HA HA!
TOOK YOU LONG ENOUGH, JENA. YOU OUGHT TO KNOW BY NOW...
...NOBODY MIXES LOVE AND WAR BETTER THAN ME!

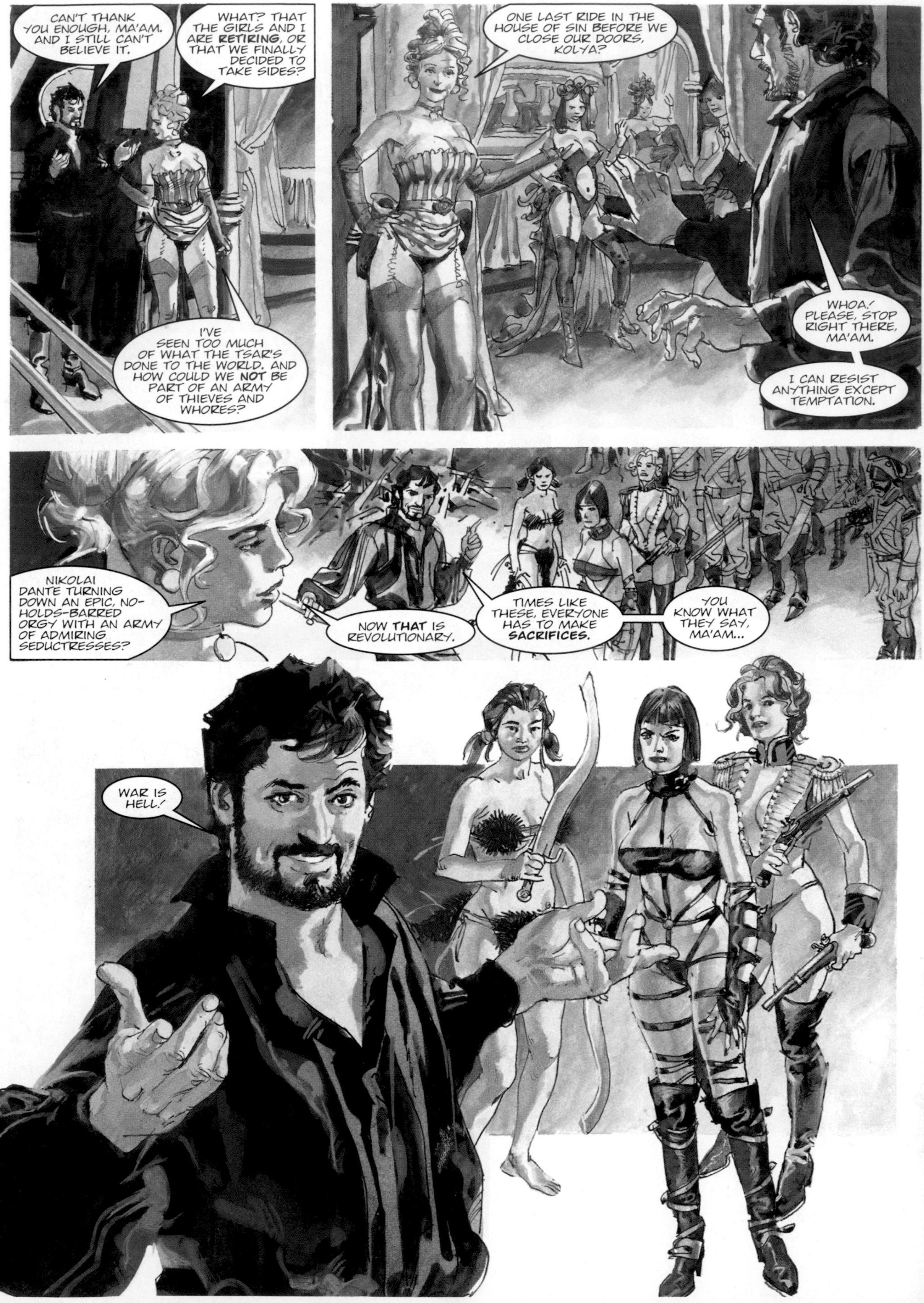
CAN'T THANK YOU ENOUGH, MA'AM. AND I STILL CAN'T BELIEVE IT.
WHAT? THAT THE GIRLS AND I ARE **RETIRING**, OR THAT WE FINALLY DECIDED TO TAKE SIDES?
I'VE SEEN TOO MUCH OF WHAT THE TSAR'S DONE TO THE WORLD, AND HOW COULD WE **NOT** BE PART OF AN ARMY OF THIEVES AND WHORES?
ONE LAST RIDE IN THE HOUSE OF SIN BEFORE WE CLOSE OUR DOORS, KOLYA?
WHOA! PLEASE, STOP RIGHT THERE, MA'AM.
I CAN RESIST ANYTHING EXCEPT TEMPTATION.
NIKOLAI DANTE TURNING DOWN AN EPIC, NO-HOLDS-BARRED ORGY WITH AN ARMY OF ADMIRING SEDUCTRESSES?
NOW **THAT** IS REVOLUTIONARY.
TIMES LIKE THESE, EVERYONE HAS TO MAKE **SACRIFICES**.
YOU KNOW WHAT THEY SAY, MA'AM...
WAR IS HELL!

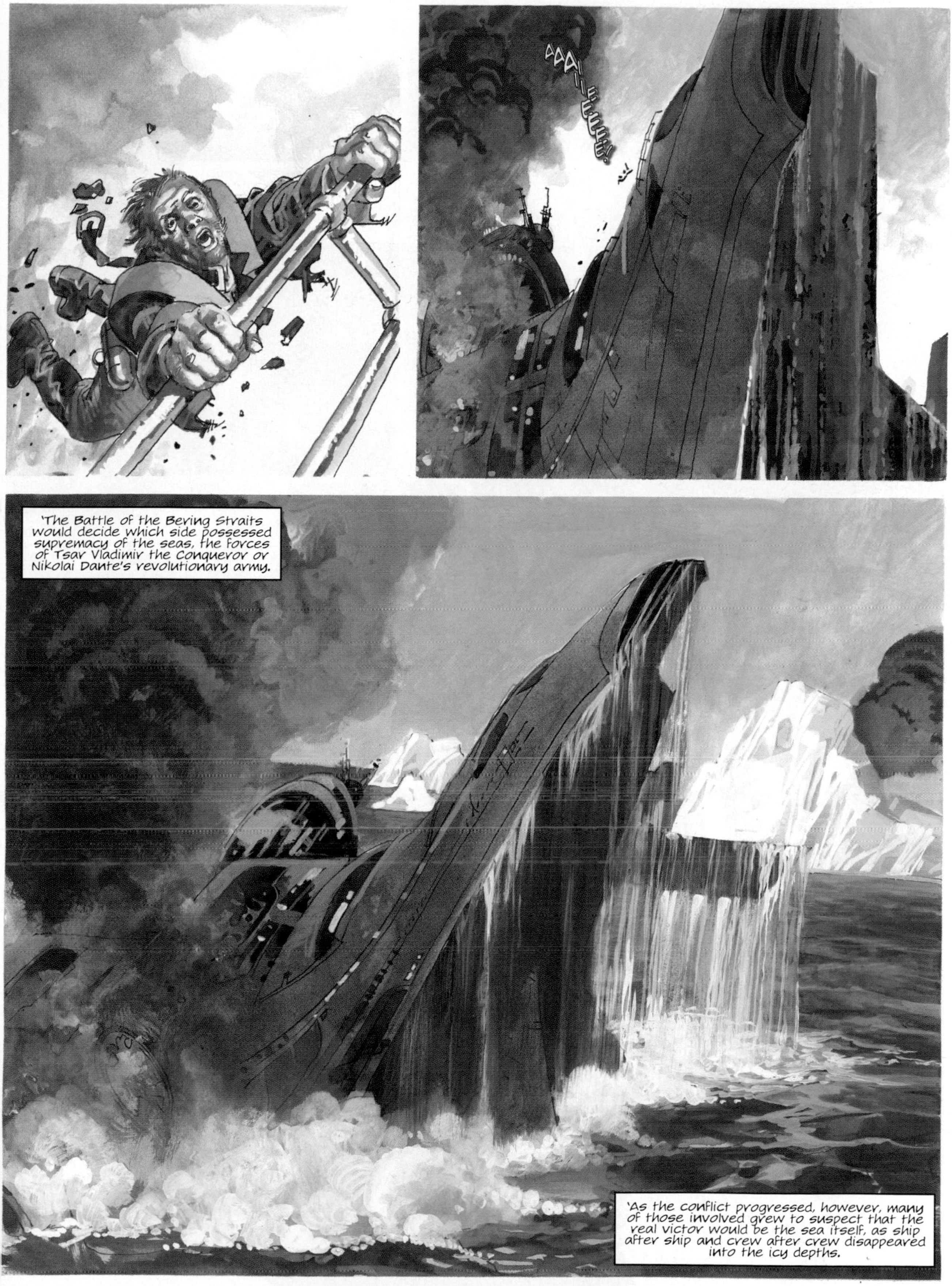
AAAIIIEEEEE!
'The Battle of the Bering Straits would decide which side possessed supremacy of the seas, the forces of Tsar Vladimir the Conqueror or Nikolai Dante's revolutionary army.
'As the conflict progressed, however, many of those involved grew to suspect that the real victor would be the sea itself, as ship after ship and crew after crew disappeared into the icy depths.

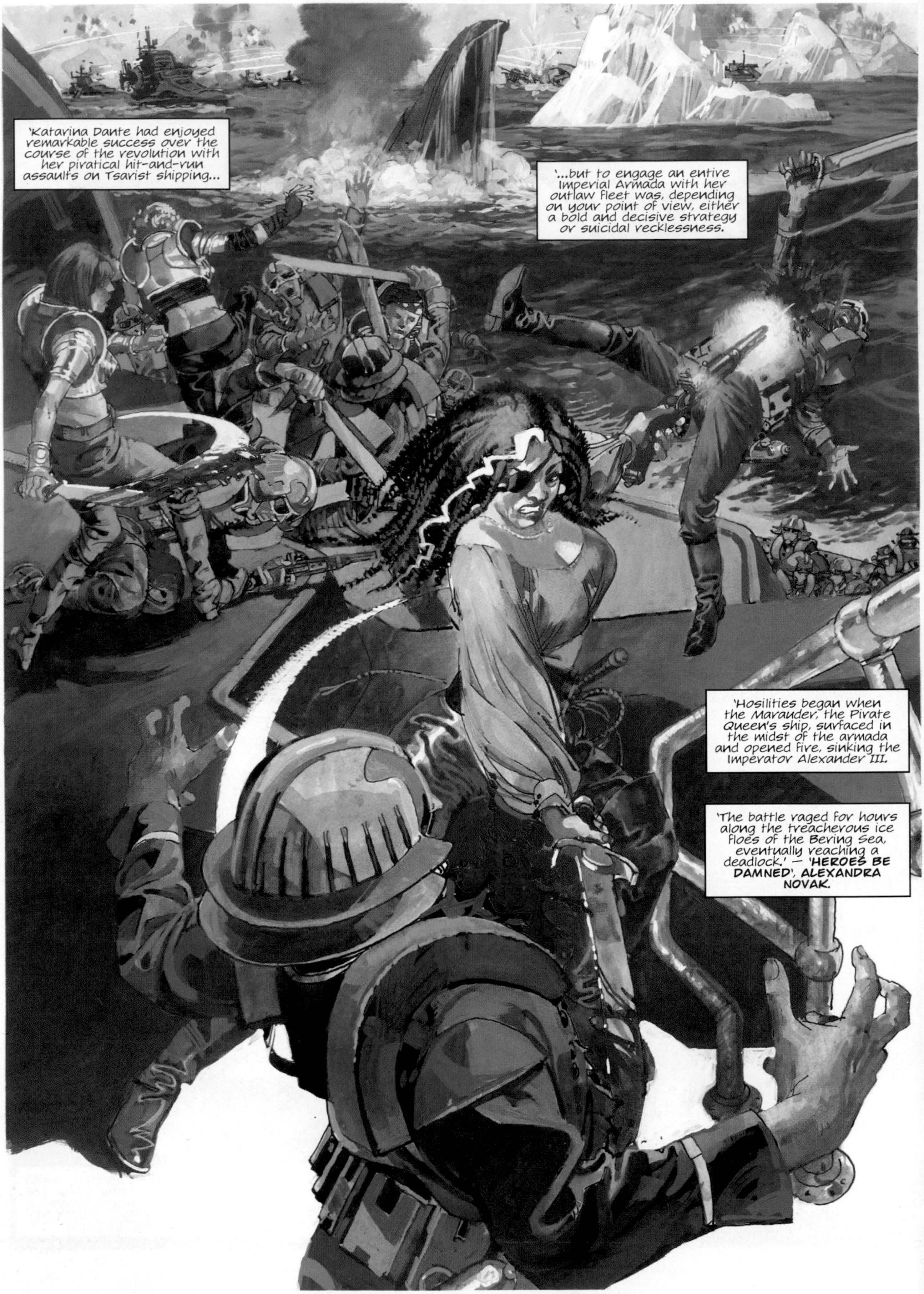
'Katarina Dante had enjoyed remarkable success over the course of the revolution with her piratical hit-and-run assaults on Tsarist shipping...
'...but to engage an entire Imperial Armada with her outlaw fleet was, depending on your point of view, either a bold and decisive strategy or suicidal recklessness.
'Hosilities began when the Marauder, the Pirate Queen's ship, surfaced in the midst of the armada and opened fire, sinking the Imperator Alexander III.
'The battle raged for hours along the treacherous ice floes of the Bering Sea, eventually reaching a deadlock.' — 'HEROES BE DAMNED', ALEXANDRA NOVAK.

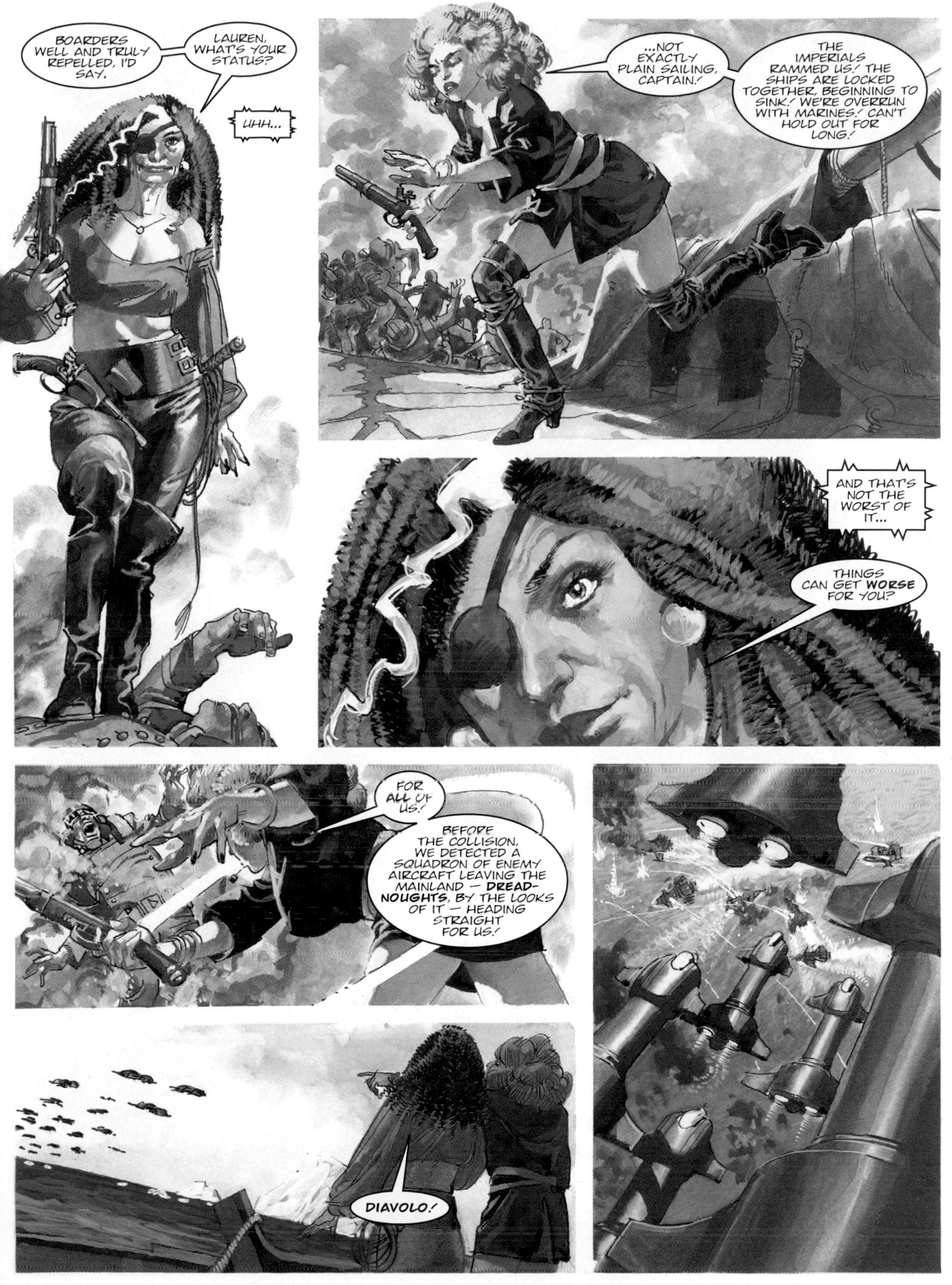
BOARDERS WELL AND TRULY REPELLED, I'D SAY.
LAUREN, WHAT'S YOUR STATUS?
UHH...
...NOT EXACTLY PLAIN SAILING, CAPTAIN!
THE IMPERIALS RAMMED US! THE SHIPS ARE LOCKED TOGETHER, BEGINNING TO SINK! WE'RE OVERRUN WITH MARINES! CAN'T HOLD OUT FOR LONG!
AND THAT'S NOT THE WORST OF IT...
THINGS CAN GET **WORSE** FOR YOU?
FOR **ALL** OF US!
BEFORE THE COLLISION, WE DETECTED A SQUADRON OF ENEMY AIRCRAFT LEAVING THE MAINLAND — **DREAD-NOUGHTS**, BY THE LOOKS OF IT — HEADING STRAIGHT FOR US!
DIAVOLO!

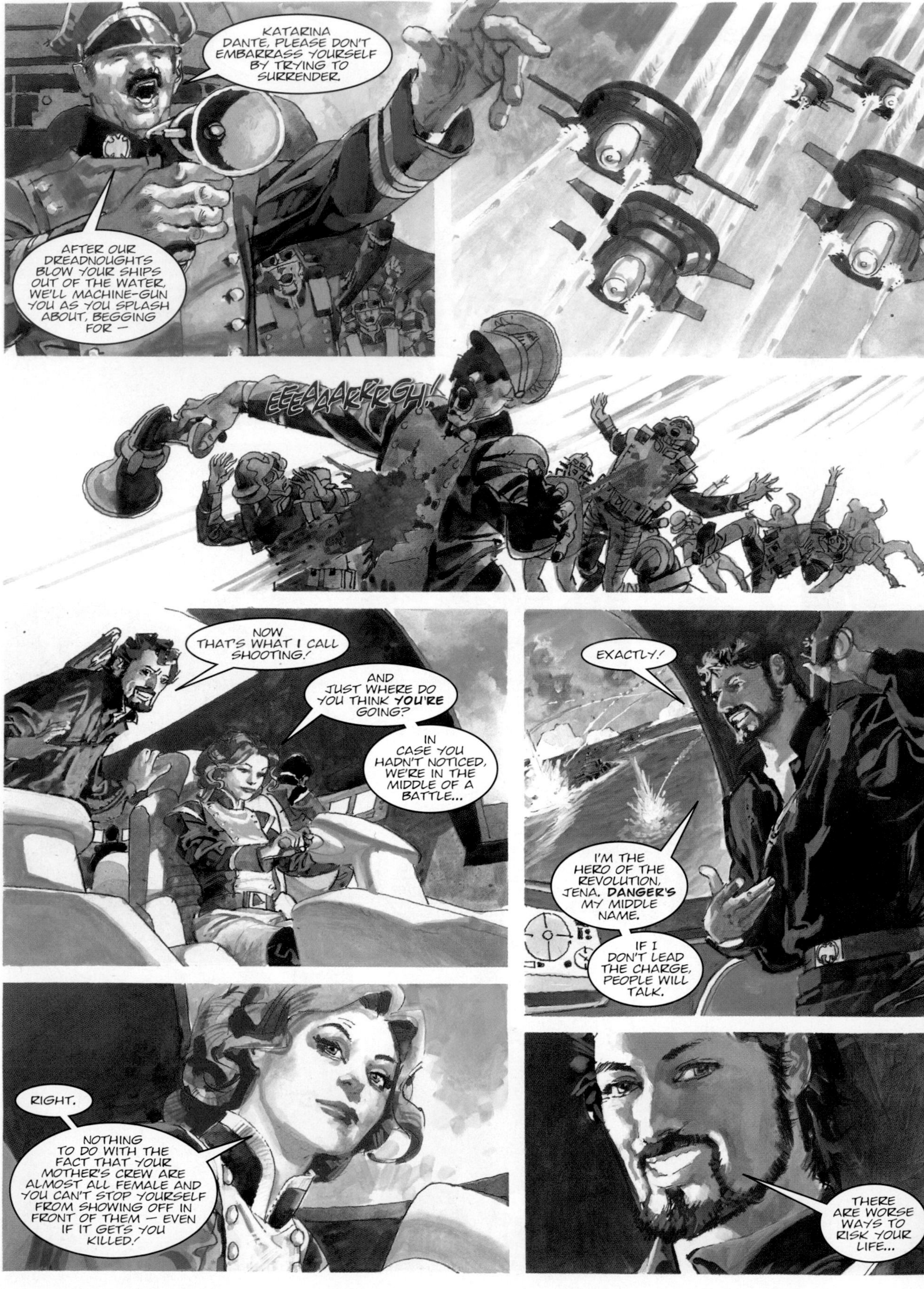
KATARINA DANTE, PLEASE DON'T EMBARRASS YOURSELF BY TRYING TO SURRENDER.
AFTER OUR DREADNOUGHTS BLOW YOUR SHIPS OUT OF THE WATER, WE'LL MACHINE-GUN YOU AS YOU SPLASH ABOUT, BEGGING FOR —
EEEAAARRRGH!
NOW THAT'S WHAT I CALL SHOOTING!
AND JUST WHERE DO YOU THINK YOU'RE GOING?
IN CASE YOU HADN'T NOTICED, WE'RE IN THE MIDDLE OF A BATTLE...
EXACTLY!
I'M THE HERO OF THE REVOLUTION, JENA. DANGER'S MY MIDDLE NAME.
IF I DON'T LEAD THE CHARGE, PEOPLE WILL TALK.
RIGHT.
NOTHING TO DO WITH THE FACT THAT YOUR MOTHER'S CREW ARE ALMOST ALL FEMALE AND YOU CAN'T STOP YOURSELF FROM SHOWING OFF IN FRONT OF THEM — EVEN IF IT GETS YOU KILLED!
THERE ARE WORSE WAYS TO RISK YOUR LIFE...

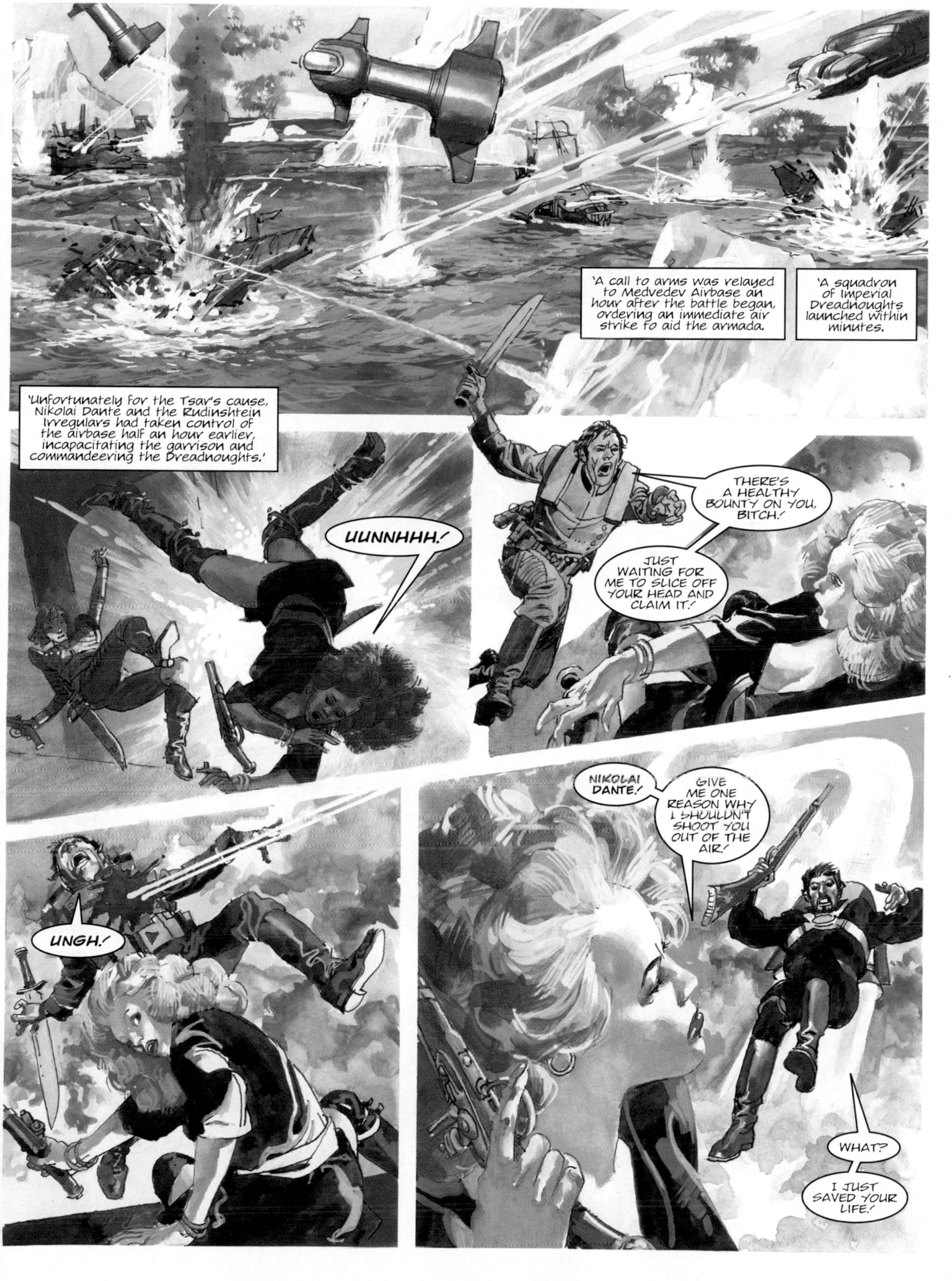
'A call to arms was relayed to Medvedev Airbase an hour after the battle began, ordering an immediate air strike to aid the armada.
'A squadron of Imperial Dreadnoughts launched within minutes.
'Unfortunately for the Tsar's cause, Nikolai Dante and the Rudinshtein Irregulars had taken control of the airbase half an hour earlier, incapacitating the garrison and commandeering the Dreadnoughts.'
UUNNHHH!
THERE'S A HEALTHY BOUNTY ON YOU, BITCH!
JUST WAITING FOR ME TO SLICE OFF YOUR HEAD AND CLAIM IT!
UNGH!
NIKOLAI DANTE!
GIVE ME ONE REASON WHY I SHOULDN'T SHOOT YOU OUT OF THE AIR!
WHAT?
I JUST SAVED YOUR LIFE!

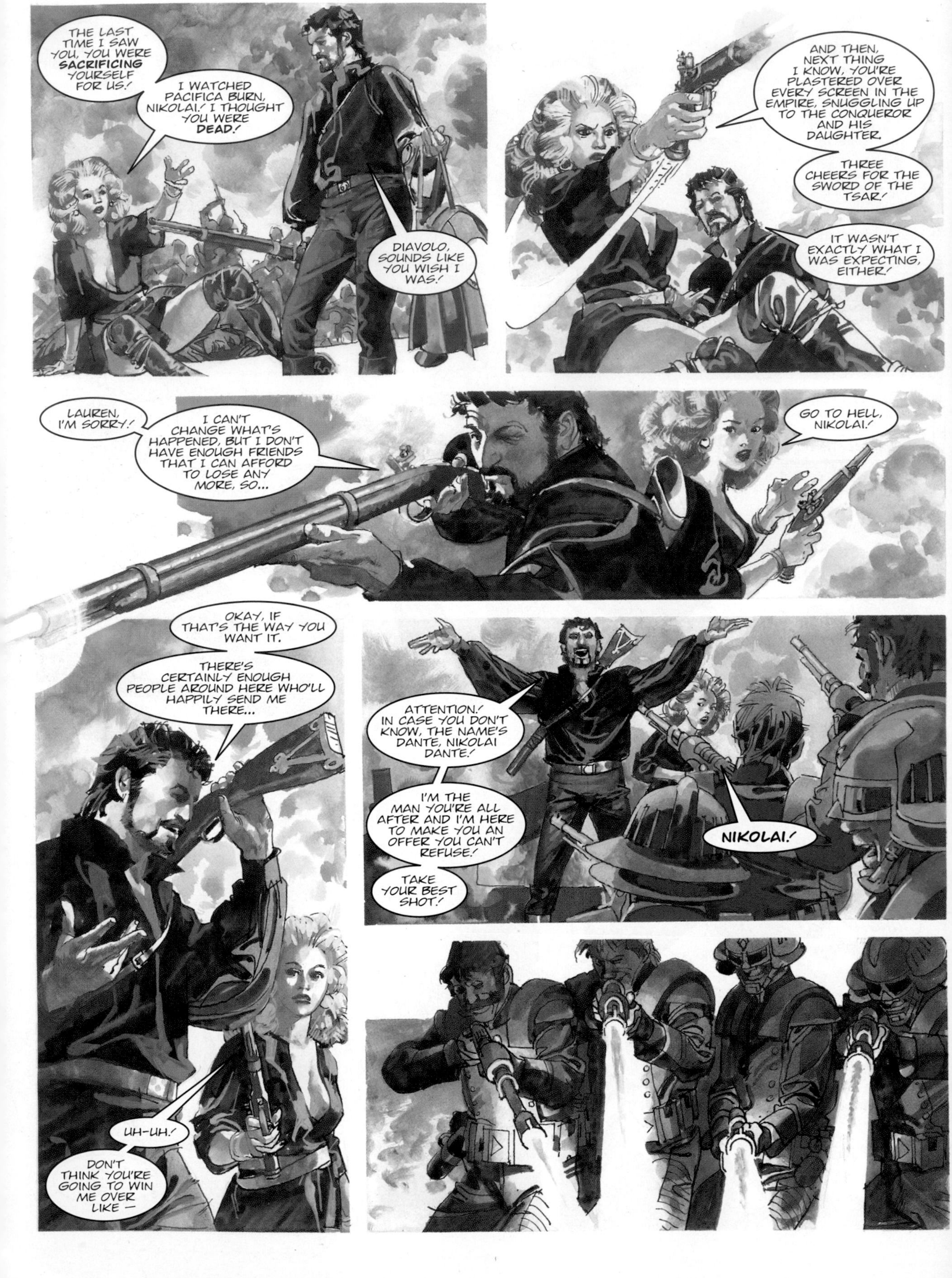
THE LAST TIME I SAW YOU, YOU WERE **SACRIFICING** YOURSELF FOR US!
I WATCHED PACIFICA BURN, NIKOLAI! I THOUGHT YOU WERE **DEAD**!
DIAVOLO, SOUNDS LIKE YOU WISH I WAS!
AND THEN, NEXT THING I KNOW, YOU'RE PLASTERED OVER EVERY SCREEN IN THE EMPIRE, SNUGGLING UP TO THE CONQUEROR AND HIS DAUGHTER.
THREE CHEERS FOR THE SWORD OF THE TSAR!
IT WASN'T EXACTLY WHAT I WAS EXPECTING, EITHER!
LAUREN, I'M SORRY!
I CAN'T CHANGE WHAT'S HAPPENED, BUT I DON'T HAVE ENOUGH FRIENDS THAT I CAN AFFORD TO LOSE ANY MORE, SO...
GO TO HELL, NIKOLAI!
OKAY, IF THAT'S THE WAY YOU WANT IT.
THERE'S CERTAINLY ENOUGH PEOPLE AROUND HERE WHO'LL HAPPILY SEND ME THERE...
UH-UH!
DON'T THINK YOU'RE GOING TO WIN ME OVER LIKE —
ATTENTION! IN CASE YOU DON'T KNOW, THE NAME'S DANTE, NIKOLAI DANTE!
I'M THE MAN YOU'RE ALL AFTER AND I'M HERE TO MAKE YOU AN OFFER YOU CAN'T REFUSE!
TAKE YOUR BEST SHOT!
NIKOLAI!

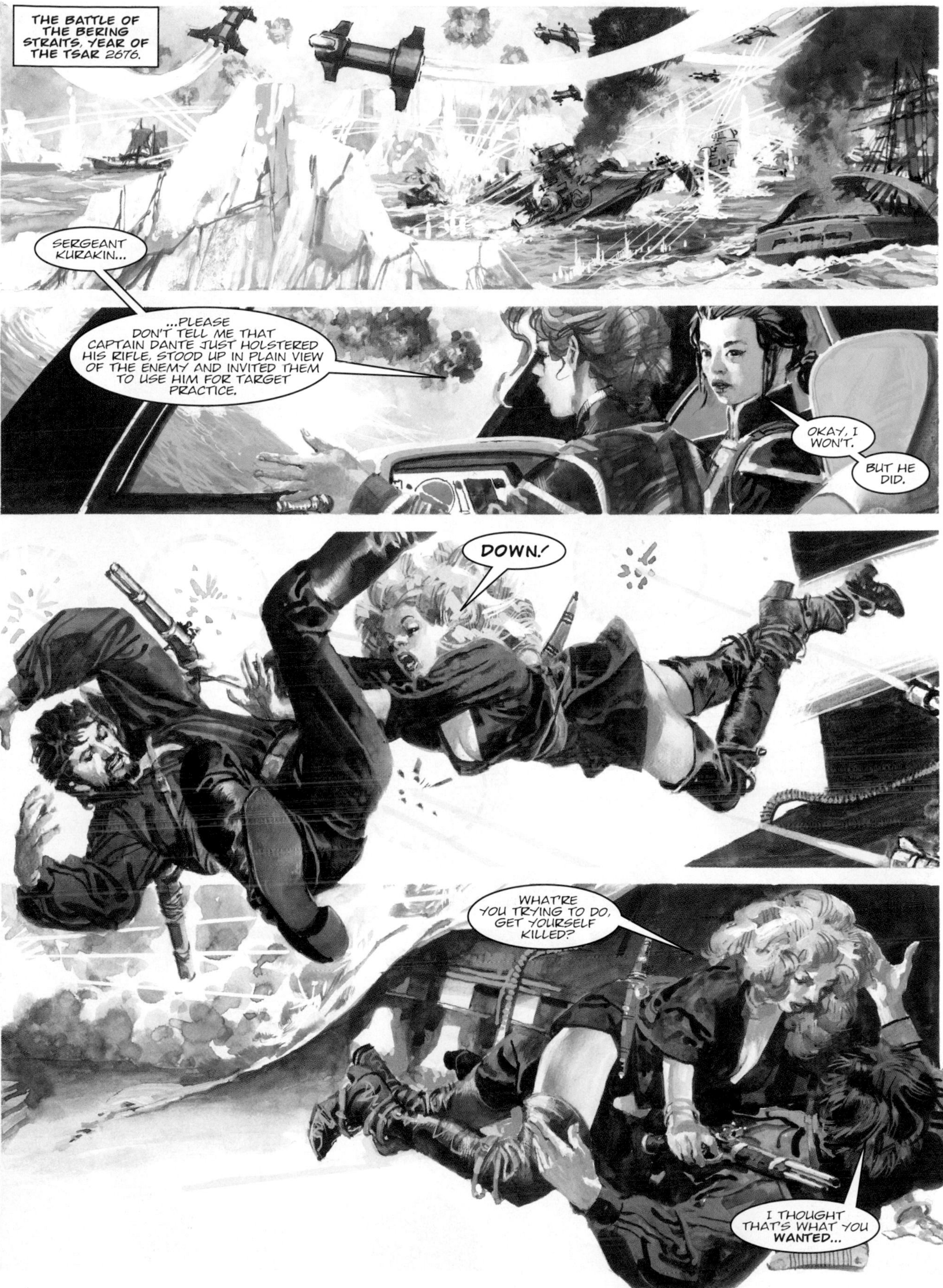
THE BATTLE OF THE BERING STRAITS, YEAR OF THE TSAR 2676.
SERGEANT KURAKIN...
...PLEASE DON'T TELL ME THAT CAPTAIN DANTE JUST HOLSTERED HIS RIFLE, STOOD UP IN PLAIN VIEW OF THE ENEMY AND INVITED THEM TO USE HIM FOR TARGET PRACTICE.
OKAY, I WON'T.
BUT HE DID.
DOWN!
WHAT'RE YOU TRYING TO DO, GET YOURSELF KILLED?
I THOUGHT THAT'S WHAT YOU WANTED...

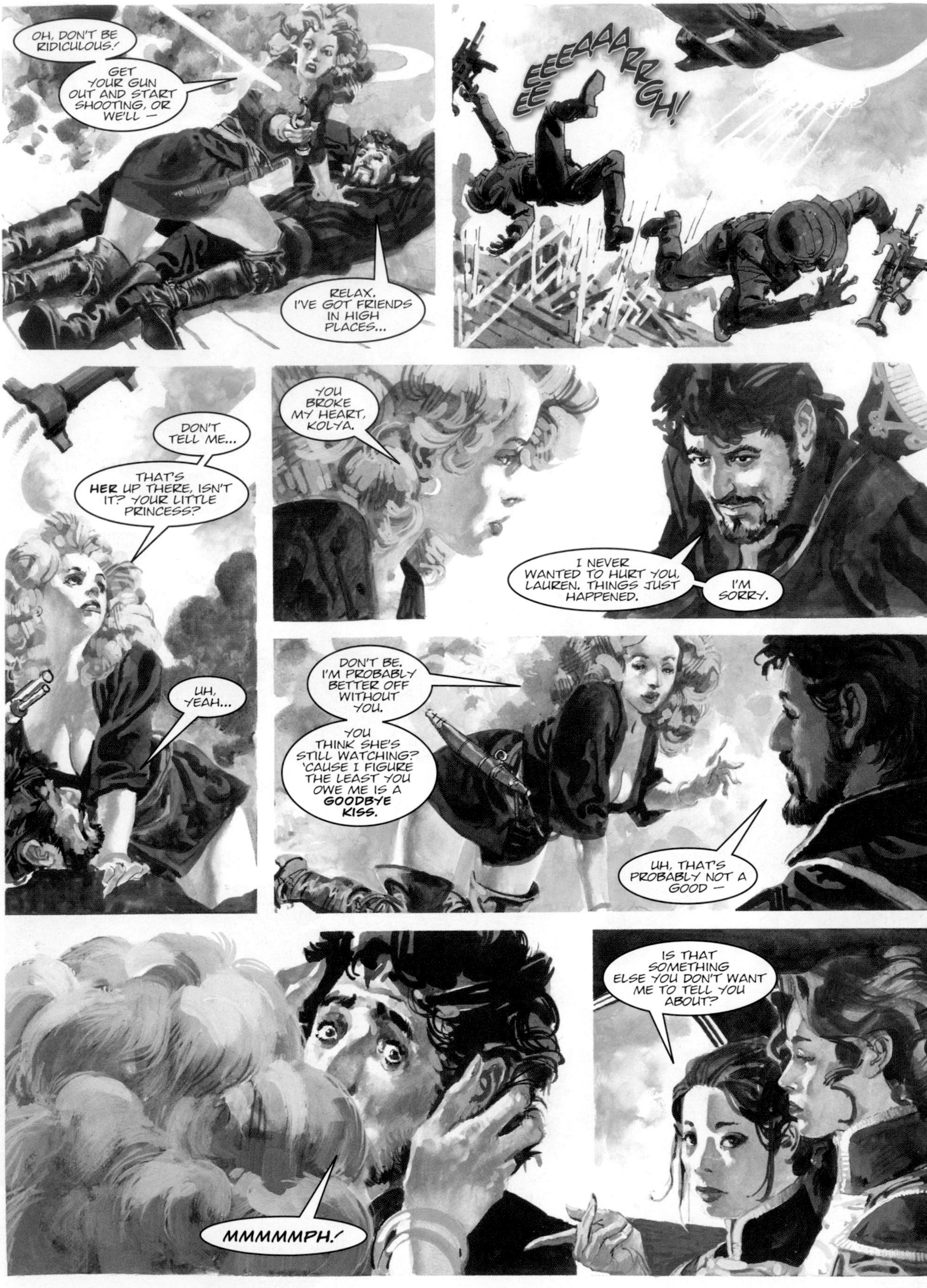

OH, DON'T BE RIDICULOUS!
GET YOUR GUN OUT AND START SHOOTING, OR WE'LL —
RELAX. I'VE GOT FRIENDS IN HIGH PLACES...
EEEEAAAARRGH!
DON'T TELL ME...
THAT'S **HER** UP THERE, ISN'T IT? YOUR LITTLE PRINCESS?
UH, YEAH...
YOU BROKE MY HEART, KOLYA.
I NEVER WANTED TO HURT YOU, LAUREN. THINGS JUST HAPPENED.
I'M SORRY.
DON'T BE. I'M PROBABLY BETTER OFF WITHOUT YOU.
YOU THINK SHE'S STILL WATCHING? 'CAUSE I FIGURE THE LEAST YOU OWE ME IS A **GOODBYE KISS.**
UH, THAT'S PROBABLY NOT A GOOD —
MMMMMPH!
IS THAT SOMETHING ELSE YOU DON'T WANT ME TO TELL YOU ABOUT?

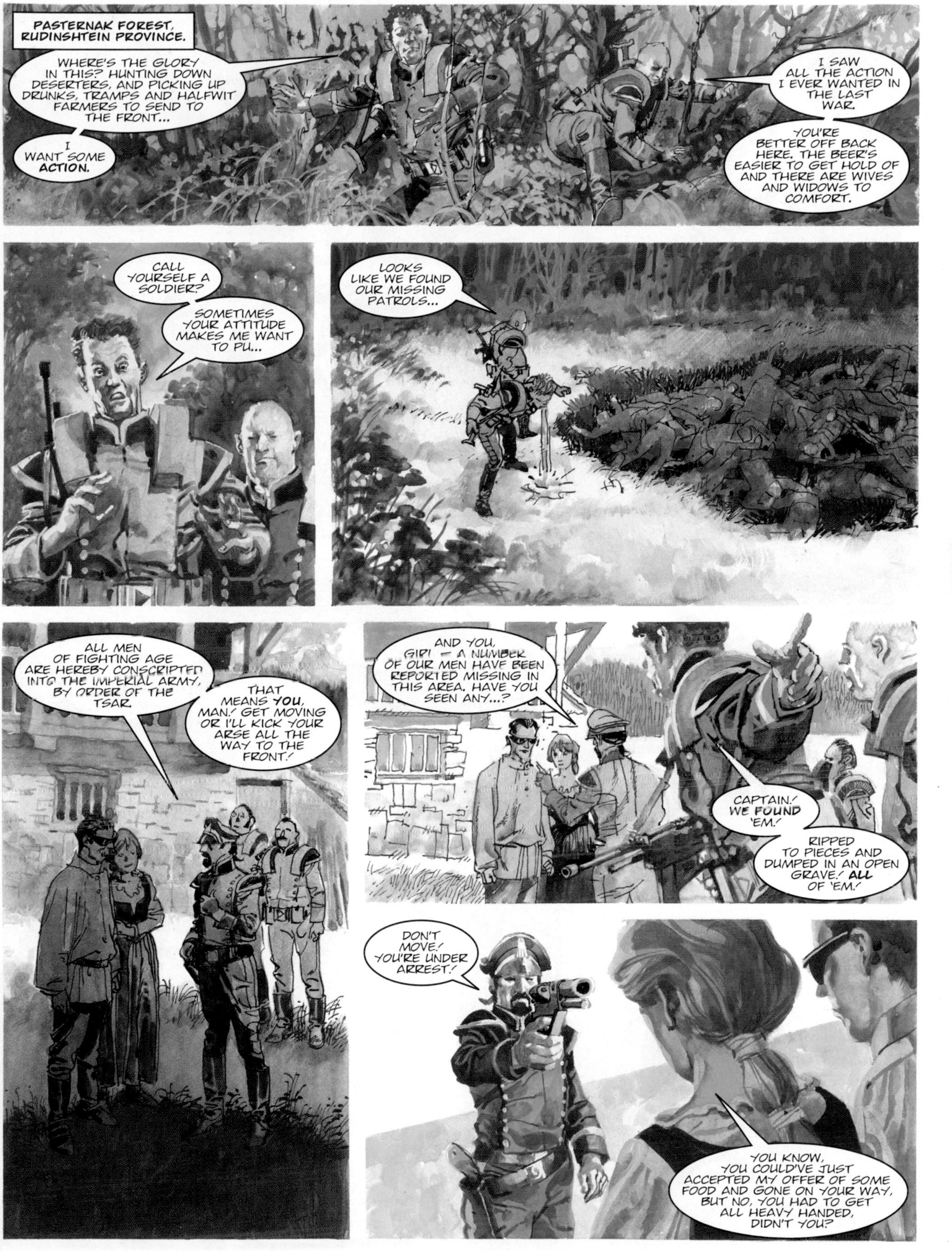

PASTERNAK FOREST, RUDINSHTEIN PROVINCE.
WHERE'S THE GLORY IN THIS? HUNTING DOWN DESERTERS, AND PICKING UP DRUNKS, TRAMPS AND HALFWIT FARMERS TO SEND TO THE FRONT...
I WANT SOME **ACTION.**
I SAW ALL THE ACTION I EVER WANTED IN THE LAST WAR.
YOU'RE BETTER OFF BACK HERE. THE BEER'S EASIER TO GET HOLD OF AND THERE ARE WIVES AND WIDOWS TO COMFORT.
CALL YOURSELF A SOLDIER?
SOMETIMES YOUR ATTITUDE MAKES ME WANT TO PU...
LOOKS LIKE WE FOUND OUR MISSING PATROLS...
ALL MEN OF FIGHTING AGE ARE HEREBY CONSCRIPTED INTO THE IMPERIAL ARMY, BY ORDER OF THE TSAR.
THAT MEANS **YOU**, MAN.! GET MOVING OR I'LL KICK YOUR ARSE ALL THE WAY TO THE FRONT.!
AND YOU, GIRL -- A NUMBER OF OUR MEN HAVE BEEN REPORTED MISSING IN THIS AREA. HAVE YOU SEEN ANY...?
CAPTAIN.! WE **FOUND** 'EM.!
RIPPED TO PIECES AND DUMPED IN AN OPEN GRAVE.! **ALL** OF 'EM.!
DON'T MOVE.! YOU'RE UNDER ARREST.!
YOU KNOW, YOU COULD'VE JUST ACCEPTED MY OFFER OF SOME FOOD AND GONE ON YOUR WAY, BUT NO, YOU HAD TO GET ALL HEAVY HANDED, DIDN'T YOU?

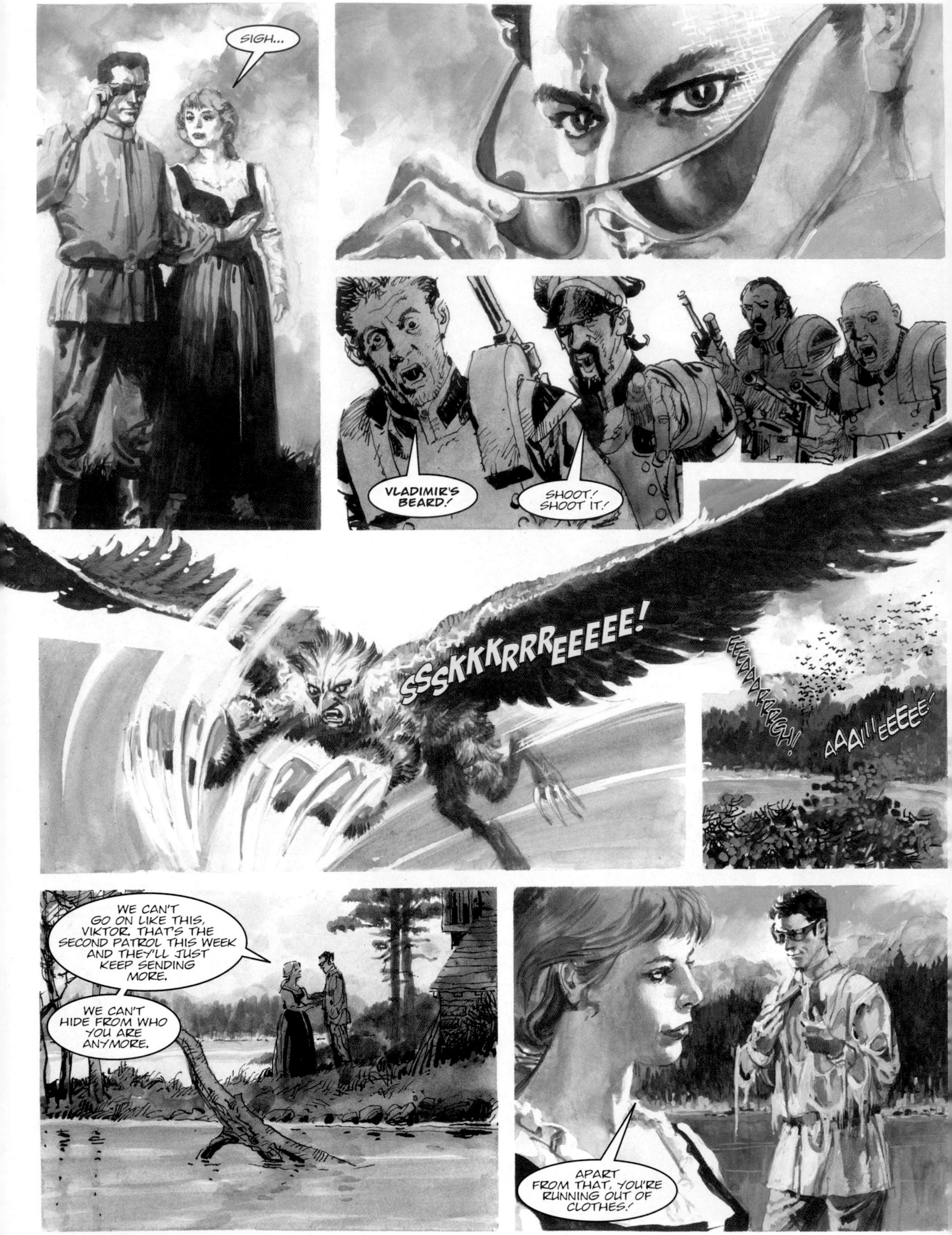
SIGH...
VLADIMIR'S BEARD!
SHOOT! SHOOT IT!
SSSKKKRRREEEEE!
EEEDDDRRRGGH!
AAAIIIEEEEE!
WE CAN'T GO ON LIKE THIS, VIKTOR. THAT'S THE SECOND PATROL THIS WEEK AND THEY'LL JUST KEEP SENDING MORE.
WE CAN'T HIDE FROM WHO YOU ARE ANYMORE.
APART FROM THAT, YOU'RE RUNNING OUT OF CLOTHES!

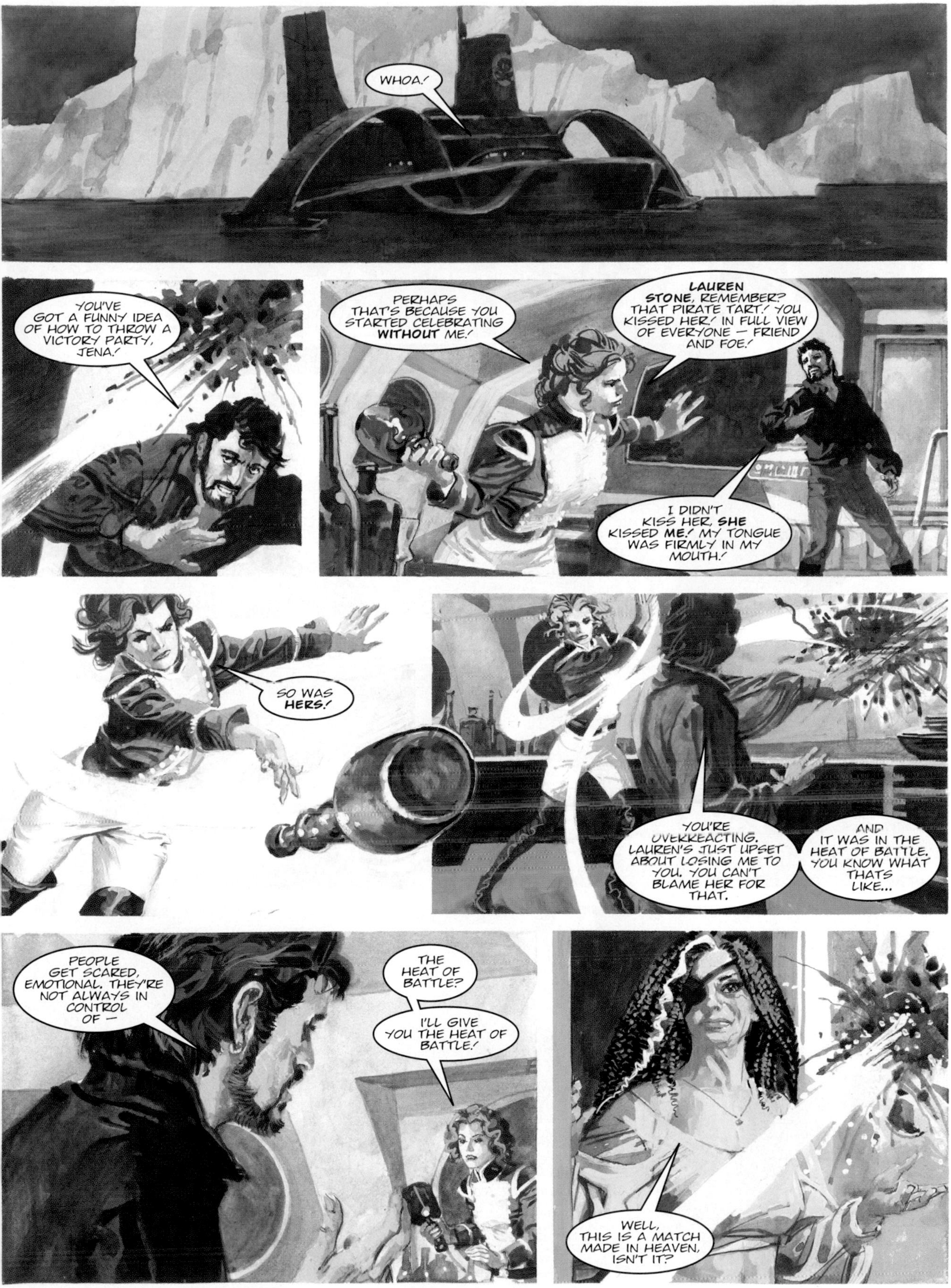
WHOA!
YOU'VE GOT A FUNNY IDEA OF HOW TO THROW A VICTORY PARTY, JENA!
PERHAPS THAT'S BECAUSE YOU STARTED CELEBRATING WITHOUT ME!
LAUREN STONE, REMEMBER? THAT PIRATE TART! YOU KISSED HER! IN FULL VIEW OF EVERYONE — FRIEND AND FOE!
I DIDN'T KISS HER, SHE KISSED ME! MY TONGUE WAS FIRMLY IN MY MOUTH!
SO WAS HERS!
YOU'RE OVERREACTING. LAUREN'S JUST UPSET ABOUT LOSING ME TO YOU. YOU CAN'T BLAME HER FOR THAT.
AND IT WAS IN THE HEAT OF BATTLE. YOU KNOW WHAT THATS LIKE...
PEOPLE GET SCARED, EMOTIONAL. THEY'RE NOT ALWAYS IN CONTROL OF —
THE HEAT OF BATTLE?
I'LL GIVE YOU THE HEAT OF BATTLE!
WELL, THIS IS A MATCH MADE IN HEAVEN, ISN'T IT?

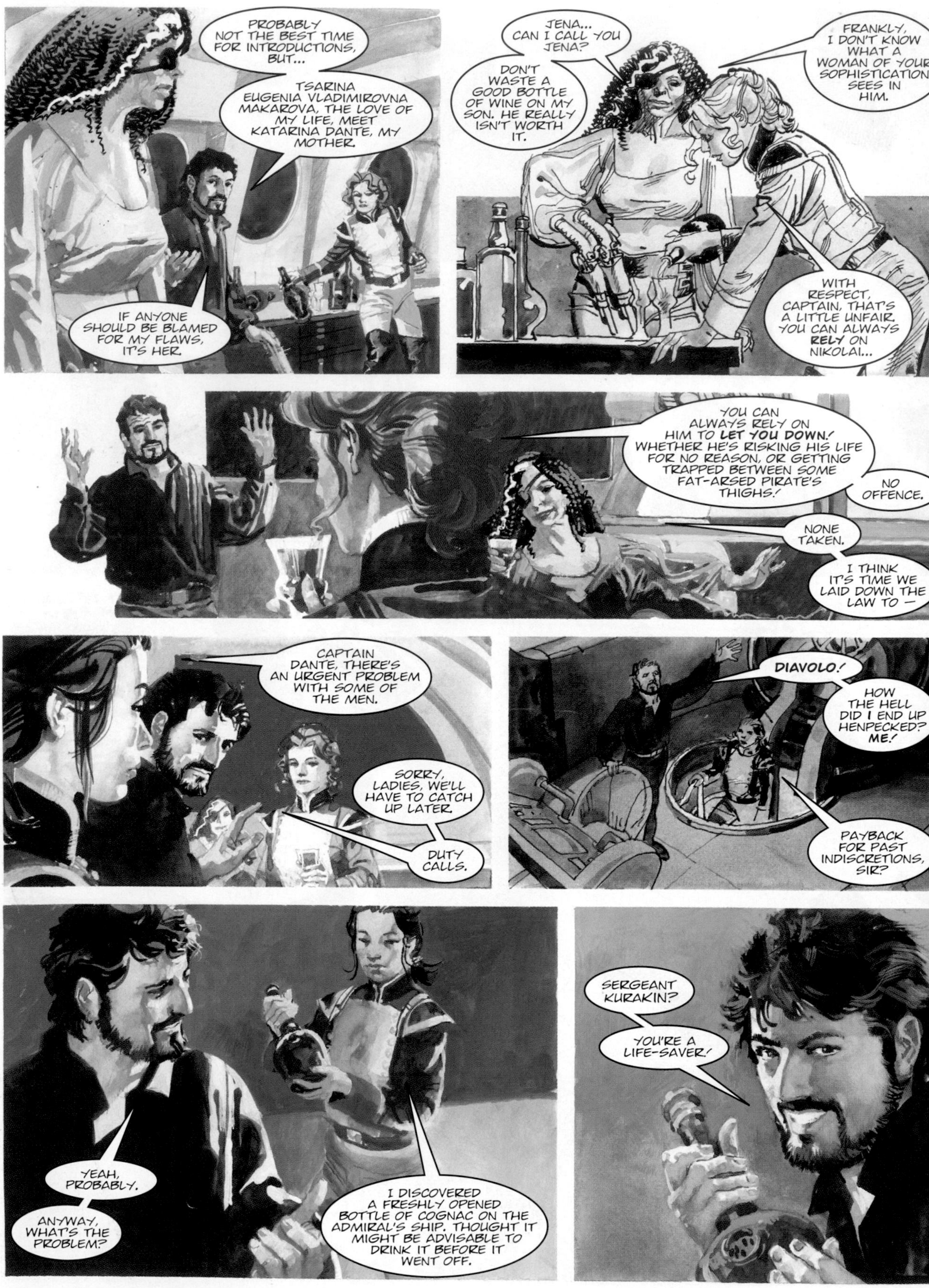
PROBABLY NOT THE BEST TIME FOR INTRODUCTIONS, BUT...
TSARINA EUGENIA VLADIMIROVNA MAKAROVA, THE LOVE OF MY LIFE, MEET KATARINA DANTE, MY MOTHER.
IF ANYONE SHOULD BE BLAMED FOR MY FLAWS, IT'S HER.
JENA... CAN I CALL YOU JENA?
DON'T WASTE A GOOD BOTTLE OF WINE ON MY SON. HE REALLY ISN'T WORTH IT.
FRANKLY, I DON'T KNOW WHAT A WOMAN OF YOUR SOPHISTICATION SEES IN HIM.
WITH RESPECT, CAPTAIN, THAT'S A LITTLE UNFAIR. YOU CAN ALWAYS **RELY** ON NIKOLAI...
YOU CAN ALWAYS RELY ON HIM TO **LET YOU DOWN!** WHETHER HE'S RISKING HIS LIFE FOR NO REASON, OR GETTING TRAPPED BETWEEN SOME FAT-ARSED PIRATE'S THIGHS!
NO OFFENCE.
NONE TAKEN.
I THINK IT'S TIME WE LAID DOWN THE LAW TO —
CAPTAIN DANTE, THERE'S AN URGENT PROBLEM WITH SOME OF THE MEN.
SORRY, LADIES, WE'LL HAVE TO CATCH UP LATER.
DUTY CALLS.
DIAVOLO!
HOW THE HELL DID I END UP HENPECKED? **ME!**
PAYBACK FOR PAST INDISCRETIONS, SIR?
YEAH, PROBABLY.
ANYWAY, WHAT'S THE PROBLEM?
I DISCOVERED A FRESHLY OPENED BOTTLE OF COGNAC ON THE ADMIRAL'S SHIP. THOUGHT IT MIGHT BE ADVISABLE TO DRINK IT BEFORE IT WENT OFF.
SERGEANT KURAKIN?
YOU'RE A LIFE-SAVER!

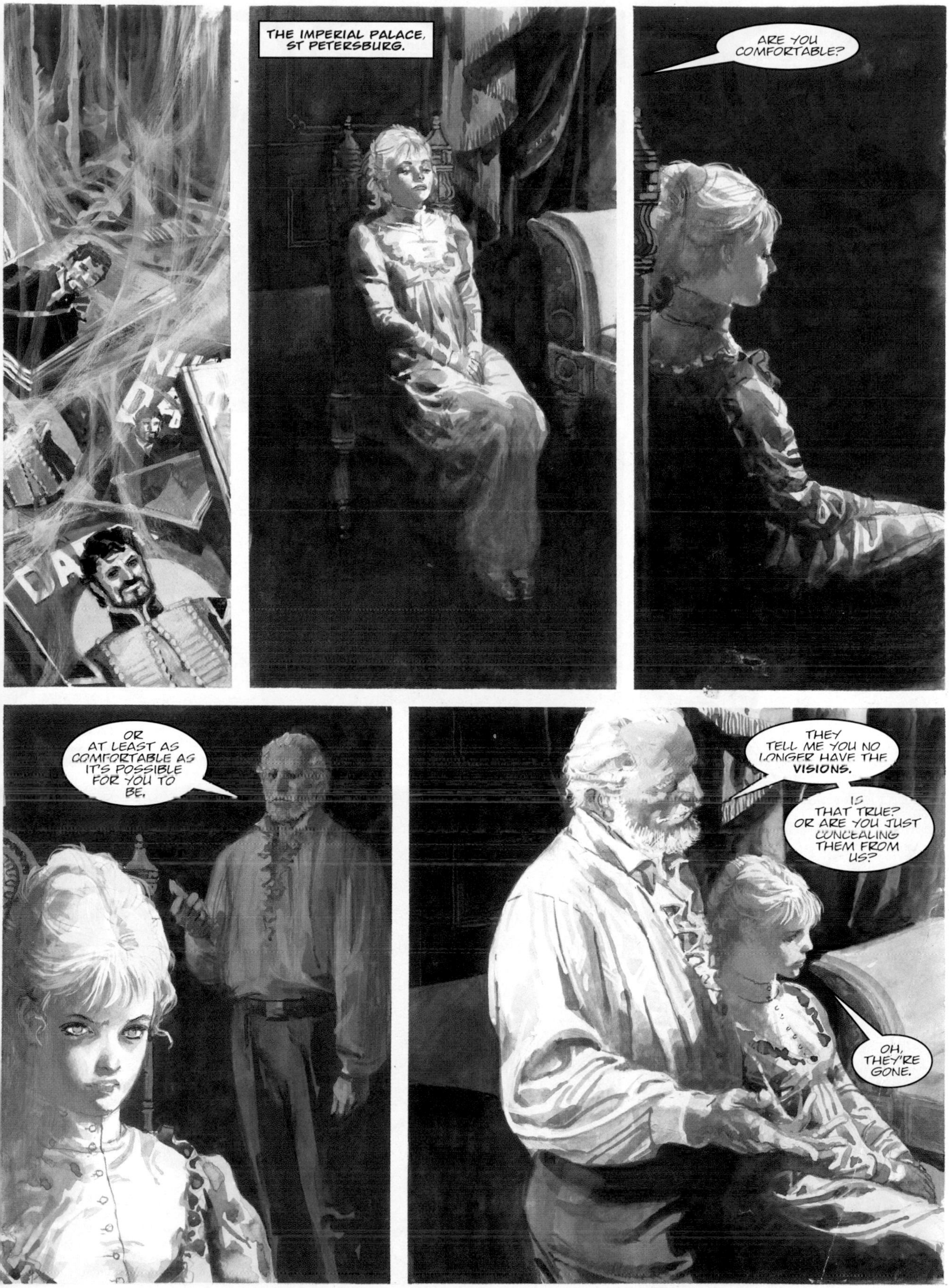
THE IMPERIAL PALACE, ST PETERSBURG.
ARE YOU COMFORTABLE?
OR AT LEAST AS COMFORTABLE AS IT'S POSSIBLE FOR YOU TO BE.
THEY TELL ME YOU NO LONGER HAVE THE VISIONS.
IS THAT TRUE? OR ARE YOU JUST CONCEALING THEM FROM US?
OH, THEY'RE GONE.

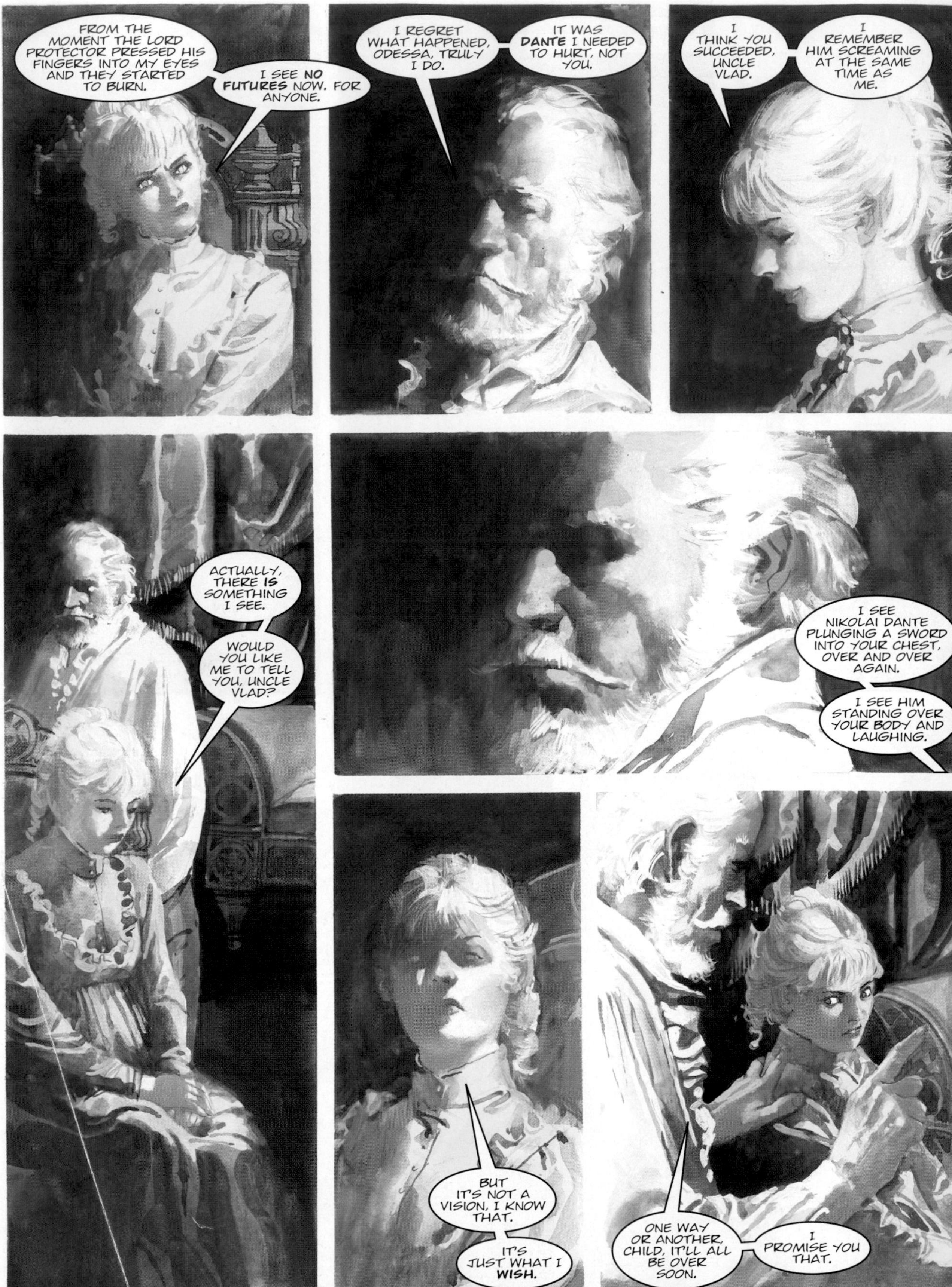
FROM THE MOMENT THE LORD PROTECTOR PRESSED HIS FINGERS INTO MY EYES AND THEY STARTED TO BURN.
I SEE NO FUTURES NOW. FOR ANYONE.
I REGRET WHAT HAPPENED, ODESSA, TRULY I DO.
IT WAS DANTE I NEEDED TO HURT, NOT YOU.
I THINK YOU SUCCEEDED, UNCLE VLAD.
I REMEMBER HIM SCREAMING AT THE SAME TIME AS ME.
ACTUALLY, THERE IS SOMETHING I SEE.
WOULD YOU LIKE ME TO TELL YOU, UNCLE VLAD?
I SEE NIKOLAI DANTE PLUNGING A SWORD INTO YOUR CHEST, OVER AND OVER AGAIN.
I SEE HIM STANDING OVER YOUR BODY AND LAUGHING.
BUT IT'S NOT A VISION, I KNOW THAT.
IT'S JUST WHAT I WISH.
ONE WAY OR ANOTHER, CHILD, IT'LL ALL BE OVER SOON.
I PROMISE YOU THAT.

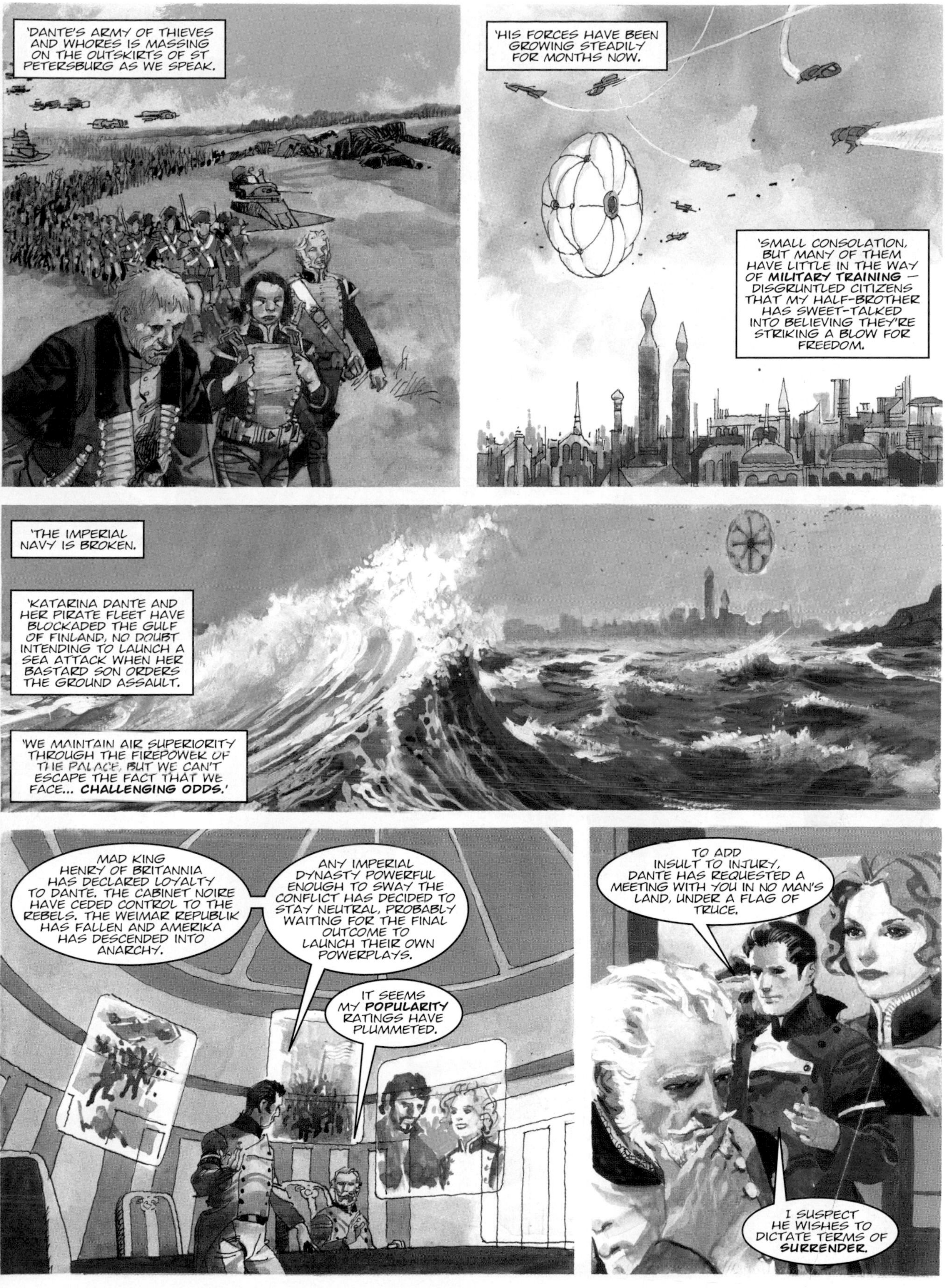

'DANTE'S ARMY OF THIEVES AND WHORES IS MASSING ON THE OUTSKIRTS OF ST PETERSBURG AS WE SPEAK.
'HIS FORCES HAVE BEEN GROWING STEADILY FOR MONTHS NOW.
'SMALL CONSOLATION, BUT MANY OF THEM HAVE LITTLE IN THE WAY OF **MILITARY TRAINING** — DISGRUNTLED CITIZENS THAT MY HALF-BROTHER HAS SWEET-TALKED INTO BELIEVING THEY'RE STRIKING A BLOW FOR FREEDOM.
'THE IMPERIAL NAVY IS BROKEN.
'KATARINA DANTE AND HER PIRATE FLEET HAVE BLOCKADED THE GULF OF FINLAND, NO DOUBT INTENDING TO LAUNCH A SEA ATTACK WHEN HER BASTARD SON ORDERS THE GROUND ASSAULT.
'WE MAINTAIN AIR SUPERIORITY THROUGH THE FIREPOWER OF THE PALACE, BUT WE CAN'T ESCAPE THE FACT THAT WE FACE... **CHALLENGING ODDS.**'
MAD KING HENRY OF BRITANNIA HAS DECLARED LOYALTY TO DANTE. THE CABINET NOIRE HAVE CEDED CONTROL TO THE REBELS. THE WEIMAR REPUBLIK HAS FALLEN AND AMERIKA HAS DESCENDED INTO ANARCHY.
ANY IMPERIAL DYNASTY POWERFUL ENOUGH TO SWAY THE CONFLICT HAS DECIDED TO STAY NEUTRAL, PROBABLY WAITING FOR THE FINAL OUTCOME TO LAUNCH THEIR OWN POWERPLAYS.
IT SEEMS MY **POPULARITY** RATINGS HAVE PLUMMETED.
TO ADD INSULT TO INJURY, DANTE HAS REQUESTED A MEETING WITH YOU IN NO MAN'S LAND, UNDER A FLAG OF TRUCE.
I SUSPECT HE WISHES TO DICTATE TERMS OF **SURRENDER.**

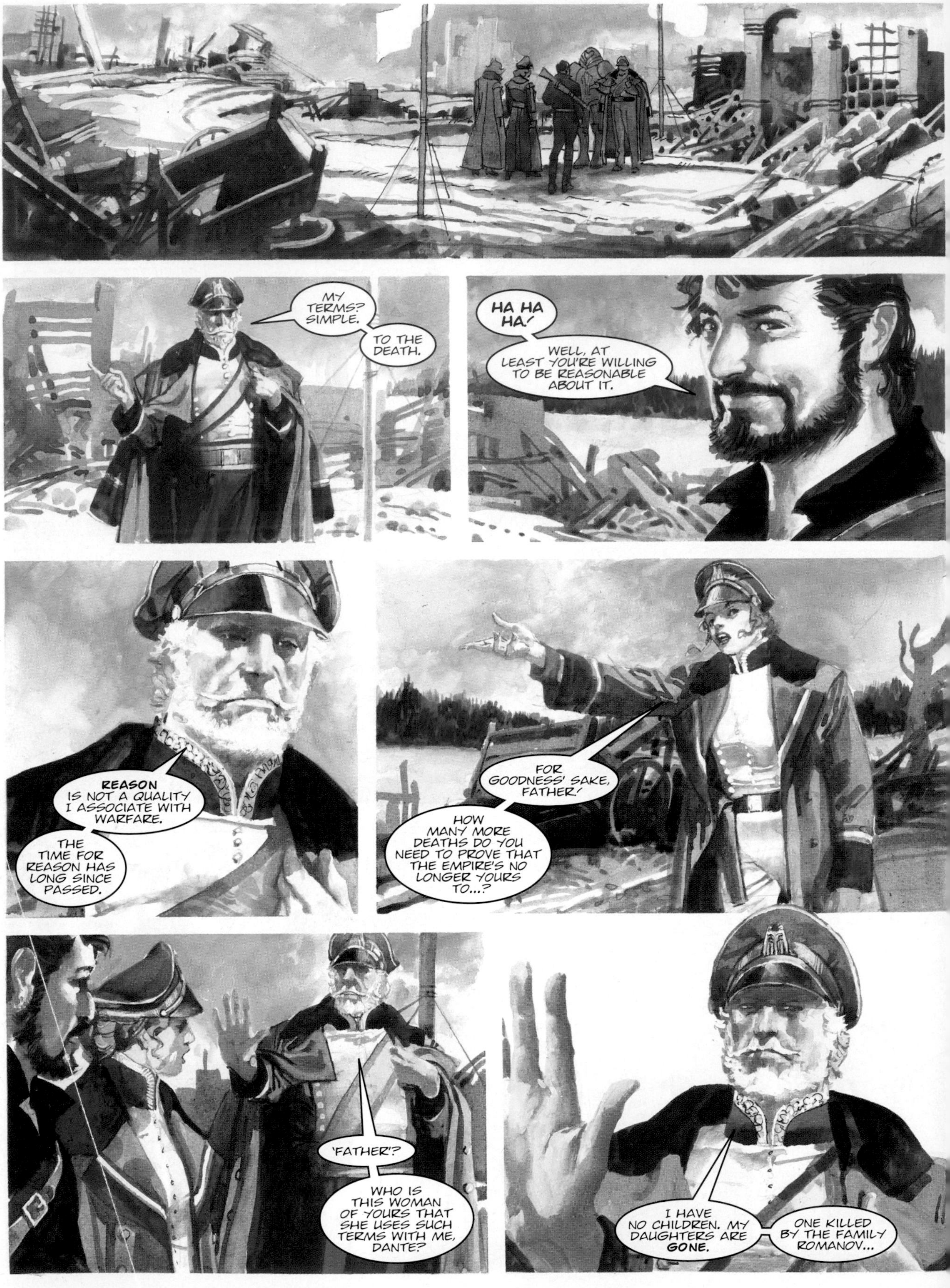
MY TERMS? SIMPLE.
TO THE DEATH.
HA HA HA!
WELL, AT LEAST YOU'RE WILLING TO BE REASONABLE ABOUT IT.
REASON IS NOT A QUALITY I ASSOCIATE WITH WARFARE.
THE TIME FOR REASON HAS LONG SINCE PASSED.
FOR GOODNESS' SAKE, FATHER!
HOW MANY MORE DEATHS DO YOU NEED TO PROVE THAT THE EMPIRE'S NO LONGER YOURS TO...?
'FATHER'?
WHO IS THIS WOMAN OF YOURS THAT SHE USES SUCH TERMS WITH ME, DANTE?
I HAVE NO CHILDREN. MY DAUGHTERS ARE GONE.
ONE KILLED BY THE FAMILY ROMANOV...

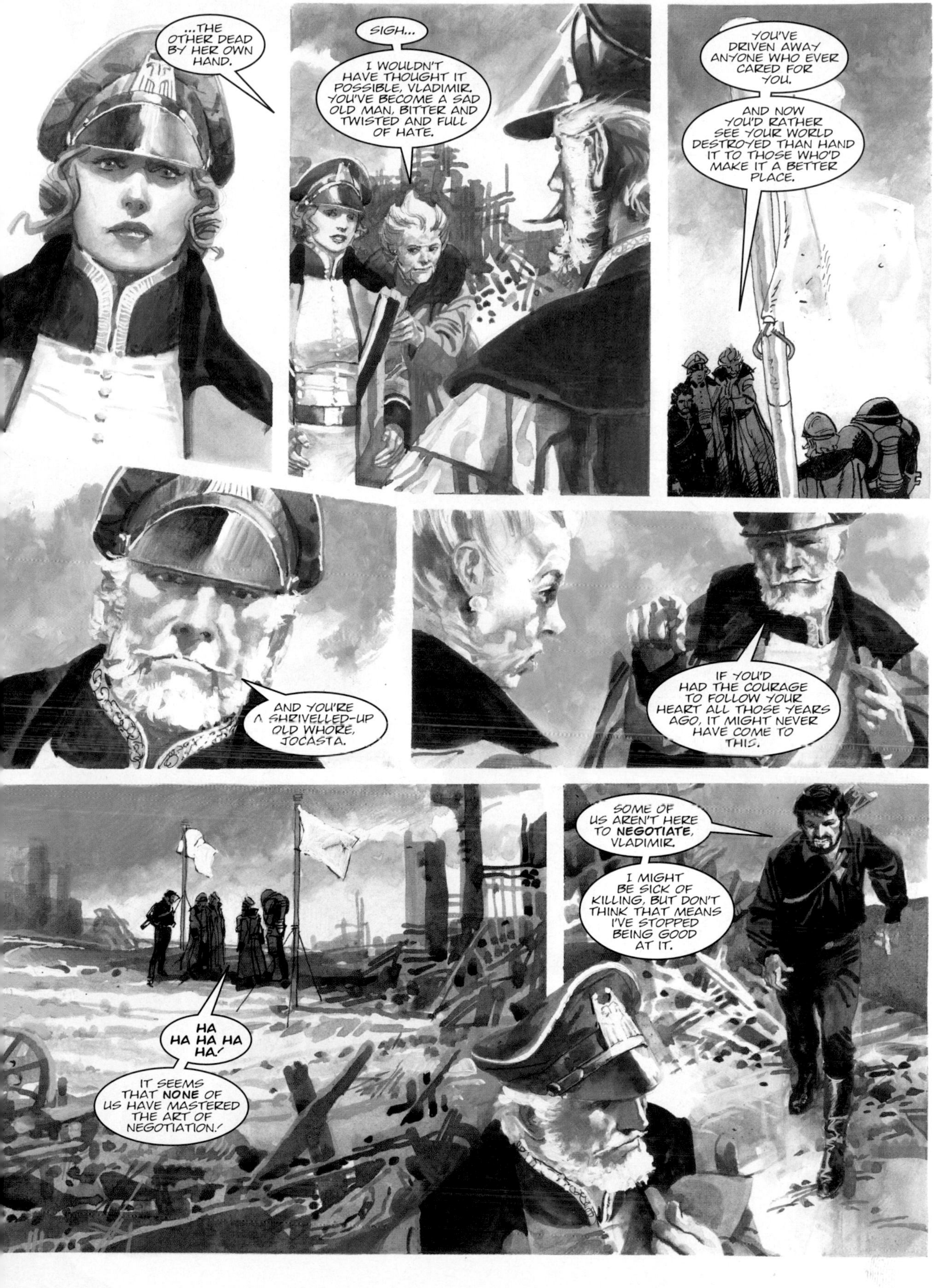

...THE OTHER DEAD BY HER OWN HAND.
SIGH...
I WOULDN'T HAVE THOUGHT IT POSSIBLE, VLADIMIR. YOU'VE BECOME A SAD OLD MAN, BITTER AND TWISTED AND FULL OF HATE.
YOU'VE DRIVEN AWAY ANYONE WHO EVER CARED FOR YOU.
AND NOW YOU'D RATHER SEE YOUR WORLD DESTROYED THAN HAND IT TO THOSE WHO'D MAKE IT A BETTER PLACE.
AND YOU'RE A SHRIVELLED-UP OLD WHORE, JOCASTA.
IF YOU'D HAD THE COURAGE TO FOLLOW YOUR HEART ALL THOSE YEARS AGO, IT MIGHT NEVER HAVE COME TO THIS.
HA HA HA HA HA!
IT SEEMS THAT NONE OF US HAVE MASTERED THE ART OF NEGOTIATION!
SOME OF US AREN'T HERE TO NEGOTIATE, VLADIMIR.
I MIGHT BE SICK OF KILLING, BUT DON'T THINK THAT MEANS I'VE STOPPED BEING GOOD AT IT.

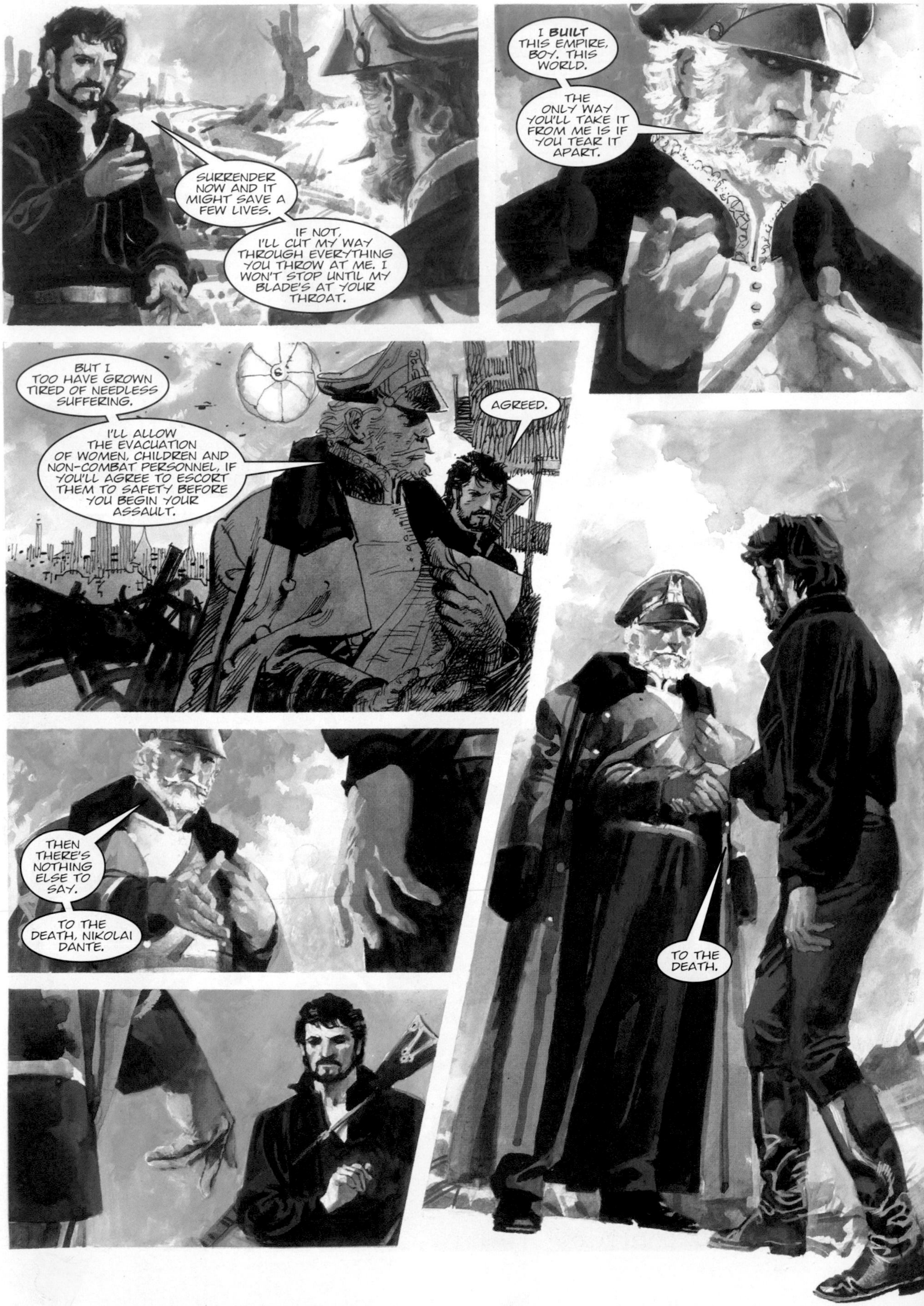
SURRENDER NOW AND IT MIGHT SAVE A FEW LIVES.
IF NOT, I'LL CUT MY WAY THROUGH EVERYTHING YOU THROW AT ME. I WON'T STOP UNTIL MY BLADE'S AT YOUR THROAT.
I **BUILT** THIS EMPIRE, BOY. THIS WORLD.
THE ONLY WAY YOU'LL TAKE IT FROM ME IS IF YOU TEAR IT APART.
BUT I TOO HAVE GROWN TIRED OF NEEDLESS SUFFERING.
I'LL ALLOW THE EVACUATION OF WOMEN, CHILDREN AND NON-COMBAT PERSONNEL, IF YOU'LL AGREE TO ESCORT THEM TO SAFETY BEFORE YOU BEGIN YOUR ASSAULT.
AGREED.
THEN THERE'S NOTHING ELSE TO SAY.
TO THE DEATH, NIKOLAI DANTE.
TO THE DEATH.

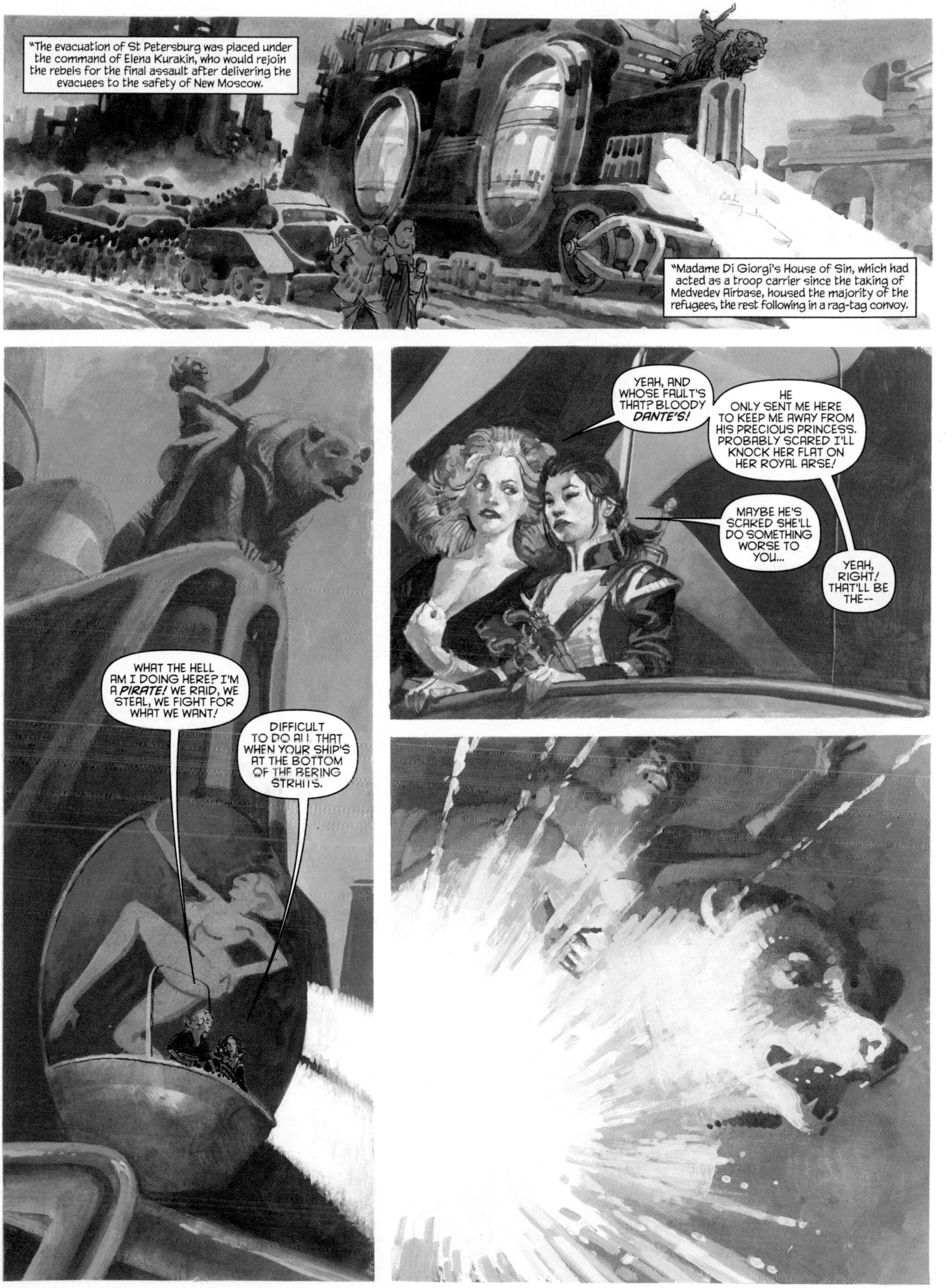

"The evacuation of St Petersburg was placed under the command of Elena Kurakin, who would rejoin the rebels for the final assault after delivering the evacuees to the safety of New Moscow.
"Madame Di Giorgi's House of Sin, which had acted as a troop carrier since the taking of Medvedev Airbase, housed the majority of the refugees, the rest following in a rag-tag convoy.
WHAT THE HELL AM I DOING HERE? I'M A ***PIRATE!*** WE RAID, WE STEAL, WE FIGHT FOR WHAT WE WANT!
DIFFICULT TO DO ALL THAT WHEN YOUR SHIP'S AT THE BOTTOM OF THE BERING STRAITS.
YEAH, AND WHOSE FAULT'S THAT? BLOODY ***DANTE'S!***
HE ONLY SENT ME HERE TO KEEP ME AWAY FROM HIS PRECIOUS PRINCESS. PROBABLY SCARED I'LL KNOCK HER FLAT ON HER ROYAL ARSE!
MAYBE HE'S SCARED SHE'LL DO SOMETHING WORSE TO YOU...
YEAH, RIGHT! THAT'LL BE THE--

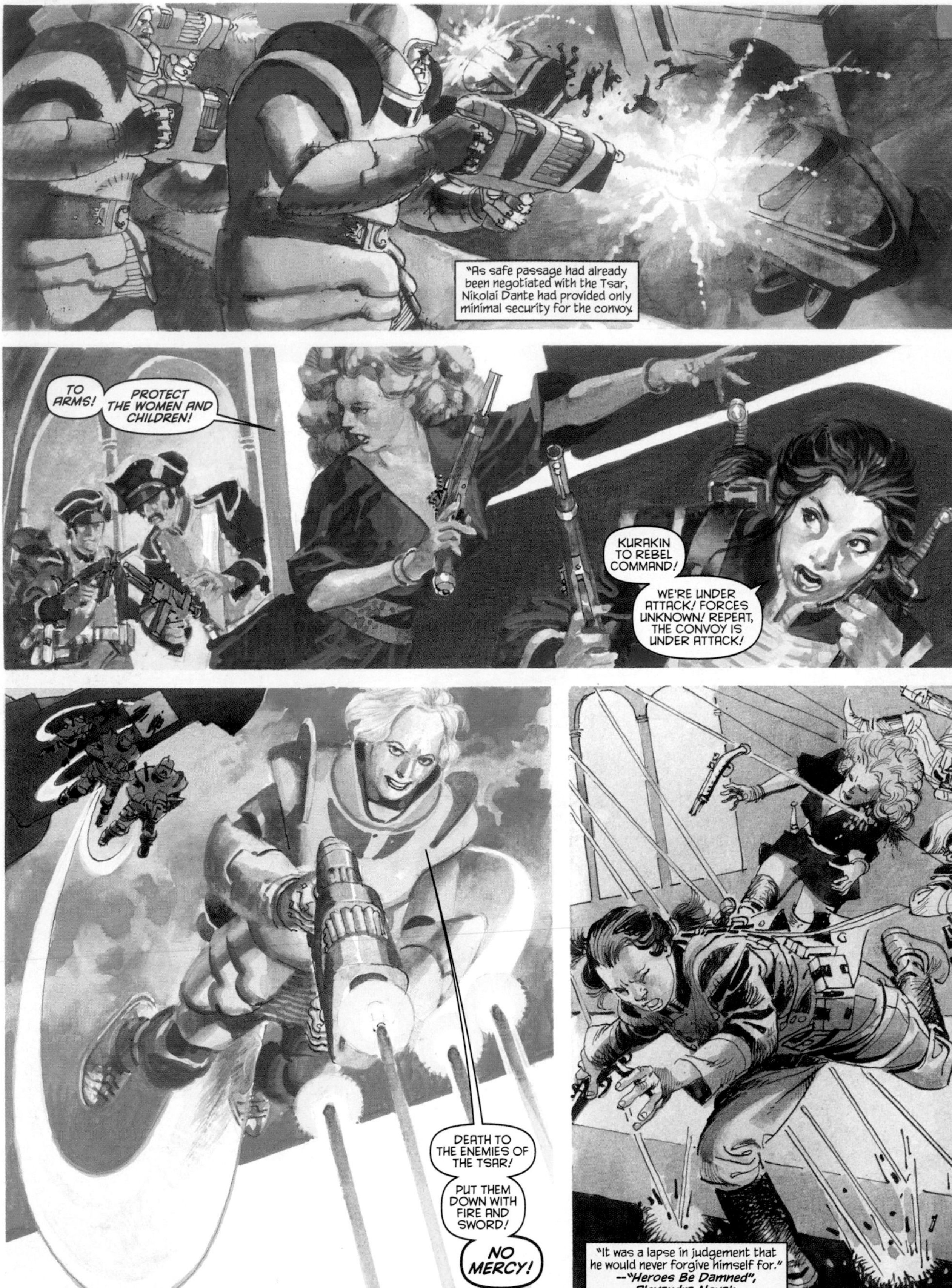
"As safe passage had already been negotiated with the Tsar, Nikolai Dante had provided only minimal security for the convoy.
TO ARMS!
PROTECT THE WOMEN AND CHILDREN!
KURAKIN TO REBEL COMMAND!
WE'RE UNDER ATTACK! FORCES UNKNOWN! REPEAT, THE CONVOY IS UNDER ATTACK!
DEATH TO THE ENEMIES OF THE TSAR!
PUT THEM DOWN WITH FIRE AND SWORD!
NO MERCY!
"It was a lapse in judgement that he would never forgive himself for." --"Heroes Be Damned", Alexandra Novak.

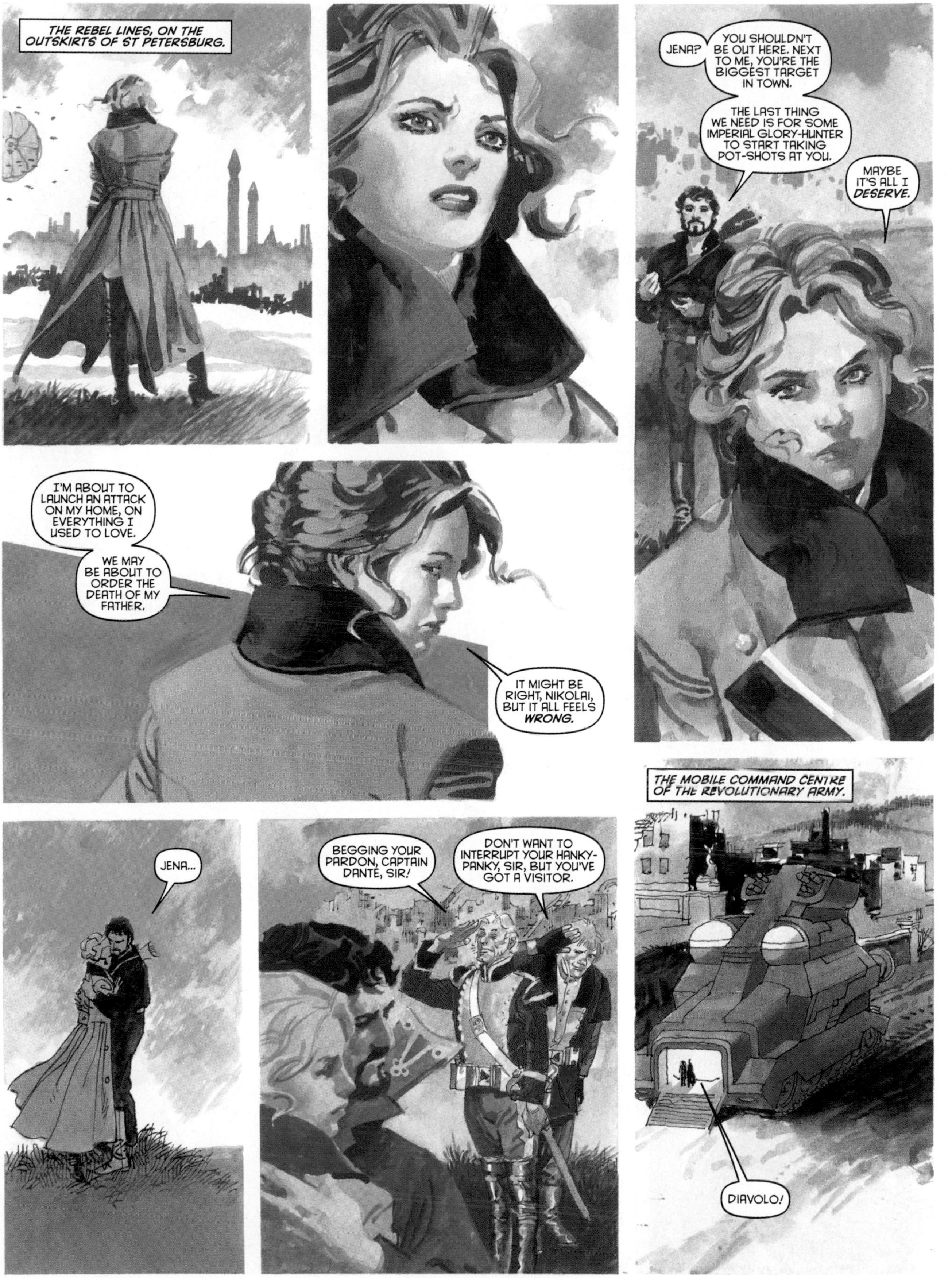
THE REBEL LINES, ON THE OUTSKIRTS OF ST PETERSBURG.
JENA?
YOU SHOULDN'T BE OUT HERE. NEXT TO ME, YOU'RE THE BIGGEST TARGET IN TOWN.
THE LAST THING WE NEED IS FOR SOME IMPERIAL GLORY-HUNTER TO START TAKING POT-SHOTS AT YOU.
MAYBE IT'S ALL I DESERVE.
I'M ABOUT TO LAUNCH AN ATTACK ON MY HOME, ON EVERYTHING I USED TO LOVE.
WE MAY BE ABOUT TO ORDER THE DEATH OF MY FATHER.
IT MIGHT BE RIGHT, NIKOLAI, BUT IT ALL FEELS WRONG.
JENA...
BEGGING YOUR PARDON, CAPTAIN DANTE, SIR!
DON'T WANT TO INTERRUPT YOUR HANKY-PANKY, SIR, BUT YOU'VE GOT A VISITOR.
THE MOBILE COMMAND CENTRE OF THE REVOLUTIONARY ARMY.
DIAVOLO!

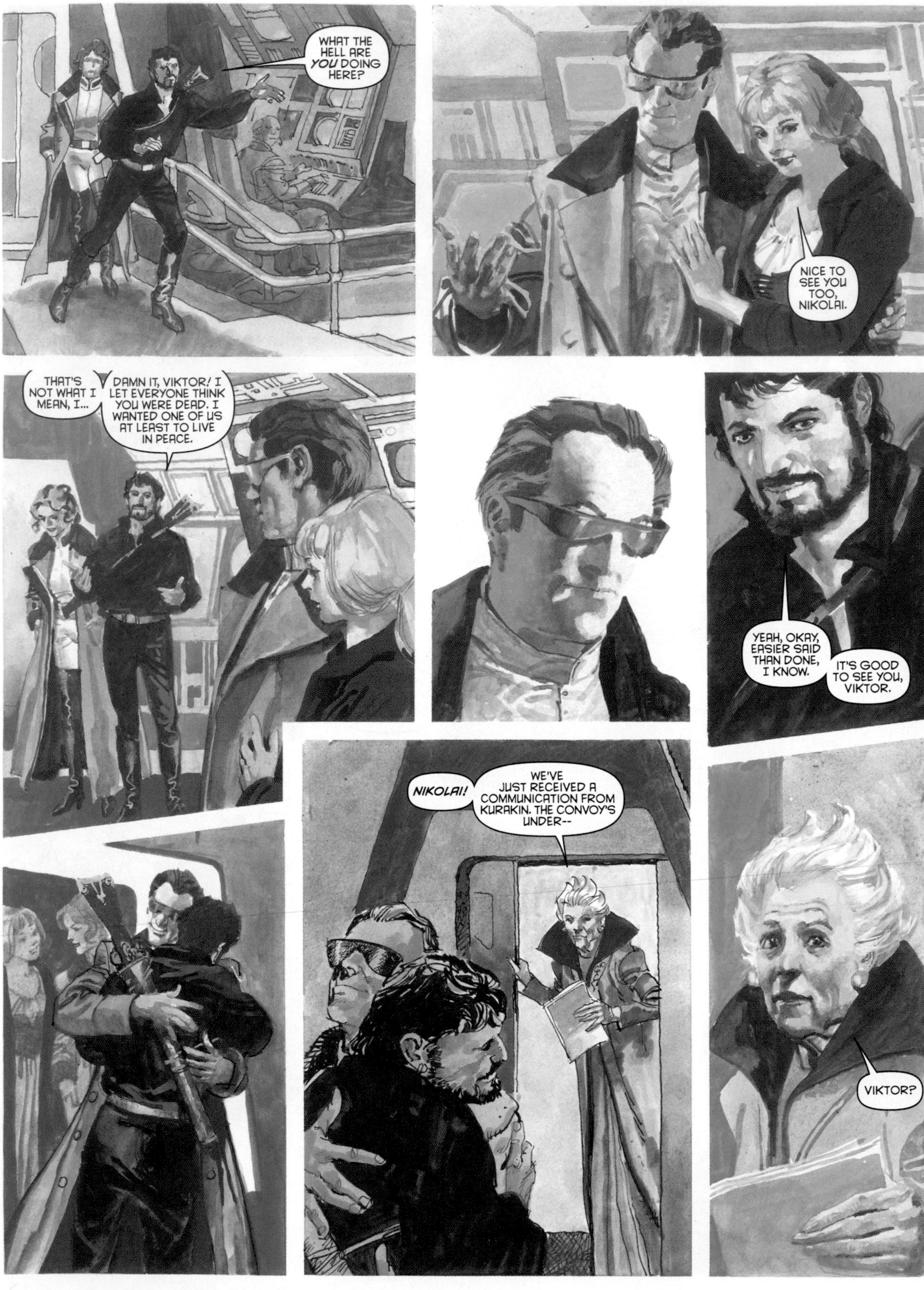
WHAT THE HELL ARE *YOU* DOING HERE?
NICE TO SEE YOU TOO, NIKOLAI.
THAT'S NOT WHAT I MEAN, I...
DAMN IT, VIKTOR! I LET EVERYONE THINK YOU WERE DEAD. I WANTED ONE OF US AT LEAST TO LIVE IN PEACE.
YEAH, OKAY, EASIER SAID THAN DONE, I KNOW.
IT'S GOOD TO SEE YOU, VIKTOR.
NIKOLAI!
WE'VE JUST RECEIVED A COMMUNICATION FROM KURAKIN. THE CONVOY'S UNDER--
VIKTOR?

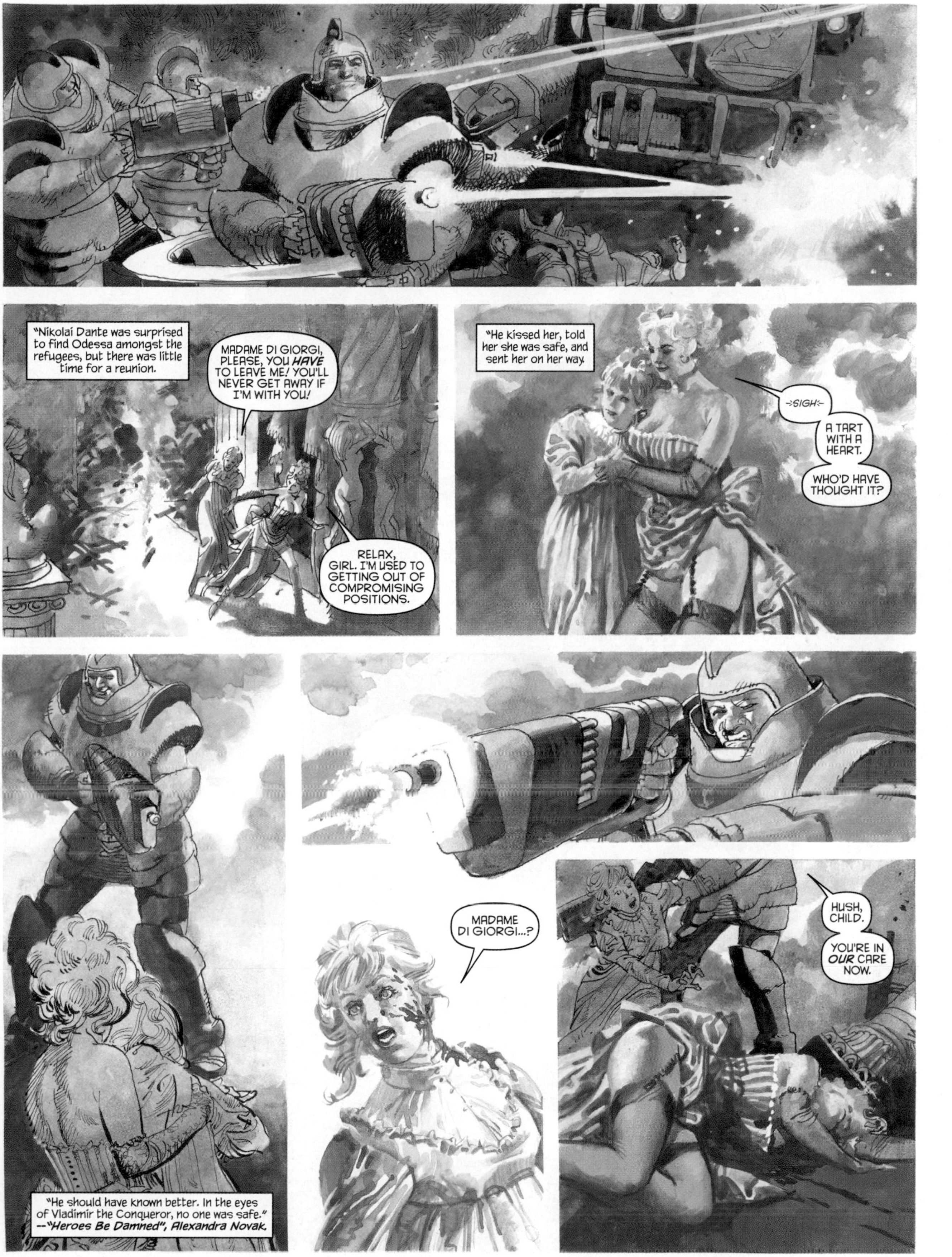
"Nikolai Dante was surprised to find Odessa amongst the refugees, but there was little time for a reunion.
MADAME DI GIORGI, PLEASE, YOU *HAVE* TO LEAVE ME! YOU'LL NEVER GET AWAY IF I'M WITH YOU!
RELAX, GIRL. I'M USED TO GETTING OUT OF COMPROMISING POSITIONS.
"He kissed her, told her she was safe, and sent her on her way.
~SIGH~
A TART WITH A HEART.
WHO'D HAVE THOUGHT IT?
"He should have known better. In the eyes of Vladimir the Conqueror, no one was safe."
--*"Heroes Be Damned", Alexandra Novak.*
MADAME DI GIORGI...?
HUSH, CHILD.
YOU'RE IN *OUR* CARE NOW.

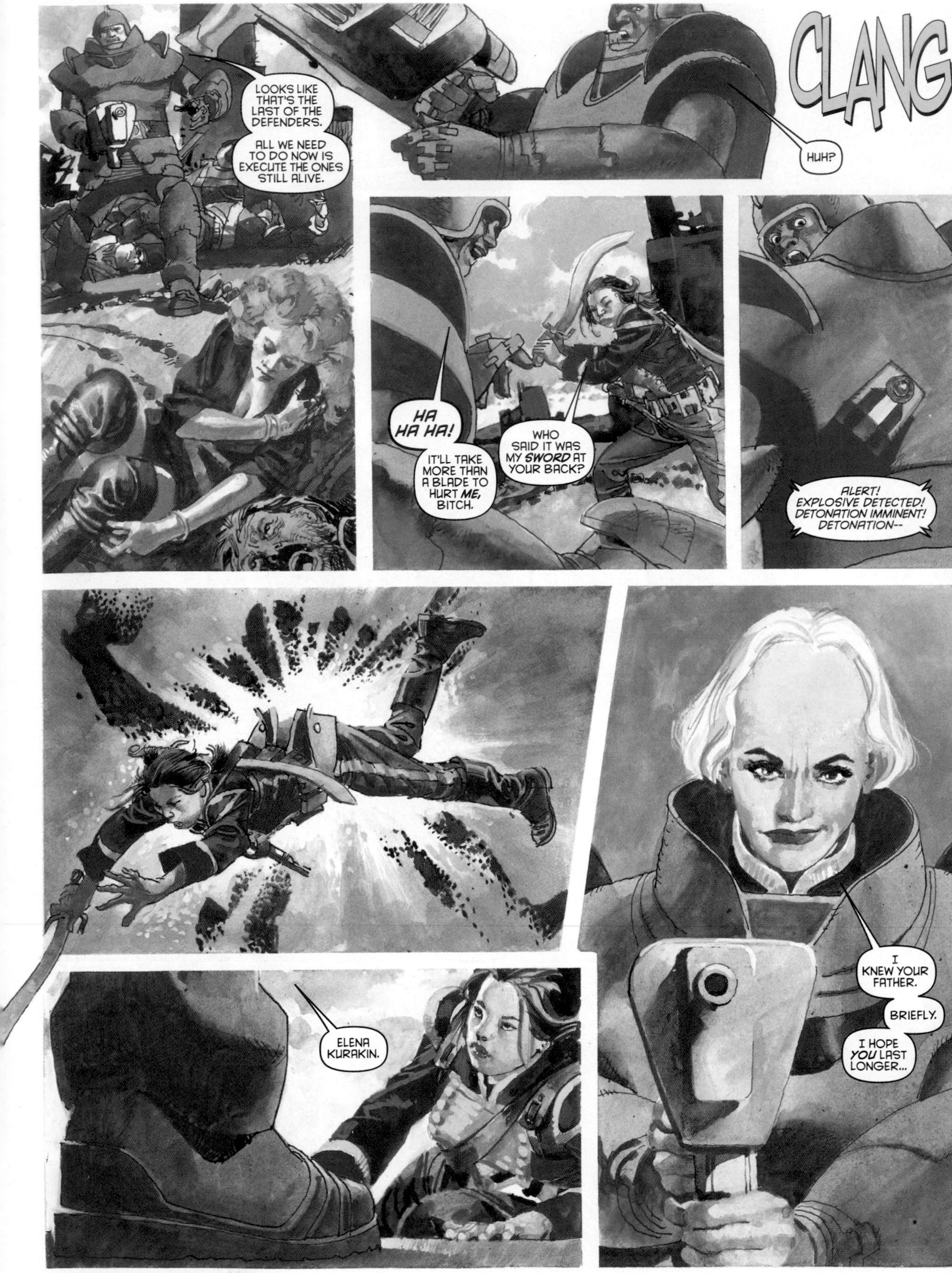
LOOKS LIKE THAT'S THE LAST OF THE DEFENDERS.
ALL WE NEED TO DO NOW IS EXECUTE THE ONES STILL ALIVE.
CLANG
HUH?
HA HA HA!
IT'LL TAKE MORE THAN A BLADE TO HURT ME, BITCH.
WHO SAID IT WAS MY SWORD AT YOUR BACK?
ALERT! EXPLOSIVE DETECTED! DETONATION IMMINENT! DETONATION--
ELENA KURAKIN.
I KNEW YOUR FATHER.
BRIEFLY.
I HOPE YOU LAST LONGER...

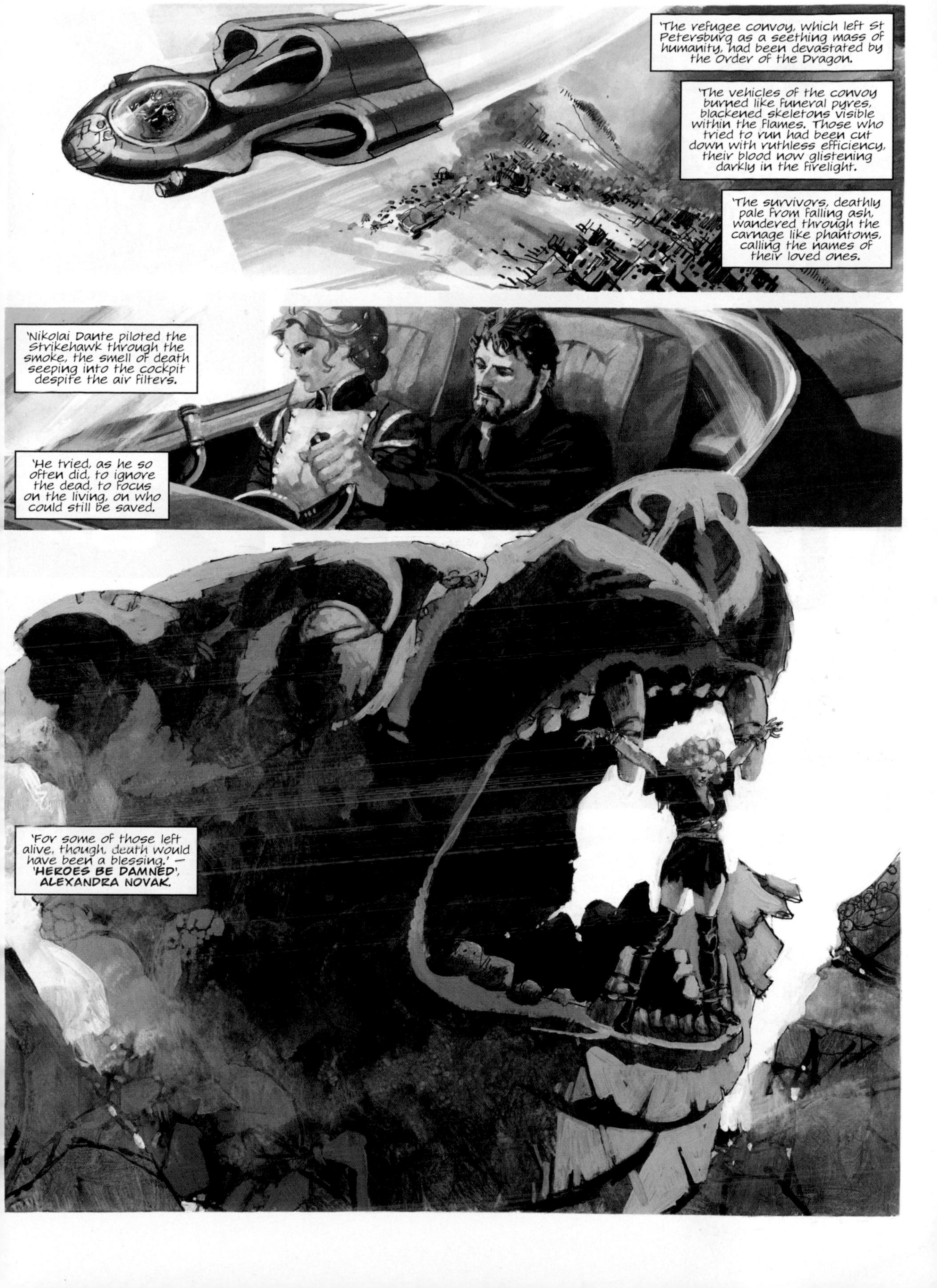
'The refugee convoy, which left St Petersburg as a seething mass of humanity, had been devastated by the Order of the Dragon.
'The vehicles of the convoy burned like funeral pyres, blackened skeletons visible within the flames. Those who tried to run had been cut down with ruthless efficiency, their blood now glistening darkly in the firelight.
'The survivors, deathly pale from falling ash, wandered through the carnage like phantoms, calling the names of their loved ones.
'Nikolai Dante piloted the Strikehawk through the smoke, the smell of death seeping into the cockpit despite the air filters.
'He tried, as he so often did, to ignore the dead, to focus on the living, on who could still be saved.
'For some of those left alive, though, death would have been a blessing.' — 'HEROES BE DAMNED', ALEXANDRA NOVAK.

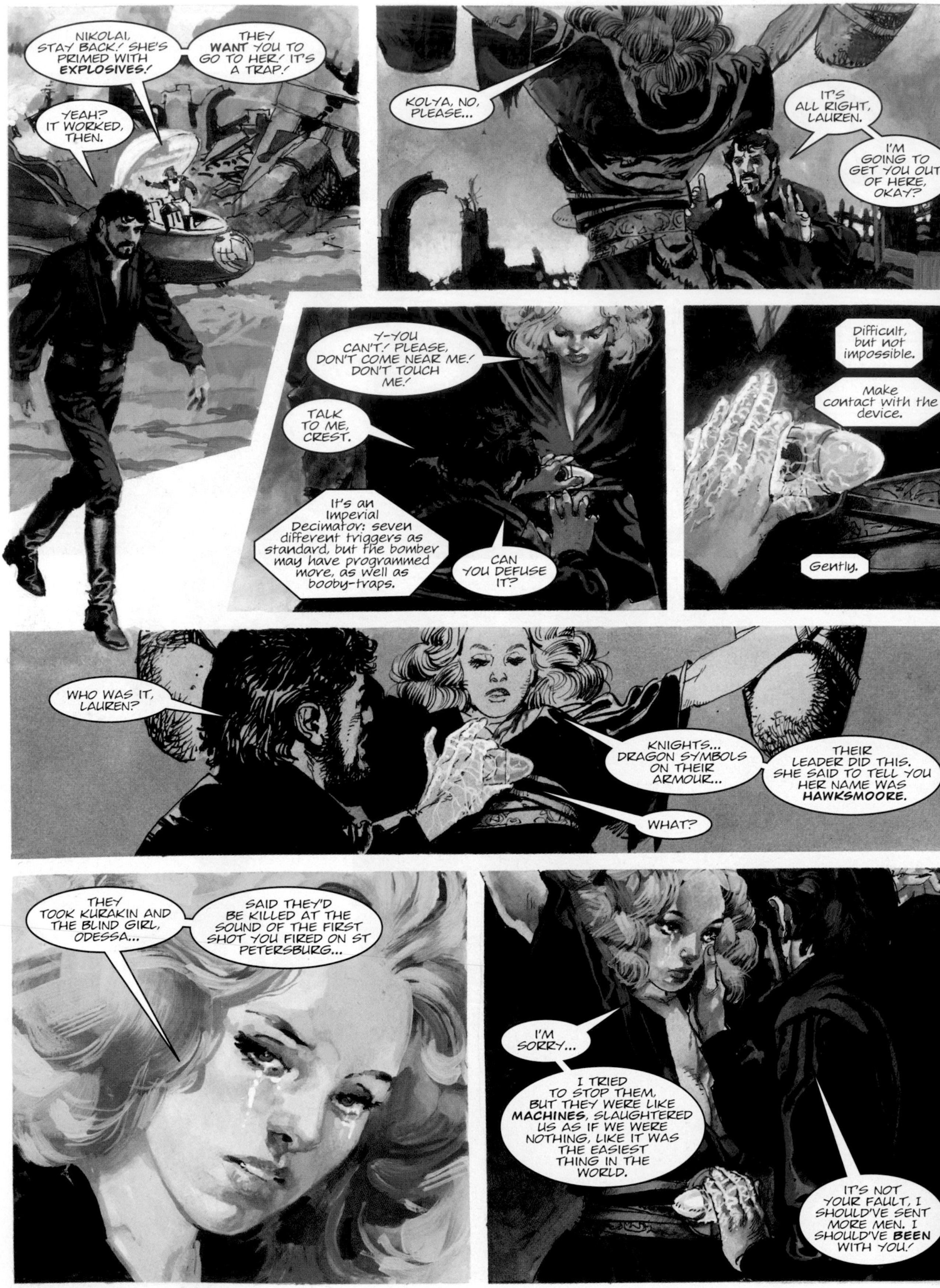
NIKOLAI, STAY BACK! SHE'S PRIMED WITH EXPLOSIVES!
THEY WANT YOU TO GO TO HER! IT'S A TRAP!
YEAH? IT WORKED, THEN.
KOLYA, NO, PLEASE...
IT'S ALL RIGHT, LAUREN.
I'M GOING TO GET YOU OUT OF HERE, OKAY?
Y-YOU CAN'T! PLEASE, DON'T COME NEAR ME! DON'T TOUCH ME!
TALK TO ME, CREST.
It's an Imperial Decimator: seven different triggers as standard, but the bomber may have programmed more, as well as booby-traps.
CAN YOU DEFUSE IT?
Difficult, but not impossible.
Make contact with the device.
Gently.
WHO WAS IT, LAUREN?
KNIGHTS... DRAGON SYMBOLS ON THEIR ARMOUR...
THEIR LEADER DID THIS. SHE SAID TO TELL YOU HER NAME WAS HAWKSMOORE.
WHAT?
THEY TOOK KURAKIN AND THE BLIND GIRL, ODESSA...
SAID THEY'D BE KILLED AT THE SOUND OF THE FIRST SHOT YOU FIRED ON ST PETERSBURG...
I'M SORRY...
I TRIED TO STOP THEM, BUT THEY WERE LIKE MACHINES, SLAUGHTERED US AS IF WE WERE NOTHING, LIKE IT WAS THE EASIEST THING IN THE WORLD.
IT'S NOT YOUR FAULT, I SHOULD'VE SENT MORE MEN. I SHOULD'VE BEEN WITH YOU!

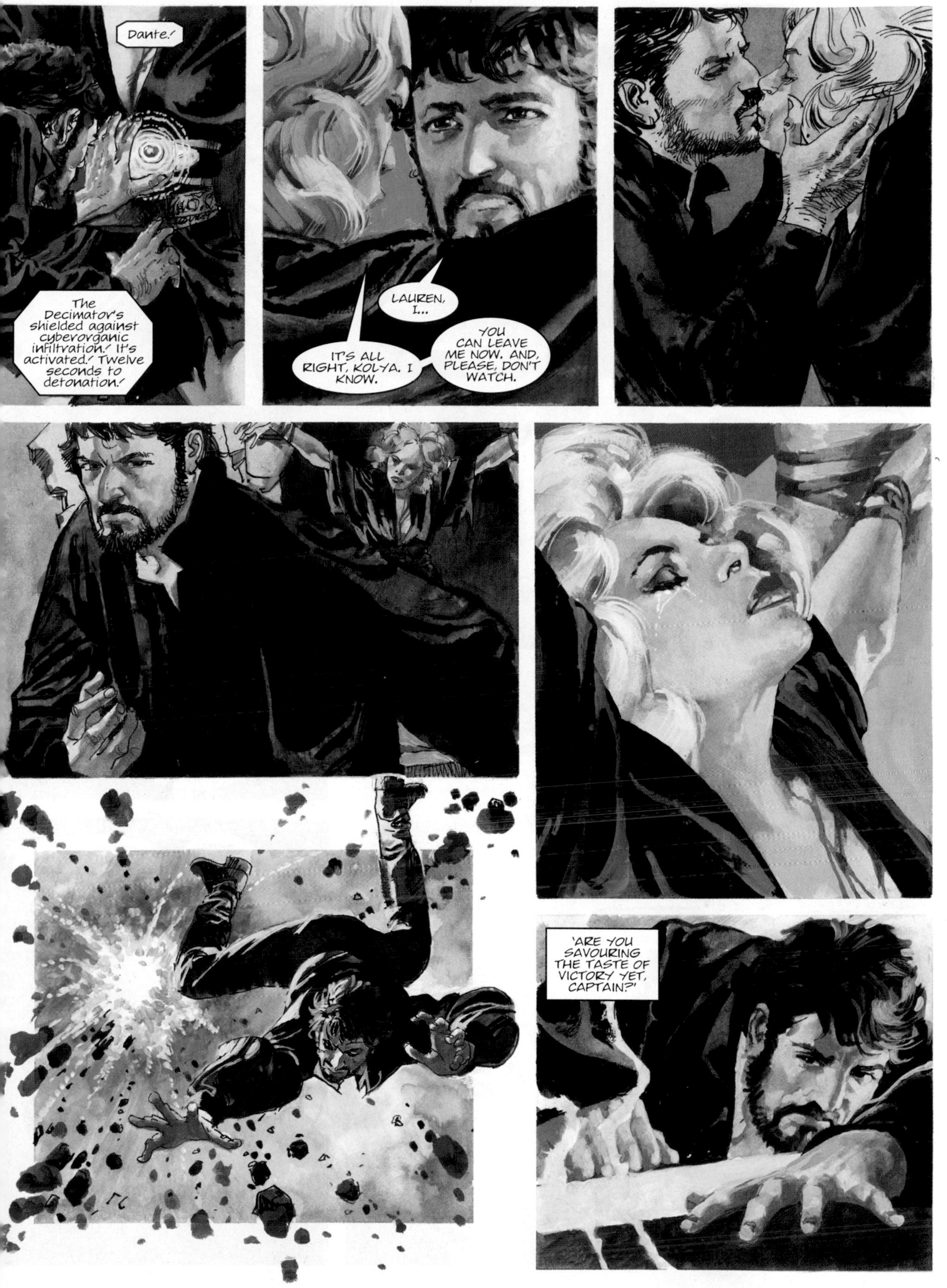

Dante.!
The Decimator's shielded against cyberorganic infiltration.! It's activated.! Twelve seconds to detonation.!
LAUREN, I...
IT'S ALL RIGHT, KOLYA. I KNOW.
YOU CAN LEAVE ME NOW. AND, PLEASE, DON'T WATCH.
'ARE YOU SAVOURING THE TASTE OF VICTORY YET, CAPTAIN?'

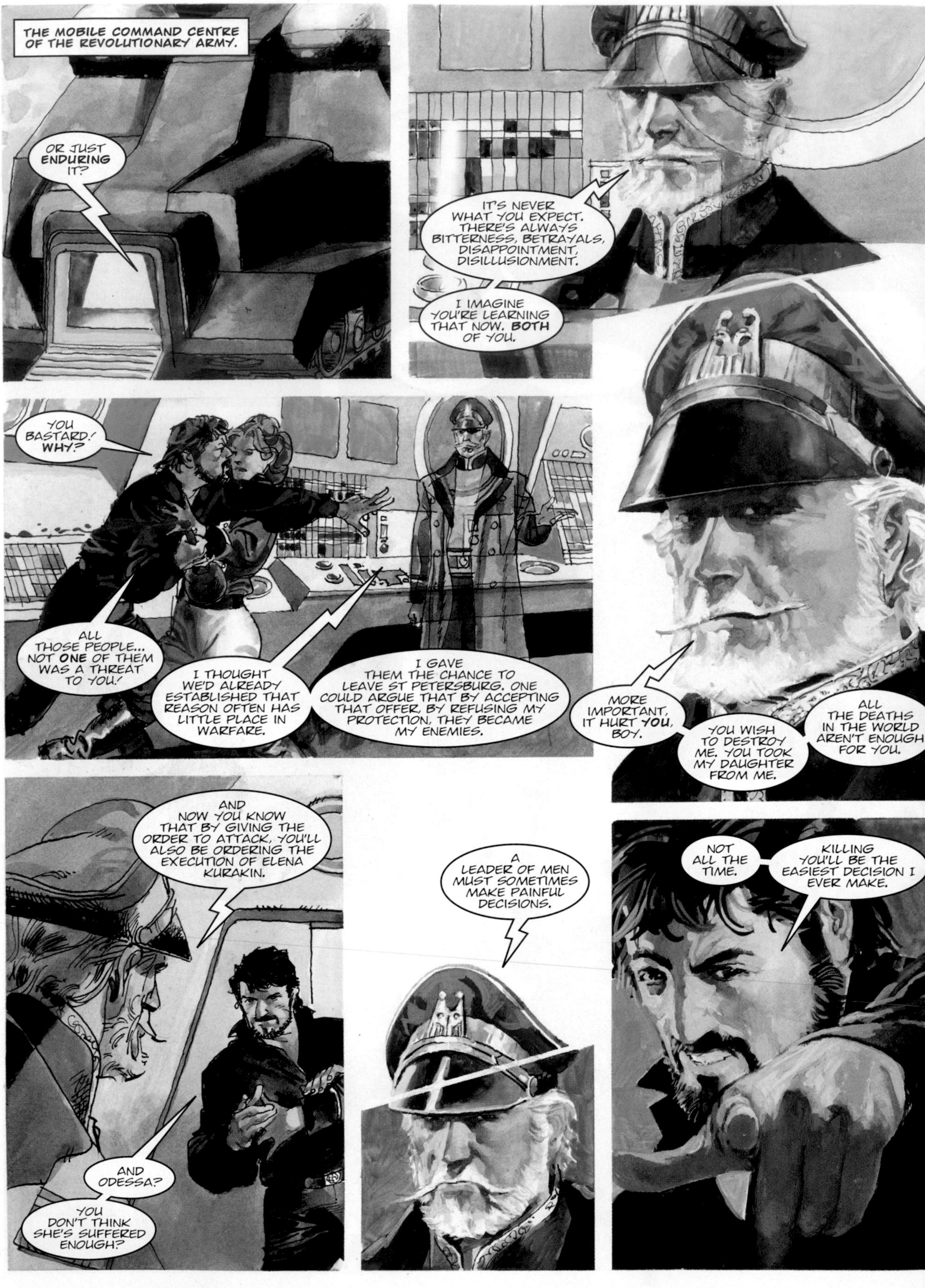
THE MOBILE COMMAND CENTRE OF THE REVOLUTIONARY ARMY.
OR JUST ENDURING IT?
IT'S NEVER WHAT YOU EXPECT. THERE'S ALWAYS BITTERNESS, BETRAYALS, DISAPPOINTMENT, DISILLUSIONMENT.
I IMAGINE YOU'RE LEARNING THAT NOW. BOTH OF YOU.
YOU BASTARD! WHY?
ALL THOSE PEOPLE... NOT ONE OF THEM WAS A THREAT TO YOU!
I THOUGHT WE'D ALREADY ESTABLISHED THAT REASON OFTEN HAS LITTLE PLACE IN WARFARE.
I GAVE THEM THE CHANCE TO LEAVE ST PETERSBURG. ONE COULD ARGUE THAT BY ACCEPTING THAT OFFER, BY REFUSING MY PROTECTION, THEY BECAME MY ENEMIES.
MORE IMPORTANT, IT HURT YOU, BOY.
YOU WISH TO DESTROY ME. YOU TOOK MY DAUGHTER FROM ME.
ALL THE DEATHS IN THE WORLD AREN'T ENOUGH FOR YOU.
AND NOW YOU KNOW THAT BY GIVING THE ORDER TO ATTACK, YOU'LL ALSO BE ORDERING THE EXECUTION OF ELENA KURAKIN.
AND ODESSA?
YOU DON'T THINK SHE'S SUFFERED ENOUGH?
A LEADER OF MEN MUST SOMETIMES MAKE PAINFUL DECISIONS.
NOT ALL THE TIME.
KILLING YOU'LL BE THE EASIEST DECISION I EVER MAKE.

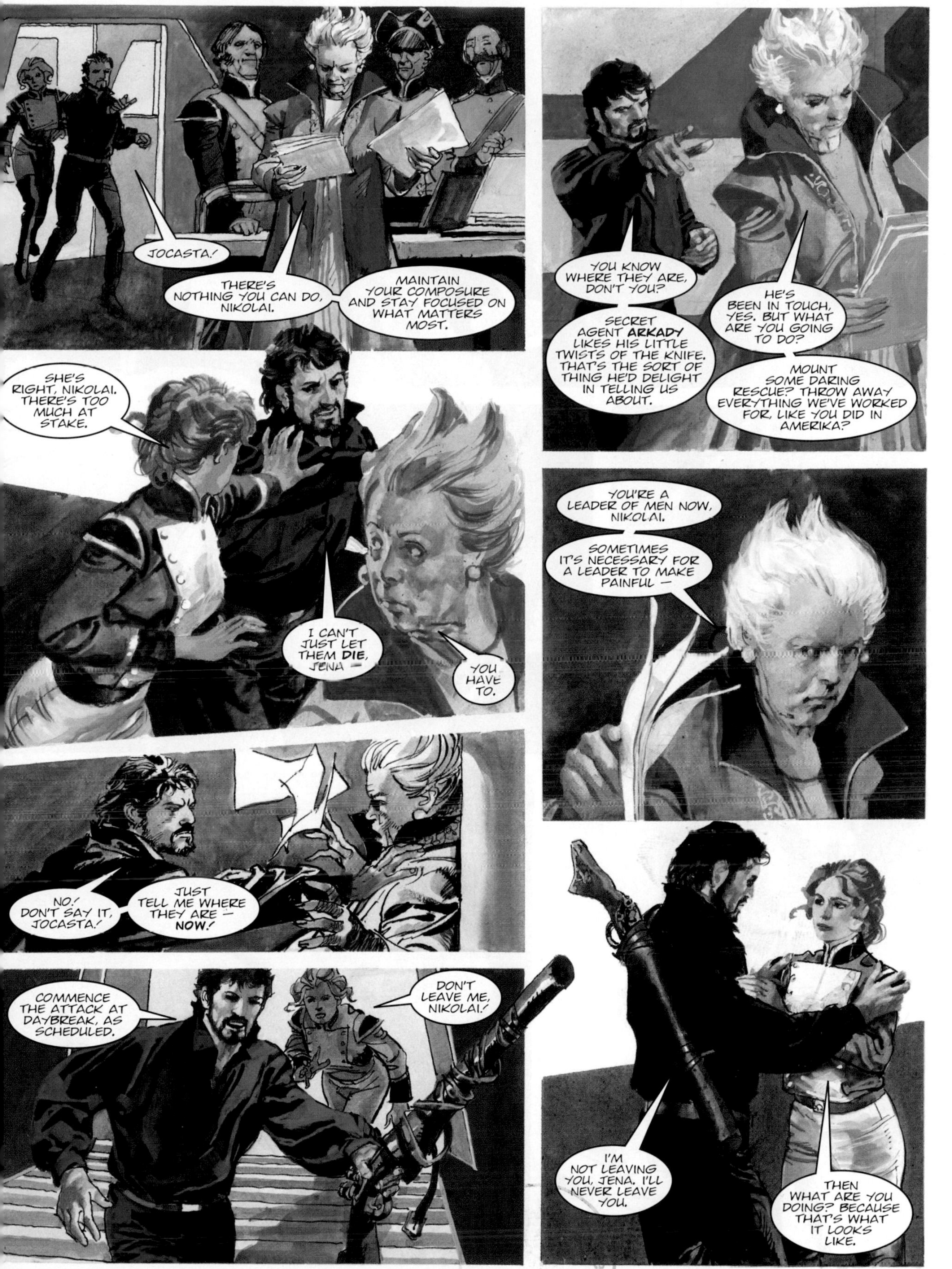

JOCASTA!
THERE'S NOTHING YOU CAN DO, NIKOLAI.
MAINTAIN YOUR COMPOSURE AND STAY FOCUSED ON WHAT MATTERS MOST.
YOU KNOW WHERE THEY ARE, DON'T YOU?
SECRET AGENT **ARKADY** LIKES HIS LITTLE TWISTS OF THE KNIFE. THAT'S THE SORT OF THING HE'D DELIGHT IN TELLING US ABOUT.
HE'S BEEN IN TOUCH, YES. BUT WHAT ARE YOU GOING TO DO?
MOUNT SOME DARING RESCUE? THROW AWAY EVERYTHING WE'VE WORKED FOR, LIKE YOU DID IN AMERIKA?
SHE'S RIGHT, NIKOLAI. THERE'S TOO MUCH AT STAKE.
I CAN'T JUST LET THEM **DIE**, JENA —
YOU HAVE TO.
YOU'RE A LEADER OF MEN NOW, NIKOLAI.
SOMETIMES IT'S NECESSARY FOR A LEADER TO MAKE PAINFUL —
NO! DON'T SAY IT, JOCASTA!
JUST TELL ME WHERE THEY ARE — **NOW**!
COMMENCE THE ATTACK AT DAYBREAK, AS SCHEDULED.
DON'T LEAVE ME, NIKOLAI!
I'M NOT LEAVING YOU, JENA. I'LL NEVER LEAVE YOU.
THEN WHAT ARE YOU DOING? BECAUSE THAT'S WHAT IT LOOKS LIKE.

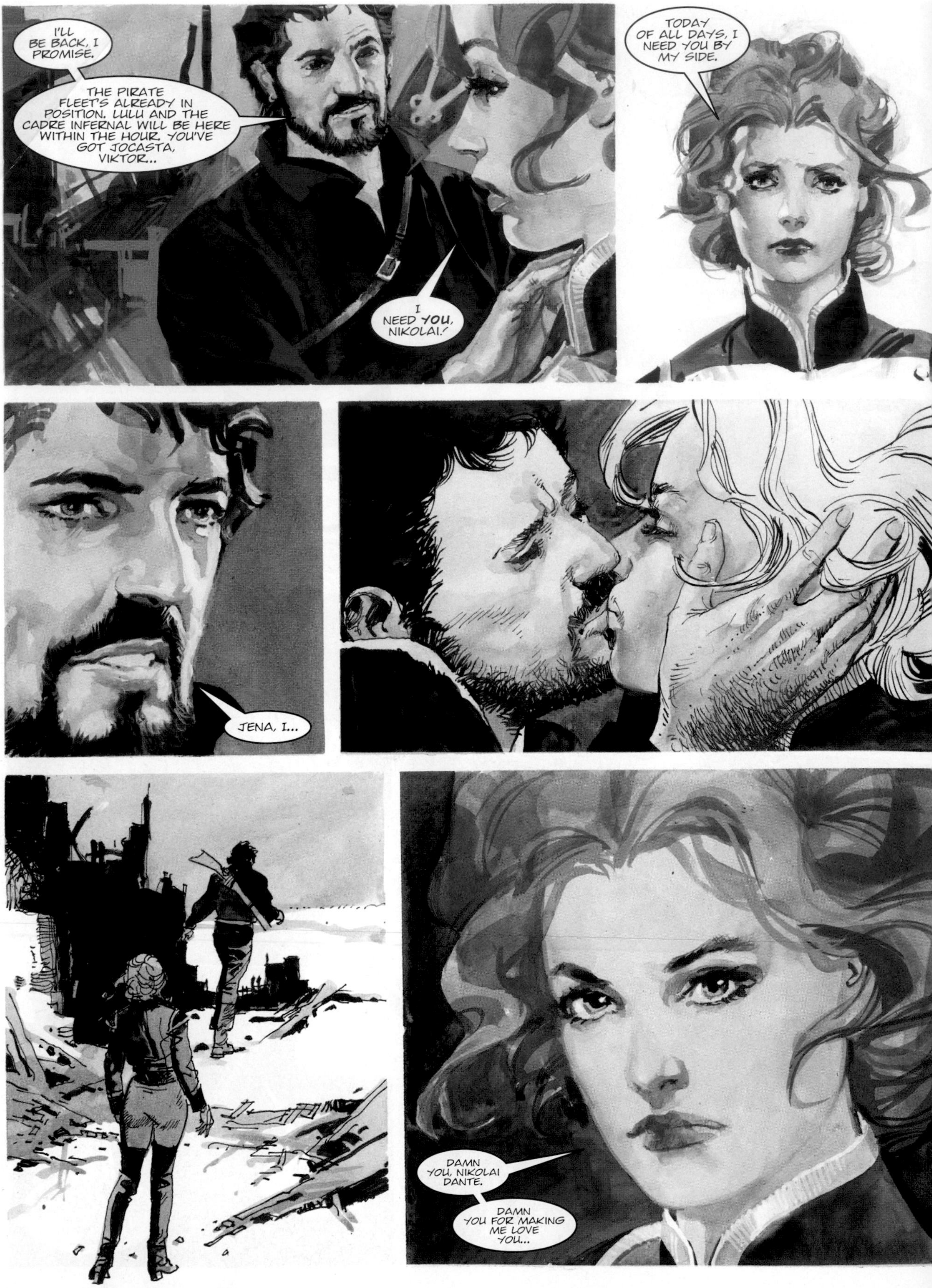
I'LL BE BACK, I PROMISE.
THE PIRATE FLEET'S ALREADY IN POSITION. LULU AND THE CADRE INFERNAL WILL BE HERE WITHIN THE HOUR. YOU'VE GOT JOCASTA, VIKTOR...
I NEED **YOU**, NIKOLAI!
TODAY OF ALL DAYS, I NEED YOU BY MY SIDE.
JENA, I...
DAMN YOU, NIKOLAI DANTE.
DAMN YOU FOR MAKING ME LOVE YOU...

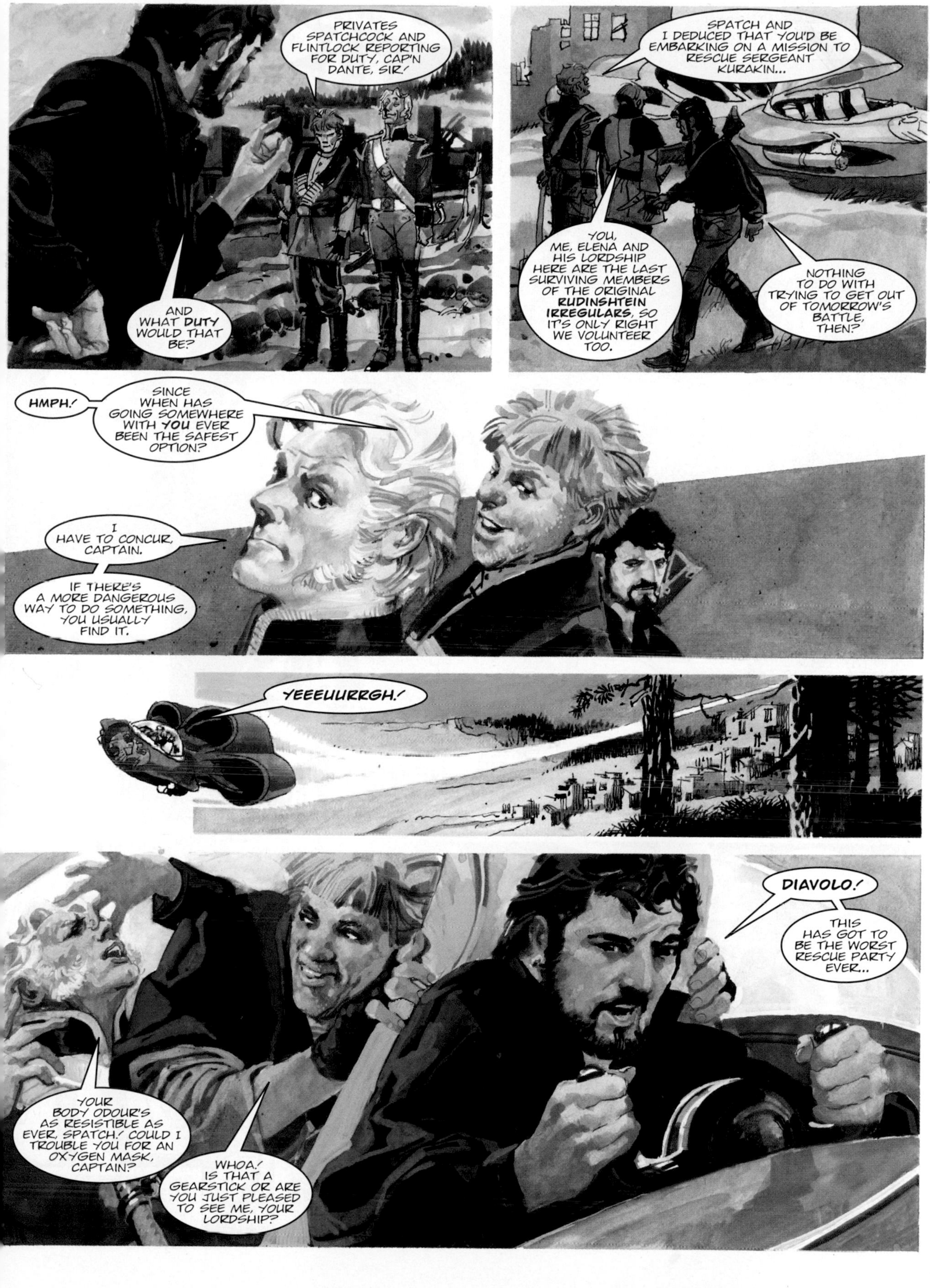

PRIVATES SPATCHCOCK AND FLINTLOCK REPORTING FOR DUTY, CAP'N DANTE, SIR!
AND WHAT **DUTY** WOULD THAT BE?
SPATCH AND I DEDUCED THAT YOU'D BE EMBARKING ON A MISSION TO RESCUE SERGEANT KURAKIN...
YOU, ME, ELENA AND HIS LORDSHIP HERE ARE THE LAST SURVIVING MEMBERS OF THE ORIGINAL **RUDINSHTEIN IRREGULARS**, SO IT'S ONLY RIGHT WE VOLUNTEER TOO.
NOTHING TO DO WITH TRYING TO GET OUT OF TOMORROW'S BATTLE, THEN?
HMPH!
SINCE WHEN HAS GOING SOMEWHERE WITH **YOU** EVER BEEN THE SAFEST OPTION?
I HAVE TO CONCUR, CAPTAIN.
IF THERE'S A MORE DANGEROUS WAY TO DO SOMETHING, YOU USUALLY FIND IT.
YEEEUURRGH!
DIAVOLO!
THIS HAS GOT TO BE THE WORST RESCUE PARTY EVER...
YOUR BODY ODOUR'S AS RESISTIBLE AS EVER, SPATCH! COULD I TROUBLE YOU FOR AN OXYGEN MASK, CAPTAIN?
WHOA! IS THAT A GEARSTICK OR ARE YOU JUST PLEASED TO SEE ME, YOUR LORDSHIP?

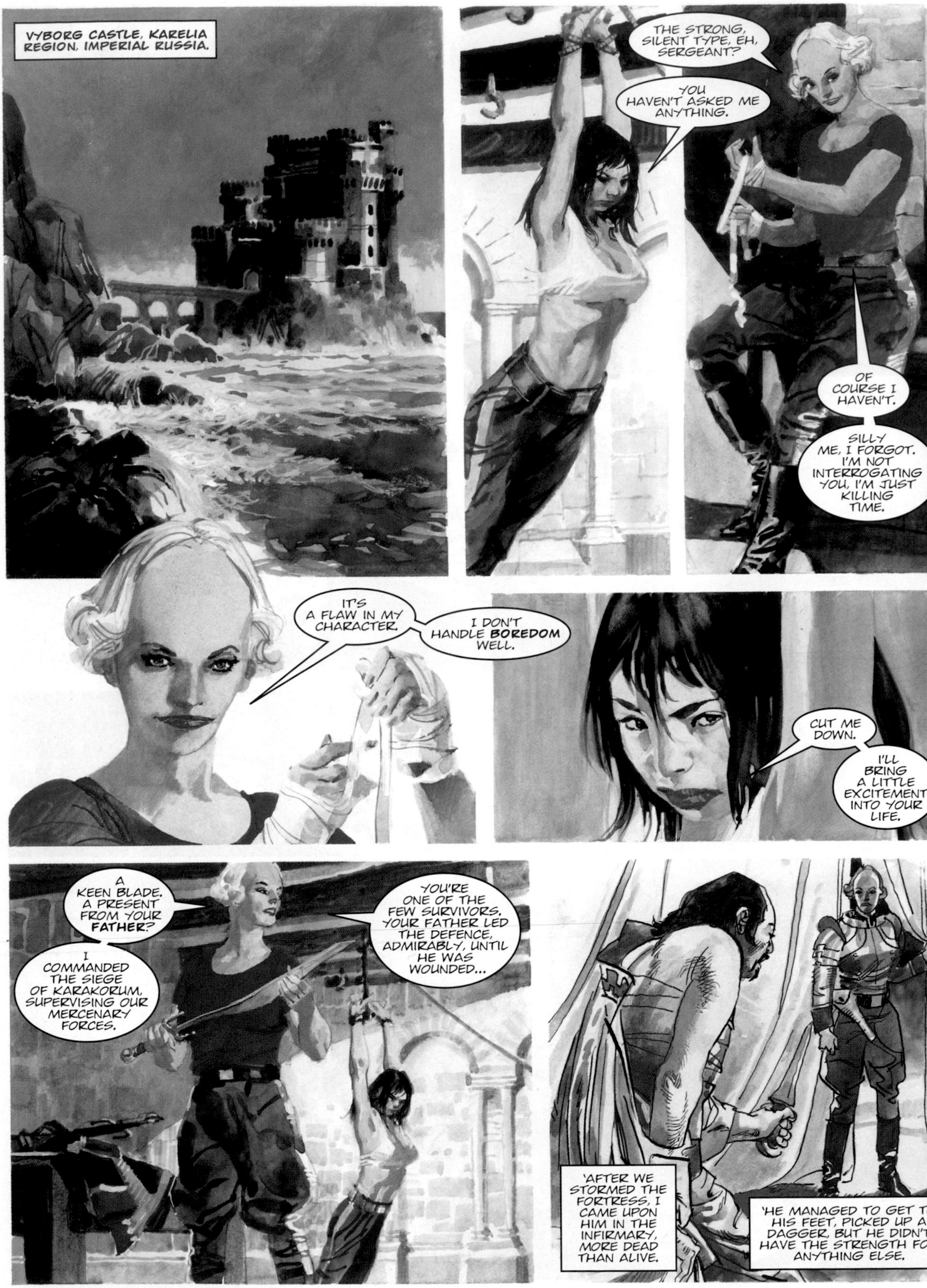
VYBORG CASTLE, KARELIA REGION, IMPERIAL RUSSIA.
THE STRONG, SILENT TYPE, EH, SERGEANT?
YOU HAVEN'T ASKED ME ANYTHING.
OF COURSE I HAVEN'T.
SILLY ME, I FORGOT. I'M NOT INTERROGATING YOU, I'M JUST KILLING TIME.
IT'S A FLAW IN MY CHARACTER.
I DON'T HANDLE BOREDOM WELL.
CUT ME DOWN.
I'LL BRING A LITTLE EXCITEMENT INTO YOUR LIFE.
A KEEN BLADE. A PRESENT FROM YOUR FATHER?
I COMMANDED THE SIEGE OF KARAKORUM, SUPERVISING OUR MERCENARY FORCES.
YOU'RE ONE OF THE FEW SURVIVORS. YOUR FATHER LED THE DEFENCE, ADMIRABLY, UNTIL HE WAS WOUNDED...
'AFTER WE STORMED THE FORTRESS, I CAME UPON HIM IN THE INFIRMARY, MORE DEAD THAN ALIVE.
'HE MANAGED TO GET TO HIS FEET, PICKED UP A DAGGER, BUT HE DIDN'T HAVE THE STRENGTH FOR ANYTHING ELSE.

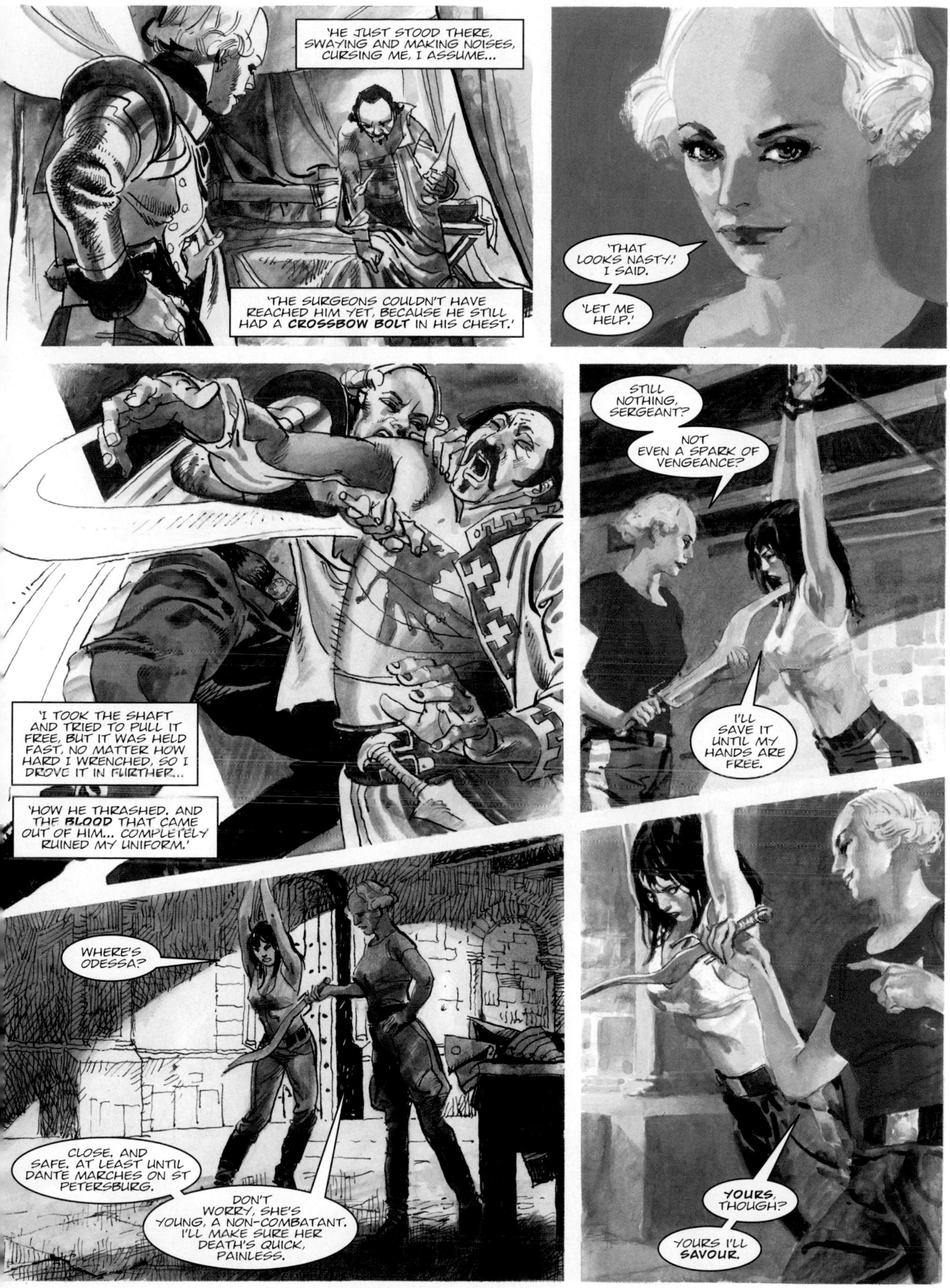
'HE JUST STOOD THERE, SWAYING AND MAKING NOISES, CURSING ME, I ASSUME...
'THE SURGEONS COULDN'T HAVE REACHED HIM YET, BECAUSE HE STILL HAD A **CROSSBOW BOLT** IN HIS CHEST.'
'THAT LOOKS NASTY,' I SAID.
'LET ME HELP.'
'I TOOK THE SHAFT AND TRIED TO PULL IT FREE, BUT IT WAS HELD FAST, NO MATTER HOW HARD I WRENCHED, SO I DROVE IT IN FURTHER...
'HOW HE THRASHED. AND THE **BLOOD** THAT CAME OUT OF HIM... COMPLETELY RUINED MY UNIFORM.'
STILL NOTHING, SERGEANT?
NOT EVEN A SPARK OF VENGEANCE?
I'LL SAVE IT UNTIL MY HANDS ARE FREE.
WHERE'S ODESSA?
CLOSE. AND SAFE. AT LEAST UNTIL DANTE MARCHES ON ST PETERSBURG.
DON'T WORRY, SHE'S YOUNG, A NON-COMBATANT. I'LL MAKE SURE HER DEATH'S QUICK, PAINLESS.
YOURS, THOUGH?
YOURS I'LL **SAVOUR**.

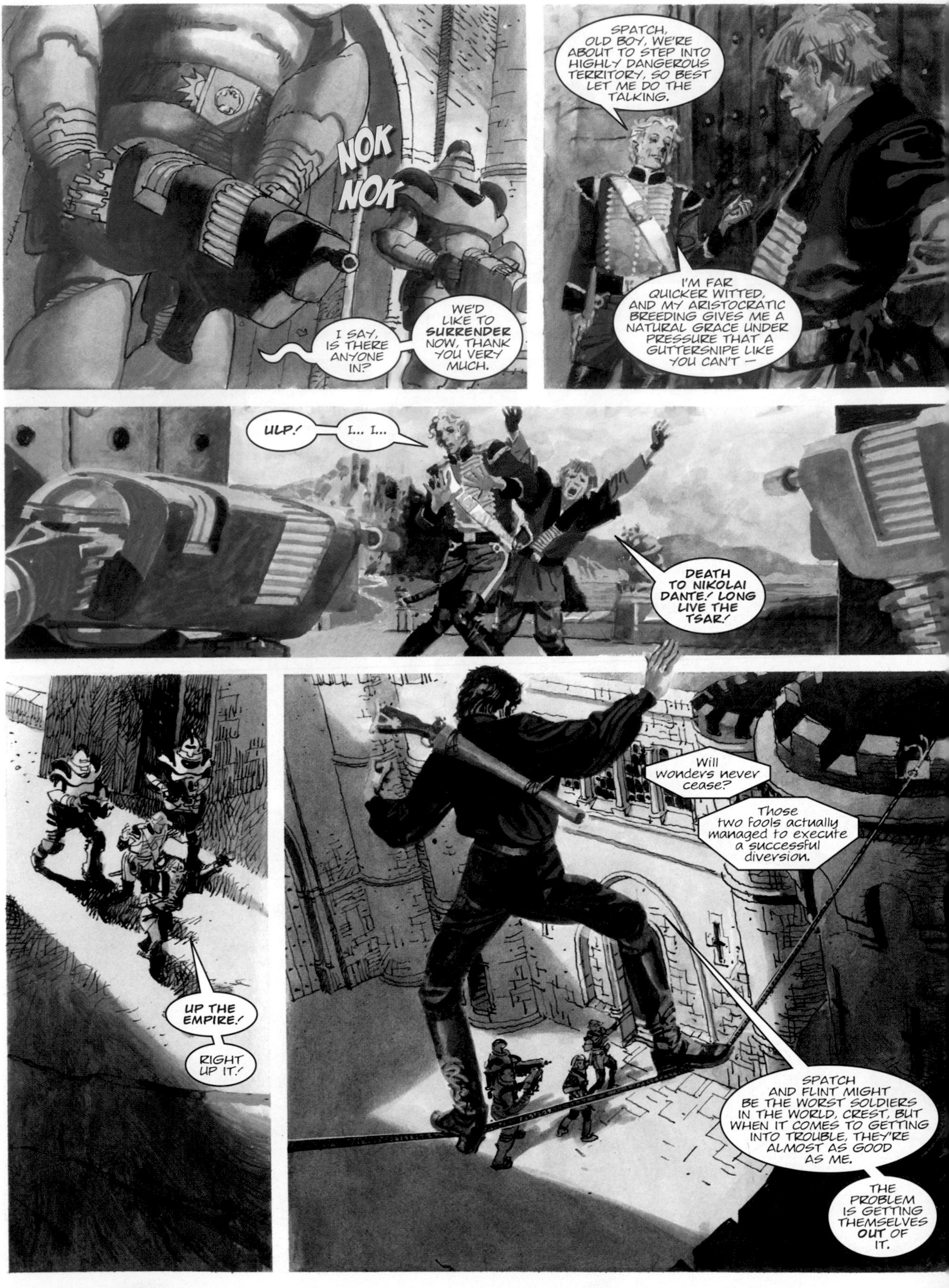
NOK NOK
I SAY, IS THERE ANYONE IN?
WE'D LIKE TO **SURRENDER** NOW, THANK YOU VERY MUCH.
SPATCH, OLD BOY, WE'RE ABOUT TO STEP INTO HIGHLY DANGEROUS TERRITORY, SO BEST LET ME DO THE TALKING.
I'M FAR QUICKER WITTED, AND MY ARISTOCRATIC BREEDING GIVES ME A NATURAL GRACE UNDER PRESSURE THAT A GUTTERSNIPE LIKE YOU CAN'T —
ULP!
I... I...
DEATH TO NIKOLAI DANTE! LONG LIVE THE TSAR!
UP THE EMPIRE!
RIGHT UP IT!
Will wonders never cease?
Those two fools actually managed to execute a successful diversion.
SPATCH AND FLINT MIGHT BE THE WORST SOLDIERS IN THE WORLD, CREST, BUT WHEN IT COMES TO GETTING INTO TROUBLE, THEY'RE ALMOST AS GOOD AS ME.
THE PROBLEM IS GETTING THEMSELVES **OUT** OF IT.

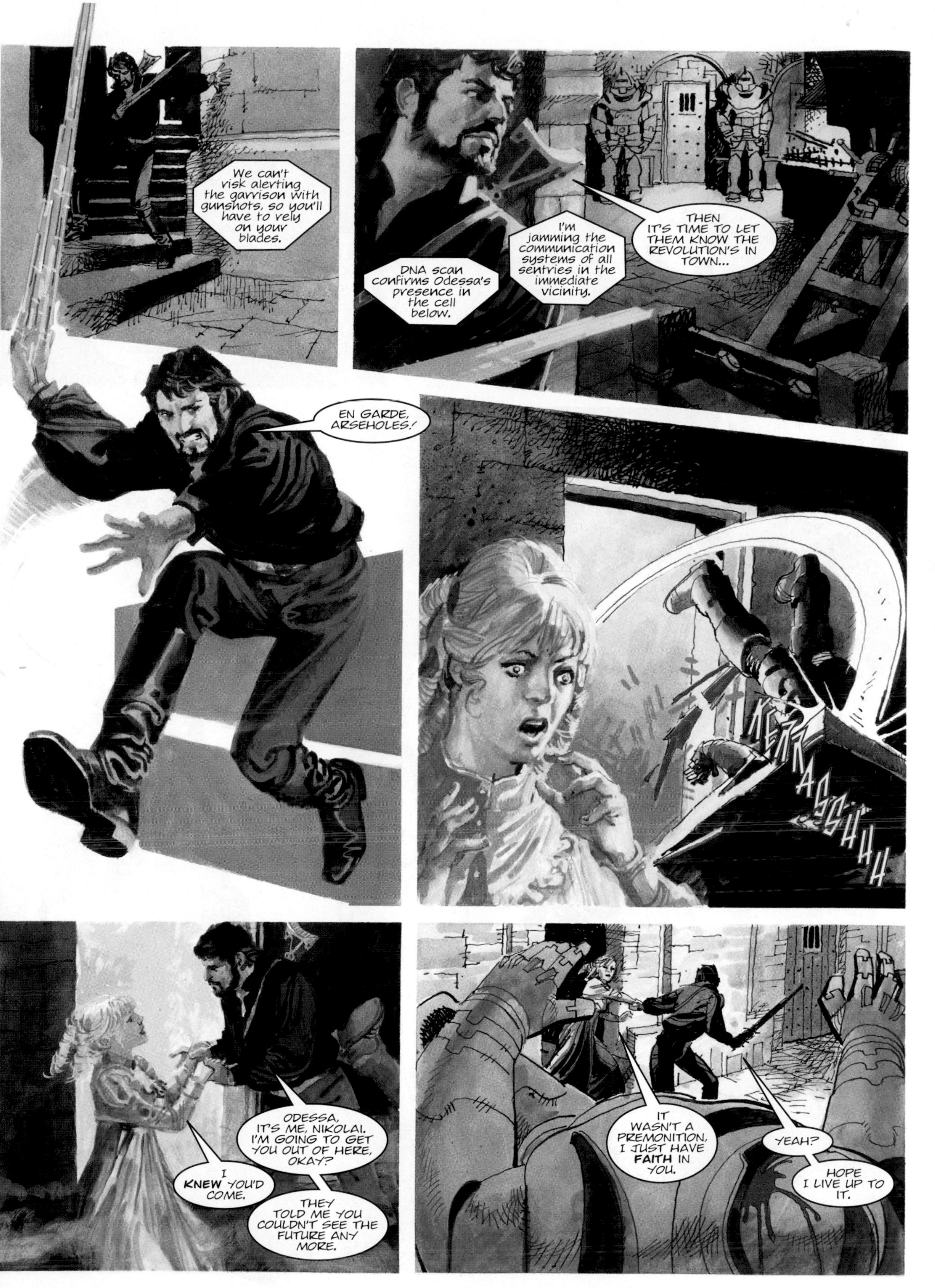

We can't risk alerting the garrison with gunshots, so you'll have to rely on your blades.
DNA scan confirms Odessa's presence in the cell below.
I'm jamming the communication systems of all sentries in the immediate vicinity.
THEN IT'S TIME TO LET THEM KNOW THE REVOLUTION'S IN TOWN...
EN GARDE, ARSEHOLES!
KERRASSHHH
ODESSA, IT'S ME, NIKOLAI. I'M GOING TO GET YOU OUT OF HERE, OKAY?
I **KNEW** YOU'D COME.
THEY TOLD ME YOU COULDN'T SEE THE FUTURE ANY MORE.
IT WASN'T A PREMONITION, I JUST HAVE **FAITH** IN YOU.
YEAH?
HOPE I LIVE UP TO IT.

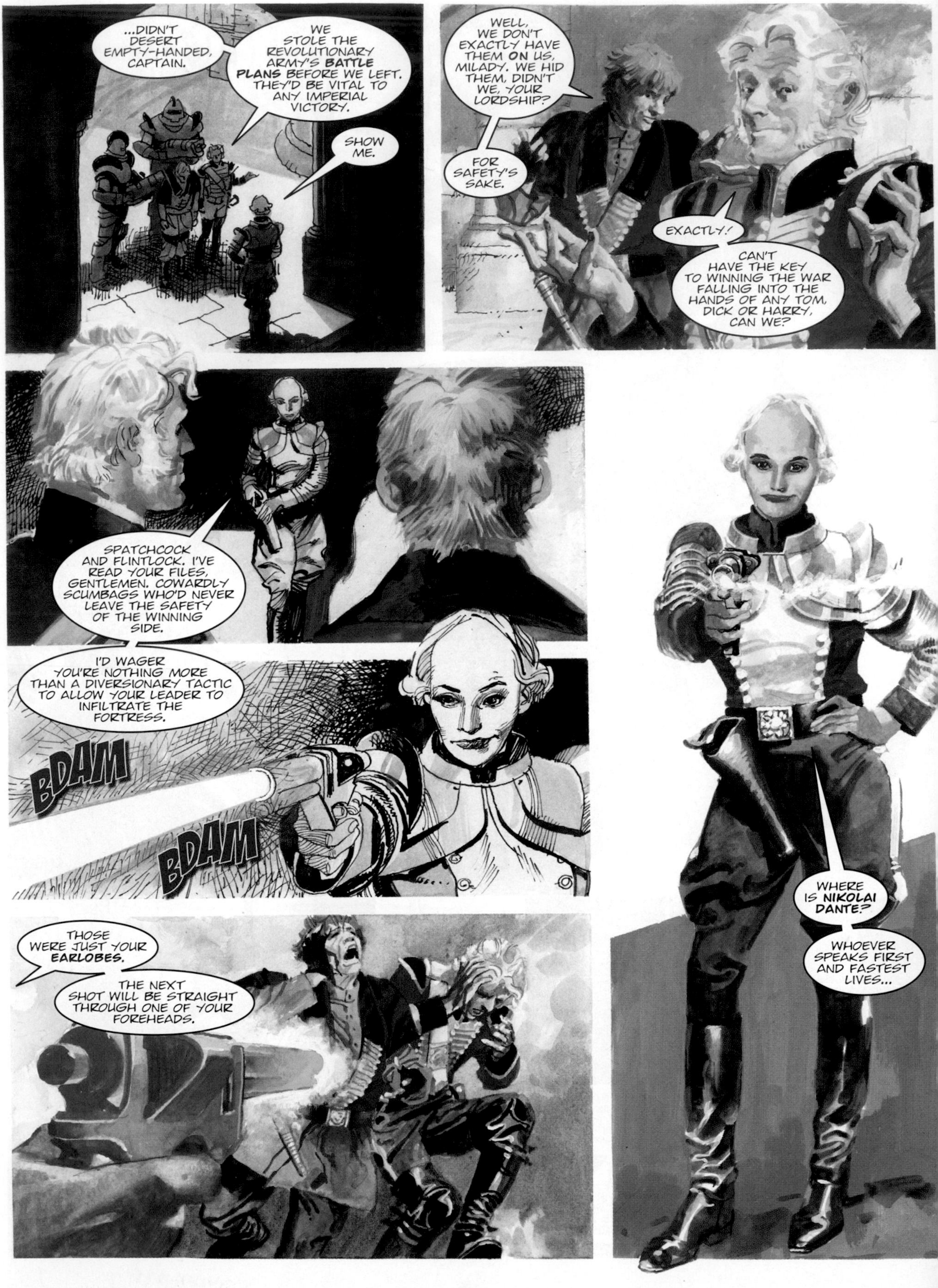

...DIDN'T DESERT EMPTY-HANDED, CAPTAIN.
WE STOLE THE REVOLUTIONARY ARMY'S BATTLE PLANS BEFORE WE LEFT. THEY'D BE VITAL TO ANY IMPERIAL VICTORY.
SHOW ME.
WELL, WE DON'T EXACTLY HAVE THEM ON US, MILADY. WE HID THEM, DIDN'T WE, YOUR LORDSHIP?
FOR SAFETY'S SAKE.
EXACTLY!
CAN'T HAVE THE KEY TO WINNING THE WAR FALLING INTO THE HANDS OF ANY TOM, DICK OR HARRY, CAN WE?
SPATCHCOCK AND FLINTLOCK. I'VE READ YOUR FILES, GENTLEMEN. COWARDLY SCUMBAGS WHO'D NEVER LEAVE THE SAFETY OF THE WINNING SIDE.
I'D WAGER YOU'RE NOTHING MORE THAN A DIVERSIONARY TACTIC TO ALLOW YOUR LEADER TO INFILTRATE THE FORTRESS.
BDAM
BDAM
THOSE WERE JUST YOUR EARLOBES.
THE NEXT SHOT WILL BE STRAIGHT THROUGH ONE OF YOUR FOREHEADS.
WHERE IS NIKOLAI DANTE?
WHOEVER SPEAKS FIRST AND FASTEST LIVES...

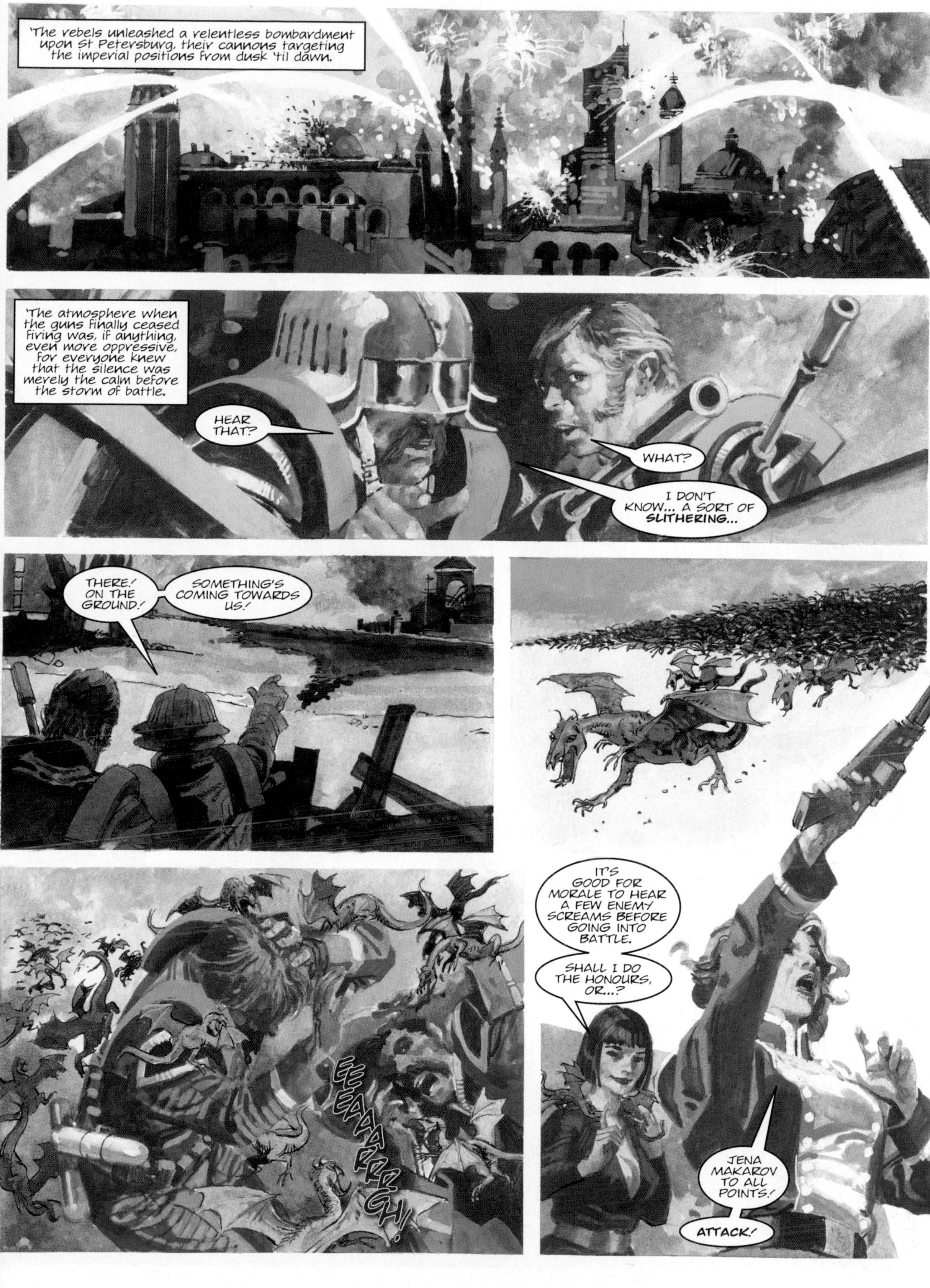
'The rebels unleashed a relentless bombardment upon St Petersburg, their cannons targeting the imperial positions from dusk 'til dawn.
'The atmosphere when the guns finally ceased firing was, if anything, even more oppressive, for everyone knew that the silence was merely the calm before the storm of battle.
HEAR THAT?
WHAT?
I DON'T KNOW... A SORT OF SLITHERING...
THERE! ON THE GROUND!
SOMETHING'S COMING TOWARDS US!
EEEAAAARRRGH!
IT'S GOOD FOR MORALE TO HEAR A FEW ENEMY SCREAMS BEFORE GOING INTO BATTLE.
SHALL I DO THE HONOURS, OR...?
JENA MAKAROV TO ALL POINTS!
ATTACK!

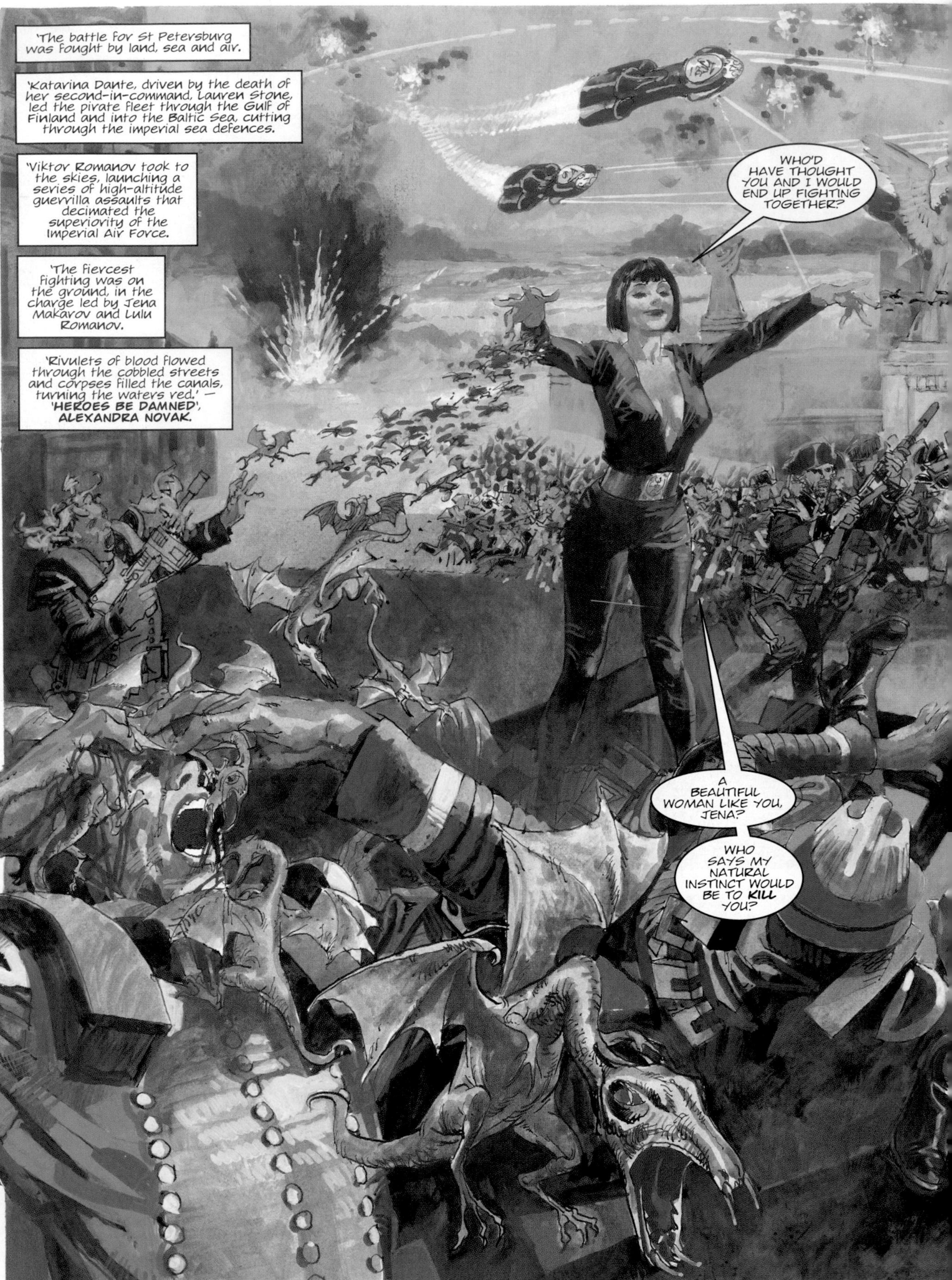
'The battle for St Petersburg was fought by land, sea and air.
'Katarina Dante, driven by the death of her second-in-command, Lauren Stone, led the pirate fleet through the Gulf of Finland and into the Baltic Sea, cutting through the imperial sea defences.
'Viktor Romanov took to the skies, launching a series of high-altitude guerrilla assaults that decimated the superiority of the Imperial Air Force.
'The fiercest fighting was on the ground, in the charge led by Jena Makarov and Lulu Romanov.
'Rivulets of blood flowed through the cobbled streets and corpses filled the canals, turning the waters red.' — 'HEROES BE DAMNED', ALEXANDRA NOVAK.
WHO'D HAVE THOUGHT YOU AND I WOULD END UP FIGHTING TOGETHER?
A BEAUTIFUL WOMAN LIKE YOU, JENA?
WHO SAYS MY NATURAL INSTINCT WOULD BE TO KILL YOU?

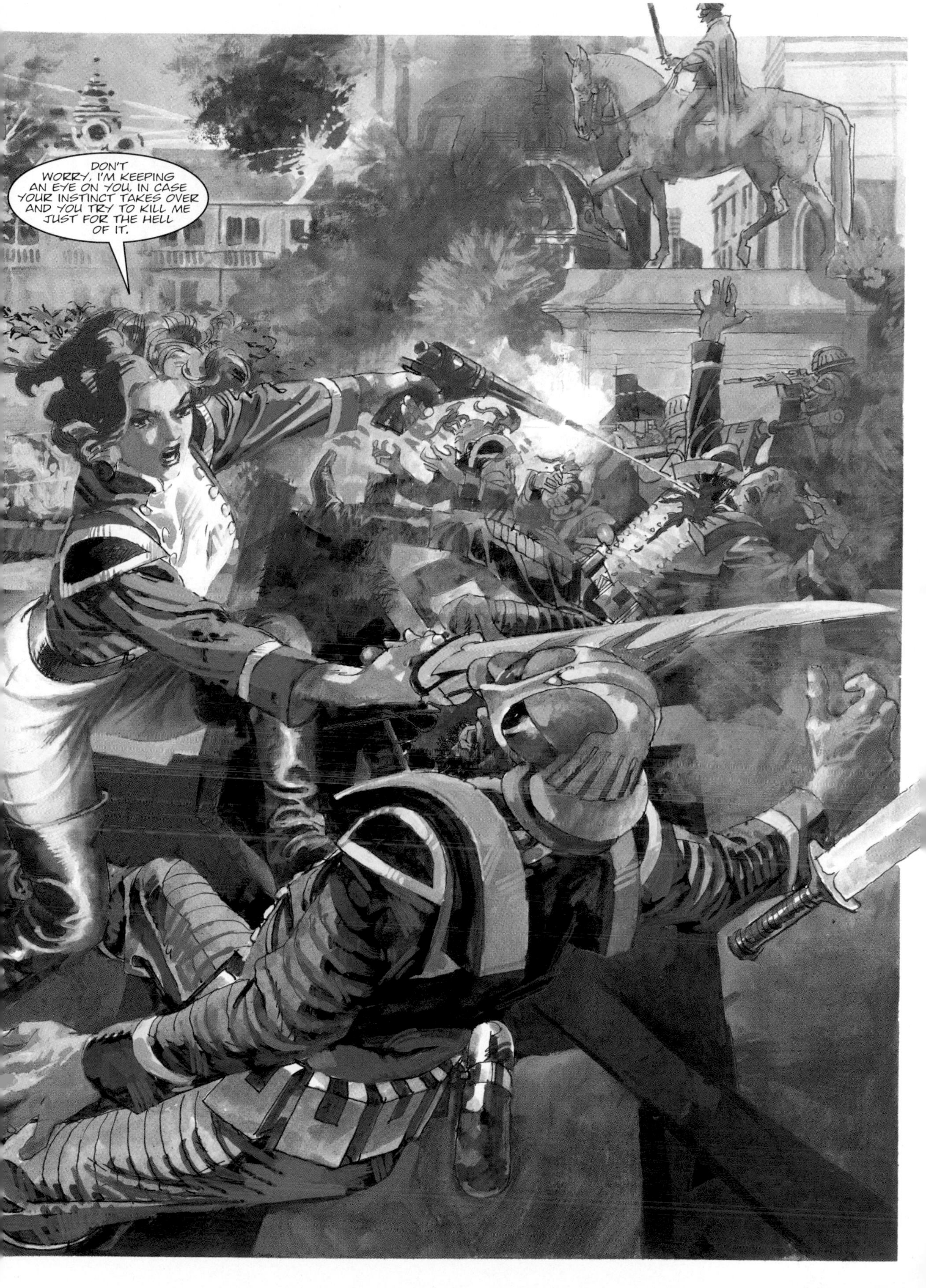
DON'T WORRY, I'M KEEPING AN EYE ON YOU, IN CASE YOUR INSTINCT TAKES OVER AND YOU TRY TO KILL ME JUST FOR THE HELL OF IT.

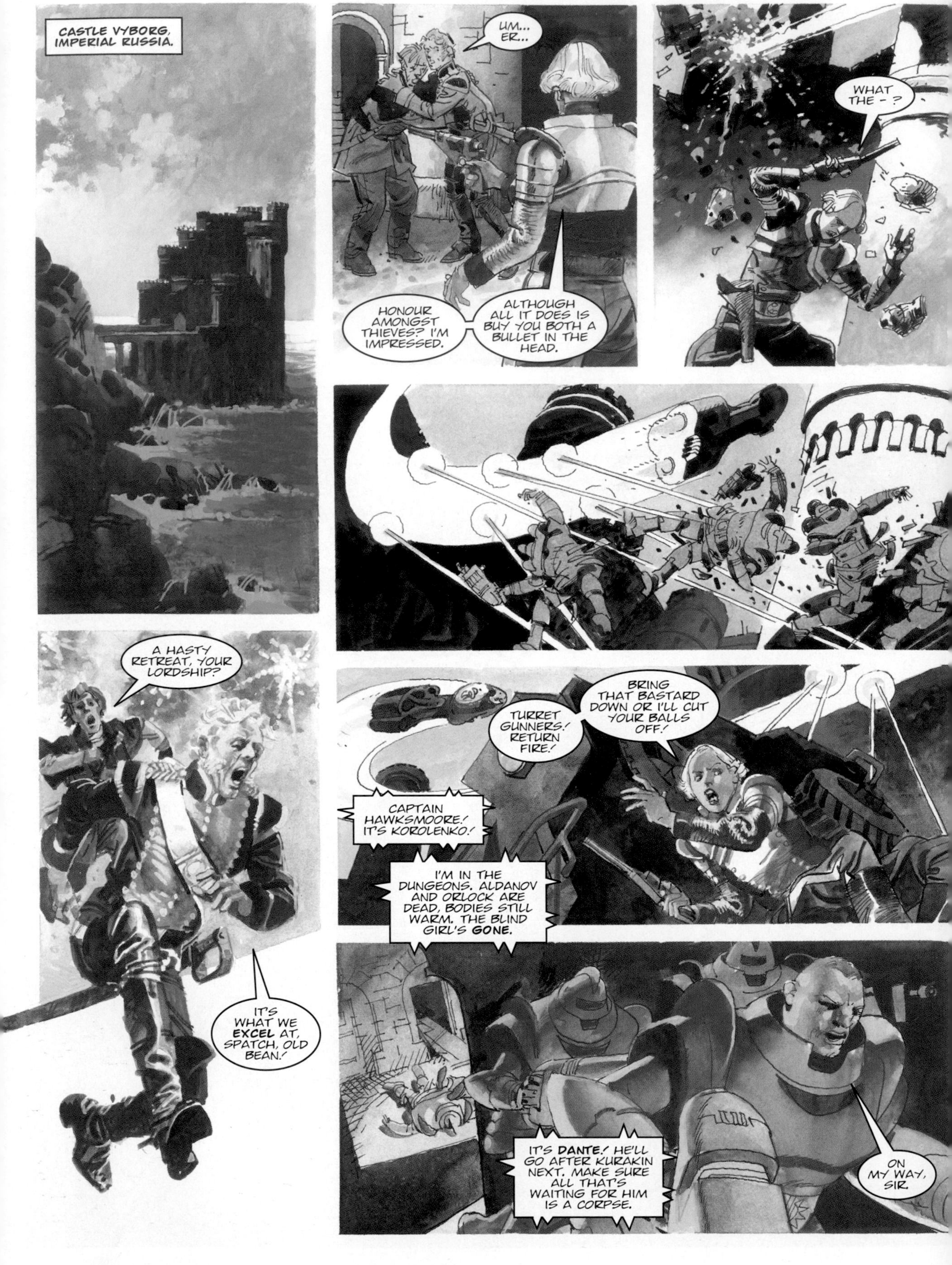
CASTLE VYBORG, IMPERIAL RUSSIA.
UM... ER...
HONOUR AMONGST THIEVES? I'M IMPRESSED.
ALTHOUGH ALL IT DOES IS BUY YOU BOTH A BULLET IN THE HEAD.
WHAT THE - ?
A HASTY RETREAT, YOUR LORDSHIP?
IT'S WHAT WE EXCEL AT, SPATCH, OLD BEAN!
TURRET GUNNERS! RETURN FIRE!
BRING THAT BASTARD DOWN OR I'LL CUT YOUR BALLS OFF!
CAPTAIN HAWKSMOORE! IT'S KOROLENKO!
I'M IN THE DUNGEONS. ALDANOV AND ORLOCK ARE DEAD, BODIES STILL WARM. THE BLIND GIRL'S GONE.
IT'S DANTE! HE'LL GO AFTER KURAKIN NEXT. MAKE SURE ALL THAT'S WAITING FOR HIM IS A CORPSE.
ON MY WAY, SIR.

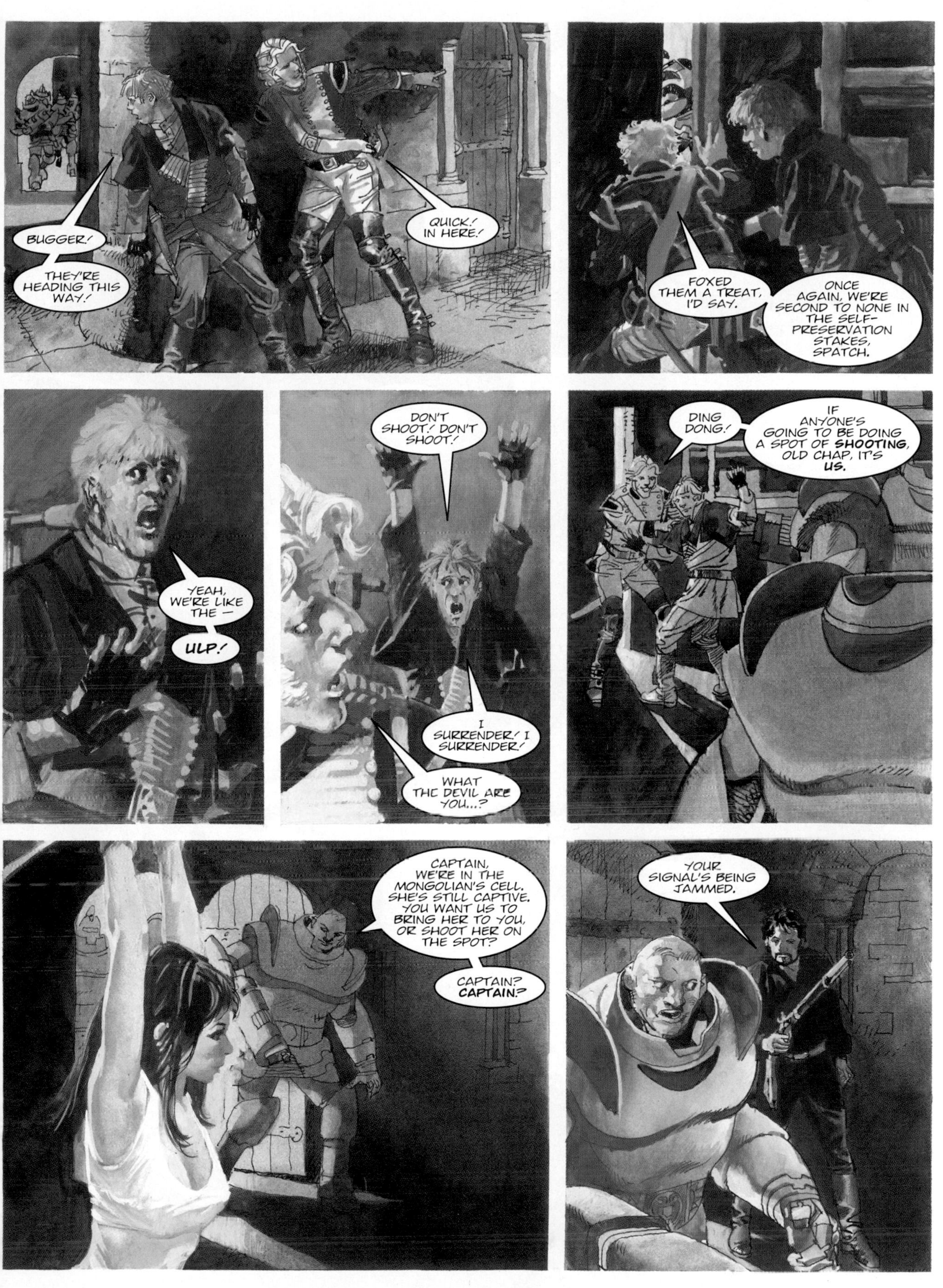
BUGGER!
THEY'RE HEADING THIS WAY!
QUICK! IN HERE!
FOXED THEM A TREAT, I'D SAY.
ONCE AGAIN, WE'RE SECOND TO NONE IN THE SELF-PRESERVATION STAKES, SPATCH.
YEAH, WE'RE LIKE THE —
ULP!
DON'T SHOOT! DON'T SHOOT!
I SURRENDER! I SURRENDER!
WHAT THE DEVIL ARE YOU...?
DING DONG!
IF ANYONE'S GOING TO BE DOING A SPOT OF SHOOTING, OLD CHAP, IT'S US.
CAPTAIN, WE'RE IN THE MONGOLIAN'S CELL. SHE'S STILL CAPTIVE. YOU WANT US TO BRING HER TO YOU, OR SHOOT HER ON THE SPOT?
CAPTAIN? CAPTAIN?
YOUR SIGNAL'S BEING JAMMED.

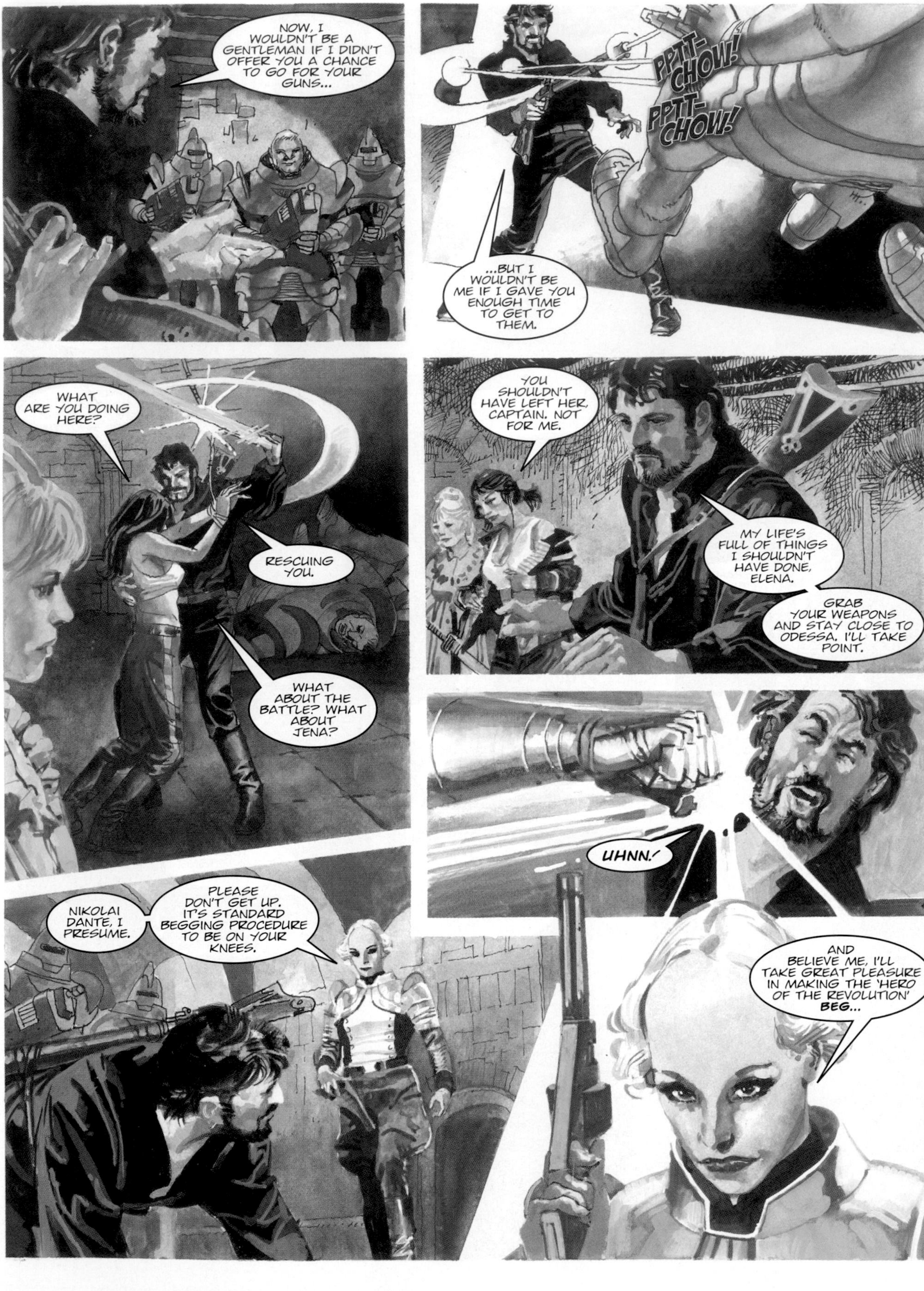
NOW, I WOULDN'T BE A GENTLEMAN IF I DIDN'T OFFER YOU A CHANCE TO GO FOR YOUR GUNS...
PPTT-CHOW!
PPTT-CHOW!
...BUT I WOULDN'T BE ME IF I GAVE YOU ENOUGH TIME TO GET TO THEM.
WHAT ARE YOU DOING HERE?
RESCUING YOU.
WHAT ABOUT THE BATTLE? WHAT ABOUT JENA?
YOU SHOULDN'T HAVE LEFT HER, CAPTAIN. NOT FOR ME.
MY LIFE'S FULL OF THINGS I SHOULDN'T HAVE DONE, ELENA.
GRAB YOUR WEAPONS AND STAY CLOSE TO ODESSA. I'LL TAKE POINT.
UHNN.!
NIKOLAI DANTE, I PRESUME.
PLEASE DON'T GET UP. IT'S STANDARD BEGGING PROCEDURE TO BE ON YOUR KNEES.
AND BELIEVE ME, I'LL TAKE GREAT PLEASURE IN MAKING THE 'HERO OF THE REVOLUTION' BEG...

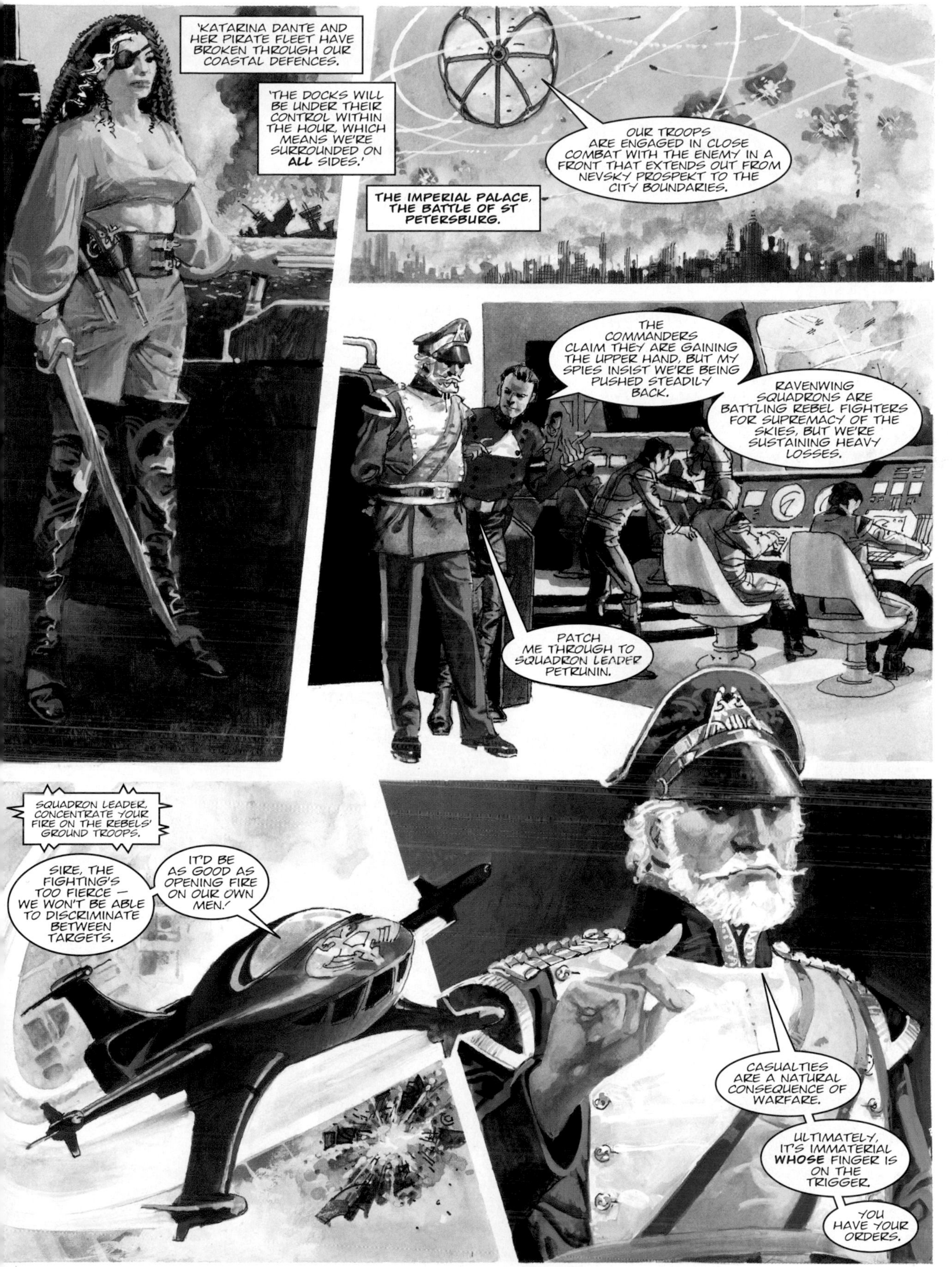
'KATARINA DANTE AND HER PIRATE FLEET HAVE BROKEN THROUGH OUR COASTAL DEFENCES.
'THE DOCKS WILL BE UNDER THEIR CONTROL WITHIN THE HOUR, WHICH MEANS WE'RE SURROUNDED ON ALL SIDES.'
THE IMPERIAL PALACE, THE BATTLE OF ST PETERSBURG.
OUR TROOPS ARE ENGAGED IN CLOSE COMBAT WITH THE ENEMY IN A FRONT THAT EXTENDS OUT FROM NEVSKY PROSPEKT TO THE CITY BOUNDARIES.
THE COMMANDERS CLAIM THEY ARE GAINING THE UPPER HAND, BUT MY SPIES INSIST WE'RE BEING PUSHED STEADILY BACK.
RAVENWING SQUADRONS ARE BATTLING REBEL FIGHTERS FOR SUPREMACY OF THE SKIES, BUT WE'RE SUSTAINING HEAVY LOSSES.
PATCH ME THROUGH TO SQUADRON LEADER PETRUNIN.
SQUADRON LEADER, CONCENTRATE YOUR FIRE ON THE REBELS' GROUND TROOPS.
SIRE, THE FIGHTING'S TOO FIERCE — WE WON'T BE ABLE TO DISCRIMINATE BETWEEN TARGETS.
IT'D BE AS GOOD AS OPENING FIRE ON OUR OWN MEN.'
CASUALTIES ARE A NATURAL CONSEQUENCE OF WARFARE.
ULTIMATELY, IT'S IMMATERIAL WHOSE FINGER IS ON THE TRIGGER.
YOU HAVE YOUR ORDERS.

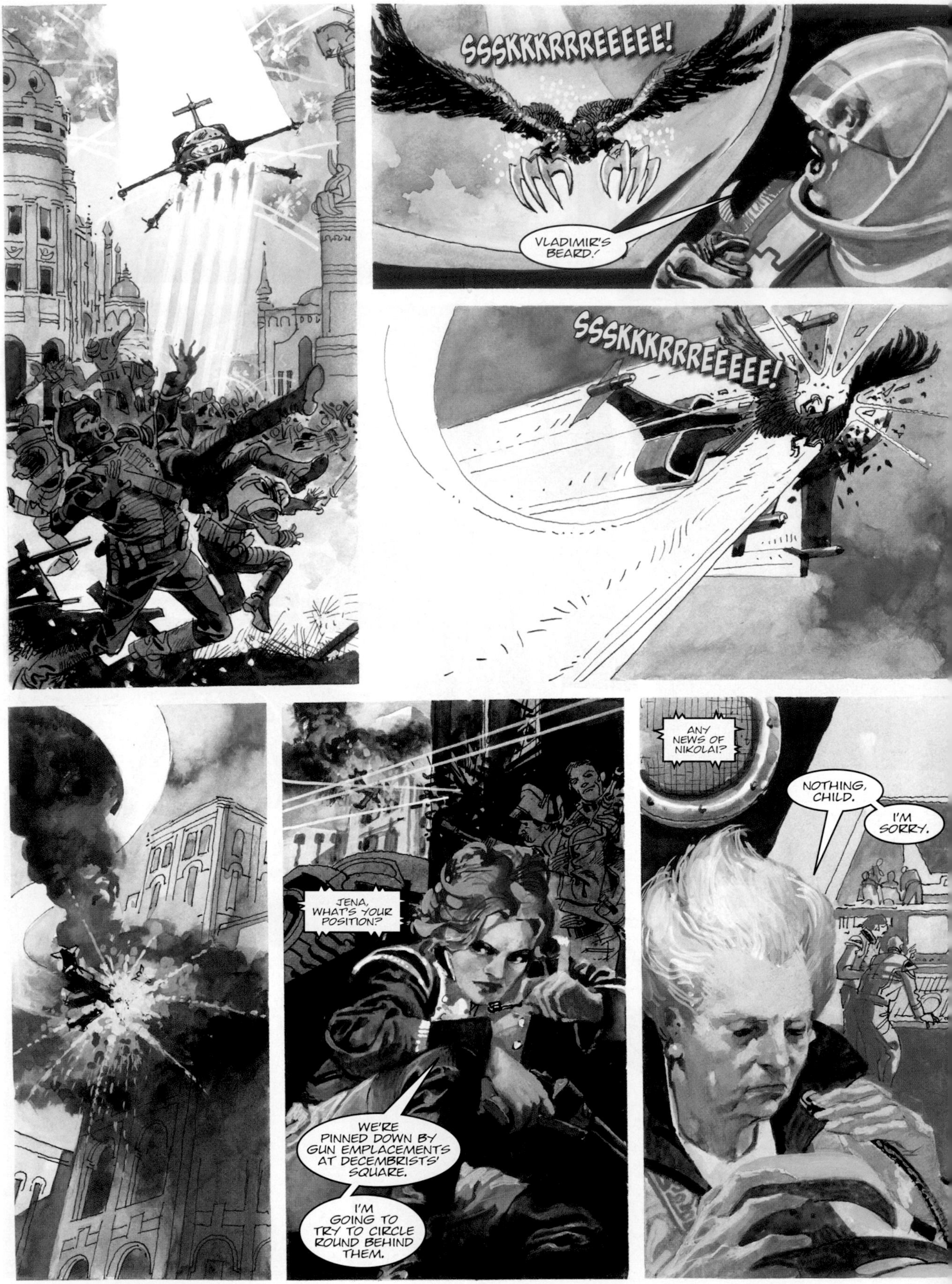
SSSKKKRRREEEEE!
VLADIMIR'S BEARD!
SSSKKKRRREEEEE!
JENA, WHAT'S YOUR POSITION?
WE'RE PINNED DOWN BY GUN EMPLACEMENTS AT DECEMBRISTS' SQUARE.
I'M GOING TO TRY TO CIRCLE ROUND BEHIND THEM.
ANY NEWS OF NIKOLAI?
NOTHING, CHILD.
I'M SORRY.

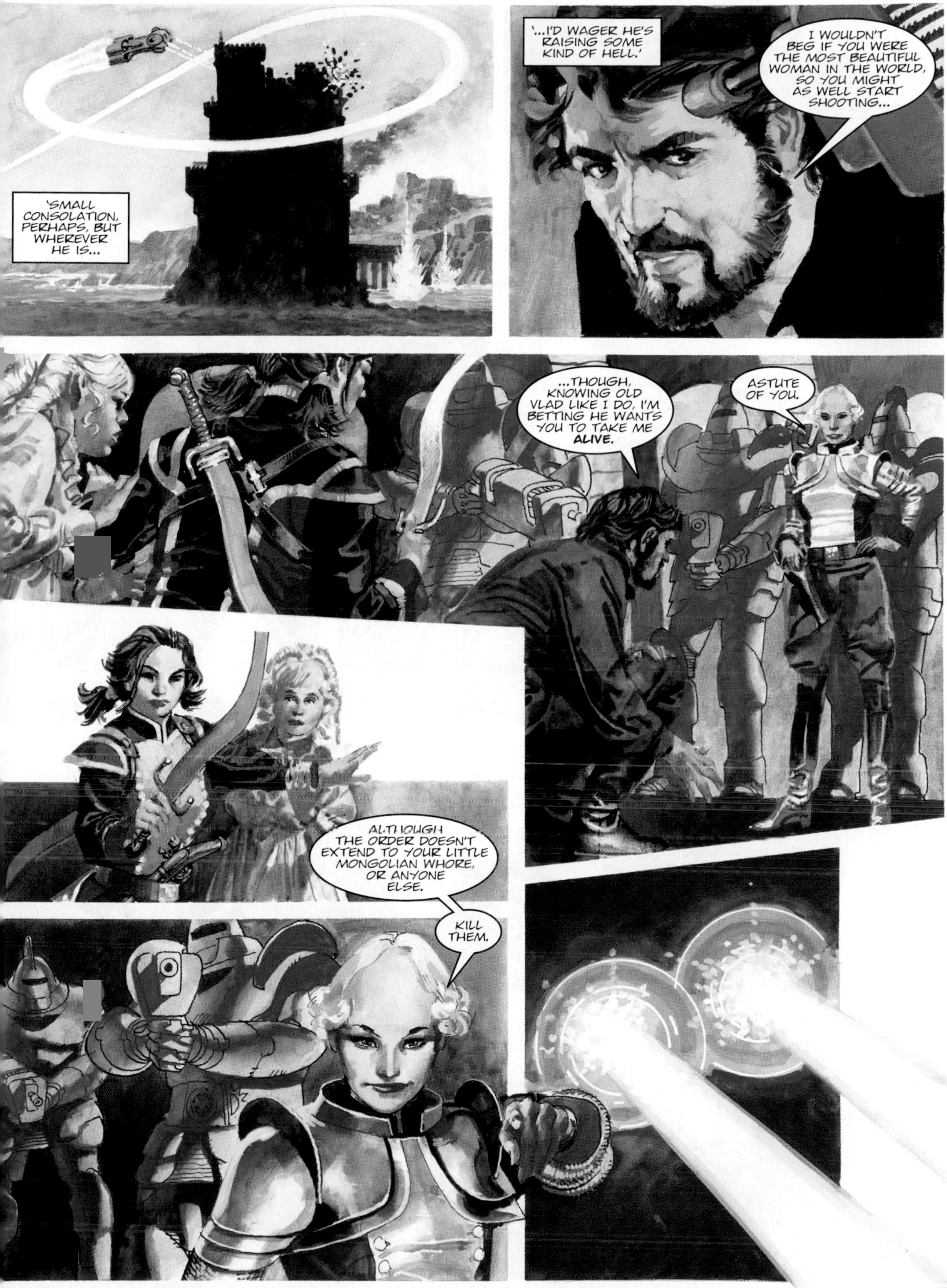

'SMALL CONSOLATION, PERHAPS, BUT WHEREVER HE IS...
'...I'D WAGER HE'S RAISING SOME KIND OF HELL.'
I WOULDN'T BEG IF YOU WERE THE MOST BEAUTIFUL WOMAN IN THE WORLD, SO YOU MIGHT AS WELL START SHOOTING...
...THOUGH, KNOWING OLD VLAD LIKE I DO, I'M BETTING HE WANTS YOU TO TAKE ME **ALIVE.**
ASTUTE OF YOU.
ALTHOUGH THE ORDER DOESN'T EXTEND TO YOUR LITTLE MONGOLIAN WHORE, OR ANYONE ELSE.
KILL THEM.

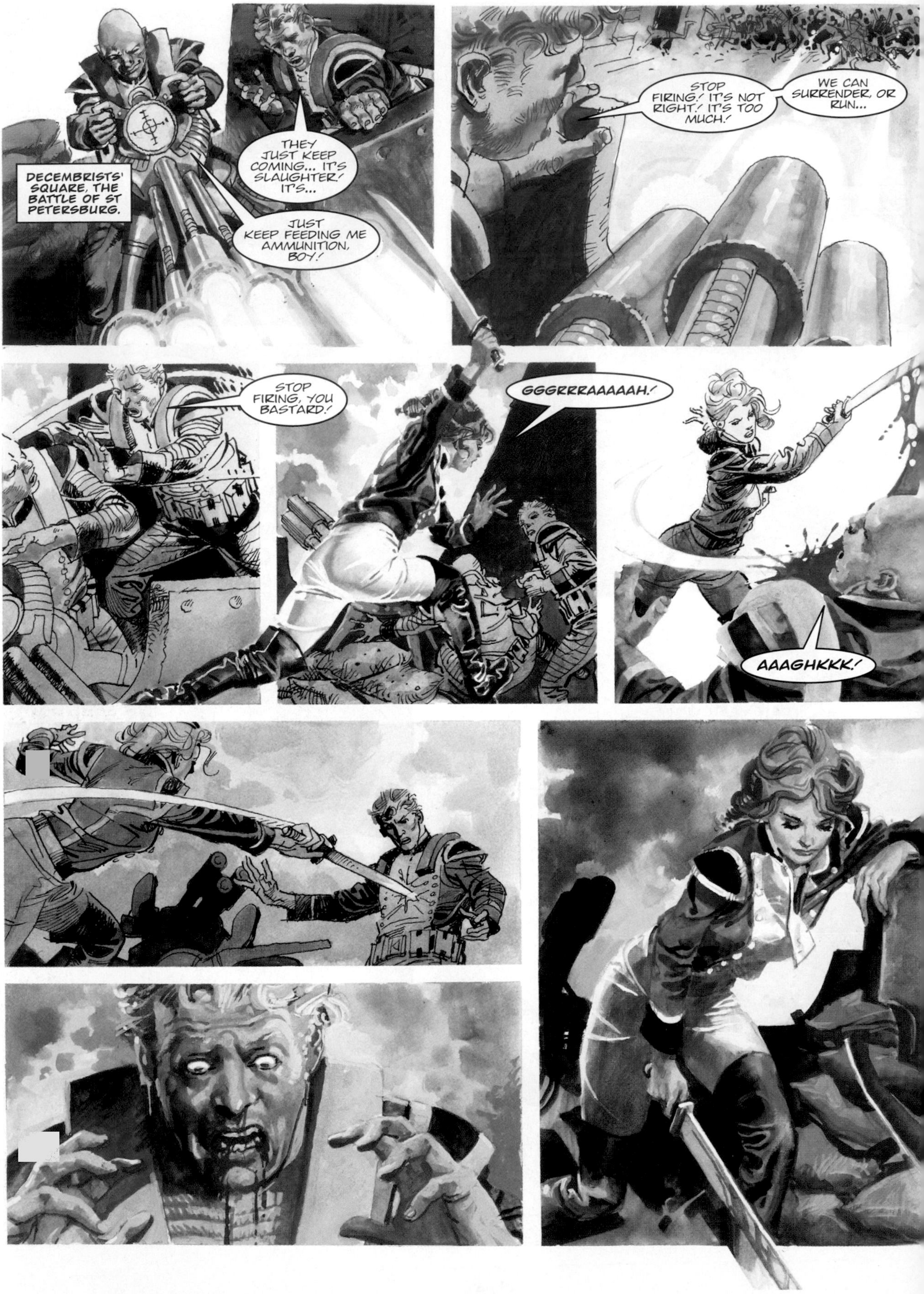
DECEMBRISTS' SQUARE, THE BATTLE OF ST PETERSBURG.
THEY JUST KEEP COMING... IT'S SLAUGHTER! IT'S...
JUST KEEP FEEDING ME AMMUNITION, BOY!
STOP FIRING! IT'S NOT RIGHT! IT'S TOO MUCH!
WE CAN SURRENDER, OR RUN...
STOP FIRING, YOU BASTARD!
GGGRRRAAAAAH!
AAAGHKKK!

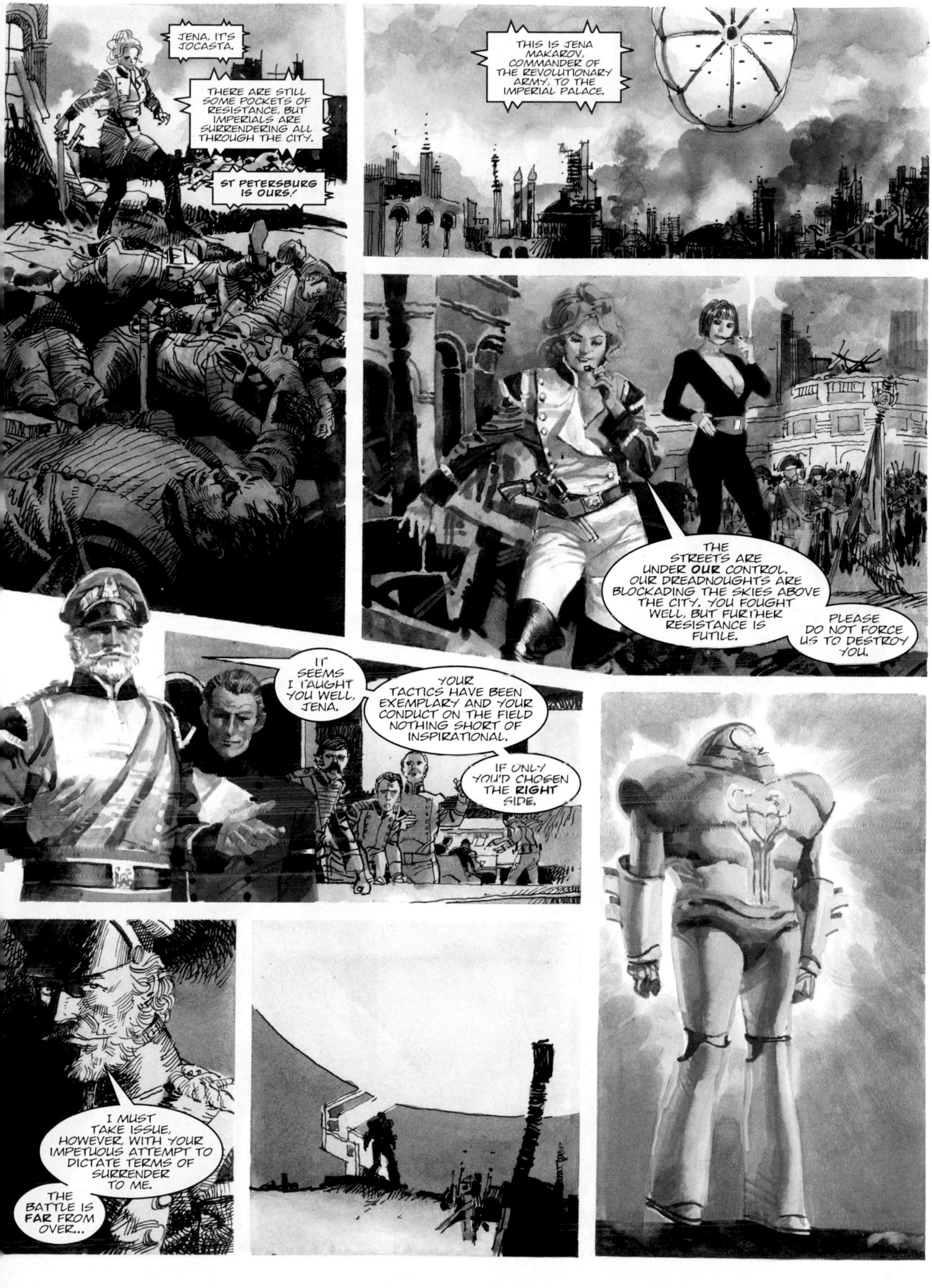
JENA, IT'S JOCASTA.
THERE ARE STILL SOME POCKETS OF RESISTANCE, BUT IMPERIALS ARE SURRENDERING ALL THROUGH THE CITY.
ST PETERSBURG IS OURS!
THIS IS JENA MAKAROV, COMMANDER OF THE REVOLUTIONARY ARMY, TO THE IMPERIAL PALACE.
THE STREETS ARE UNDER OUR CONTROL. OUR DREADNOUGHTS ARE BLOCKADING THE SKIES ABOVE THE CITY. YOU FOUGHT WELL, BUT FURTHER RESISTANCE IS FUTILE.
PLEASE DO NOT FORCE US TO DESTROY YOU.
IT SEEMS I TAUGHT YOU WELL, JENA.
YOUR TACTICS HAVE BEEN EXEMPLARY AND YOUR CONDUCT ON THE FIELD NOTHING SHORT OF INSPIRATIONAL.
IF ONLY YOU'D CHOSEN THE RIGHT SIDE.
I MUST TAKE ISSUE, HOWEVER, WITH YOUR IMPETUOUS ATTEMPT TO DICTATE TERMS OF SURRENDER TO ME.
THE BATTLE IS FAR FROM OVER...

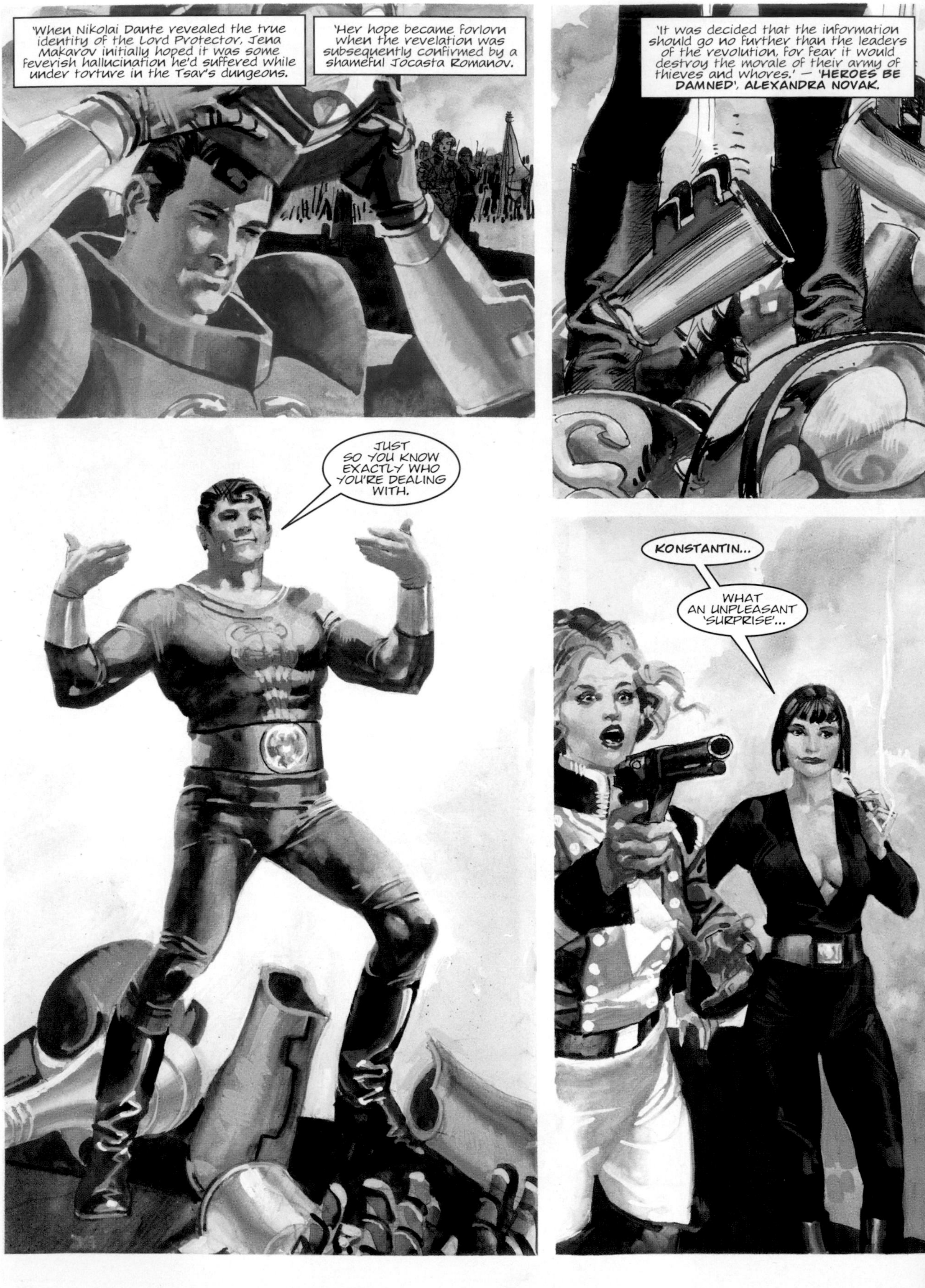
'When Nikolai Dante revealed the true identity of the Lord Protector, Jena Makarov initially hoped it was some feverish hallucination he'd suffered while under torture in the Tsar's dungeons.
'Her hope became forlorn when the revelation was subsequently confirmed by a shameful Jocasta Romanov.
'It was decided that the information should go no further than the leaders of the revolution, for fear it would destroy the morale of their army of thieves and whores.' — 'HEROES BE DAMNED', ALEXANDRA NOVAK.
JUST SO YOU KNOW EXACTLY WHO YOU'RE DEALING WITH.
KONSTANTIN...
WHAT AN UNPLEASANT 'SURPRISE'...

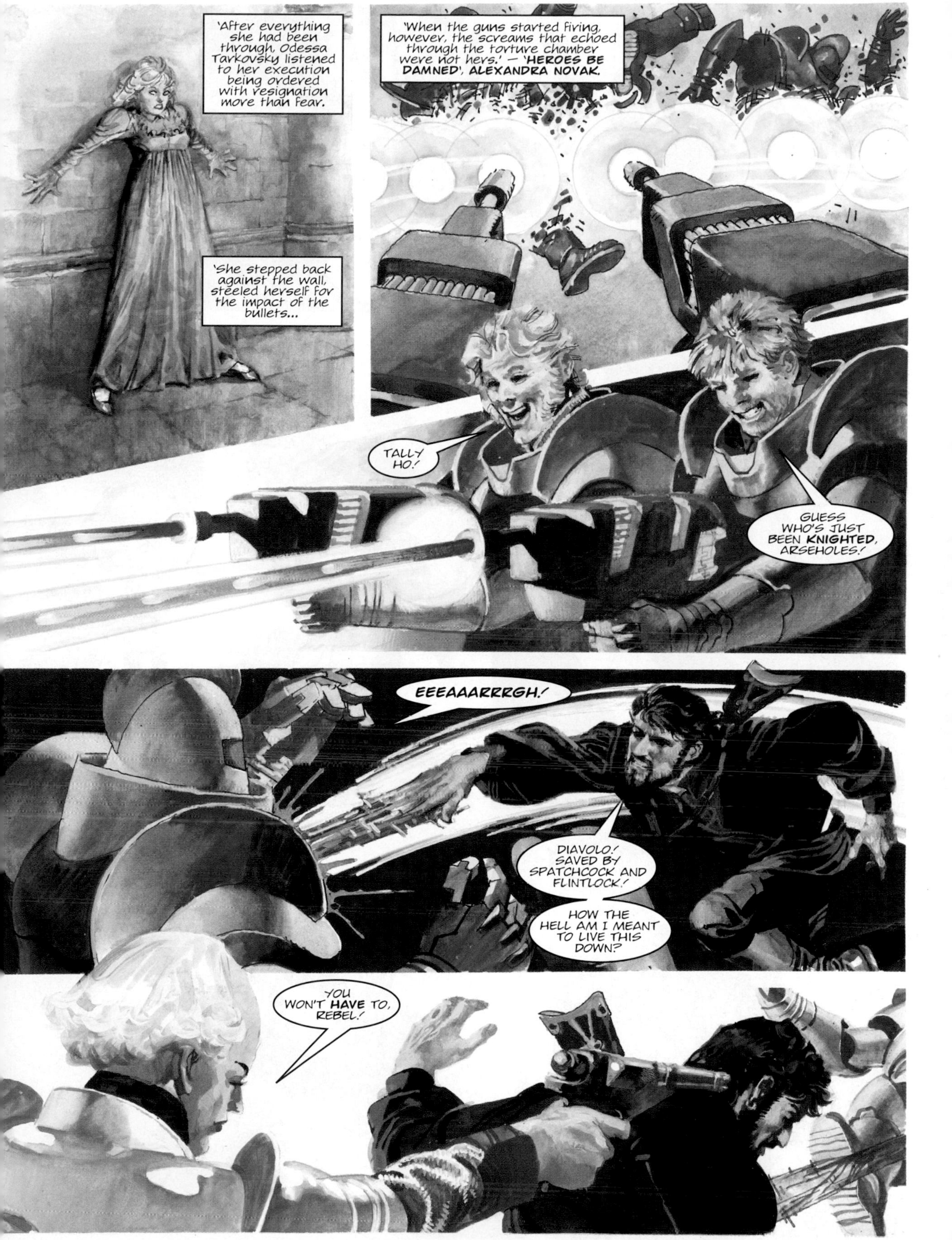
'After everything she had been through, Odessa Tarkovsky listened to her execution being ordered with resignation more than fear.
'She stepped back against the wall, steeled herself for the impact of the bullets...
'When the guns started firing, however, the screams that echoed through the torture chamber were not hers.' — '**HEROES BE DAMNED**', **ALEXANDRA NOVAK.**
TALLY HO.!
GUESS WHO'S JUST BEEN **KNIGHTED**, ARSEHOLES.!
EEEAAARRRGH.!
DIAVOLO.! SAVED BY SPATCHCOCK AND FLINTLOCK.!
HOW THE HELL AM I MEANT TO LIVE THIS DOWN?
YOU WON'T **HAVE** TO, REBEL.!

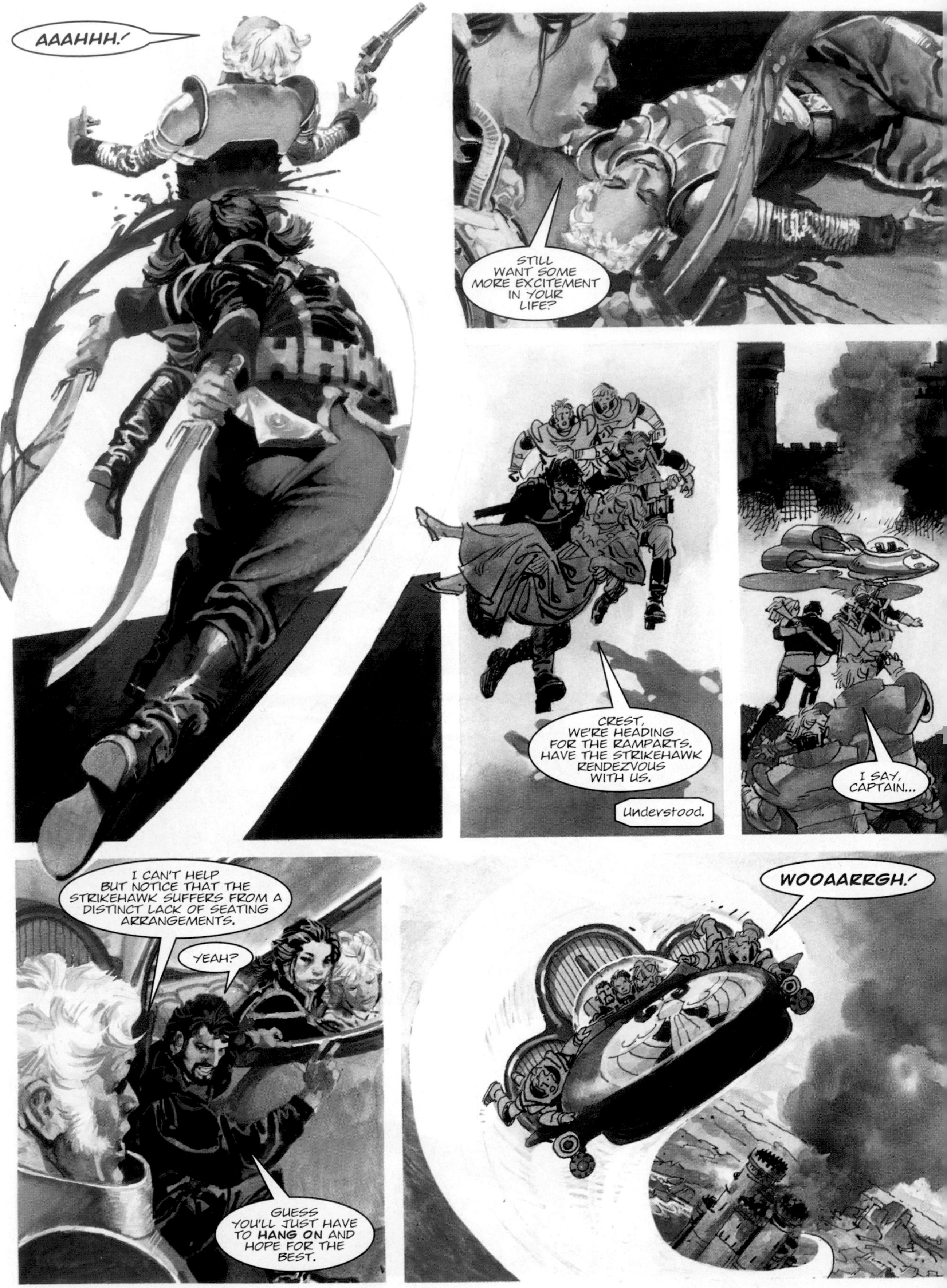
AAAHHH.!
STILL WANT SOME MORE EXCITEMENT IN YOUR LIFE?
CREST, WE'RE HEADING FOR THE RAMPARTS. HAVE THE STRIKEHAWK RENDEZVOUS WITH US.
Understood.
I SAY, CAPTAIN...
I CAN'T HELP BUT NOTICE THAT THE STRIKEHAWK SUFFERS FROM A DISTINCT LACK OF SEATING ARRANGEMENTS.
YEAH?
GUESS YOU'LL JUST HAVE TO HANG ON AND HOPE FOR THE BEST.
WOOAARRGH.!

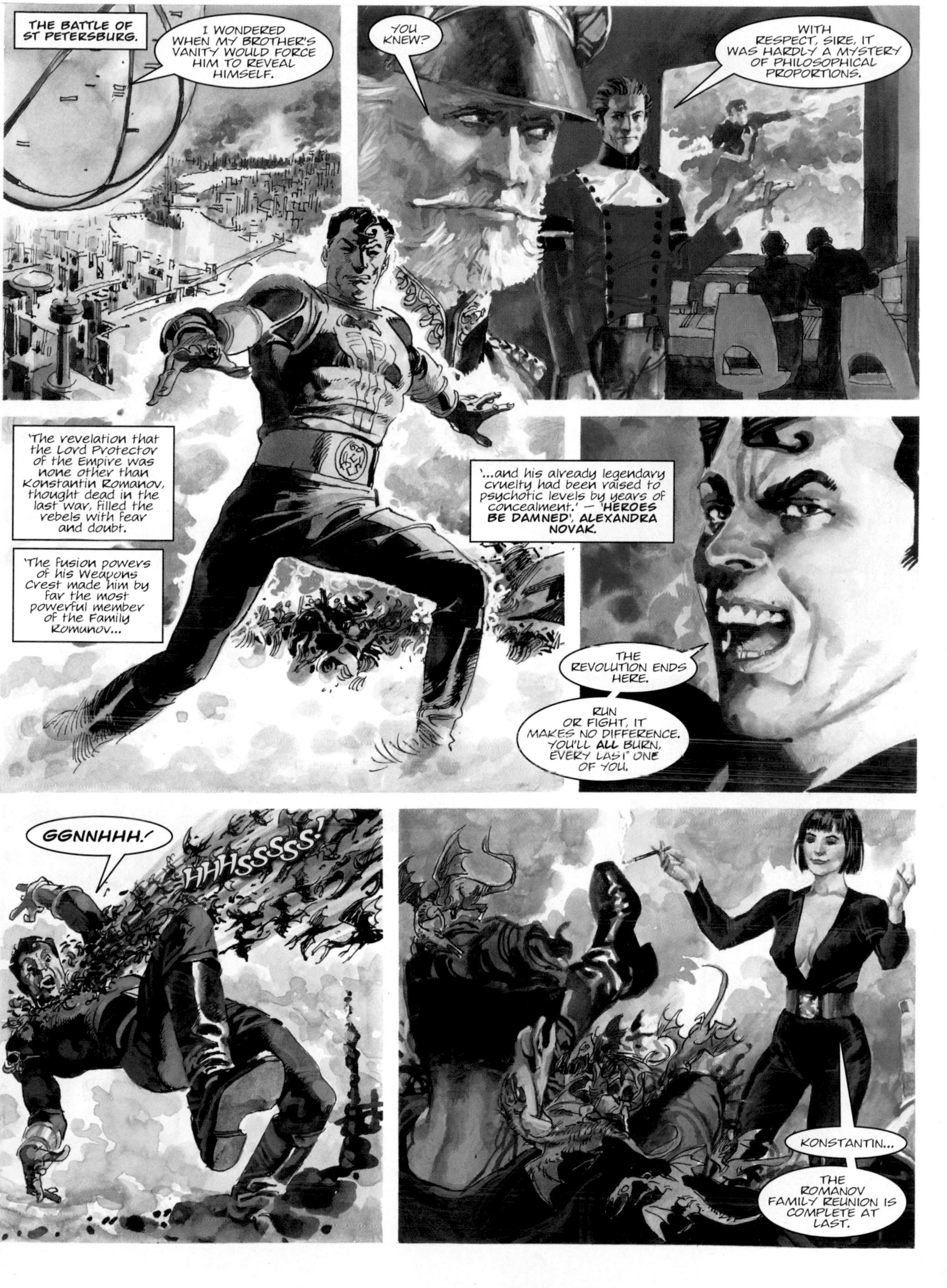

THE BATTLE OF ST PETERSBURG.
I WONDERED WHEN MY BROTHER'S VANITY WOULD FORCE HIM TO REVEAL HIMSELF.
YOU KNEW?
WITH RESPECT, SIRE, IT WAS HARDLY A MYSTERY OF PHILOSOPHICAL PROPORTIONS.
'The revelation that the Lord Protector of the Empire was none other than Konstantin Romanov, thought dead in the last war, filled the rebels with fear and doubt.
'The fusion powers of his Weapons Crest made him by far the most powerful member of the Family Romanov...
'...and his already legendary cruelty had been raised to psychotic levels by years of concealment.' — **'HEROES BE DAMNED', ALEXANDRA NOVAK.**
THE REVOLUTION ENDS HERE.
RUN OR FIGHT, IT MAKES NO DIFFERENCE. YOU'LL **ALL** BURN, EVERY LAST ONE OF YOU.
GGNNHHH!
HHHSSSSS!
KONSTANTIN...
THE ROMANOV FAMILY REUNION IS COMPLETE AT LAST.

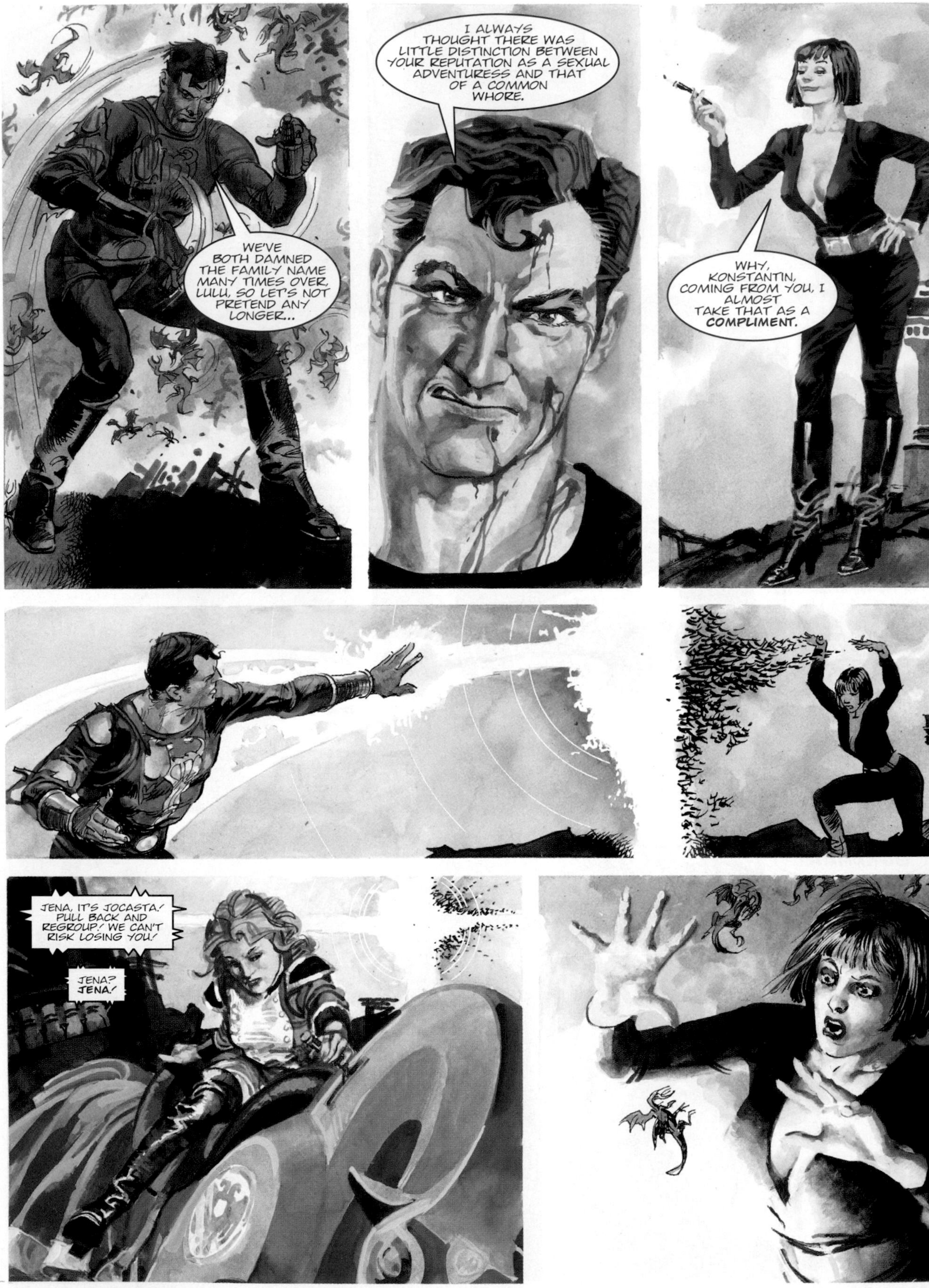
WE'VE BOTH DAMNED THE FAMILY NAME MANY TIMES OVER, LULU, SO LET'S NOT PRETEND ANY LONGER...
I ALWAYS THOUGHT THERE WAS LITTLE DISTINCTION BETWEEN YOUR REPUTATION AS A SEXUAL ADVENTURESS AND THAT OF A COMMON WHORE.
WHY, KONSTANTIN, COMING FROM YOU, I ALMOST TAKE THAT AS A **COMPLIMENT**.
JENA, IT'S JOCASTA! PULL BACK AND REGROUP! WE CAN'T RISK LOSING YOU!
JENA? **JENA!**

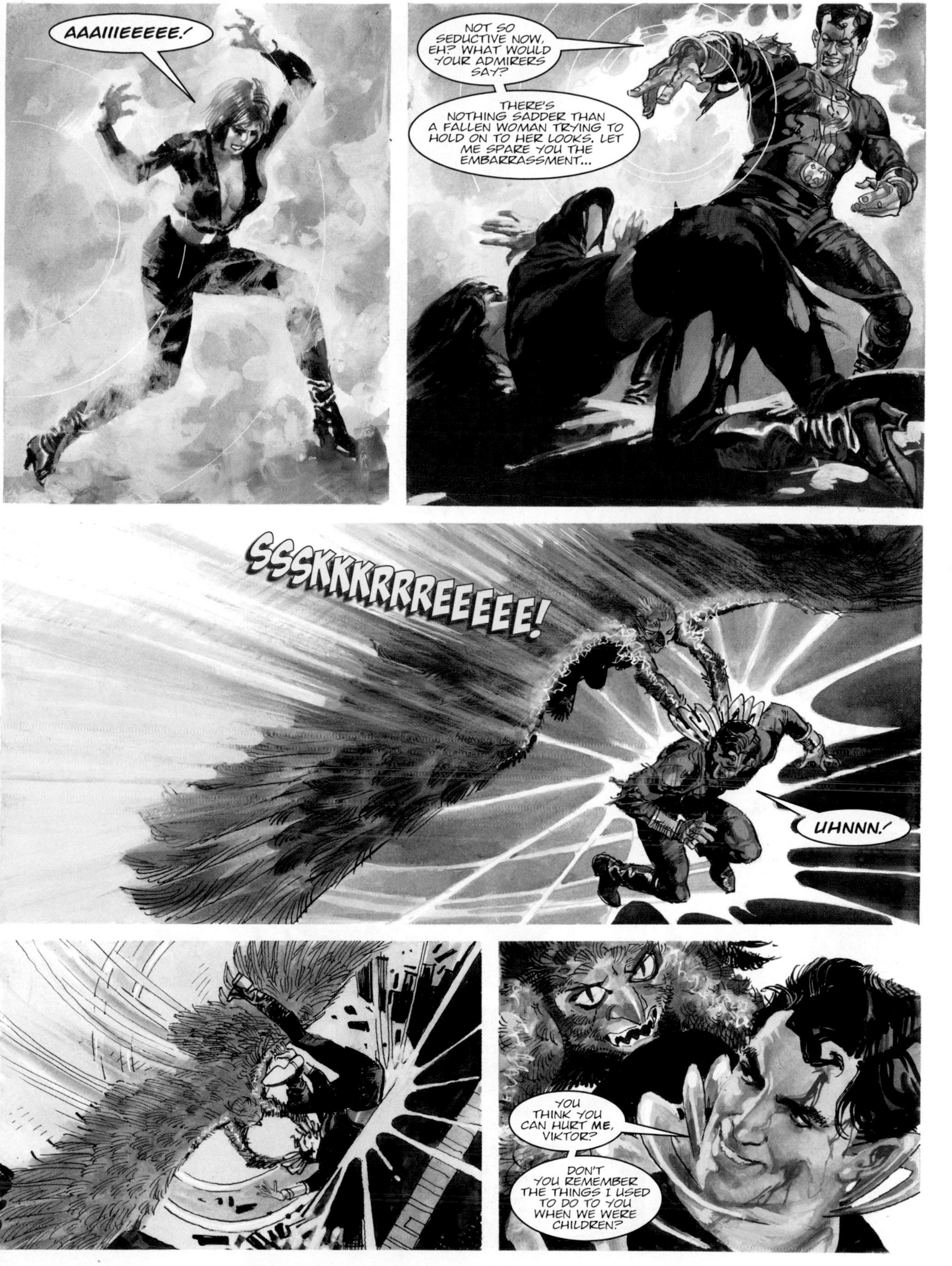
AAAIIIEEEEE.!
NOT SO SEDUCTIVE NOW, EH? WHAT WOULD YOUR ADMIRERS SAY?
THERE'S NOTHING SADDER THAN A FALLEN WOMAN TRYING TO HOLD ON TO HER LOOKS. LET ME SPARE YOU THE EMBARRASSMENT...
SSSKKKRRREEEEEE!
UHNNN.!
YOU THINK YOU CAN HURT ME, VIKTOR?
DON'T YOU REMEMBER THE THINGS I USED TO DO TO YOU WHEN WE WERE CHILDREN?

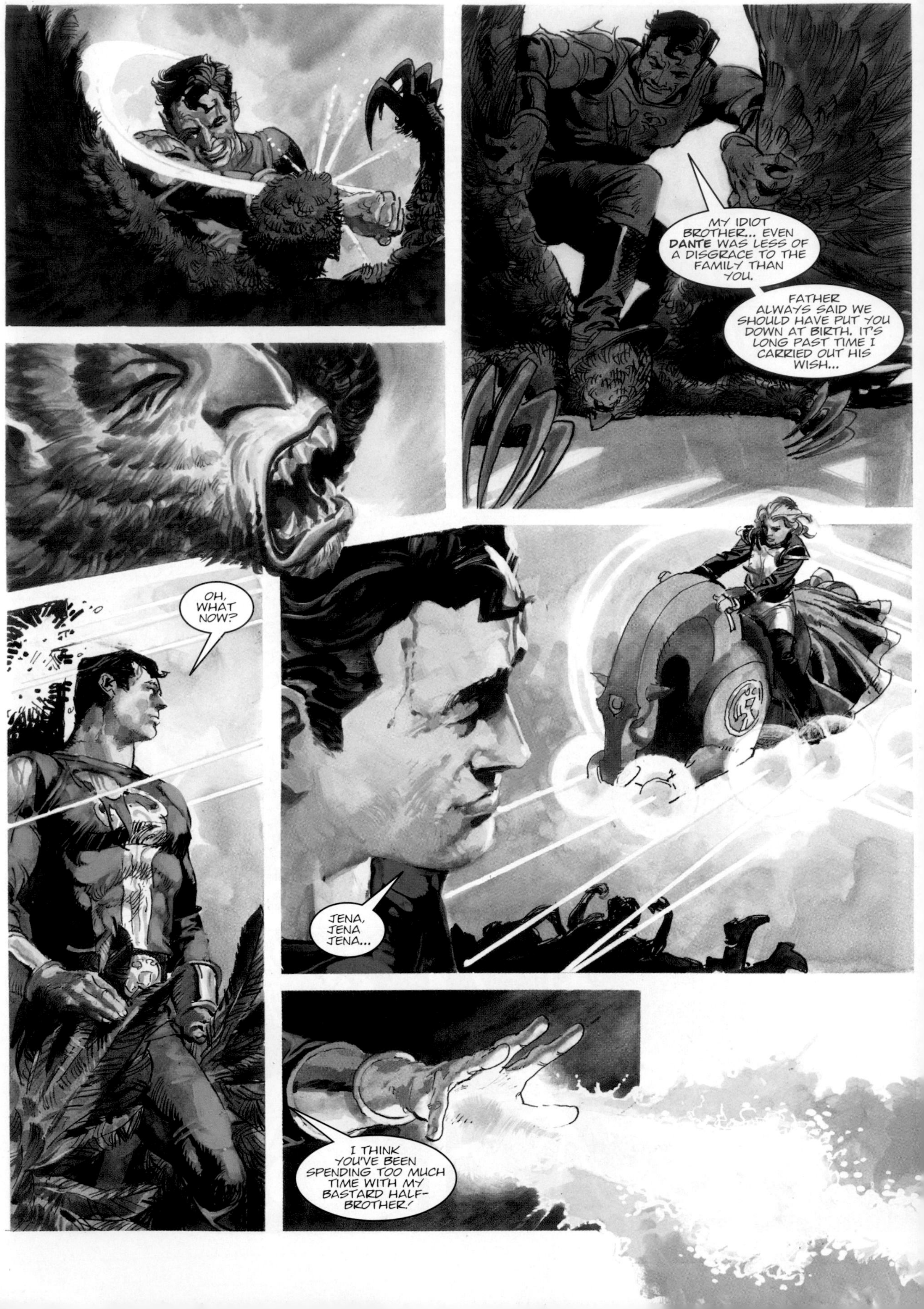
MY IDIOT BROTHER... EVEN DANTE WAS LESS OF A DISGRACE TO THE FAMILY THAN YOU.
FATHER ALWAYS SAID WE SHOULD HAVE PUT YOU DOWN AT BIRTH. IT'S LONG PAST TIME I CARRIED OUT HIS WISH...
OH, WHAT NOW?
JENA, JENA JENA...
I THINK YOU'VE BEEN SPENDING TOO MUCH TIME WITH MY BASTARD HALF-BROTHER!

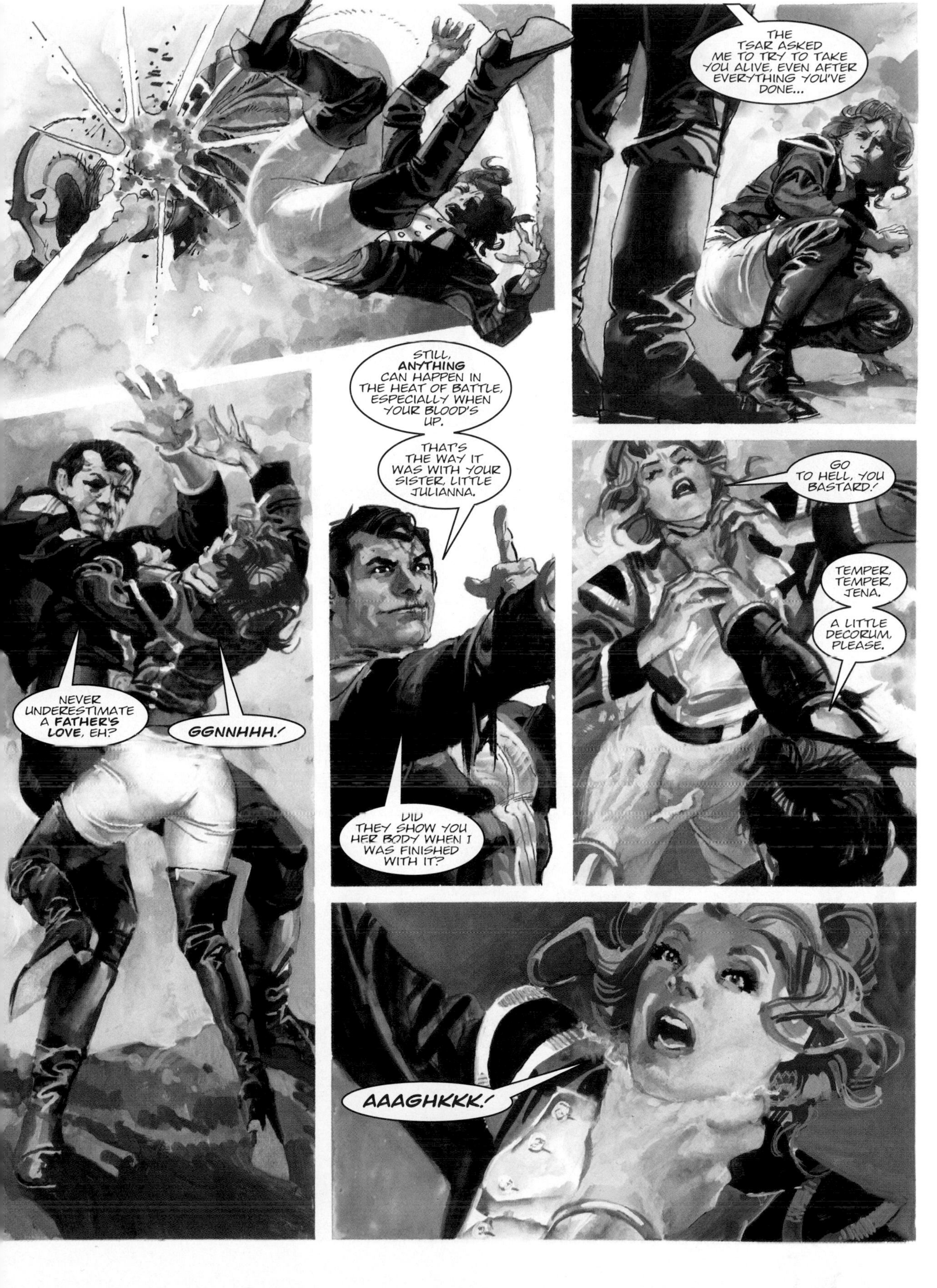
THE TSAR ASKED ME TO TRY TO TAKE YOU ALIVE, EVEN AFTER EVERYTHING YOU'VE DONE...
STILL, **ANYTHING** CAN HAPPEN IN THE HEAT OF BATTLE, ESPECIALLY WHEN YOUR BLOOD'S UP.
THAT'S THE WAY IT WAS WITH YOUR SISTER, LITTLE JULIANNA.
NEVER UNDERESTIMATE A **FATHER'S LOVE**, EH?
GGNNHHH.!
DID THEY SHOW YOU HER BODY WHEN I WAS FINISHED WITH IT?
GO TO HELL, YOU BASTARD.!
TEMPER, TEMPER, JENA.
A LITTLE DECORUM, PLEASE.
AAAGHKKK.!

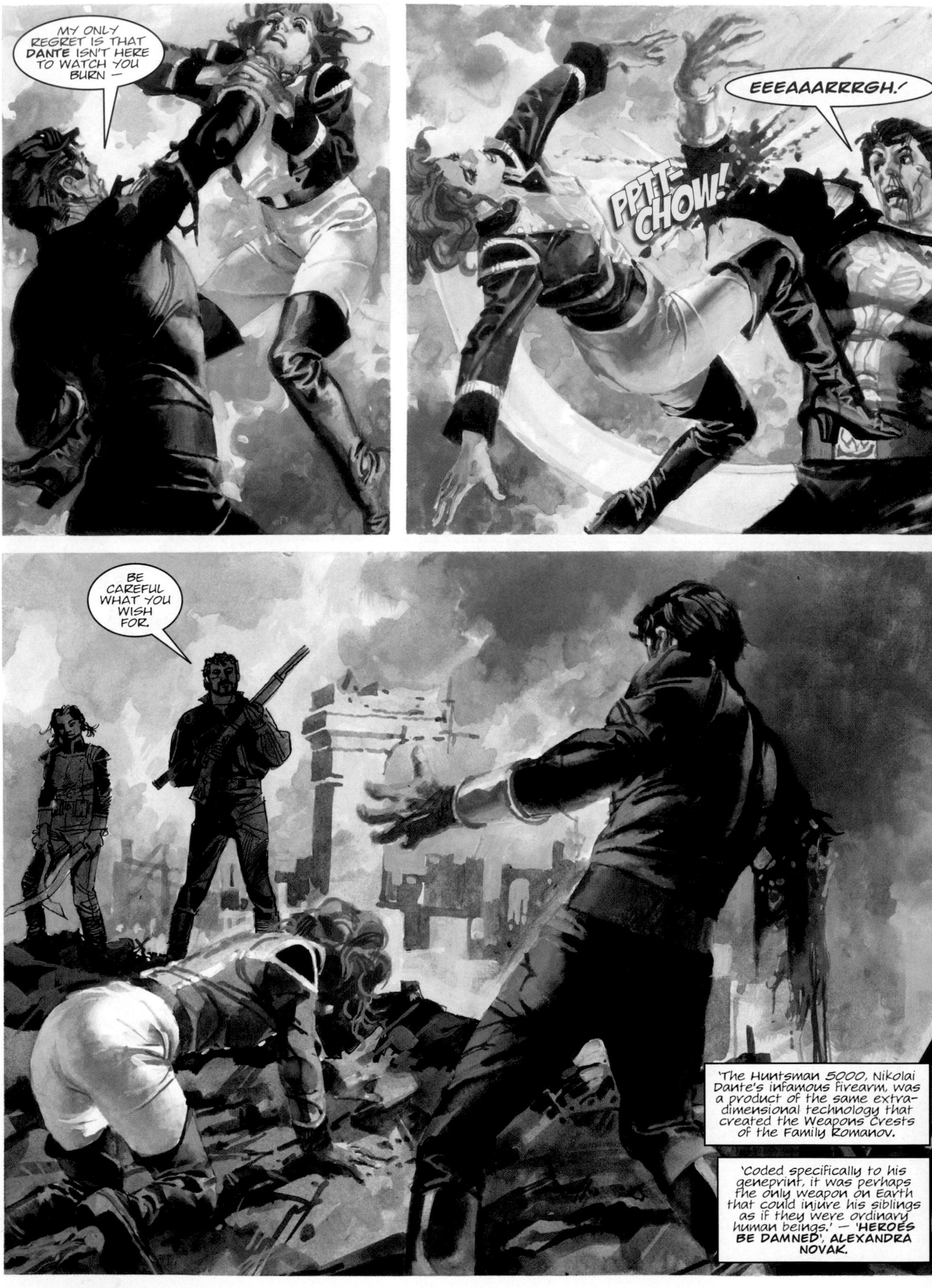
MY ONLY REGRET IS THAT DANTE ISN'T HERE TO WATCH YOU BURN —
EEEAAARRRGH.!
PPTT-CHOW!
BE CAREFUL WHAT YOU WISH FOR.
'The Huntsman 5000, Nikolai Dante's infamous firearm, was a product of the same extra-dimensional technology that created the Weapons Crests of the Family Romanov.
'Coded specifically to his geneprint, it was perhaps the only weapon on Earth that could injure his siblings as if they were ordinary human beings.' — 'HEROES BE DAMNED', ALEXANDRA NOVAK.

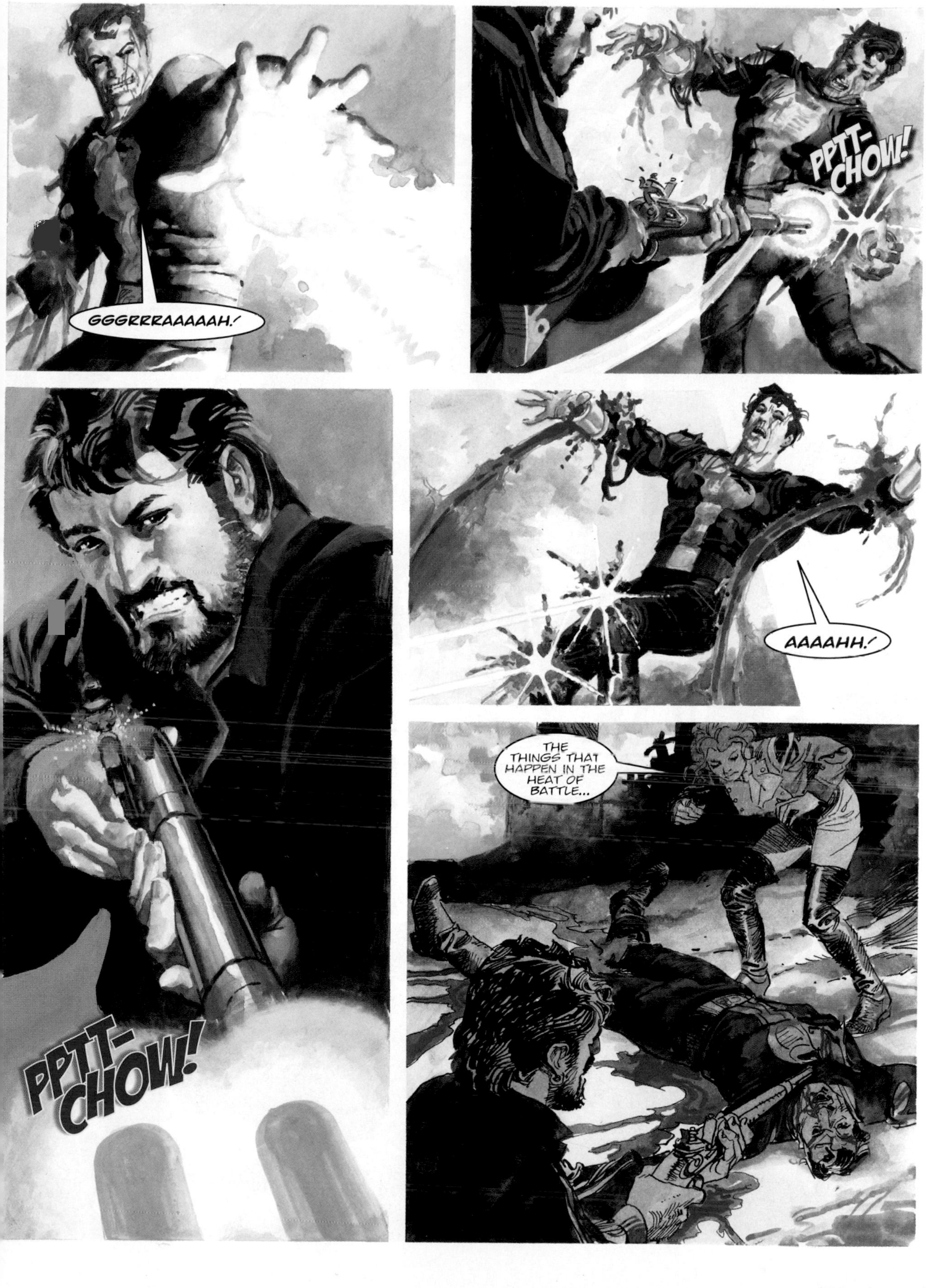
GGGRRRAAAAAH.!
PPTT-CHOW!
PPTT-CHOW!
AAAAHH.!
THE THINGS THAT HAPPEN IN THE HEAT OF BATTLE...

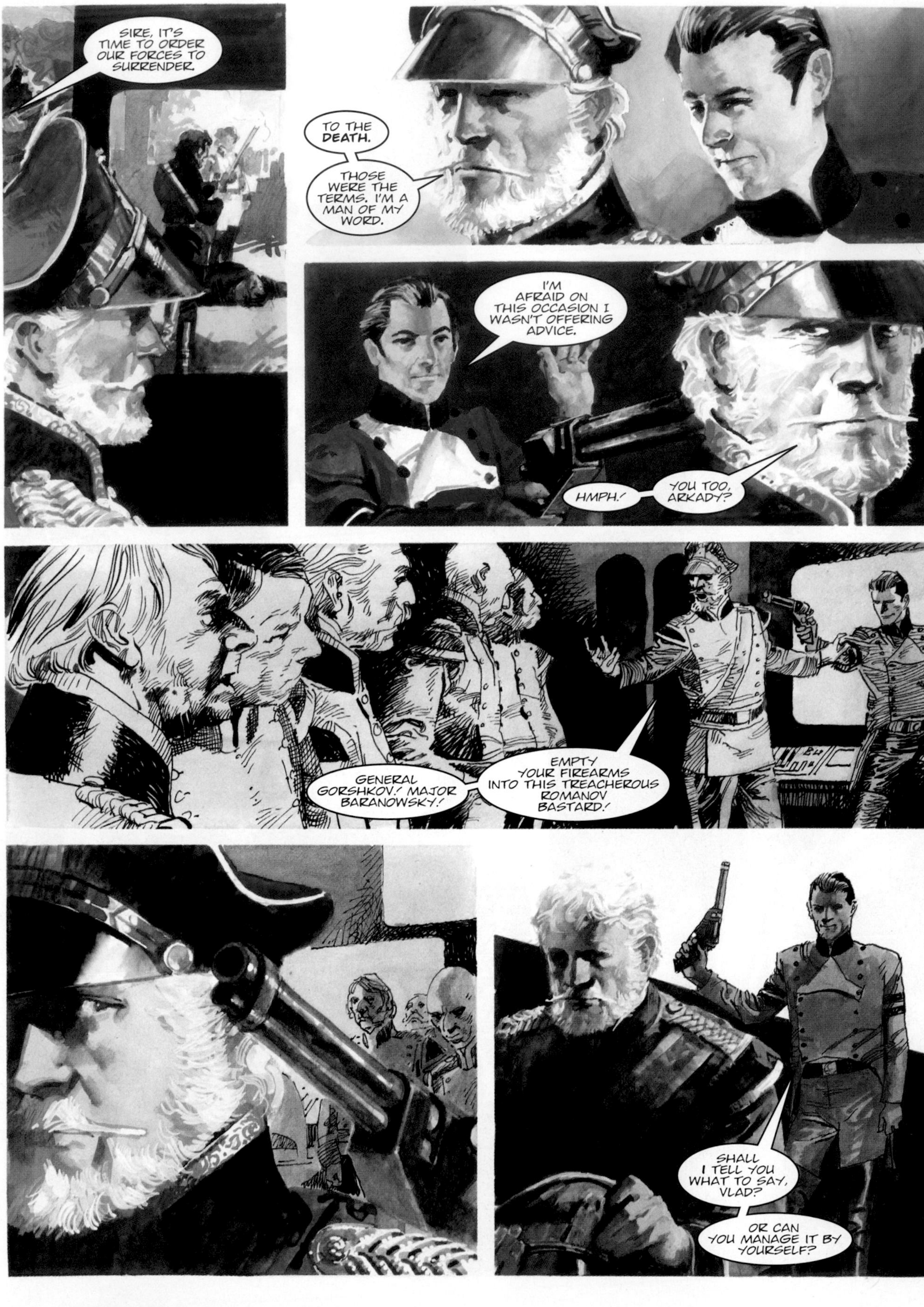
SIRE, IT'S TIME TO ORDER OUR FORCES TO SURRENDER.
TO THE DEATH.
THOSE WERE THE TERMS. I'M A MAN OF MY WORD.
I'M AFRAID ON THIS OCCASION I WASN'T OFFERING ADVICE.
YOU TOO, ARKADY?
HMPH!
GENERAL GORSHKOV! MAJOR BARANOWSKY!
EMPTY YOUR FIREARMS INTO THIS TREACHEROUS ROMANOV BASTARD!
SHALL I TELL YOU WHAT TO SAY, VLAD?
OR CAN YOU MANAGE IT BY YOURSELF?

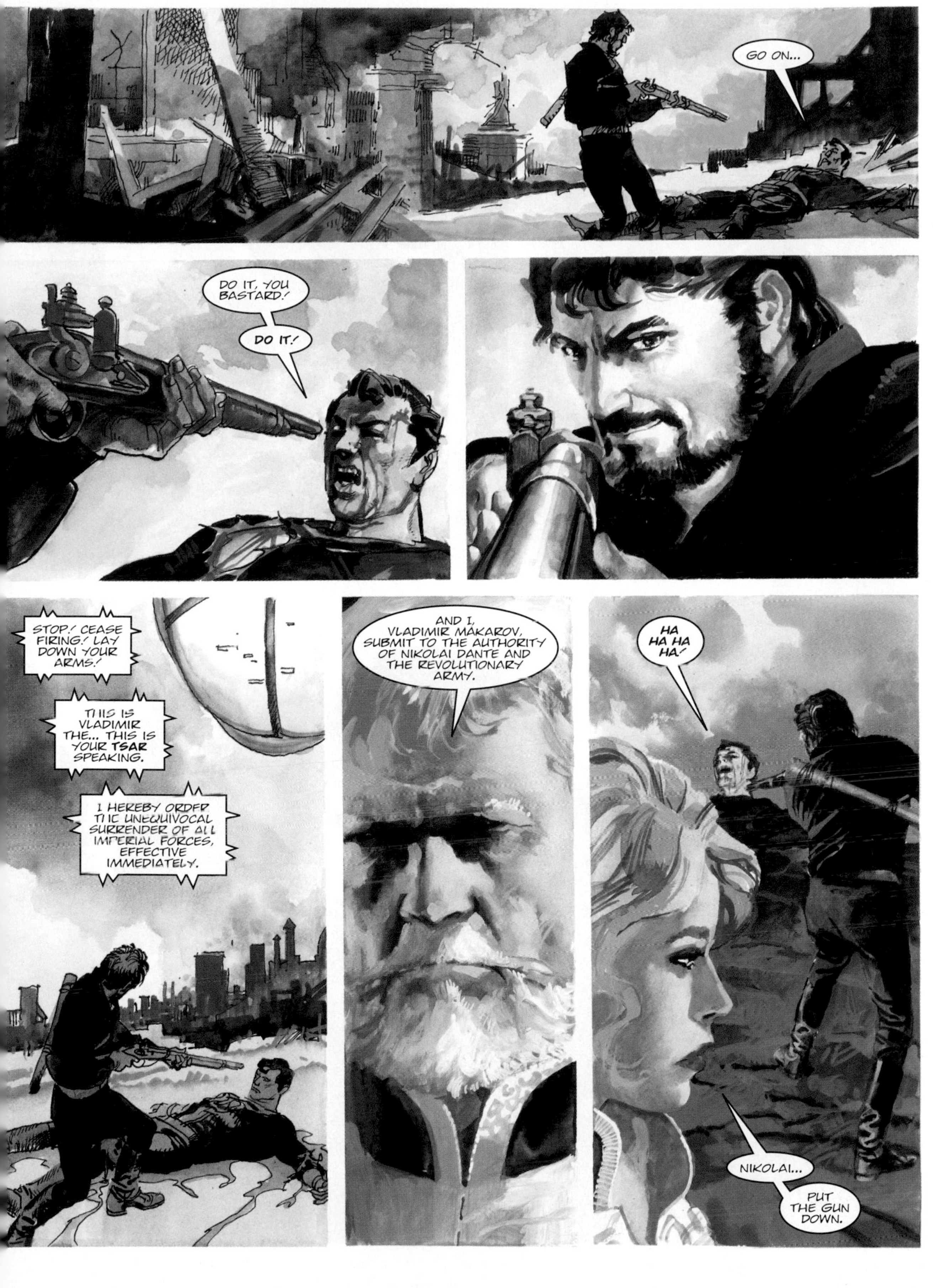
GO ON...
DO IT, YOU BASTARD!
DO IT!
STOP! CEASE FIRING! LAY DOWN YOUR ARMS!
THIS IS VLADIMIR THE... THIS IS YOUR TSAR SPEAKING.
I HEREBY ORDER THE UNEQUIVOCAL SURRENDER OF ALL IMPERIAL FORCES, EFFECTIVE IMMEDIATELY.
AND I, VLADIMIR MAKAROV, SUBMIT TO THE AUTHORITY OF NIKOLAI DANTE AND THE REVOLUTIONARY ARMY.
HA HA HA HA!
NIKOLAI...
PUT THE GUN DOWN.

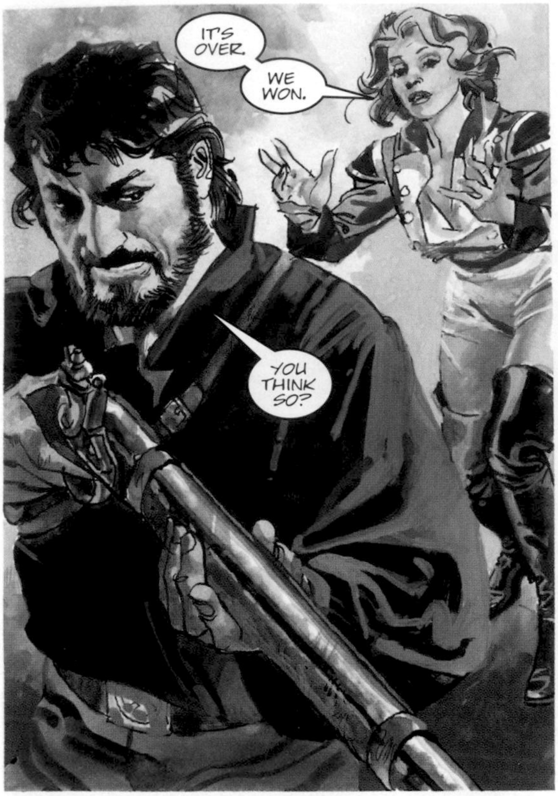
IT'S OVER. WE WON.
YOU THINK SO?

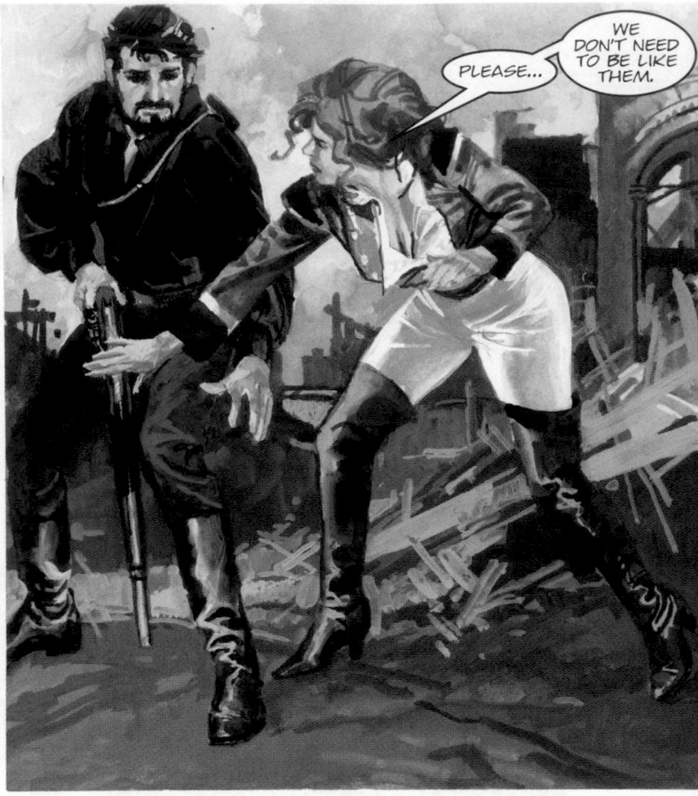
PLEASE...
WE DON'T NEED TO BE LIKE THEM.

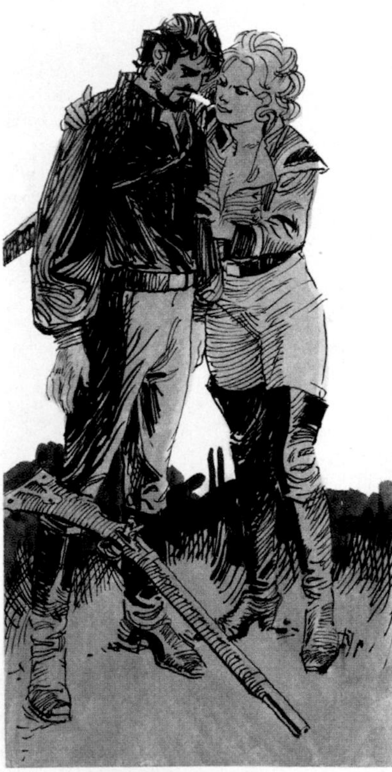

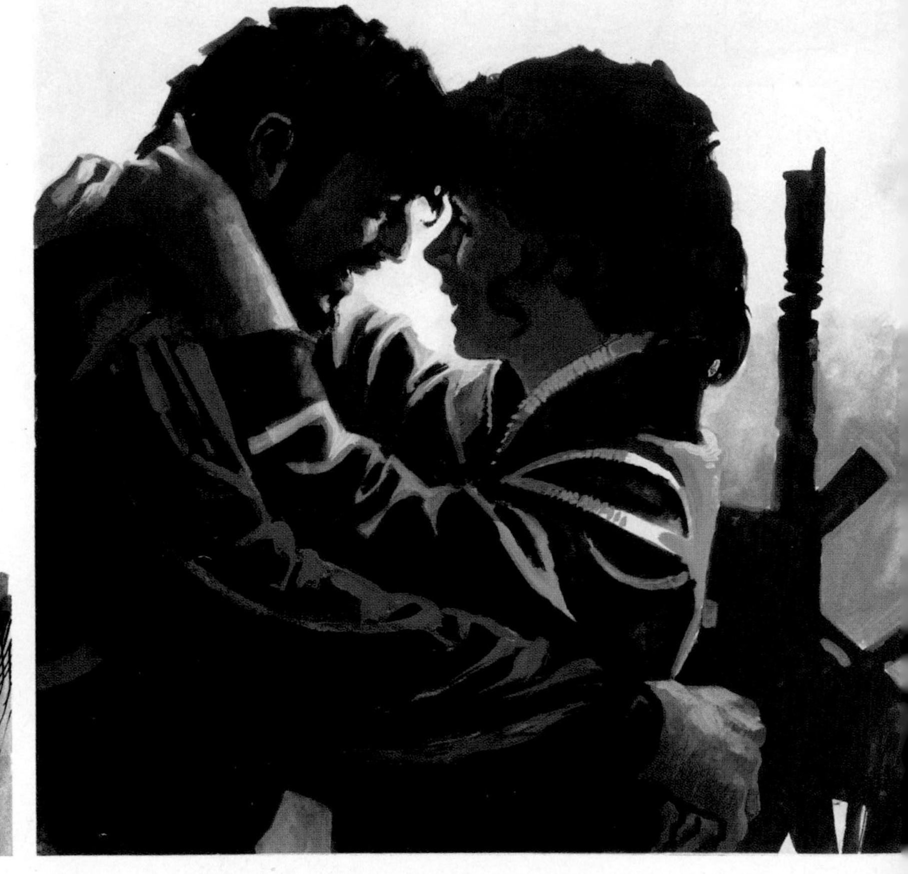

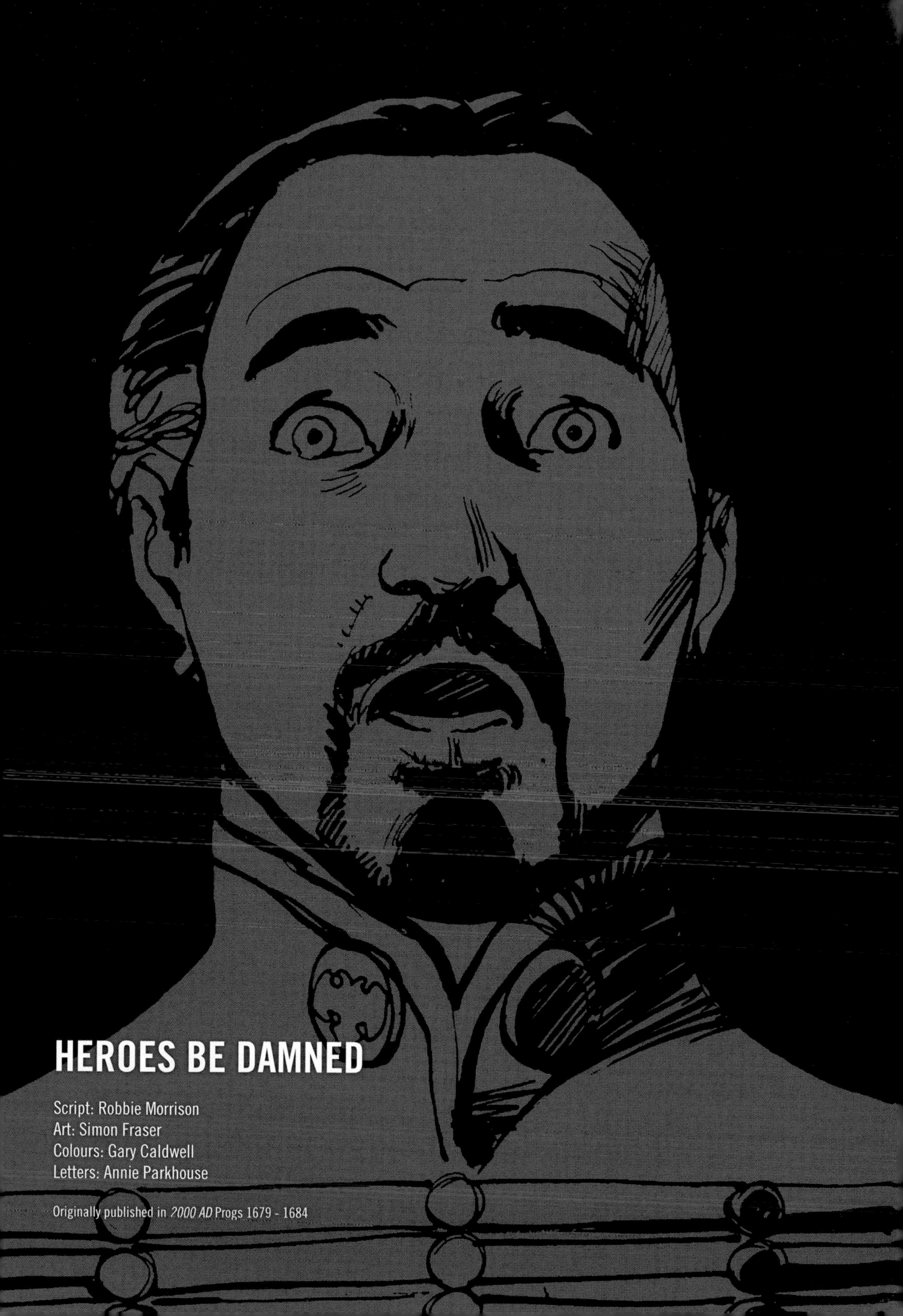

HEROES BE DAMNED

Script: Robbie Morrison
Art: Simon Fraser
Colours: Gary Caldwell
Letters: Annie Parkhouse

Originally published in *2000 AD* Progs 1679 - 1684

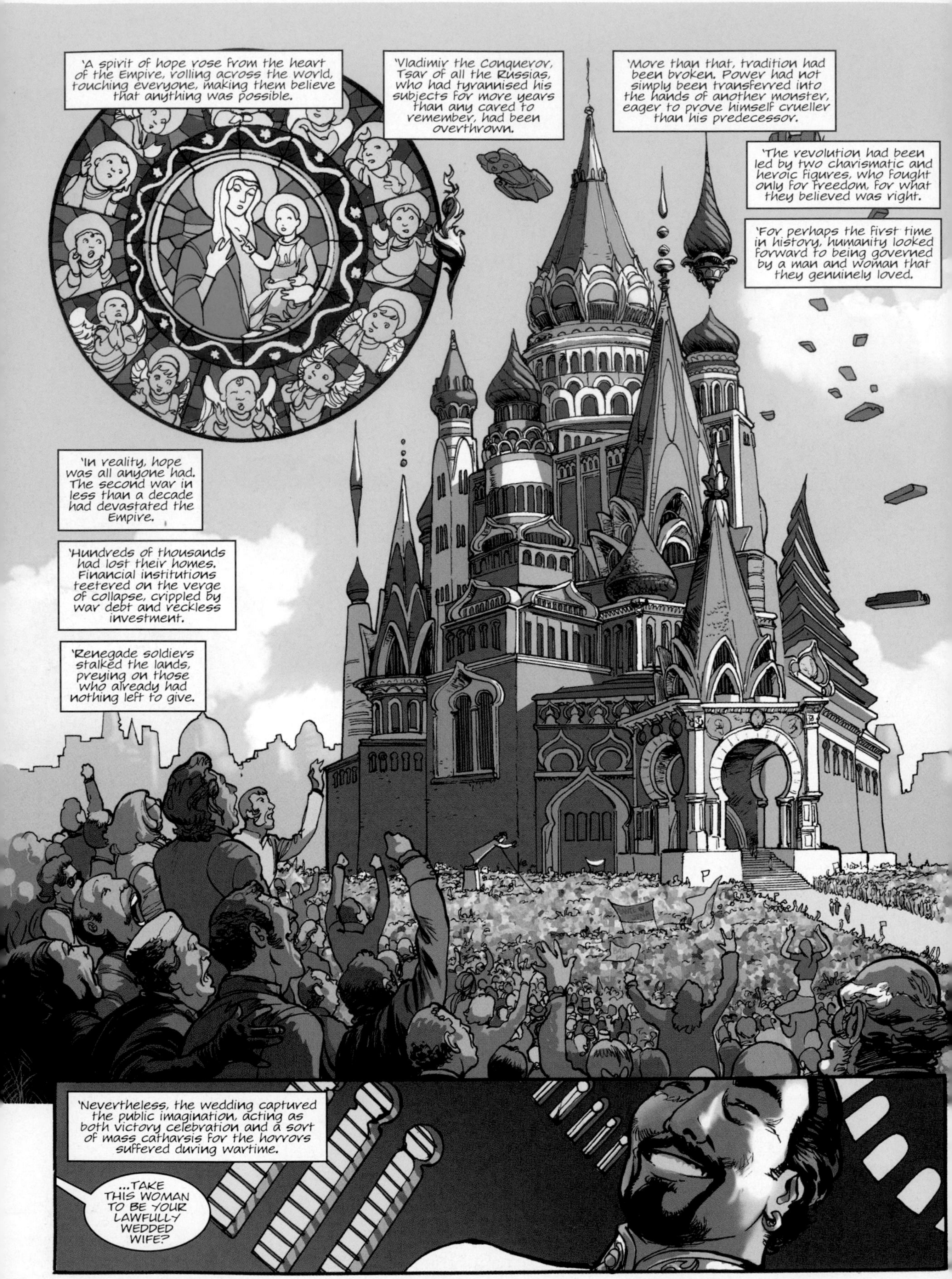
'A spirit of hope rose from the heart of the Empire, rolling across the world, touching everyone, making them believe that anything was possible.
'Vladimir the Conqueror, Tsar of all the Russias, who had tyrannised his subjects for more years than any cared to remember, had been overthrown.
'More than that, tradition had been broken. Power had not simply been transferred into the hands of another monster, eager to prove himself crueller than his predecessor.
'The revolution had been led by two charismatic and heroic figures, who fought only for freedom, for what they believed was right.
'For perhaps the first time in history, humanity looked forward to being governed by a man and woman that they genuinely loved.
'In reality, hope was all anyone had. The second war in less than a decade had devastated the Empire.
'Hundreds of thousands had lost their homes. Financial institutions teetered on the verge of collapse, crippled by war debt and reckless investment.
'Renegade soldiers stalked the lands, preying on those who already had nothing left to give.
'Nevertheless, the wedding captured the public imagination, acting as both victory celebration and a sort of mass catharsis for the horrors suffered during wartime.
...TAKE THIS WOMAN TO BE YOUR LAWFULLY WEDDED WIFE?

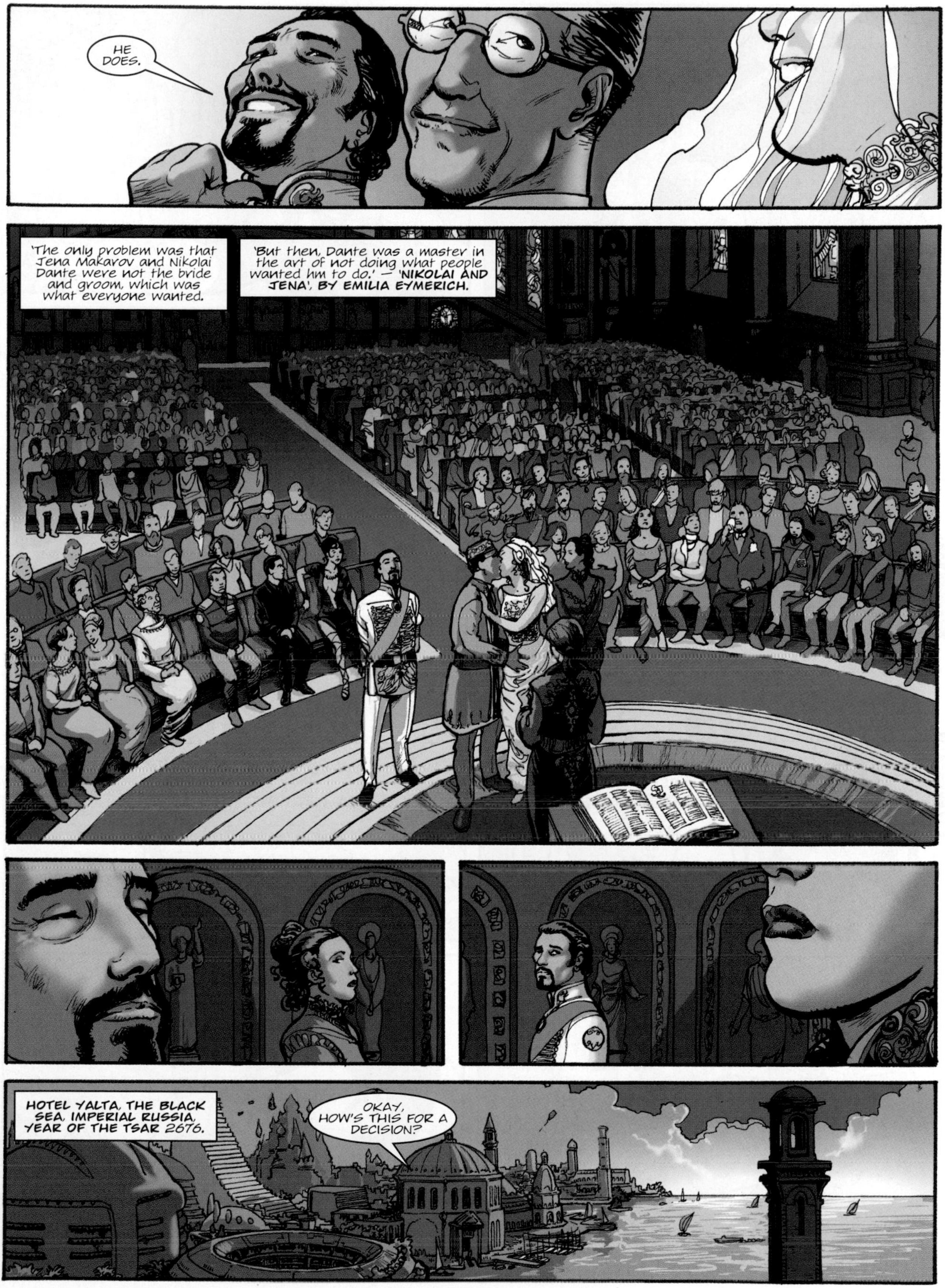
HE DOES.
'The only problem was that Jena Makarov and Nikolai Dante were not the bride and groom, which was what everyone wanted.
'But then, Dante was a master in the art of not doing what people wanted hm to do.' — 'NIKOLAI AND JENA', BY EMILIA EYMERICH.
HOTEL YALTA, THE BLACK SEA, IMPERIAL RUSSIA, YEAR OF THE TSAR 2676.
OKAY, HOW'S THIS FOR A DECISION?

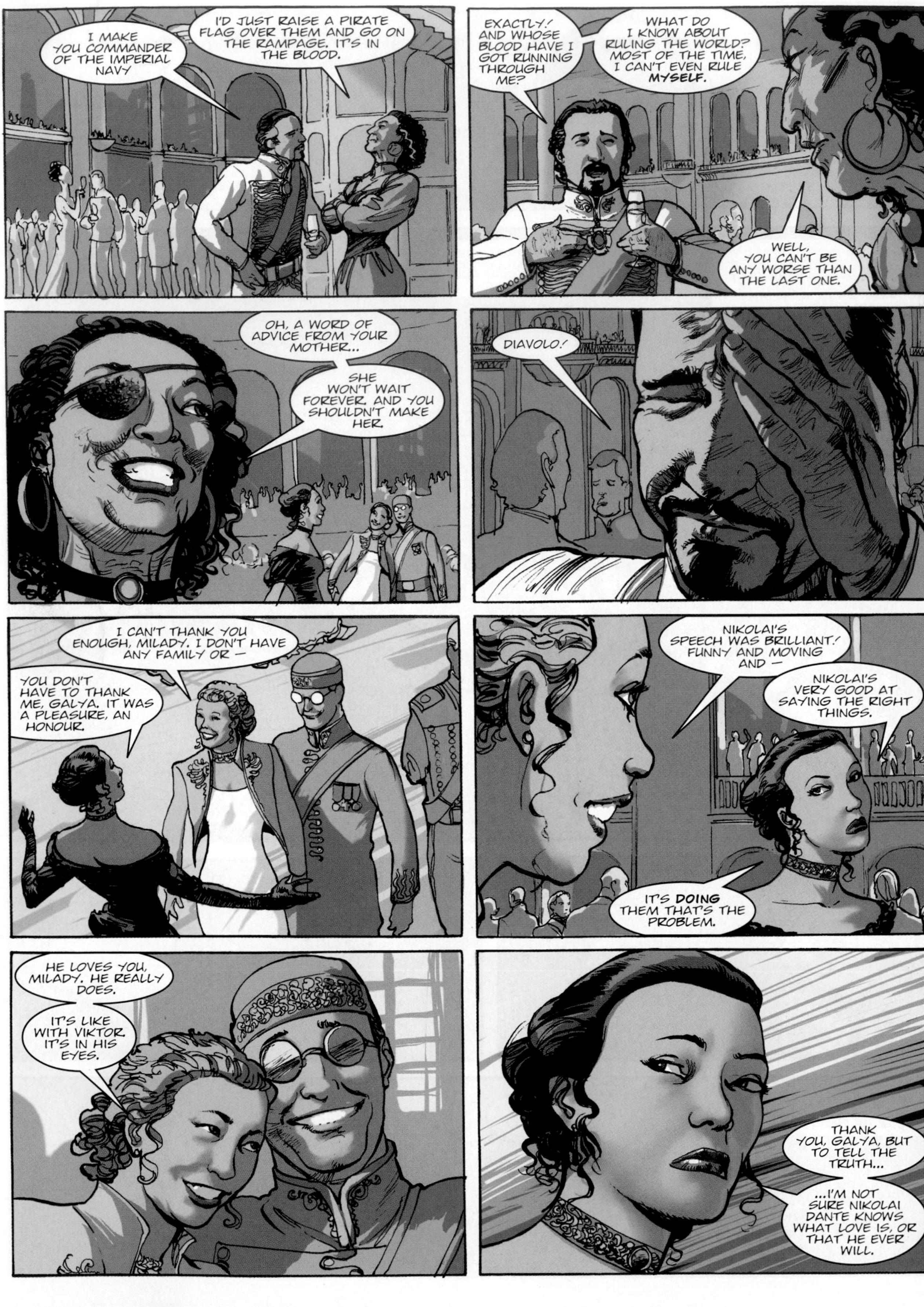
I MAKE YOU COMMANDER OF THE IMPERIAL NAVY
I'D JUST RAISE A PIRATE FLAG OVER THEM AND GO ON THE RAMPAGE. IT'S IN THE BLOOD.
EXACTLY! AND WHOSE BLOOD HAVE I GOT RUNNING THROUGH ME?
WHAT DO I KNOW ABOUT RULING THE WORLD? MOST OF THE TIME, I CAN'T EVEN RULE **MYSELF**.
WELL, YOU CAN'T BE ANY WORSE THAN THE LAST ONE.
OH, A WORD OF ADVICE FROM YOUR MOTHER...
SHE WON'T WAIT FOREVER. AND YOU SHOULDN'T MAKE HER.
DIAVOLO!
I CAN'T THANK YOU ENOUGH, MILADY. I DON'T HAVE ANY FAMILY OR —
YOU DON'T HAVE TO THANK ME, GALYA. IT WAS A PLEASURE, AN HONOUR.
NIKOLAI'S SPEECH WAS **BRILLIANT**! FUNNY AND MOVING AND —
NIKOLAI'S VERY GOOD AT SAYING THE RIGHT THINGS.
IT'S **DOING** THEM THAT'S THE PROBLEM.
HE LOVES YOU, MILADY. HE REALLY DOES.
IT'S LIKE WITH VIKTOR. IT'S IN HIS EYES.
THANK YOU, GALYA, BUT TO TELL THE TRUTH...
...I'M NOT SURE NIKOLAI DANTE KNOWS WHAT LOVE IS, OR THAT HE EVER WILL.

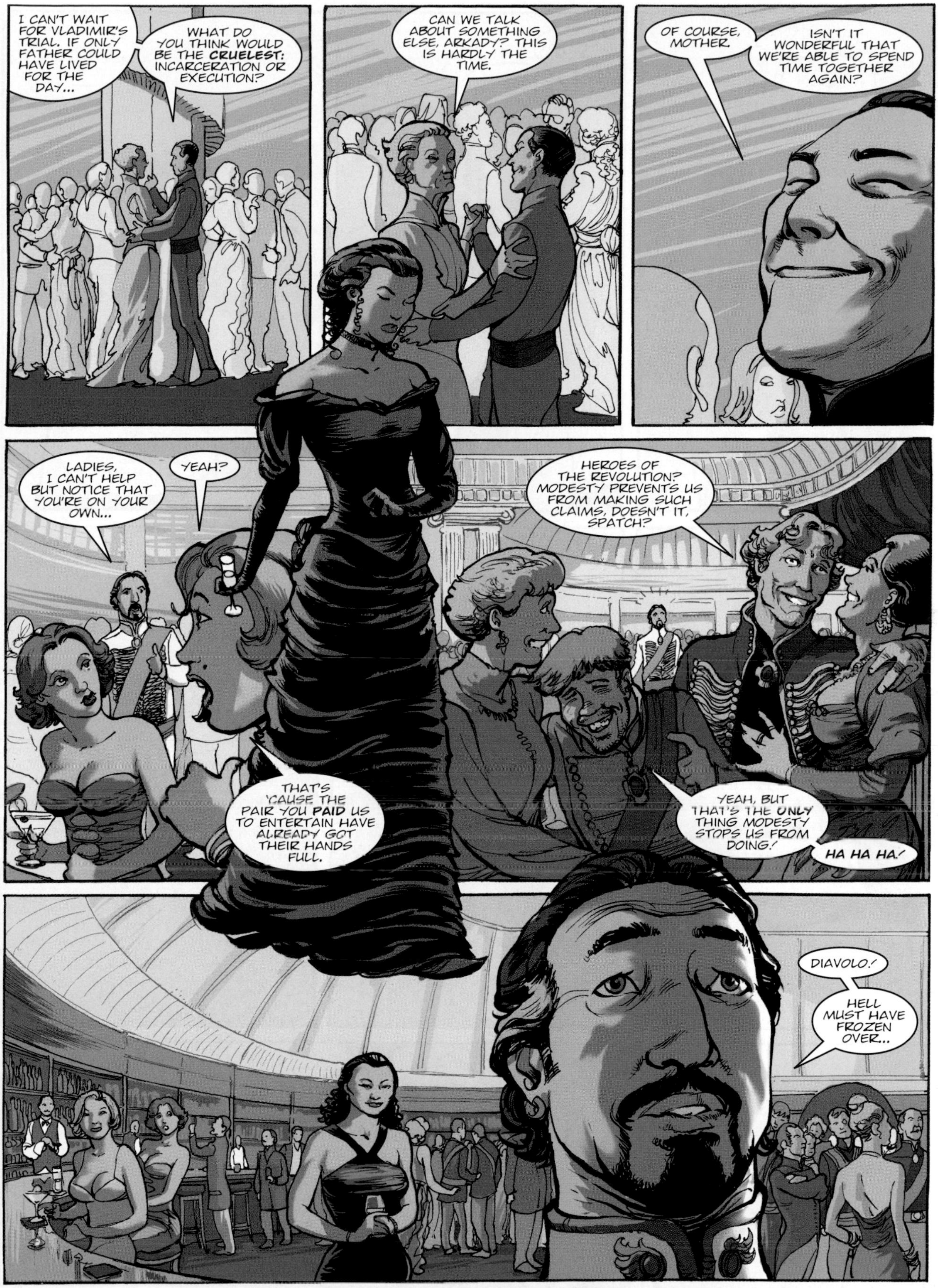
I CAN'T WAIT FOR VLADIMIR'S TRIAL. IF ONLY FATHER COULD HAVE LIVED FOR THE DAY...
WHAT DO YOU THINK WOULD BE THE **CRUELEST**: INCARCERATION OR EXECUTION?
CAN WE TALK ABOUT SOMETHING ELSE, ARKADY? THIS IS HARDLY THE TIME.
OF COURSE, MOTHER.
ISN'T IT WONDERFUL THAT WE'RE ABLE TO SPEND TIME TOGETHER AGAIN?
LADIES, I CAN'T HELP BUT NOTICE THAT YOU'RE ON YOUR OWN...
YEAH?
THAT'S 'CAUSE THE PAIR YOU **PAID** US TO ENTERTAIN HAVE ALREADY GOT THEIR HANDS FULL.
HEROES OF THE REVOLUTION? MODESTY PREVENTS US FROM MAKING SUCH CLAIMS, DOESN'T IT, SPATCH?
YEAH, BUT THAT'S THE **ONLY** THING MODESTY STOPS US FROM DOING!
HA HA HA!
DIAVOLO!
HELL MUST HAVE FROZEN OVER...

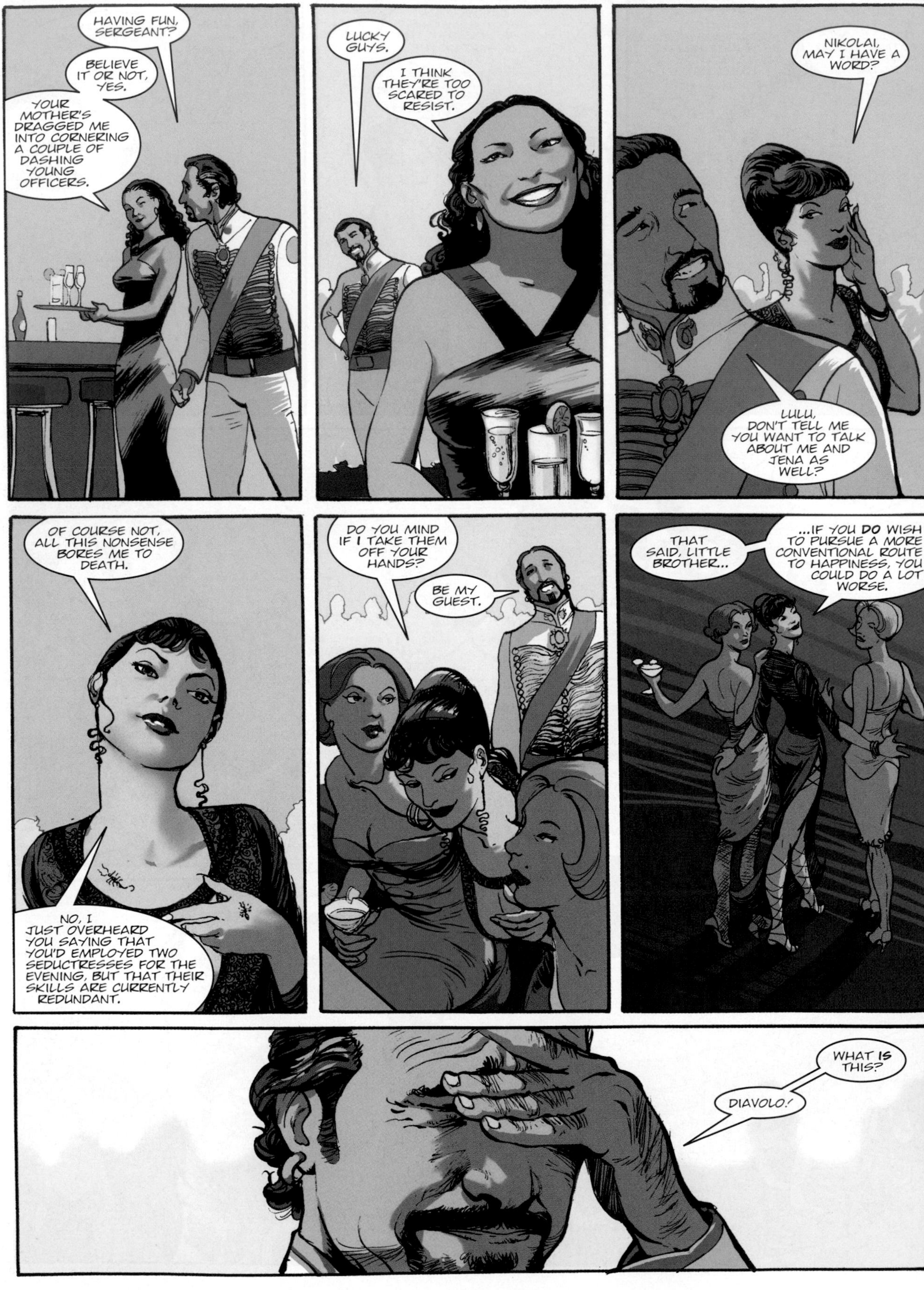
HAVING FUN, SERGEANT?
BELIEVE IT OR NOT, YES.
YOUR MOTHER'S DRAGGED ME INTO CORNERING A COUPLE OF DASHING YOUNG OFFICERS.
LUCKY GUYS.
I THINK THEY'RE TOO SCARED TO RESIST.
NIKOLAI, MAY I HAVE A WORD?
LULU, DON'T TELL ME YOU WANT TO TALK ABOUT ME AND JENA AS WELL?
OF COURSE NOT, ALL THIS NONSENSE BORES ME TO DEATH.
NO, I JUST OVERHEARD YOU SAYING THAT YOU'D EMPLOYED TWO SEDUCTRESSES FOR THE EVENING, BUT THAT THEIR SKILLS ARE CURRENTLY REDUNDANT.
DO YOU MIND IF I TAKE THEM OFF YOUR HANDS?
BE MY GUEST.
THAT SAID, LITTLE BROTHER...
...IF YOU **DO** WISH TO PURSUE A MORE CONVENTIONAL ROUTE TO HAPPINESS, YOU COULD DO A LOT WORSE.
WHAT **IS** THIS?
DIAVOLO!

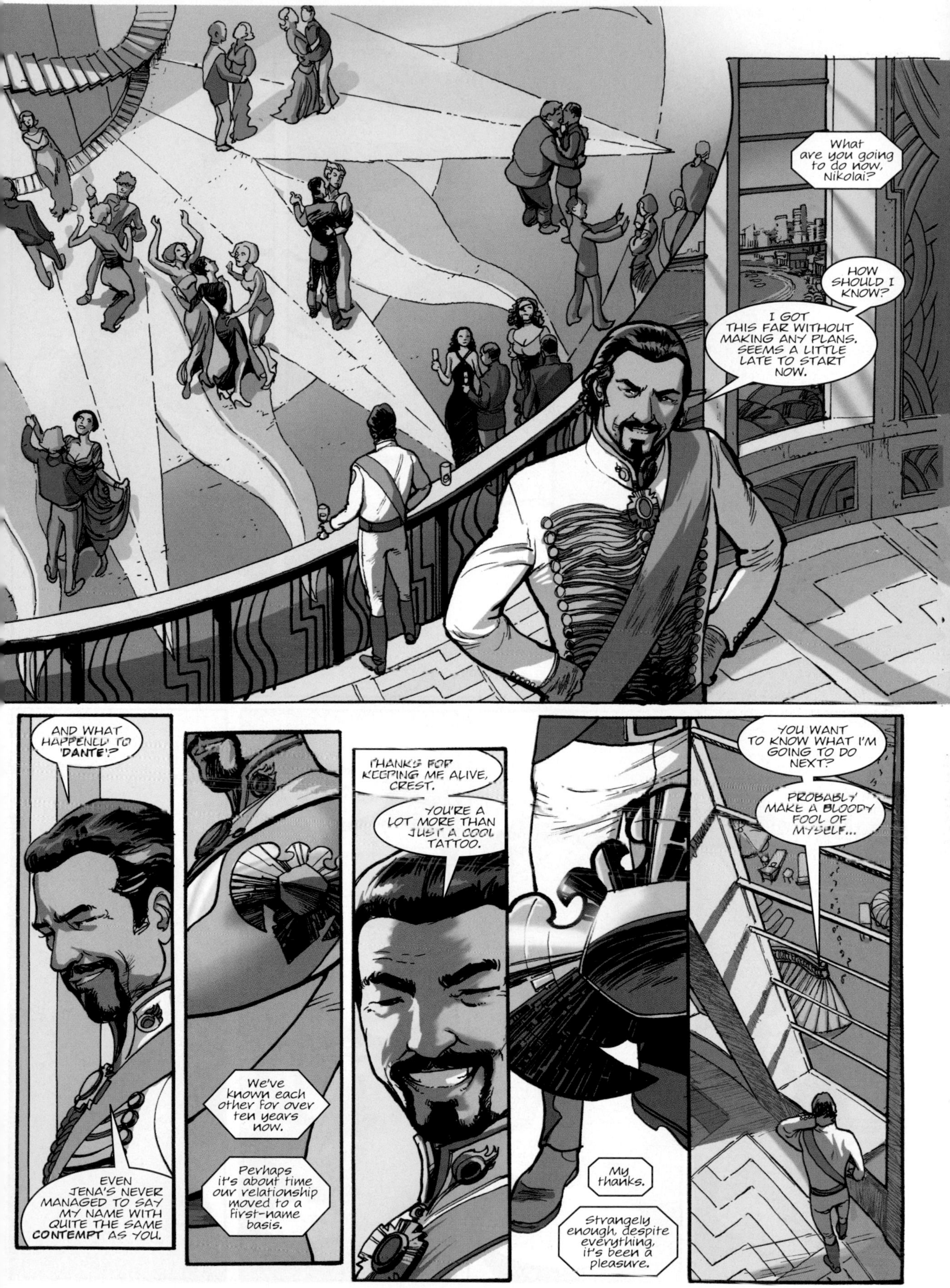

What are you going to do now, Nikolai?
HOW SHOULD I KNOW?
I GOT THIS FAR WITHOUT MAKING ANY PLANS. SEEMS A LITTLE LATE TO START NOW.
AND WHAT HAPPENED TO 'DANTE'?
EVEN JENA'S NEVER MANAGED TO SAY MY NAME WITH QUITE THE SAME CONTEMPT AS YOU.
We've known each other for over ten years now.
Perhaps it's about time our relationship moved to a first-name basis.
THANKS FOR KEEPING ME ALIVE, CREST.
YOU'RE A LOT MORE THAN JUST A COOL TATTOO.
My thanks.
Strangely enough, despite everything, it's been a pleasure.
YOU WANT TO KNOW WHAT I'M GOING TO DO NEXT?
PROBABLY MAKE A BLOODY FOOL OF MYSELF...

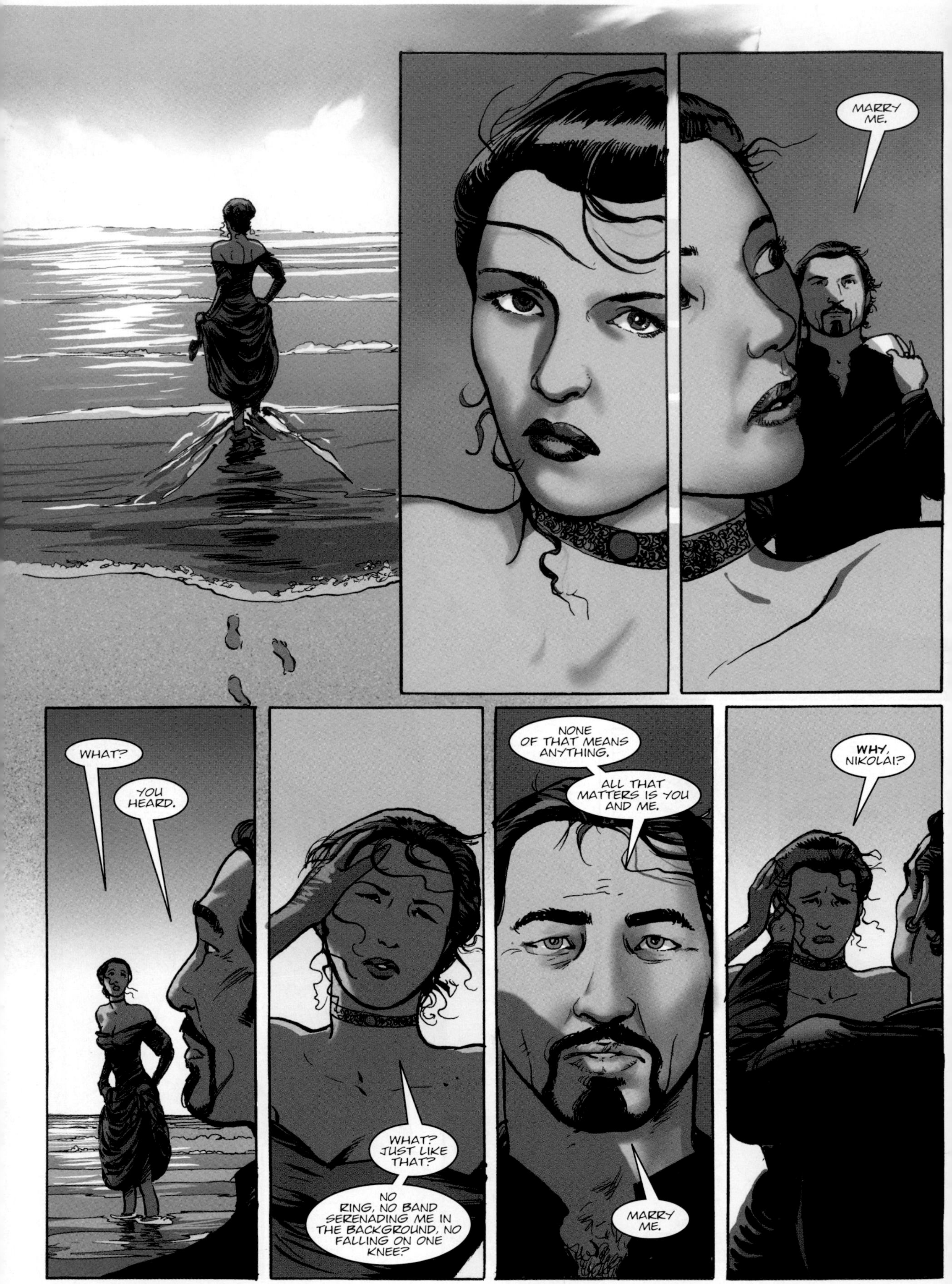
MARRY ME.
WHAT?
YOU HEARD.
WHAT? JUST LIKE THAT?
NO RING, NO BAND SERENADING ME IN THE BACKGROUND, NO FALLING ON ONE KNEE?
NONE OF THAT MEANS ANYTHING.
ALL THAT MATTERS IS YOU AND ME.
MARRY ME.
WHY, NIKOLAI?

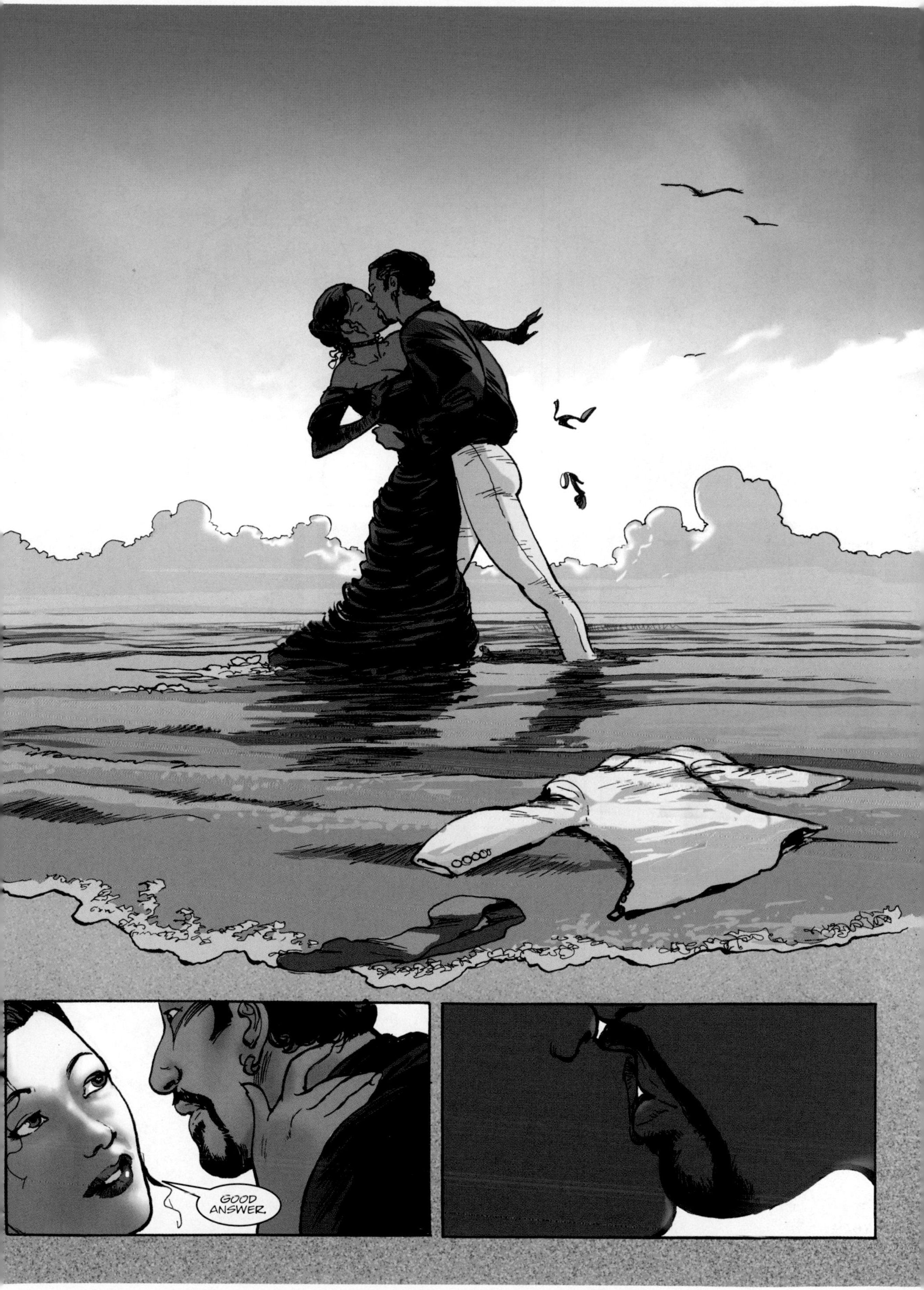
GOOD ANSWER.

'EXECUTE HIM.

'NOW.

'NO MERCY.

'NO TRIAL.

'NOTHING.'

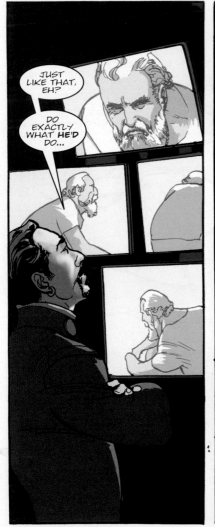

JUST LIKE THAT, EH?

DO EXACTLY WHAT **HE'D** DO...

NO, VLADIMIR THE CONQUEROR WOULD HANG YOU FROM A HOOK AND TORTURE YOU EXCRUCIATINGLY EVERY DAY FOR THE REST OF YOUR LIFE.

HE WOULD KEEP YOU ALIVE PURELY FOR THE PLEASURE OF KEEPING YOU IN AGONY.

I'M NOT TALKING ABOUT VENGEANCE, NIKOLAI, I'M TALKING ABOUT **HARSH REALITY.**

EXECUTE HIM. QUICKLY, PAINLESSLY, WHATEVER. JUST KILL HIM. IT'S THE ONLY WAY.

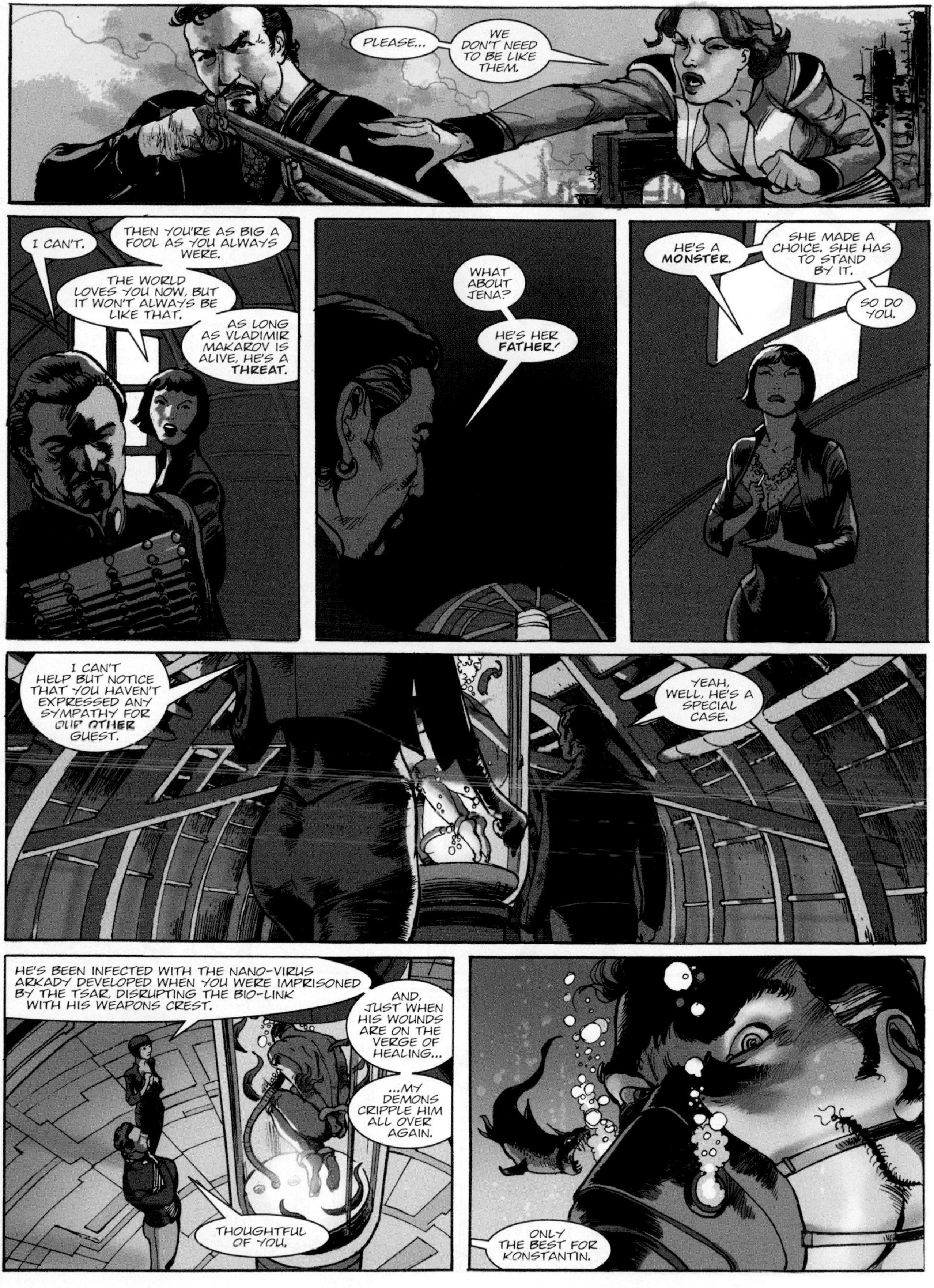
PLEASE...
WE DON'T NEED TO BE LIKE THEM.
I CAN'T.
THEN YOU'RE AS BIG A FOOL AS YOU ALWAYS WERE.
THE WORLD LOVES YOU NOW, BUT IT WON'T ALWAYS BE LIKE THAT.
AS LONG AS VLADIMIR MAKAROV IS ALIVE, HE'S A **THREAT**.
WHAT ABOUT JENA?
HE'S HER **FATHER**!
HE'S A **MONSTER**.
SHE MADE A CHOICE. SHE HAS TO STAND BY IT.
SO DO YOU.
I CAN'T HELP BUT NOTICE THAT YOU HAVEN'T EXPRESSED ANY SYMPATHY FOR OUR **OTHER** GUEST.
YEAH, WELL, HE'S A SPECIAL CASE.
HE'S BEEN INFECTED WITH THE NANO-VIRUS ARKADY DEVELOPED WHEN YOU WERE IMPRISONED BY THE TSAR, DISRUPTING THE BIO-LINK WITH HIS WEAPONS CREST.
AND, JUST WHEN HIS WOUNDS ARE ON THE VERGE OF HEALING...
...MY DEMONS CRIPPLE HIM ALL OVER AGAIN.
THOUGHTFUL OF YOU.
ONLY THE BEST FOR KONSTANTIN.

WHEN WE FIRST MET, YOU WERE A SIMPLE THIEF, DRAGGED BEFORE ME IN CHAINS.

A SLIGHT REVERSAL OF FORTUNE...

MAYBE WE JUST GOT WHAT WE BOTH DESERVED.

THINGS ARE RARELY THAT SIMPLE, NIKOLAI.

AND NOW YOU STAND IN JUDGEMENT OVER ME?

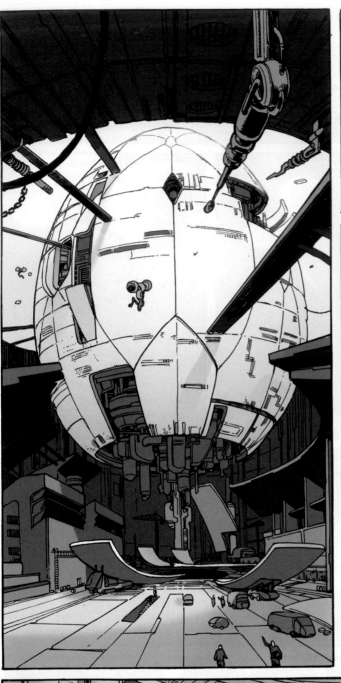

THE GRAND COURT OF THE IMPERIAL PALACE, ST PETERSBURG, YEAR OF THE TSAR 2676.

I ASSUME THAT'S WHAT THIS IS, NO?

A SHOW TRIAL TO PERSUADE MY PEOPLE THAT DEMOCRACY ONCE MORE HOLDS SWAY...

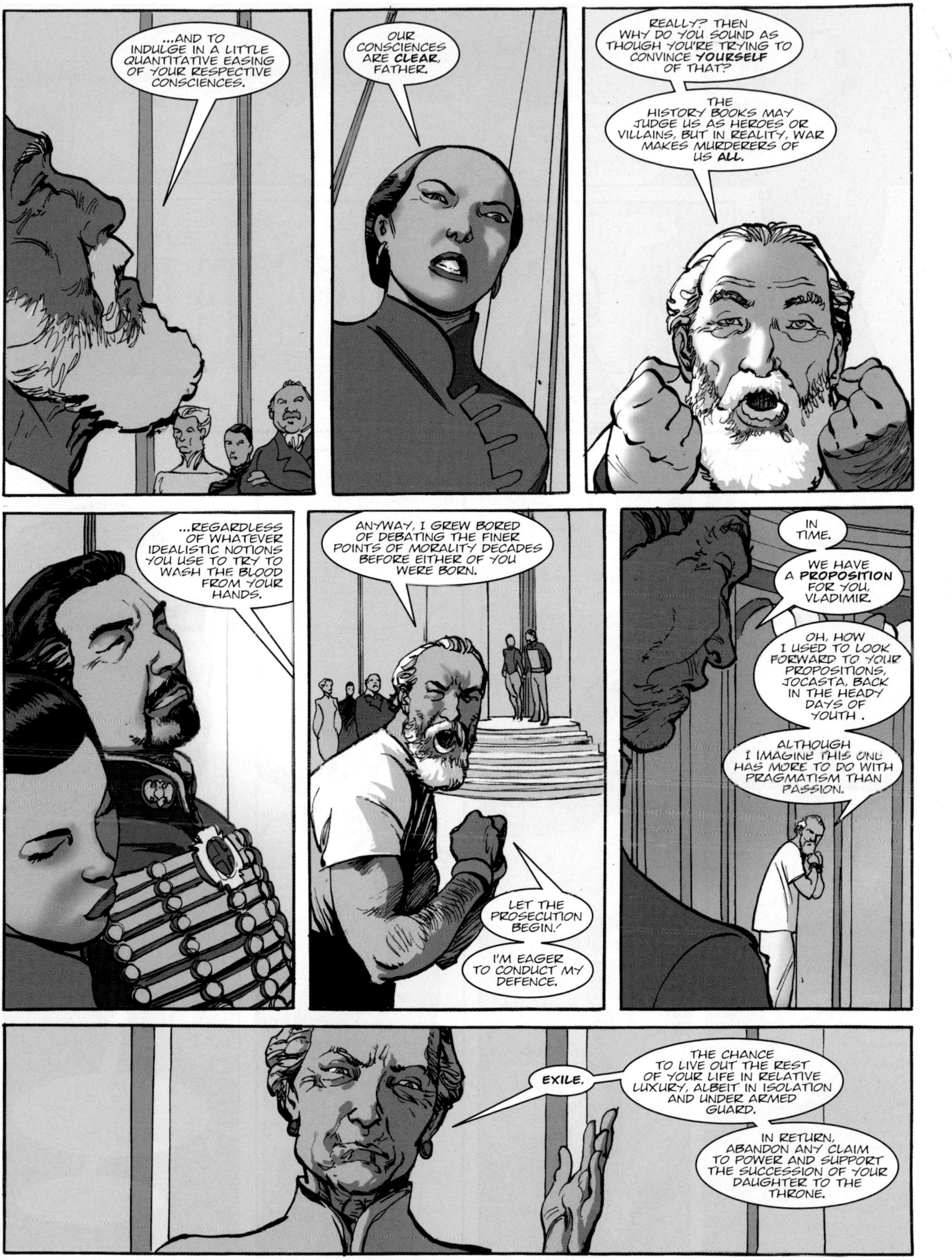
...AND TO INDULGE IN A LITTLE QUANTITATIVE EASING OF YOUR RESPECTIVE CONSCIENCES.
OUR CONSCIENCES ARE **CLEAR**, FATHER.
REALLY? THEN WHY DO YOU SOUND AS THOUGH YOU'RE TRYING TO CONVINCE **YOURSELF** OF THAT?
THE HISTORY BOOKS MAY JUDGE US AS HEROES OR VILLAINS, BUT IN REALITY, WAR MAKES MURDERERS OF US **ALL.**
...REGARDLESS OF WHATEVER IDEALISTIC NOTIONS YOU USE TO TRY TO WASH THE BLOOD FROM YOUR HANDS.
ANYWAY, I GREW BORED OF DEBATING THE FINER POINTS OF MORALITY DECADES BEFORE EITHER OF YOU WERE BORN.
LET THE PROSECUTION BEGIN!
I'M EAGER TO CONDUCT MY DEFENCE.
IN TIME.
WE HAVE A **PROPOSITION** FOR YOU, VLADIMIR.
OH, HOW I USED TO LOOK FORWARD TO YOUR PROPOSITIONS, JOCASTA, BACK IN THE HEADY DAYS OF YOUTH .
ALTHOUGH I IMAGINE THIS ONE HAS MORE TO DO WITH PRAGMATISM THAN PASSION.
EXILE.
THE CHANCE TO LIVE OUT THE REST OF YOUR LIFE IN RELATIVE LUXURY, ALBEIT IN ISOLATION AND UNDER ARMED GUARD.
IN RETURN, ABANDON ANY CLAIM TO POWER AND SUPPORT THE SUCCESSION OF YOUR DAUGHTER TO THE THRONE.

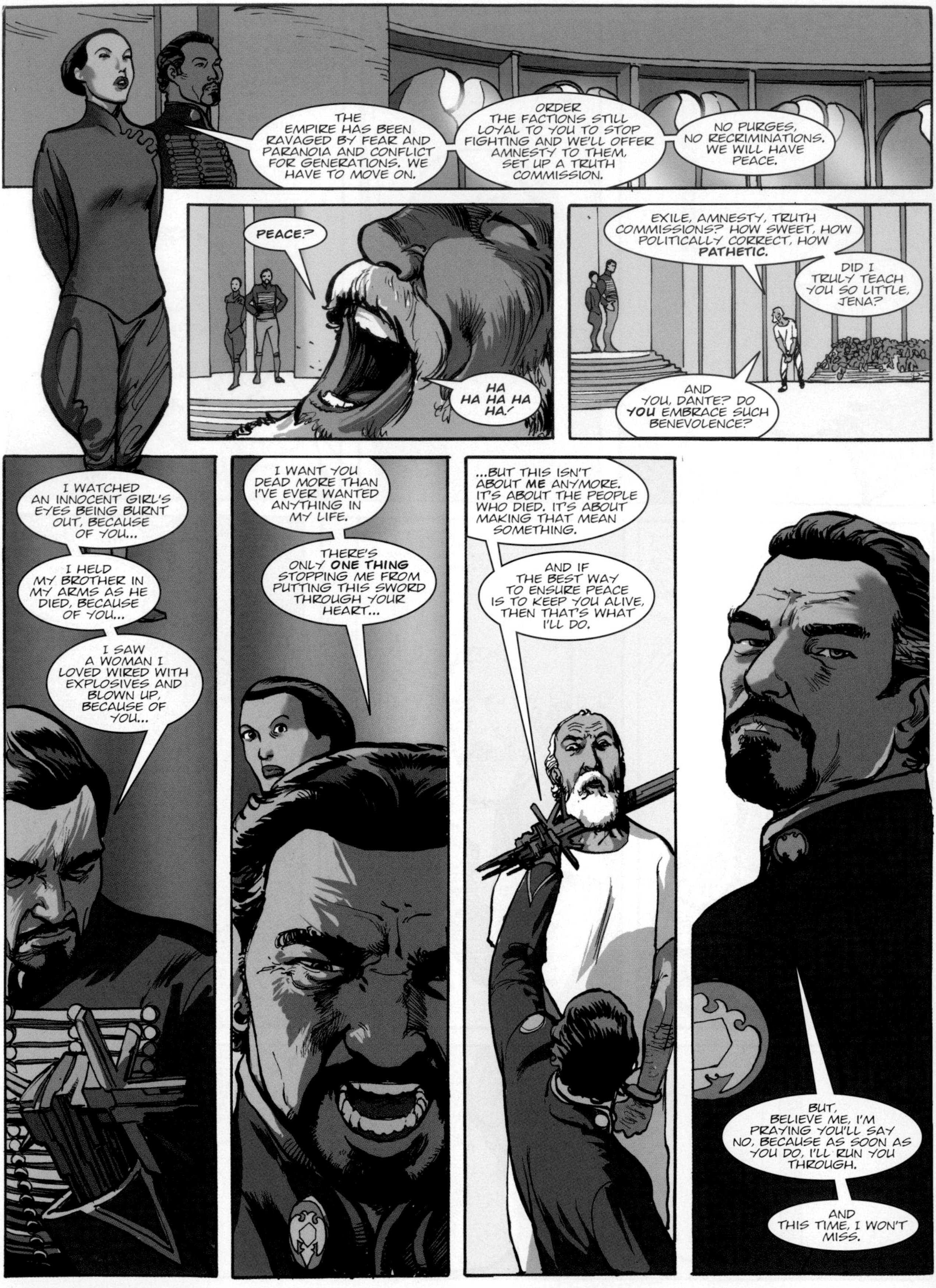

THE EMPIRE HAS BEEN RAVAGED BY FEAR AND PARANOIA AND CONFLICT FOR GENERATIONS. WE HAVE TO MOVE ON.
ORDER THE FACTIONS STILL LOYAL TO YOU TO STOP FIGHTING AND WE'LL OFFER AMNESTY TO THEM, SET UP A TRUTH COMMISSION.
NO PURGES, NO RECRIMINATIONS. WE WILL HAVE PEACE.
PEACE?
HA HA HA HA HA!
EXILE, AMNESTY, TRUTH COMMISSIONS? HOW SWEET, HOW POLITICALLY CORRECT, HOW PATHETIC.
DID I TRULY TEACH YOU SO LITTLE, JENA?
AND YOU, DANTE? DO YOU EMBRACE SUCH BENEVOLENCE?
I WATCHED AN INNOCENT GIRL'S EYES BEING BURNT OUT, BECAUSE OF YOU...
I HELD MY BROTHER IN MY ARMS AS HE DIED, BECAUSE OF YOU...
I SAW A WOMAN I LOVED WIRED WITH EXPLOSIVES AND BLOWN UP, BECAUSE OF YOU...
I WANT YOU DEAD MORE THAN I'VE EVER WANTED ANYTHING IN MY LIFE.
THERE'S ONLY ONE THING STOPPING ME FROM PUTTING THIS SWORD THROUGH YOUR HEART...
...BUT THIS ISN'T ABOUT ME ANYMORE. IT'S ABOUT THE PEOPLE WHO DIED. IT'S ABOUT MAKING THAT MEAN SOMETHING.
AND IF THE BEST WAY TO ENSURE PEACE IS TO KEEP YOU ALIVE, THEN THAT'S WHAT I'LL DO.
BUT, BELIEVE ME, I'M PRAYING YOU'LL SAY NO, BECAUSE AS SOON AS YOU DO, I'LL RUN YOU THROUGH.
AND THIS TIME, I WON'T MISS.

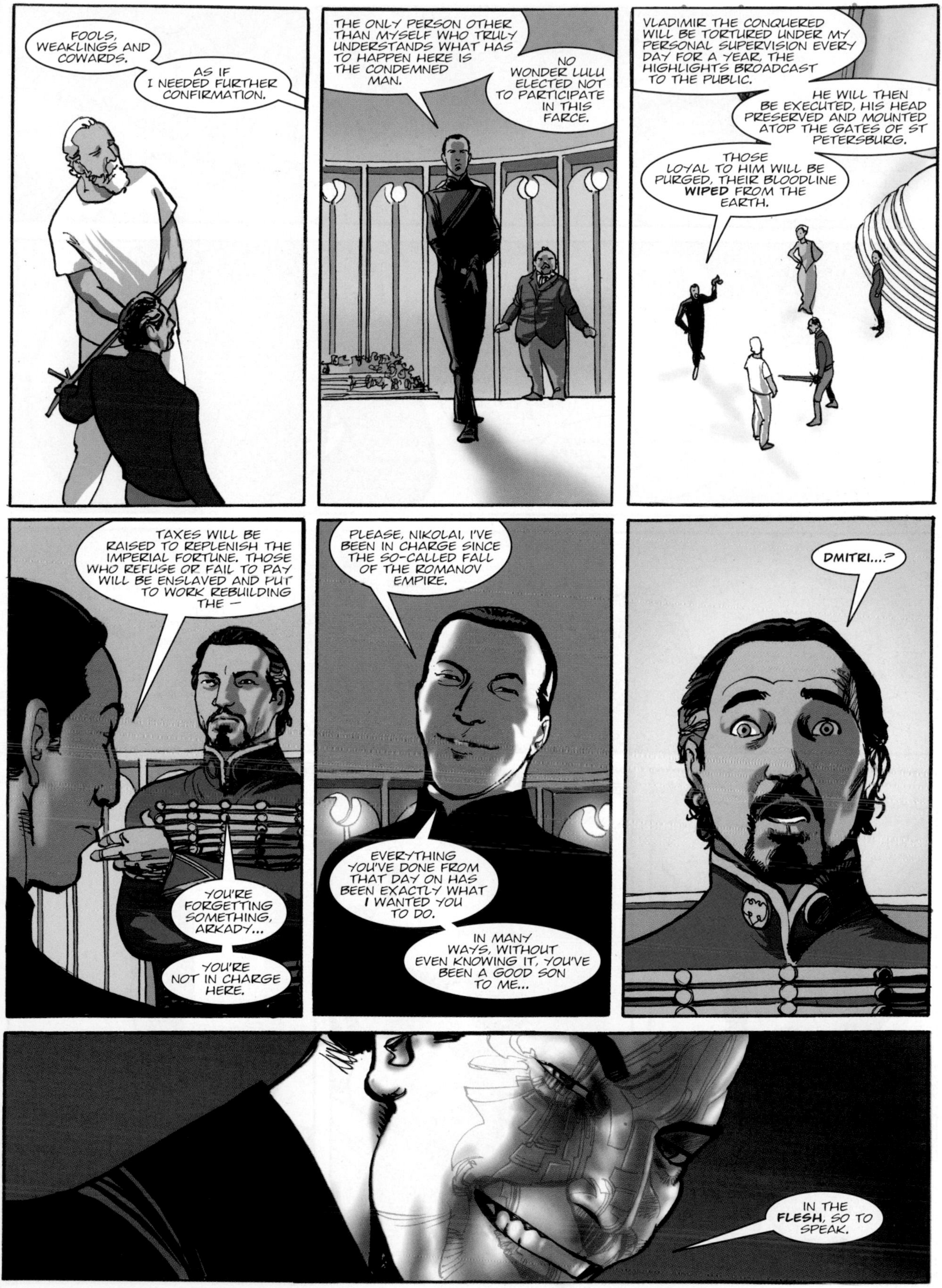
FOOLS, WEAKLINGS AND COWARDS.
AS IF I NEEDED FURTHER CONFIRMATION.
THE ONLY PERSON OTHER THAN MYSELF WHO TRULY UNDERSTANDS WHAT HAS TO HAPPEN HERE IS THE CONDEMNED MAN.
NO WONDER LULU ELECTED NOT TO PARTICIPATE IN THIS FARCE.
VLADIMIR THE CONQUERED WILL BE TORTURED UNDER MY PERSONAL SUPERVISION EVERY DAY FOR A YEAR, THE HIGHLIGHTS BROADCAST TO THE PUBLIC.
HE WILL THEN BE EXECUTED, HIS HEAD PRESERVED AND MOUNTED ATOP THE GATES OF ST PETERSBURG.
THOSE LOYAL TO HIM WILL BE PURGED, THEIR BLOODLINE **WIPED** FROM THE EARTH.
TAXES WILL BE RAISED TO REPLENISH THE IMPERIAL FORTUNE. THOSE WHO REFUSE OR FAIL TO PAY WILL BE ENSLAVED AND PUT TO WORK REBUILDING THE —
YOU'RE FORGETTING SOMETHING, ARKADY...
YOU'RE NOT IN CHARGE HERE.
PLEASE, NIKOLAI, I'VE BEEN IN CHARGE SINCE THE SO-CALLED FALL OF THE ROMANOV EMPIRE.
EVERYTHING YOU'VE DONE FROM THAT DAY ON HAS BEEN EXACTLY WHAT **I** WANTED YOU TO DO.
IN MANY WAYS, WITHOUT EVEN KNOWING IT, YOU'VE BEEN A GOOD SON TO ME...
DMITRI...?
IN THE **FLESH**, SO TO SPEAK.

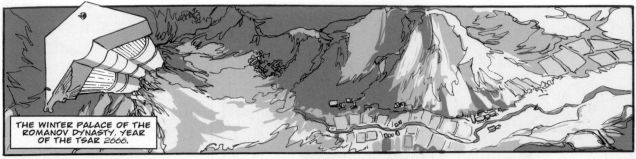

THE WINTER PALACE OF THE ROMANOV DYNASTY, YEAR OF THE TSAR 2666.

NIKOLAI DANTE, FATHER!

I DEMAND THAT YOU PUT HIM TO DEATH!

PERHAPS I WOULD HAVE, IF I'D KNOWN OF HIS EXISTENCE BEFORE NOW.

AS IT IS, HE'S MADE HIMSELF SOMETHING OF A **HERO** IN A REMARKABLY SHORT SPACE OF TIME.

HE... HE CLAIMS HE'S YOUR SON!

ONLY A ROMANOV BORN MAY BEAR THE WEAPONS CREST. ALL THE NECESSARY TESTS PROVED POSITIVE.

THE RECKLESS AND IMPETUOUS ACTIONS OF YOUTH, I'M AFRAID.

IT WAS TO BE MINE! THE CREST HE BEARS IS MINE!

YOUR BASTARD HAS STOLEN MY **BIRTHRIGHT!**

DON'T WORRY, ARKADY.

YOUR TIME WILL COME.

THIS CHANGES NOTHING.

YOU'LL ALWAYS BE MY FAVOURITE CHILD.

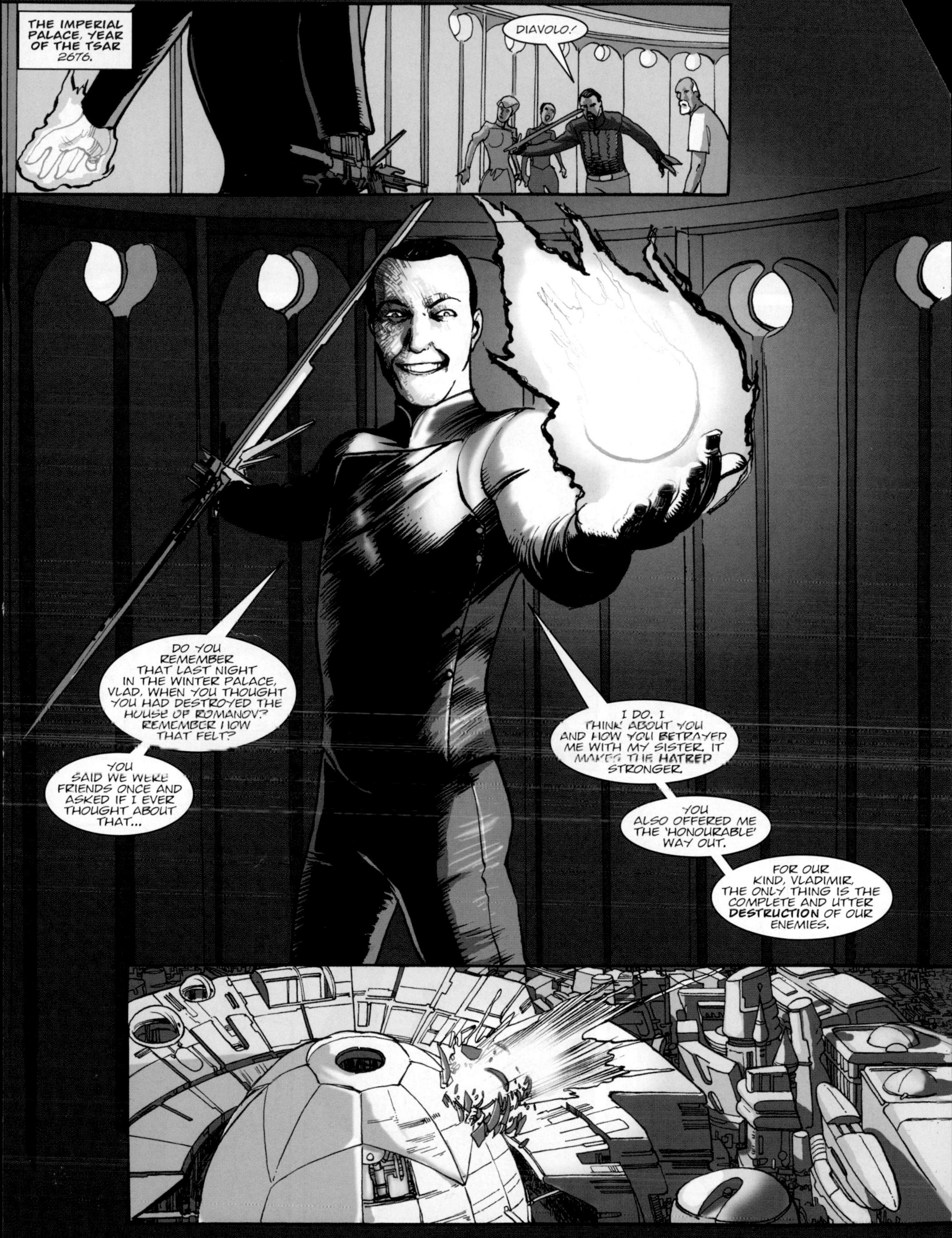
THE IMPERIAL PALACE, YEAR OF THE TSAR 2676.
DIAVOLO!
DO YOU REMEMBER THAT LAST NIGHT IN THE WINTER PALACE, VLAD, WHEN YOU THOUGHT YOU HAD DESTROYED THE HOUSE OF ROMANOV? REMEMBER HOW THAT FELT?
YOU SAID WE WERE FRIENDS ONCE AND ASKED IF I EVER THOUGHT ABOUT THAT...
I DO. I THINK ABOUT YOU AND HOW YOU BETRAYED ME WITH MY SISTER. IT MAKES THE HATRED STRONGER.
YOU ALSO OFFERED ME THE 'HONOURABLE' WAY OUT.
FOR OUR KIND, VLADIMIR, THE ONLY THING IS THE COMPLETE AND UTTER DESTRUCTION OF OUR ENEMIES.

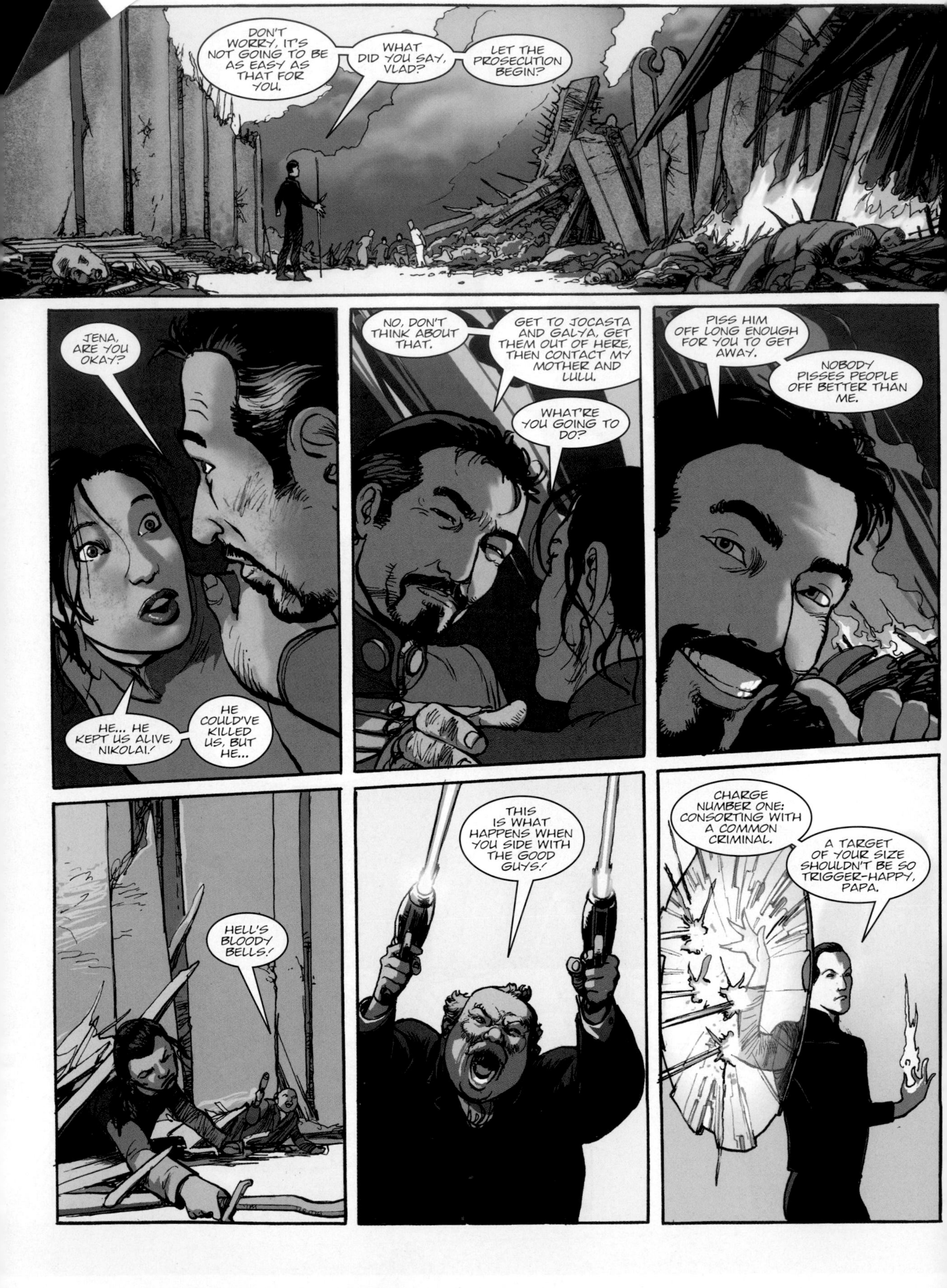
DON'T WORRY, IT'S NOT GOING TO BE AS EASY AS THAT FOR YOU.
WHAT DID YOU SAY, VLAD?
LET THE PROSECUTION BEGIN?
JENA, ARE YOU OKAY?
HE... HE KEPT US ALIVE, NIKOLAI!
HE COULD'VE KILLED US, BUT HE...
NO, DON'T THINK ABOUT THAT.
GET TO JOCASTA AND GALYA, GET THEM OUT OF HERE, THEN CONTACT MY MOTHER AND LULU.
WHAT'RE YOU GOING TO DO?
PISS HIM OFF LONG ENOUGH FOR YOU TO GET AWAY.
NOBODY PISSES PEOPLE OFF BETTER THAN ME.
HELL'S BLOODY BELLS!
THIS IS WHAT HAPPENS WHEN YOU SIDE WITH THE GOOD GUYS!
CHARGE NUMBER ONE: CONSORTING WITH A COMMON CRIMINAL.
A TARGET OF YOUR SIZE SHOULDN'T BE SO TRIGGER-HAPPY, PAPA.

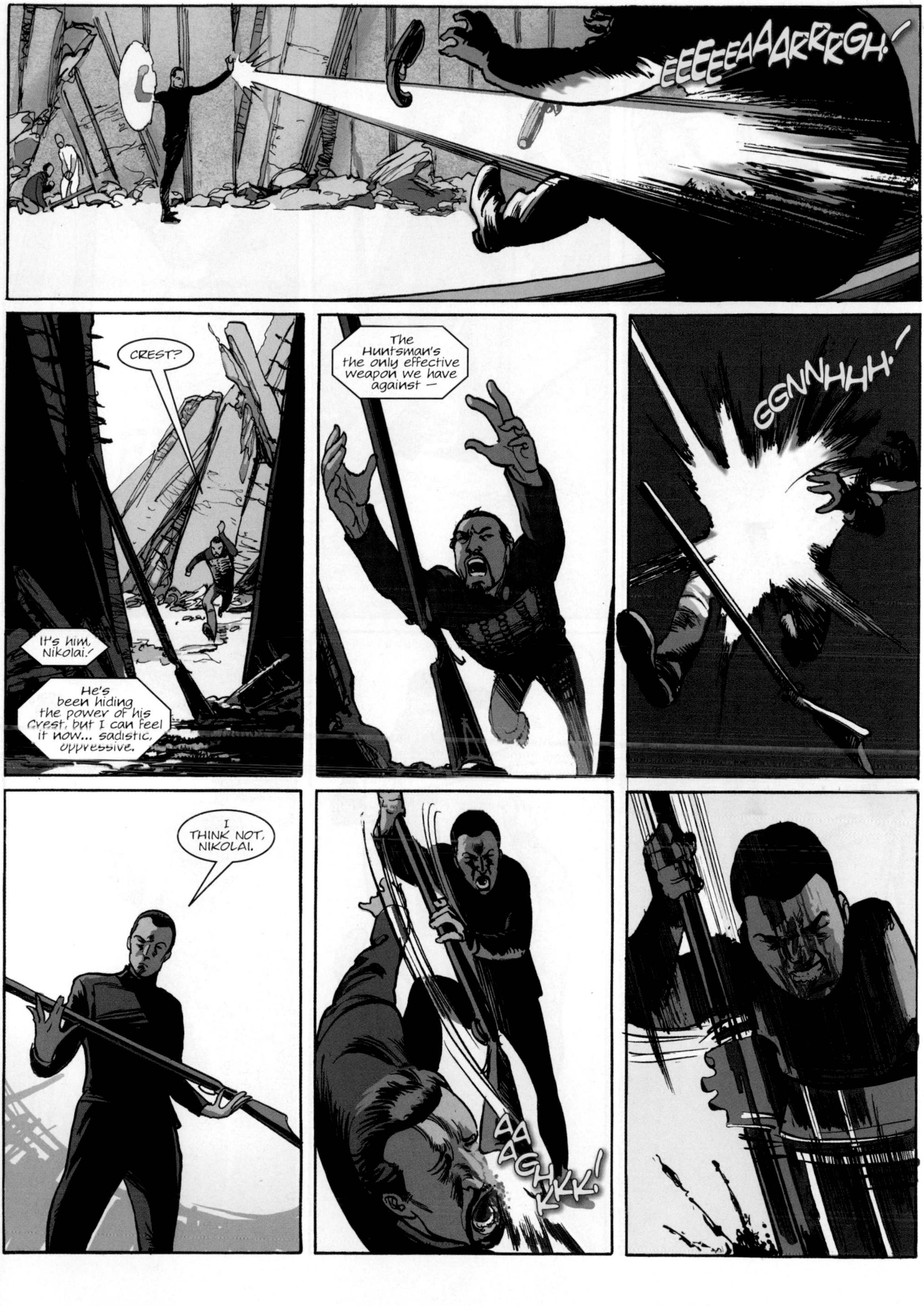
EEEEEAAARRRGH!
CREST?
It's him, Nikolai!
He's been hiding the power of his Crest, but I can feel it now... sadistic, oppressive.
The Huntsman's the only effective weapon we have against —
GGNNHHH!
I THINK NOT, NIKOLAI.
AAAGHKKK!

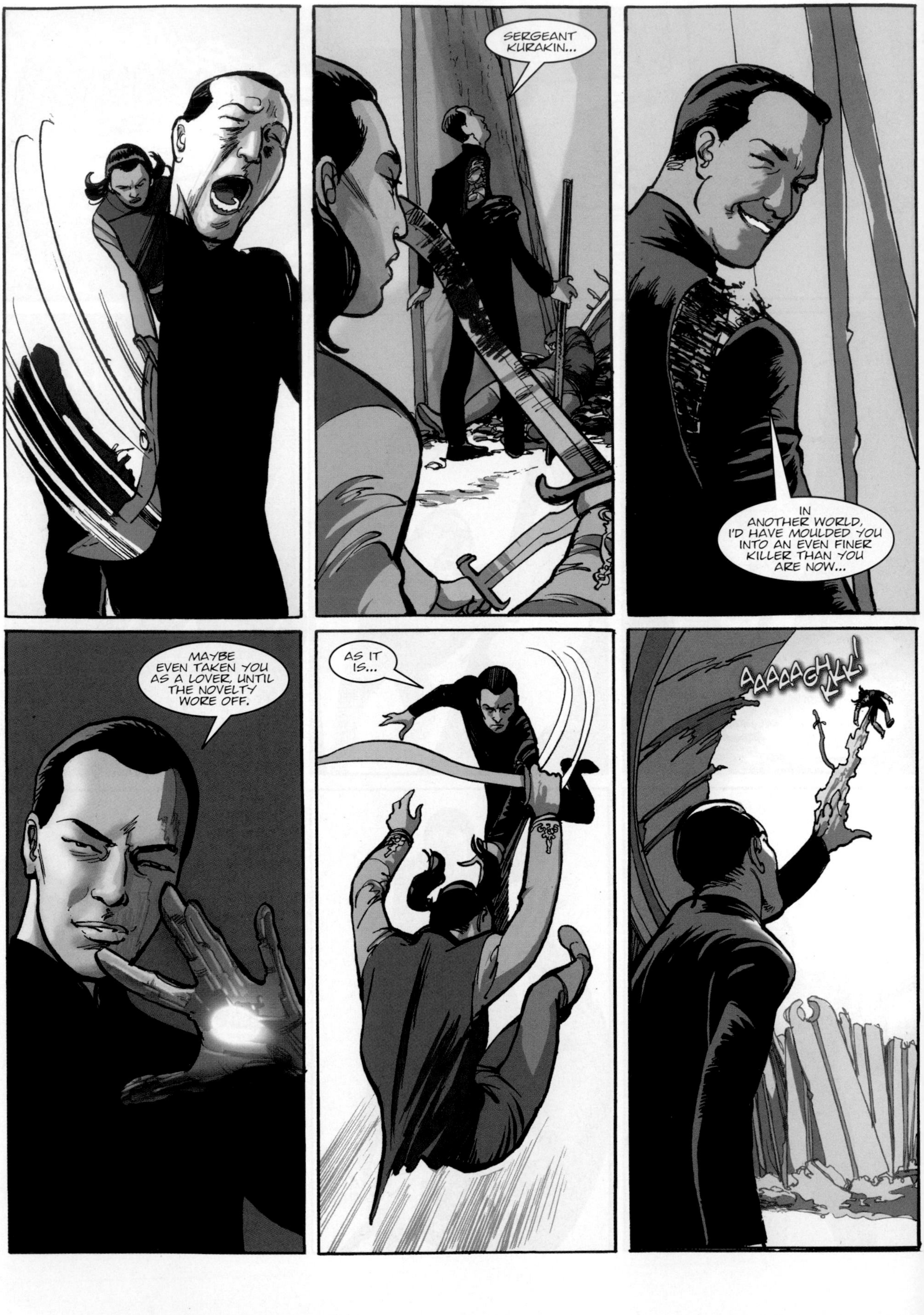
SERGEANT KURAKIN...
IN ANOTHER WORLD, I'D HAVE MOULDED YOU INTO AN EVEN FINER KILLER THAN YOU ARE NOW...
MAYBE EVEN TAKEN YOU AS A LOVER, UNTIL THE NOVELTY WORE OFF.
AS IT IS...
AAAAAGHKKK!

...THERE'S A LITTLE BIT TOO MUCH OF **DANTE** IN YOU FOR MY LIKING.

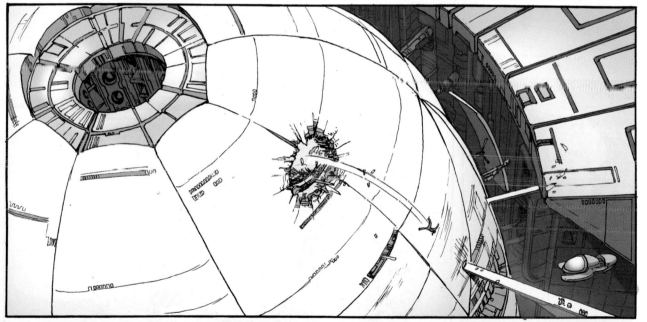

ELENA!

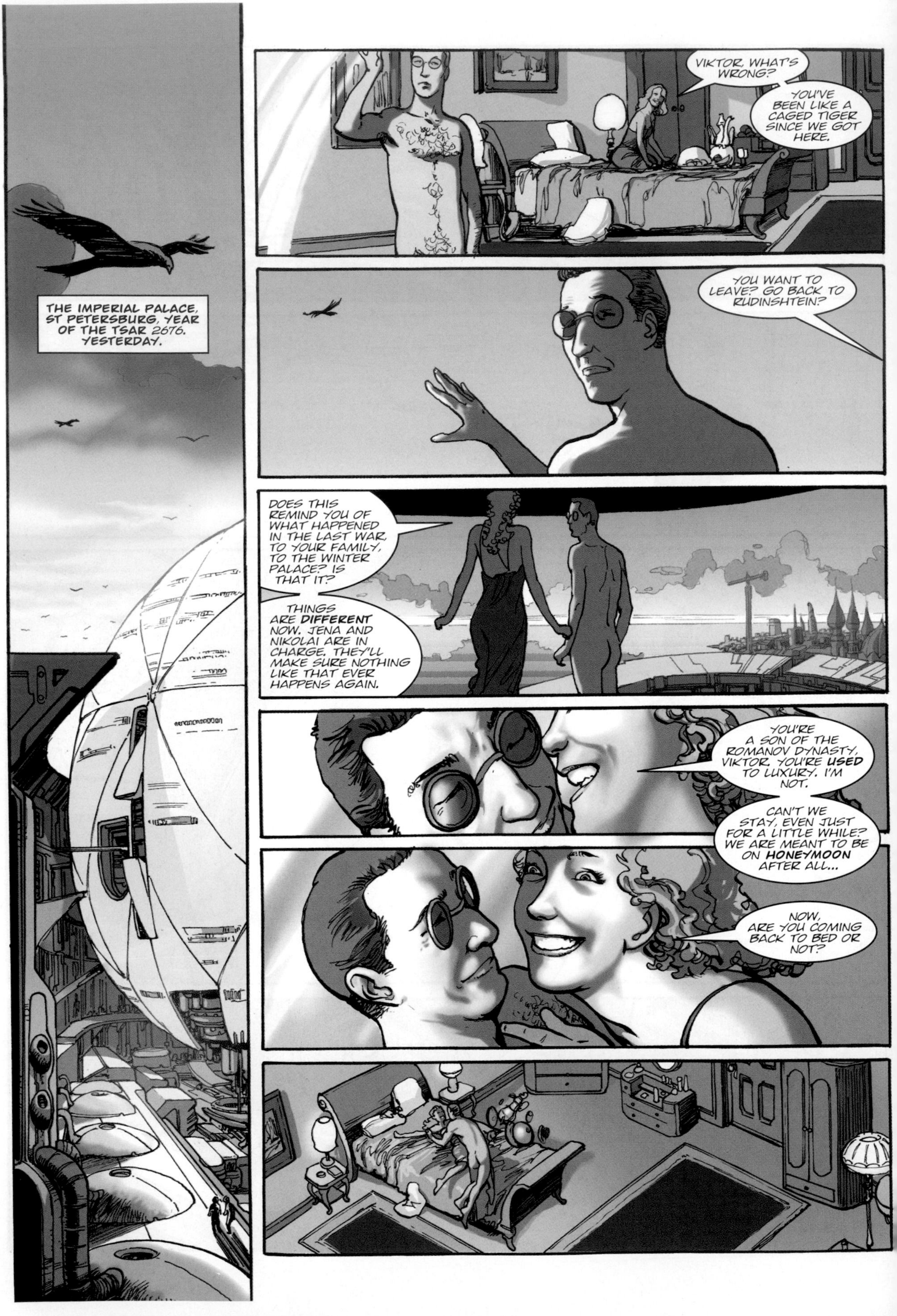

THE IMPERIAL PALACE, ST PETERSBURG, YEAR OF THE TSAR 2676. YESTERDAY.
VIKTOR, WHAT'S WRONG?
YOU'VE BEEN LIKE A CAGED TIGER SINCE WE GOT HERE.
YOU WANT TO LEAVE? GO BACK TO RUDINSHTEIN?
DOES THIS REMIND YOU OF WHAT HAPPENED IN THE LAST WAR, TO YOUR FAMILY, TO THE WINTER PALACE? IS THAT IT?
THINGS ARE **DIFFERENT** NOW. JENA AND NIKOLAI ARE IN CHARGE. THEY'LL MAKE SURE NOTHING LIKE THAT EVER HAPPENS AGAIN.
YOU'RE A SON OF THE ROMANOV DYNASTY, VIKTOR. YOU'RE **USED** TO LUXURY. I'M NOT.
CAN'T WE STAY, EVEN JUST FOR A LITTLE WHILE? WE ARE MEANT TO BE ON **HONEYMOON** AFTER ALL...
NOW, ARE YOU COMING BACK TO BED OR NOT?

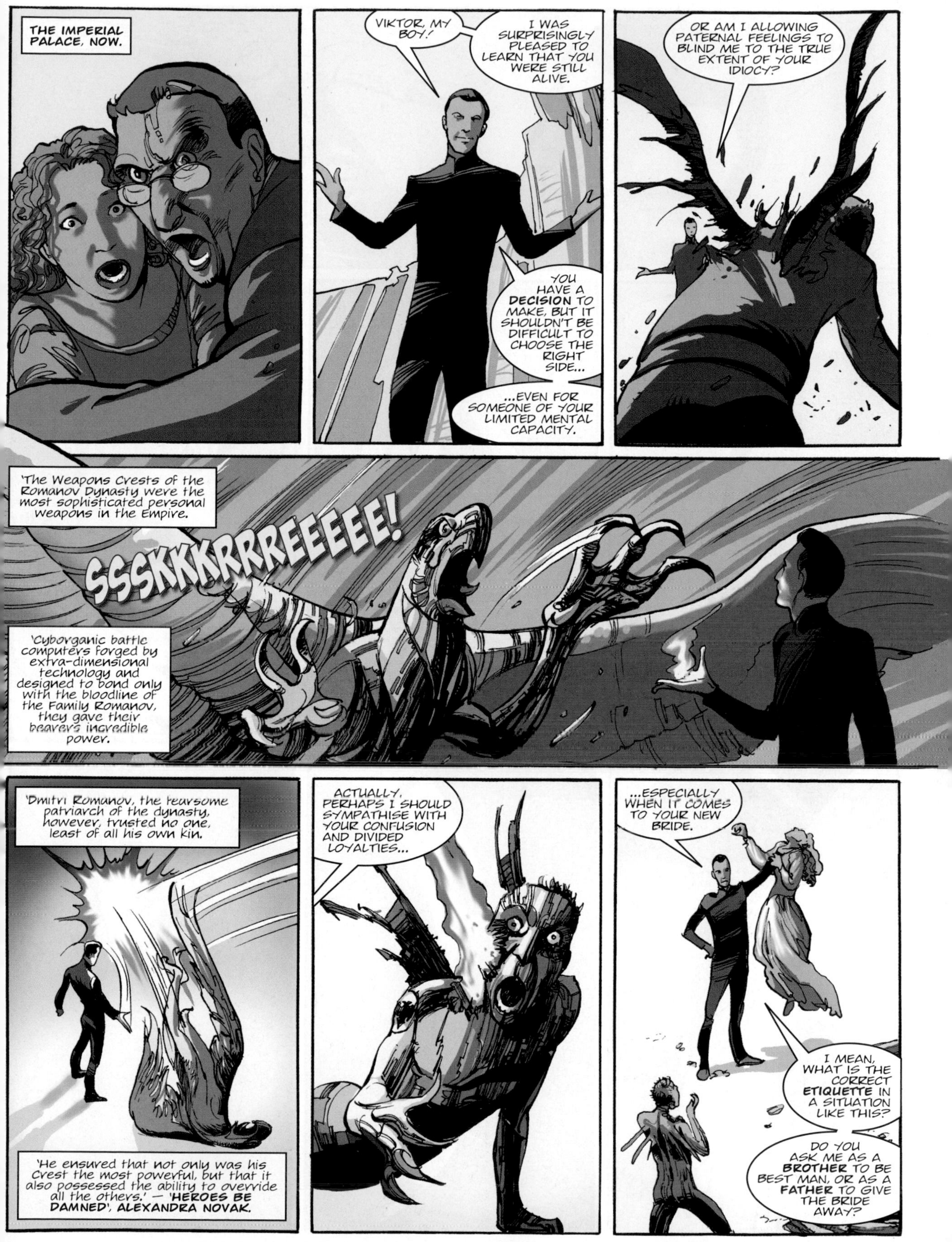
THE IMPERIAL PALACE, NOW.
VIKTOR, MY BOY!
I WAS SURPRISINGLY PLEASED TO LEARN THAT YOU WERE STILL ALIVE.
YOU HAVE A DECISION TO MAKE, BUT IT SHOULDN'T BE DIFFICULT TO CHOOSE THE RIGHT SIDE...
...EVEN FOR SOMEONE OF YOUR LIMITED MENTAL CAPACITY.
OR AM I ALLOWING PATERNAL FEELINGS TO BLIND ME TO THE TRUE EXTENT OF YOUR IDIOCY?
'The Weapons Crests of the Romanov Dynasty were the most sophisticated personal weapons in the Empire.
SSSKKKRRREEEEEE!
'Cyborganic battle computers forged by extra-dimensional technology and designed to bond only with the bloodline of the Family Romanov, they gave their bearers incredible power.
'Dmitri Romanov, the fearsome patriarch of the dynasty, however, trusted no one, least of all his own kin.
'He ensured that not only was his Crest the most powerful, but that it also possessed the ability to override all the others.' — 'HEROES BE DAMNED', ALEXANDRA NOVAK.
ACTUALLY, PERHAPS I SHOULD SYMPATHISE WITH YOUR CONFUSION AND DIVIDED LOYALTIES...
...ESPECIALLY WHEN IT COMES TO YOUR NEW BRIDE.
I MEAN, WHAT IS THE CORRECT ETIQUETTE IN A SITUATION LIKE THIS?
DO YOU ASK ME AS A BROTHER TO BE BEST MAN, OR AS A FATHER TO GIVE THE BRIDE AWAY?

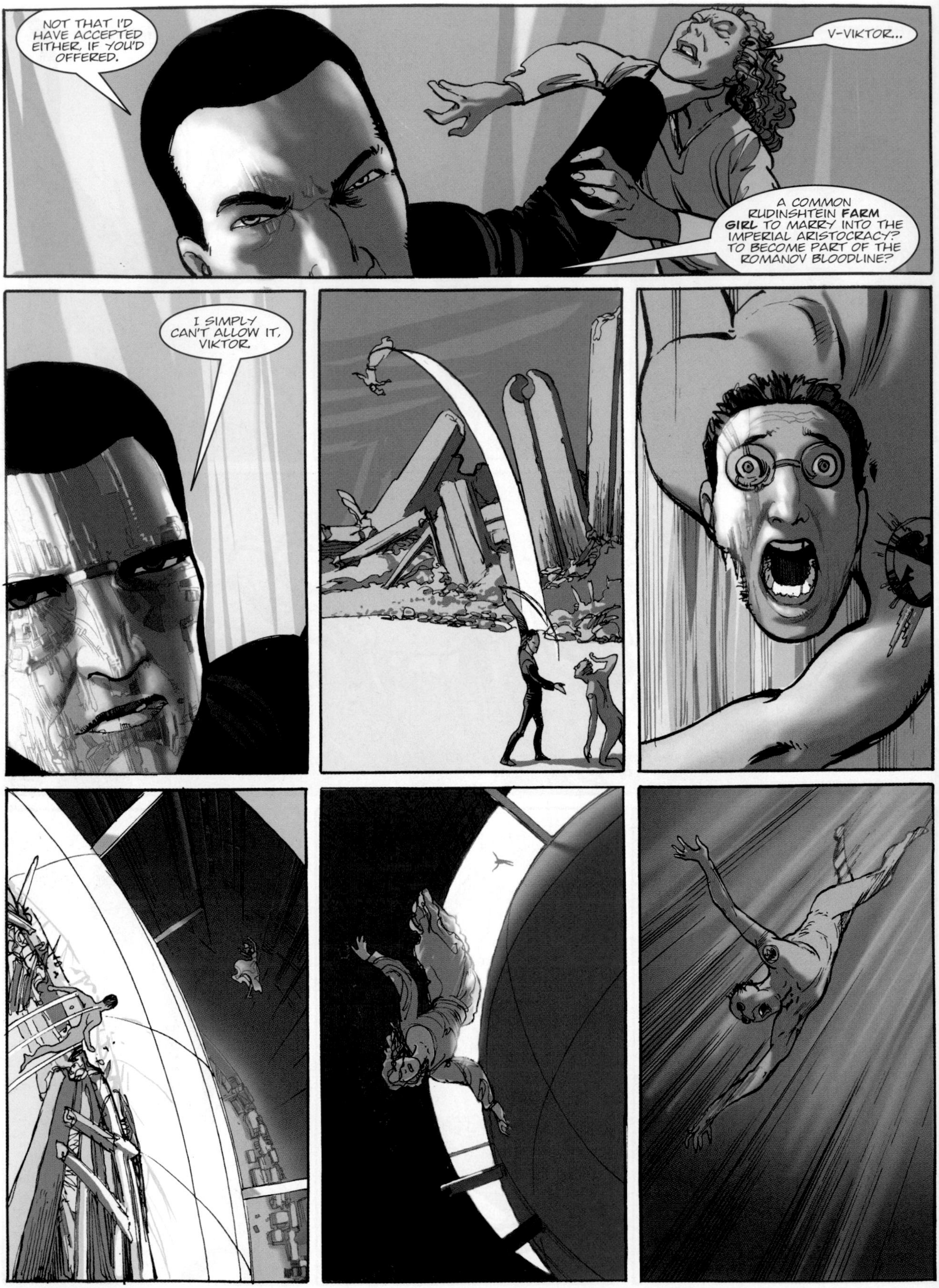
NOT THAT I'D HAVE ACCEPTED EITHER, IF YOU'D OFFERED.
V-VIKTOR...
A COMMON RUDINSHTEIN FARM GIRL TO MARRY INTO THE IMPERIAL ARISTOCRACY? TO BECOME PART OF THE ROMANOV BLOODLINE?
I SIMPLY CAN'T ALLOW IT, VIKTOR.

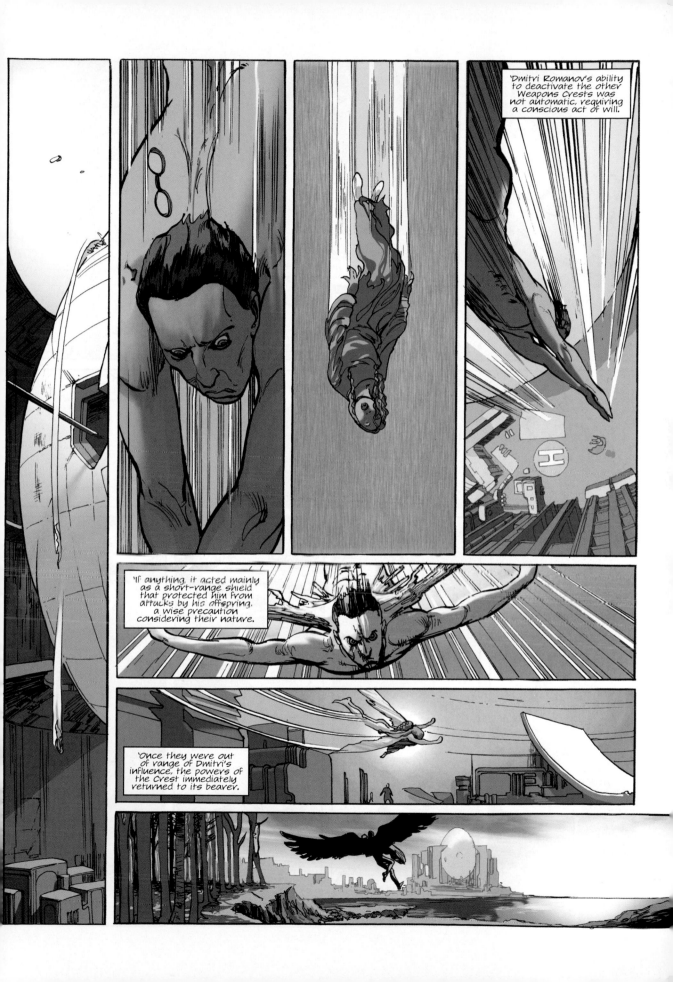

'Dmitri Romanov's ability to deactivate the other Weapons Crests was not automatic, requiring a conscious act of will.

'If anything, it acted mainly as a short-range shield that protected him from attacks by his offspring, a wise precaution considering their nature.

'Once they were out of range of Dmitri's influence, the powers of the Crest immediately returned to its bearer.

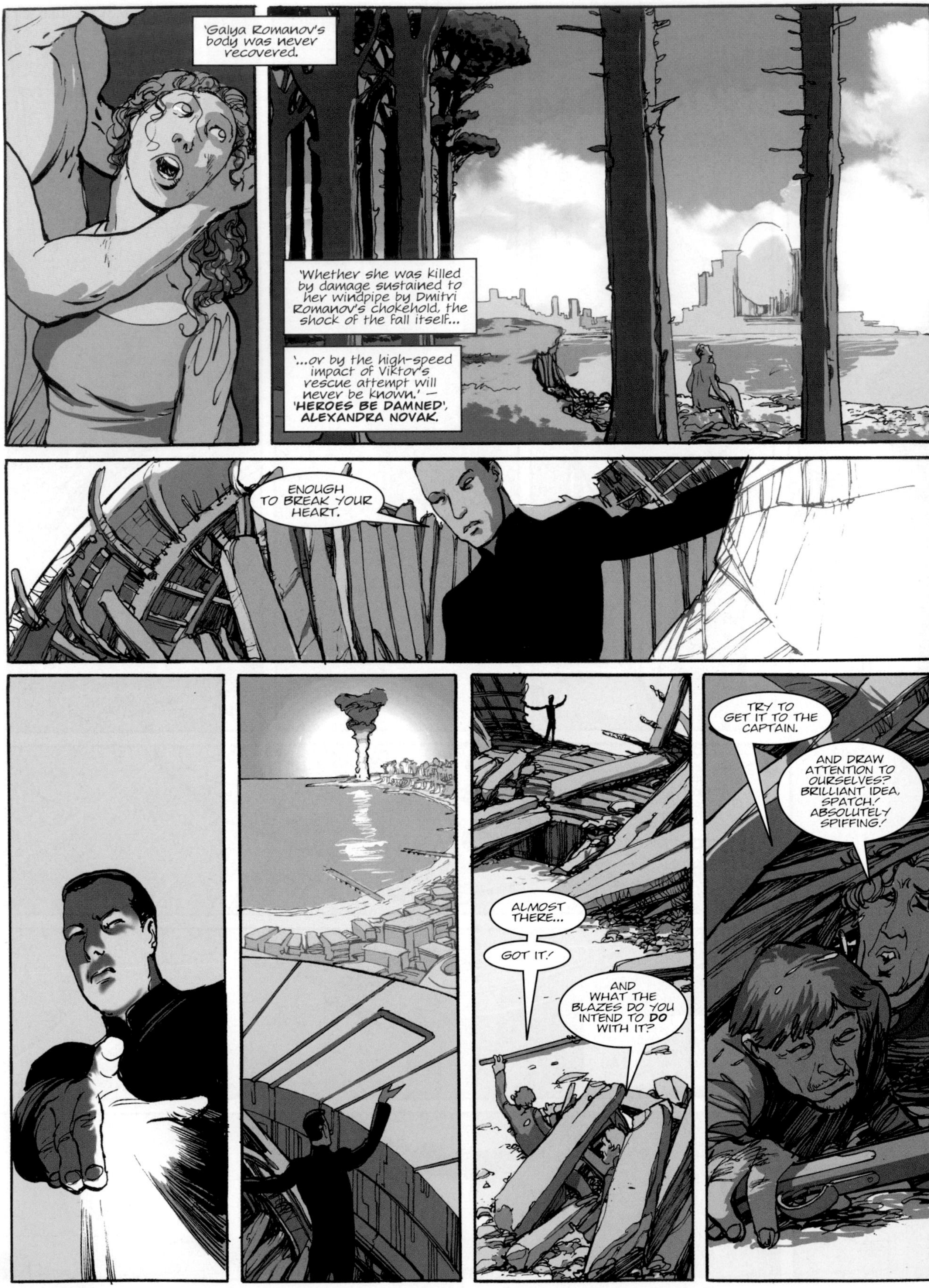

'Galya Romanov's body was never recovered.
'Whether she was killed by damage sustained to her windpipe by Dmitri Romanov's chokehold, the shock of the fall itself...
'...or by the high-speed impact of Viktor's rescue attempt will never be known.' — 'HEROES BE DAMNED', ALEXANDRA NOVAK.
ENOUGH TO BREAK YOUR HEART.
TRY TO GET IT TO THE CAPTAIN.
AND DRAW ATTENTION TO OURSELVES? BRILLIANT IDEA, SPATCH! ABSOLUTELY SPIFFING!
ALMOST THERE...
GOT IT!
AND WHAT THE BLAZES DO YOU INTEND TO DO WITH IT?

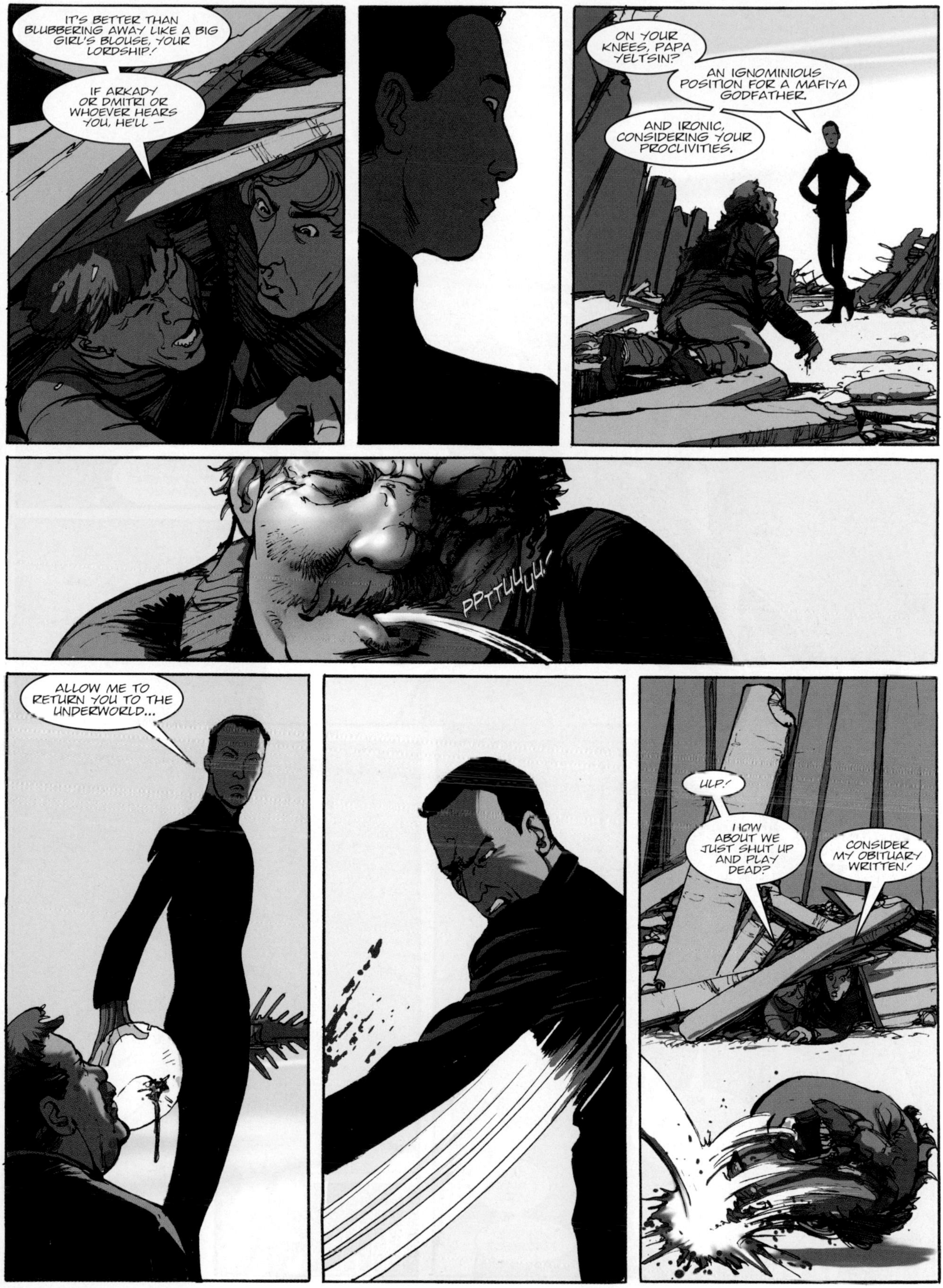
IT'S BETTER THAN BLUBBERING AWAY LIKE A BIG GIRL'S BLOUSE, YOUR LORDSHIP!
IF ARKADY OR DMITRI OR WHOEVER HEARS YOU, HE'LL —
ON YOUR KNEES, PAPA YELTSIN?
AN IGNOMINIOUS POSITION FOR A MAFIYA GODFATHER.
AND IRONIC, CONSIDERING YOUR PROCLIVITIES.
PPTTUUUU!
ALLOW ME TO RETURN YOU TO THE UNDERWORLD...
ULP!
HOW ABOUT WE JUST SHUT UP AND PLAY DEAD?
CONSIDER MY OBITUARY WRITTEN!

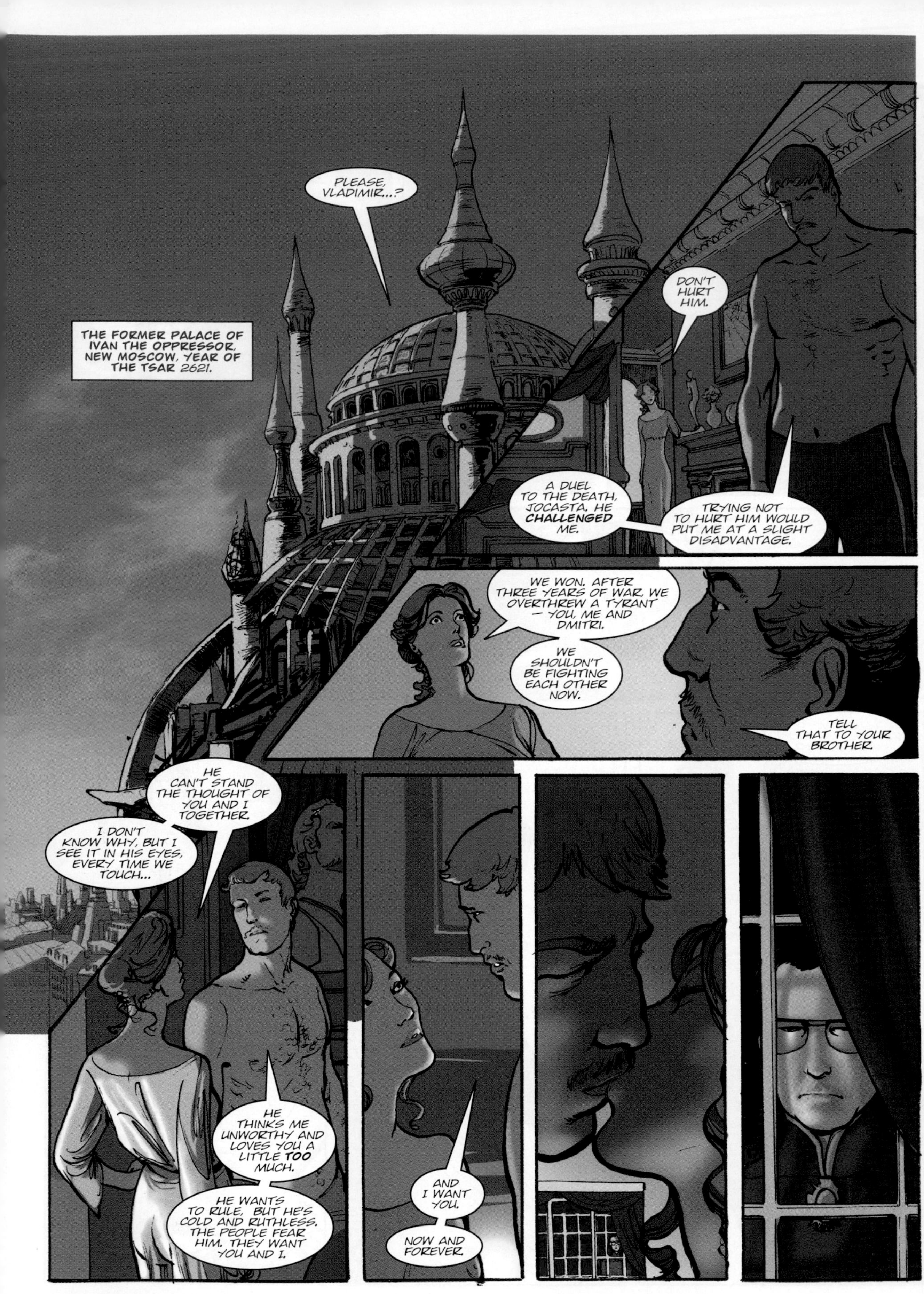
THE FORMER PALACE OF IVAN THE OPPRESSOR, NEW MOSCOW, YEAR OF THE TSAR 2621.
PLEASE, VLADIMIR...?
DON'T HURT HIM.
A DUEL TO THE DEATH, JOCASTA. HE **CHALLENGED** ME.
TRYING NOT TO HURT HIM WOULD PUT ME AT A SLIGHT DISADVANTAGE.
WE WON. AFTER THREE YEARS OF WAR, WE OVERTHREW A TYRANT — YOU, ME AND DMITRI.
WE SHOULDN'T BE FIGHTING EACH OTHER NOW.
TELL THAT TO YOUR BROTHER.
HE CAN'T STAND THE THOUGHT OF YOU AND I TOGETHER.
I DON'T KNOW WHY, BUT I SEE IT IN HIS EYES, EVERY TIME WE TOUCH...
HE THINKS ME UNWORTHY AND LOVES YOU A LITTLE **TOO** MUCH.
HE WANTS TO RULE, BUT HE'S COLD AND RUTHLESS. THE PEOPLE FEAR HIM. THEY WANT YOU AND I.
AND I WANT YOU.
NOW AND FOREVER.

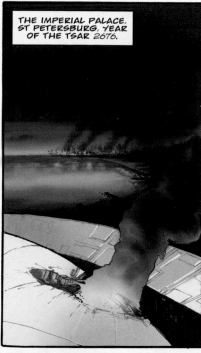

THE IMPERIAL PALACE, ST PETERSBURG, YEAR OF THE TSAR 2676.

JENA MAKAROV TO IMPERIAL COMMAND!

RESPOND, DAMN IT!

IT'S NO USE, CHILD. DMITRI'S BOUND TO BE JAMMING COMMUNICATIONS.

HE'S A MILITARY GENIUS AND HE'S FAMILIARISED HIMSELF WITH THE PALACE INFRASTRUCTURE SINCE BEING MADE COMMANDER OF THE SCARLET WRAITHS.

GOOD CALL, VLADIMIR.

NOT MY FINEST MOMENT, IT'S TRUE, ALTHOUGH THESE ARE RATHER EXCEPTIONAL —

UUUNNGH!

JOCASTA... VLADIMIR...

TIME HAS BEEN SO UNKIND TO BOTH OF YOU.

YOUNG LOVERS GROWN OLD AND BITTER AND RESENTFUL OF EACH OTHER...

JOCASTA, HELP JENA!

I'LL —

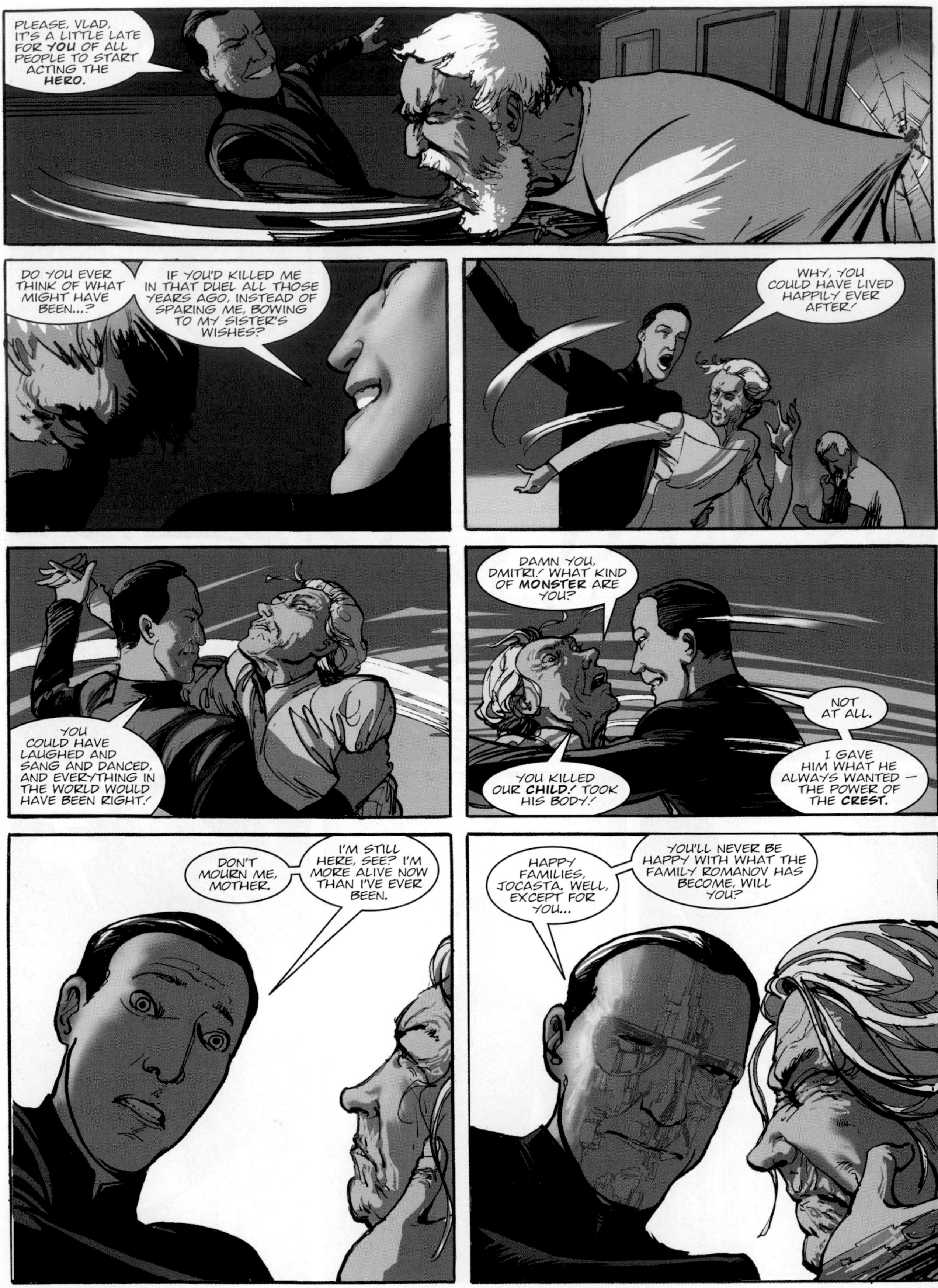
PLEASE, VLAD, IT'S A LITTLE LATE FOR YOU OF ALL PEOPLE TO START ACTING THE HERO.
DO YOU EVER THINK OF WHAT MIGHT HAVE BEEN...?
IF YOU'D KILLED ME IN THAT DUEL ALL THOSE YEARS AGO, INSTEAD OF SPARING ME, BOWING TO MY SISTER'S WISHES?
WHY, YOU COULD HAVE LIVED HAPPILY EVER AFTER!
YOU COULD HAVE LAUGHED AND SANG AND DANCED, AND EVERYTHING IN THE WORLD WOULD HAVE BEEN RIGHT!
DAMN YOU, DMITRI! WHAT KIND OF MONSTER ARE YOU?
YOU KILLED OUR CHILD! TOOK HIS BODY!
NOT AT ALL.
I GAVE HIM WHAT HE ALWAYS WANTED — THE POWER OF THE CREST.
DON'T MOURN ME, MOTHER.
I'M STILL HERE, SEE? I'M MORE ALIVE NOW THAN I'VE EVER BEEN.
HAPPY FAMILIES, JOCASTA. WELL, EXCEPT FOR YOU...
YOU'LL NEVER BE HAPPY WITH WHAT THE FAMILY ROMANOV HAS BECOME, WILL YOU?

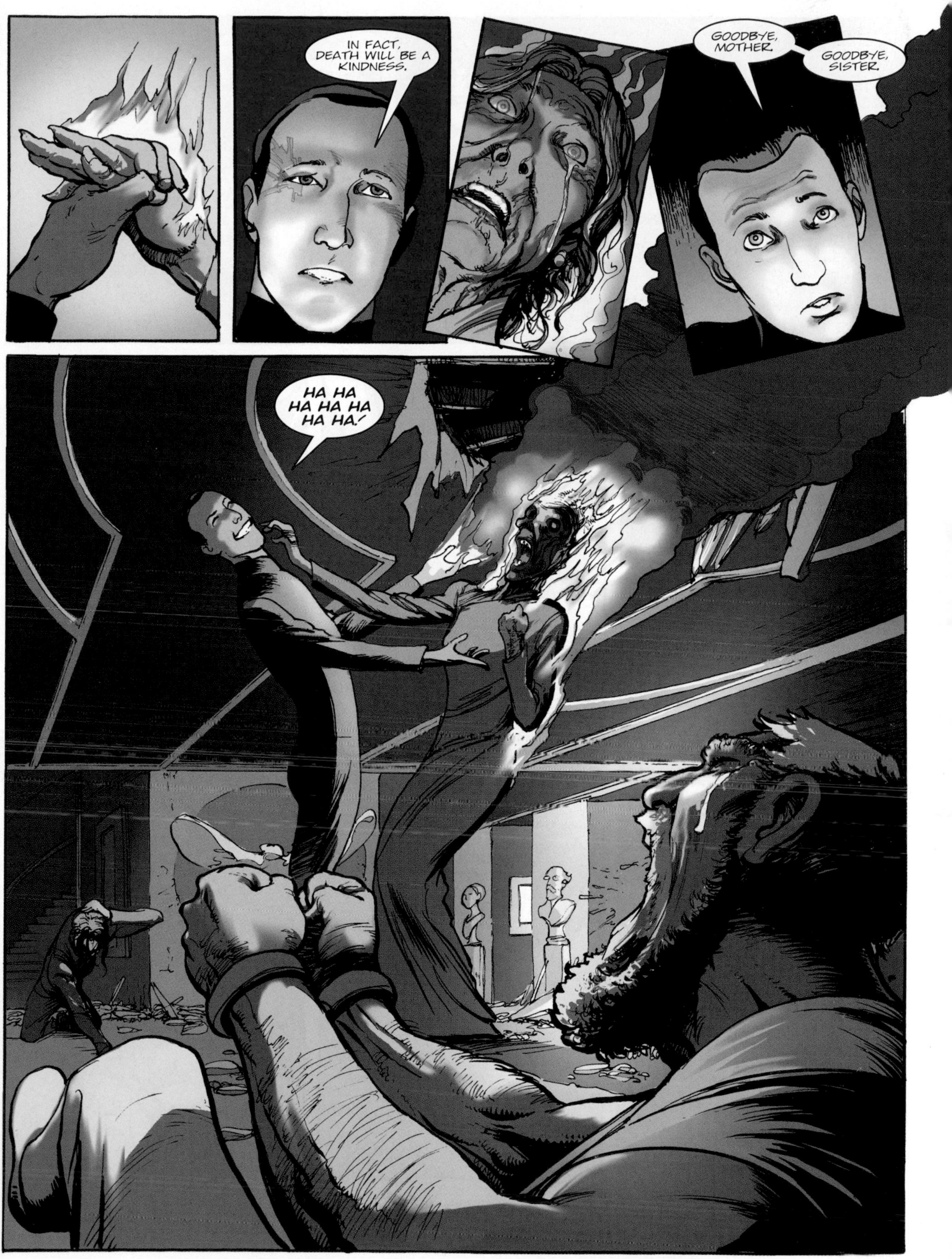
IN FACT, DEATH WILL BE A KINDNESS.
GOODBYE, MOTHER.
GOODBYE, SISTER.
HA HA HA HA HA HA HA HA.'

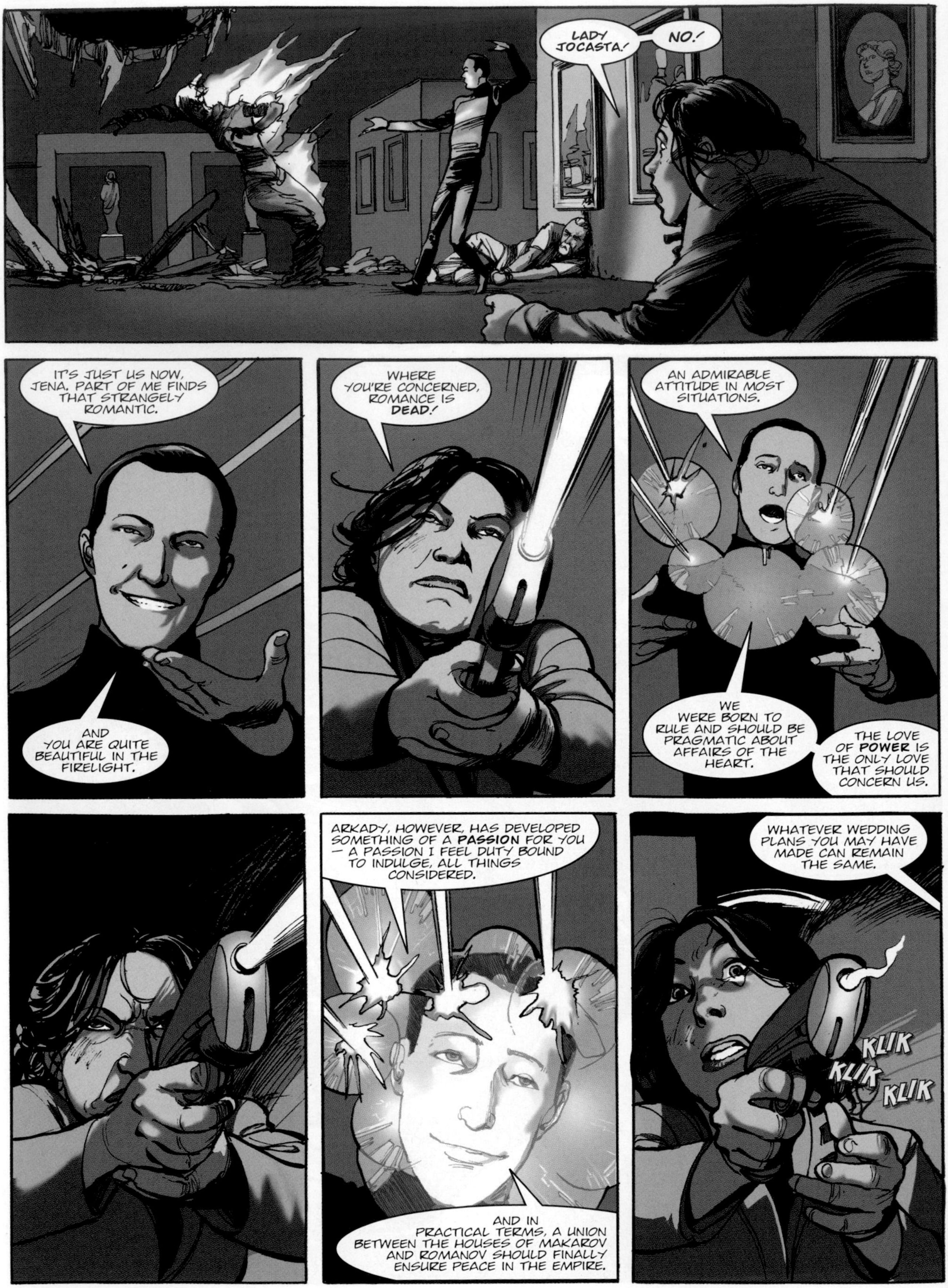
LADY JOCASTA!
NO!
IT'S JUST US NOW, JENA. PART OF ME FINDS THAT STRANGELY ROMANTIC.
AND YOU ARE QUITE BEAUTIFUL IN THE FIRELIGHT.
WHERE YOU'RE CONCERNED, ROMANCE IS DEAD!
AN ADMIRABLE ATTITUDE IN MOST SITUATIONS.
WE WERE BORN TO RULE AND SHOULD BE PRAGMATIC ABOUT AFFAIRS OF THE HEART.
THE LOVE OF POWER IS THE ONLY LOVE THAT SHOULD CONCERN US.
ARKADY, HOWEVER, HAS DEVELOPED SOMETHING OF A PASSION FOR YOU — A PASSION I FEEL DUTY BOUND TO INDULGE, ALL THINGS CONSIDERED.
AND IN PRACTICAL TERMS, A UNION BETWEEN THE HOUSES OF MAKAROV AND ROMANOV SHOULD FINALLY ENSURE PEACE IN THE EMPIRE.
WHATEVER WEDDING PLANS YOU MAY HAVE MADE CAN REMAIN THE SAME.
KLIK
KLIK
KLIK

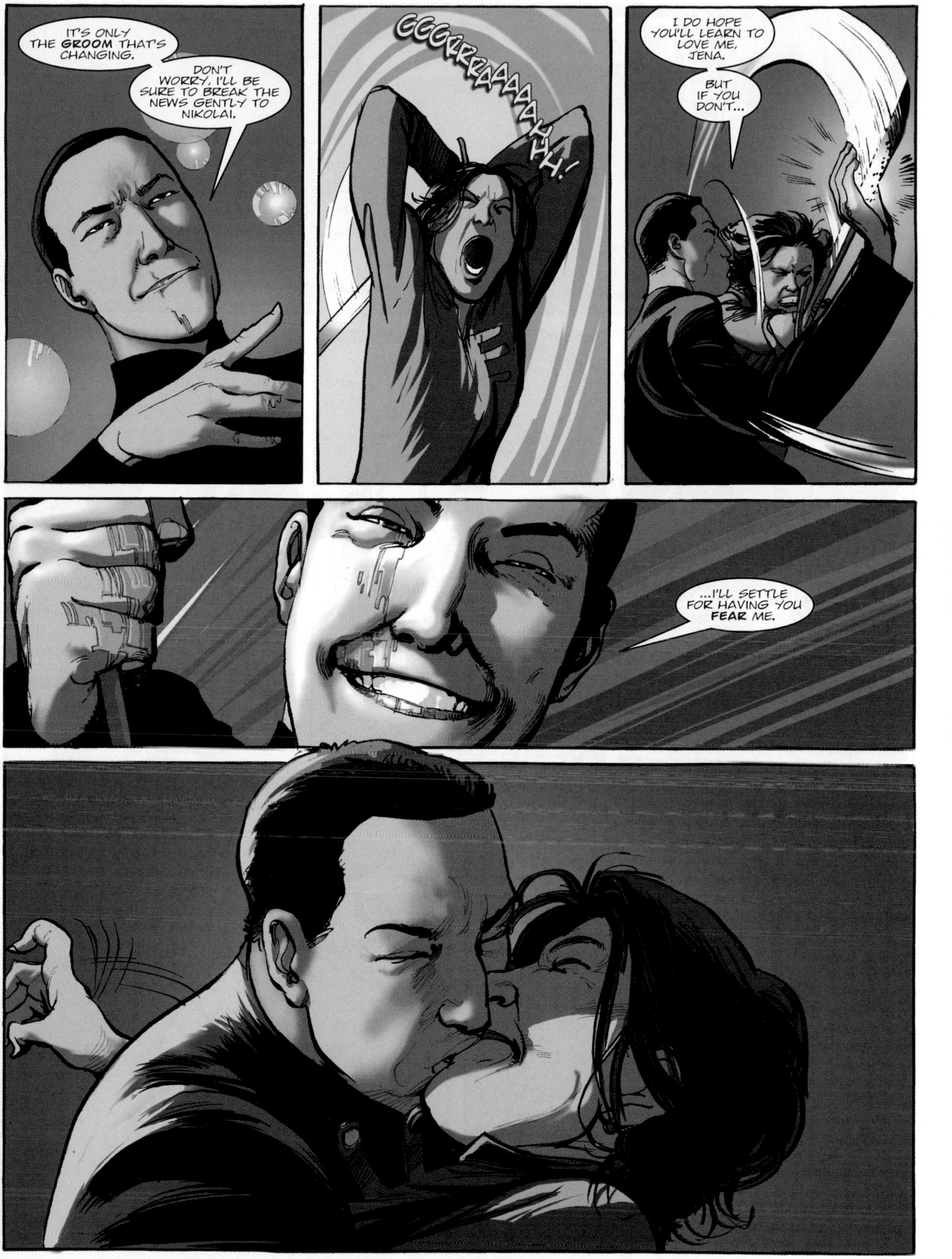
IT'S ONLY THE GROOM THAT'S CHANGING.
DON'T WORRY, I'LL BE SURE TO BREAK THE NEWS GENTLY TO NIKOLAI.
GGGRRRAAAAAHHH!
I DO HOPE YOU'LL LEARN TO LOVE ME, JENA.
BUT IF YOU DON'T...
...I'LL SETTLE FOR HAVING YOU FEAR ME.

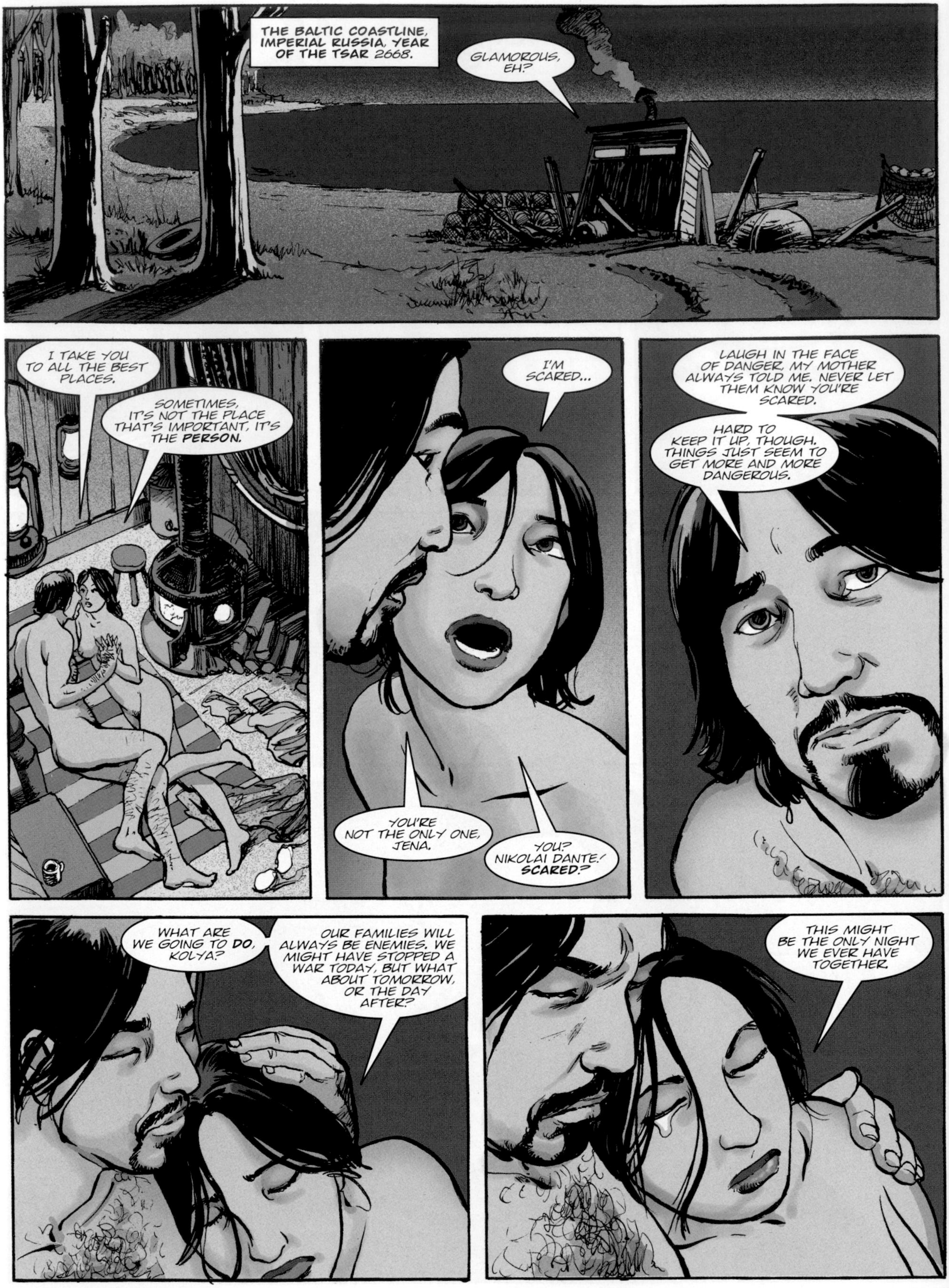

THE BALTIC COASTLINE, IMPERIAL RUSSIA, YEAR OF THE TSAR 2668.
GLAMOROUS, EH?
I TAKE YOU TO ALL THE BEST PLACES.
SOMETIMES, IT'S NOT THE PLACE THAT'S IMPORTANT, IT'S THE PERSON.
I'M SCARED...
YOU'RE NOT THE ONLY ONE, JENA.
YOU? NIKOLAI DANTE! SCARED?
LAUGH IN THE FACE OF DANGER, MY MOTHER ALWAYS TOLD ME. NEVER LET THEM KNOW YOU'RE SCARED.
HARD TO KEEP IT UP, THOUGH. THINGS JUST SEEM TO GET MORE AND MORE DANGEROUS.
WHAT ARE WE GOING TO DO, KOLYA?
OUR FAMILIES WILL ALWAYS BE ENEMIES. WE MIGHT HAVE STOPPED A WAR TODAY, BUT WHAT ABOUT TOMORROW, OR THE DAY AFTER?
THIS MIGHT BE THE ONLY NIGHT WE EVER HAVE TOGETHER.

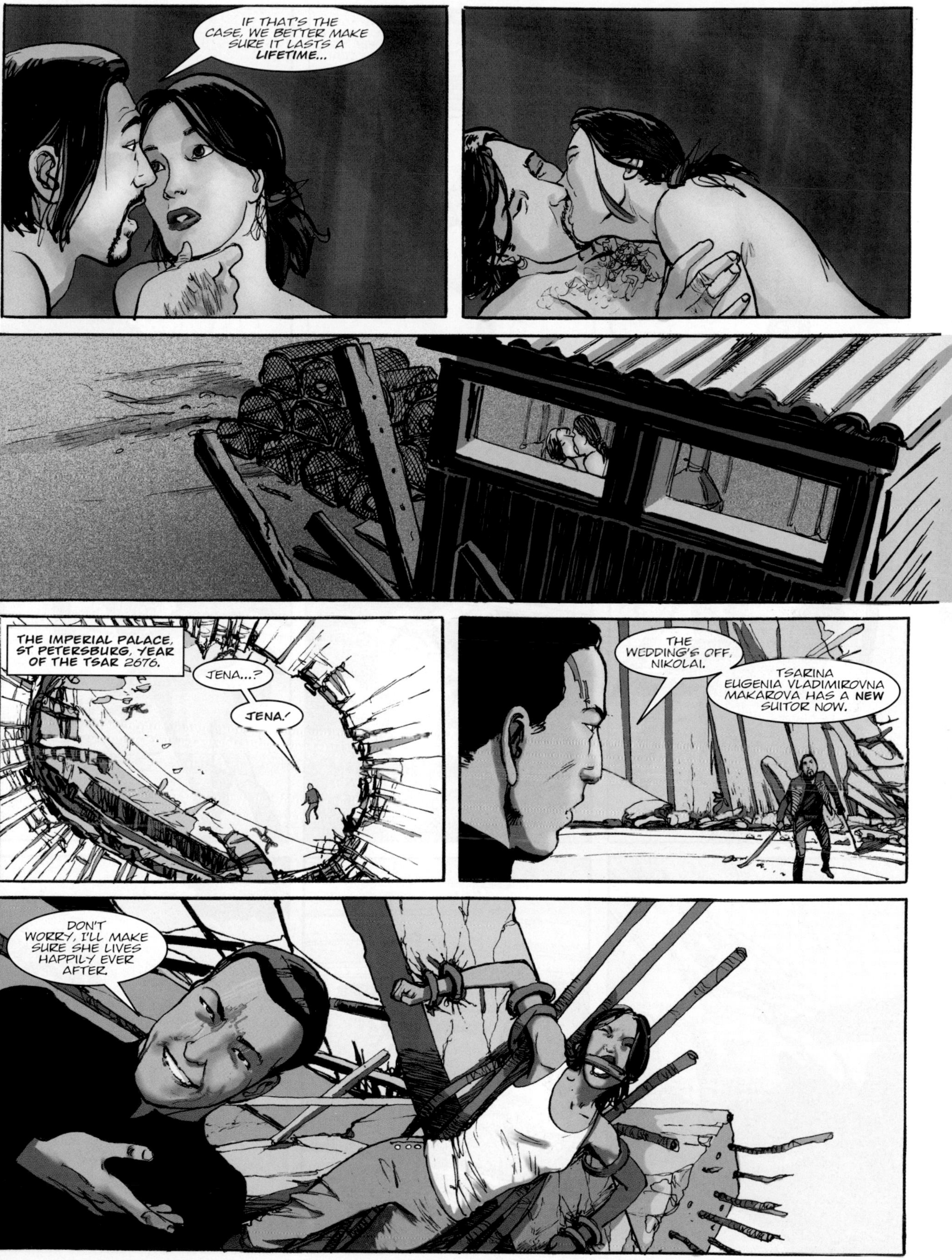

IF THAT'S THE CASE, WE BETTER MAKE SURE IT LASTS A LIFETIME...
THE IMPERIAL PALACE, ST PETERSBURG, YEAR OF THE TSAR 2676.
JENA...?
JENA!
THE WEDDING'S OFF, NIKOLAI.
TSARINA EUGENIA VLADIMIROVNA MAKAROVA HAS A NEW SUITOR NOW.
DON'T WORRY, I'LL MAKE SURE SHE LIVES HAPPILY EVER AFTER.

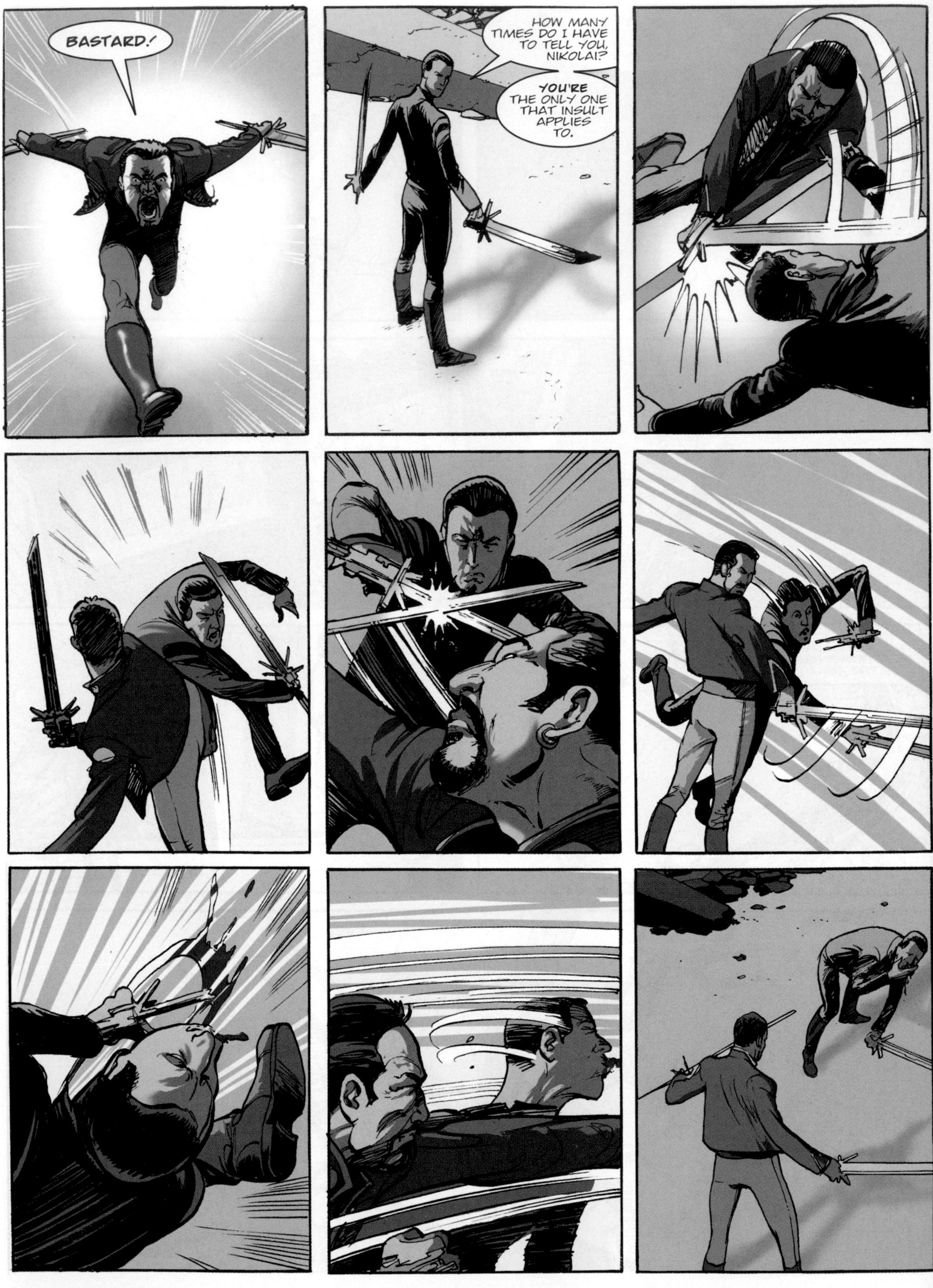
BASTARD!
HOW MANY TIMES DO I HAVE TO TELL YOU, NIKOLAI?
YOU'RE THE ONLY ONE THAT INSULT APPLIES TO.

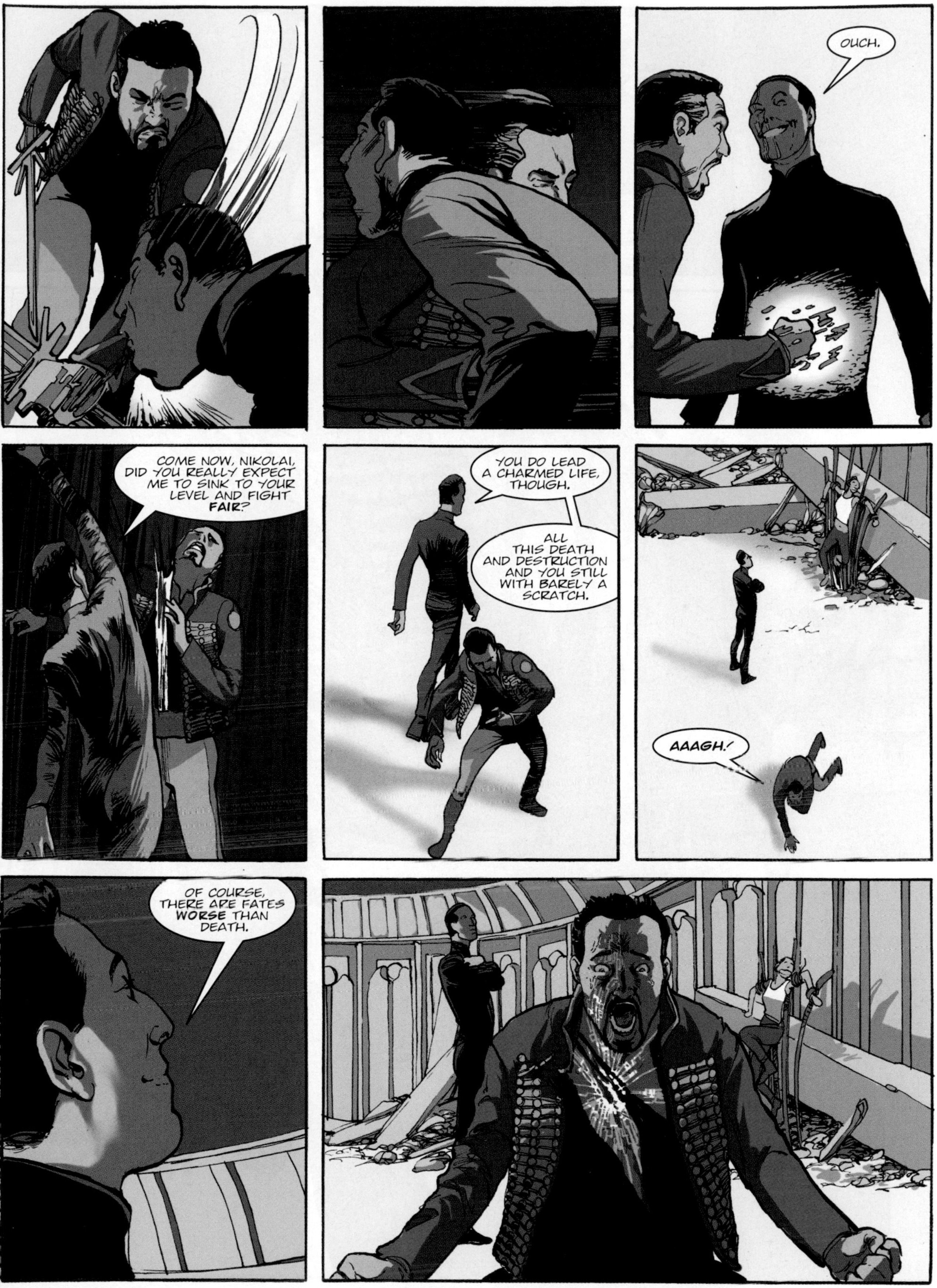
OUCH.
COME NOW, NIKOLAI, DID YOU REALLY EXPECT ME TO SINK TO YOUR LEVEL AND FIGHT FAIR?
YOU DO LEAD A CHARMED LIFE, THOUGH.
ALL THIS DEATH AND DESTRUCTION AND YOU STILL WITH BARELY A SCRATCH.
AAAGH!
OF COURSE, THERE ARE FATES WORSE THAN DEATH.

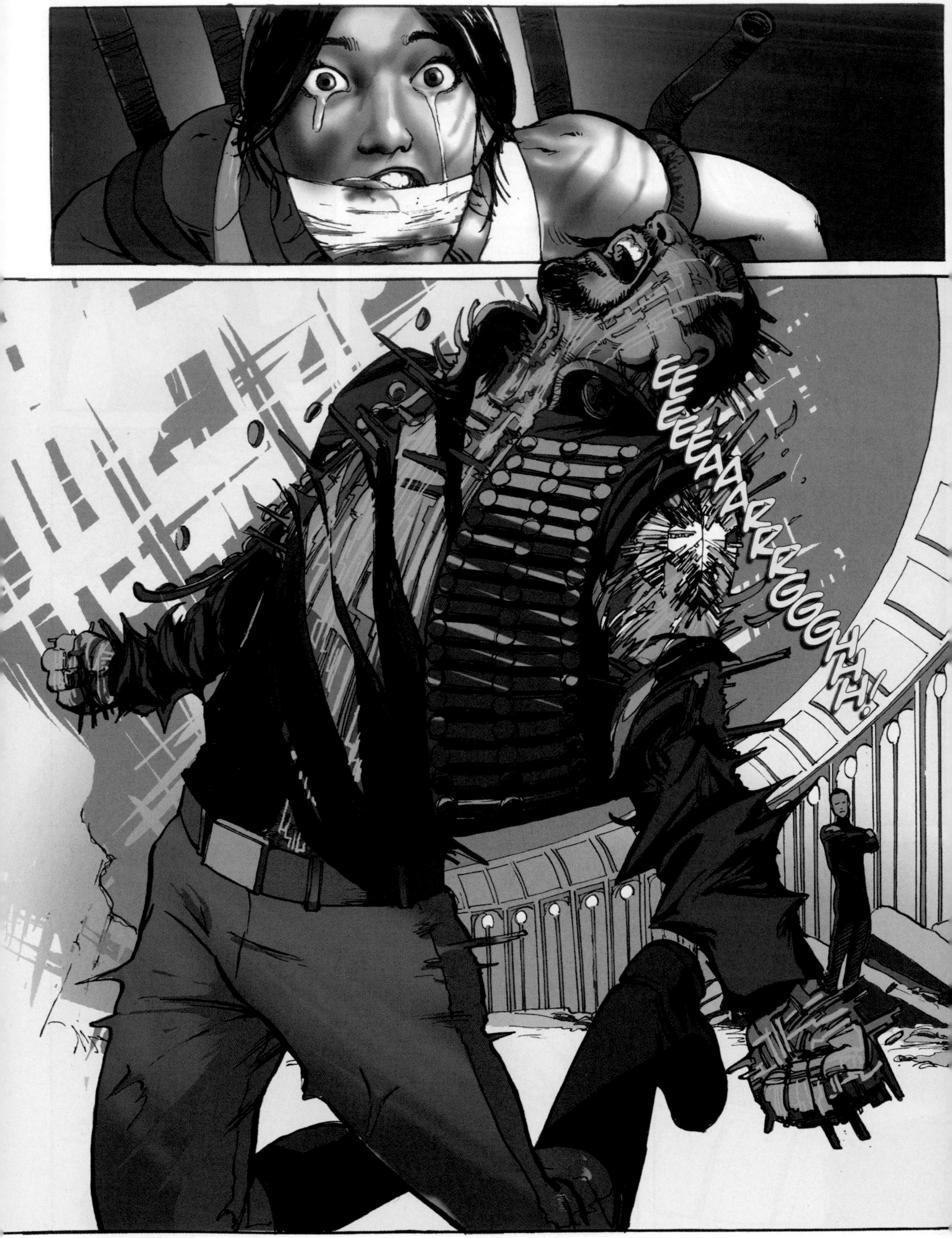
EEEEAAARRRGGGHH!

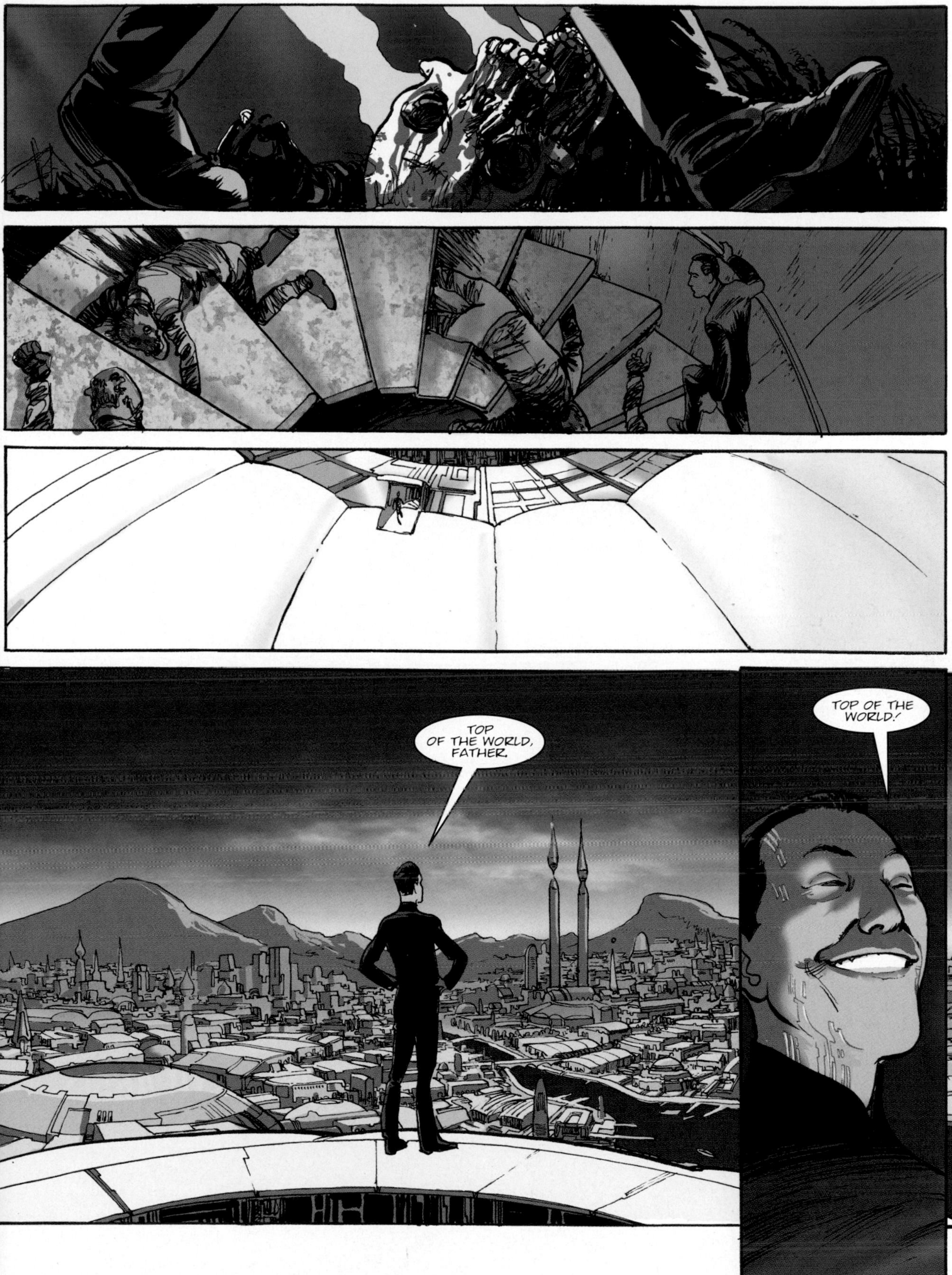
TOP OF THE WORLD, FATHER.
TOP OF THE WORLD!

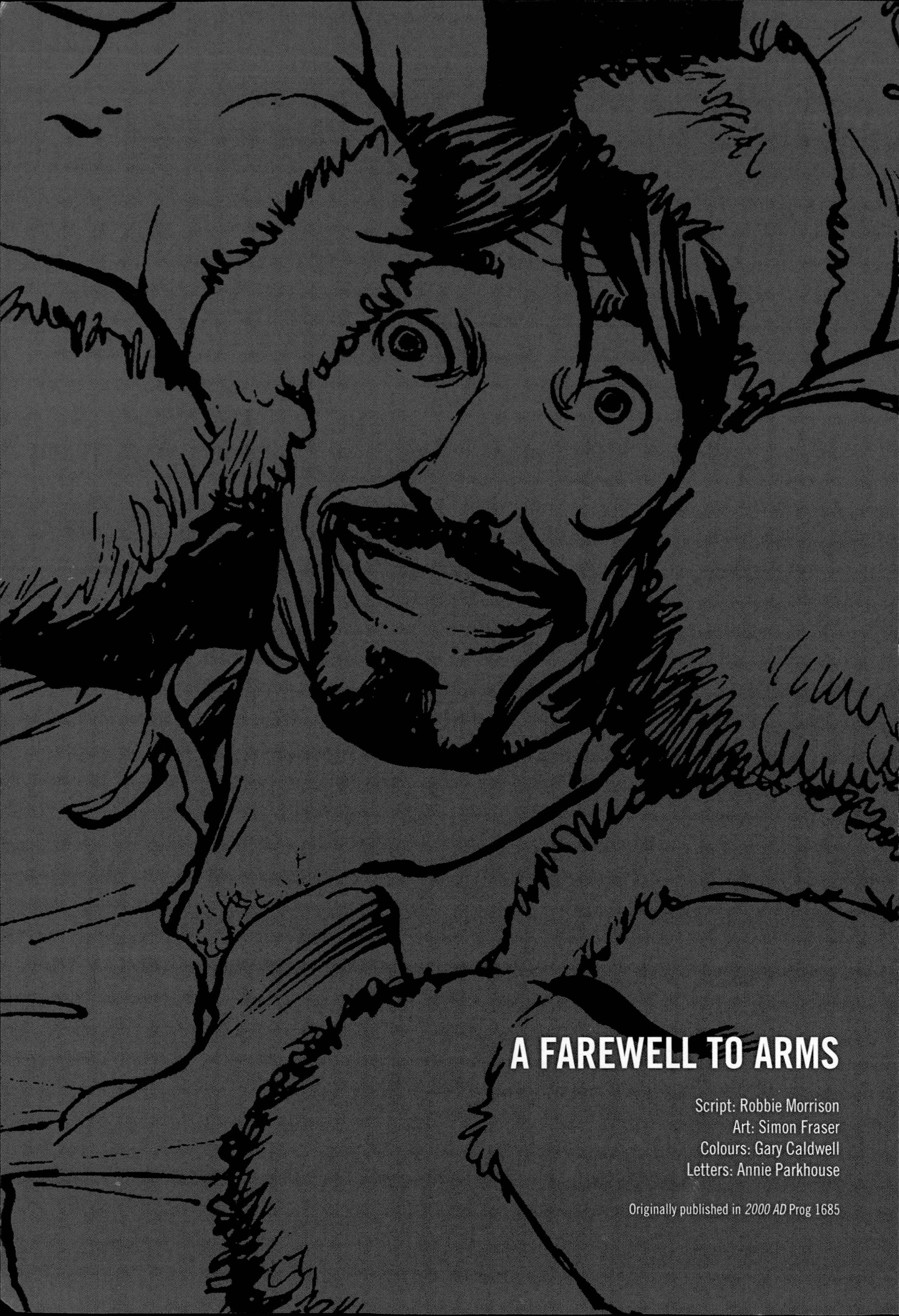

A FAREWELL TO ARMS

Script: Robbie Morrison
Art: Simon Fraser
Colours: Gary Caldwell
Letters: Annie Parkhouse

Originally published in *2000 AD* Prog 1685

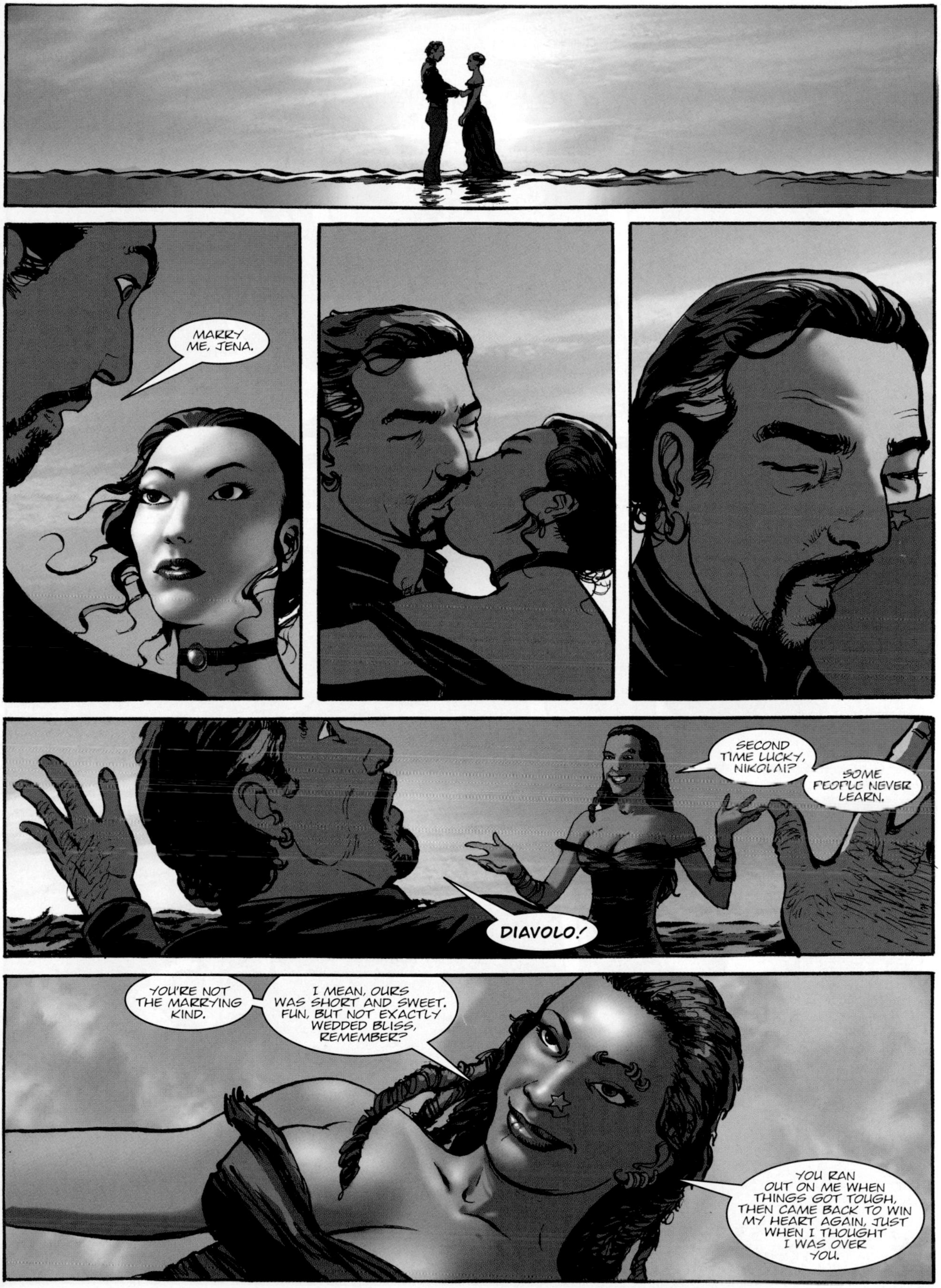
MARRY ME, JENA.
SECOND TIME LUCKY, NIKOLAI?
SOME PEOPLE NEVER LEARN.
DIAVOLO!
YOU'RE NOT THE MARRYING KIND.
I MEAN, OURS WAS SHORT AND SWEET. FUN, BUT NOT EXACTLY WEDDED BLISS, REMEMBER?
YOU RAN OUT ON ME WHEN THINGS GOT TOUGH, THEN CAME BACK TO WIN MY HEART AGAIN, JUST WHEN I THOUGHT I WAS OVER YOU.

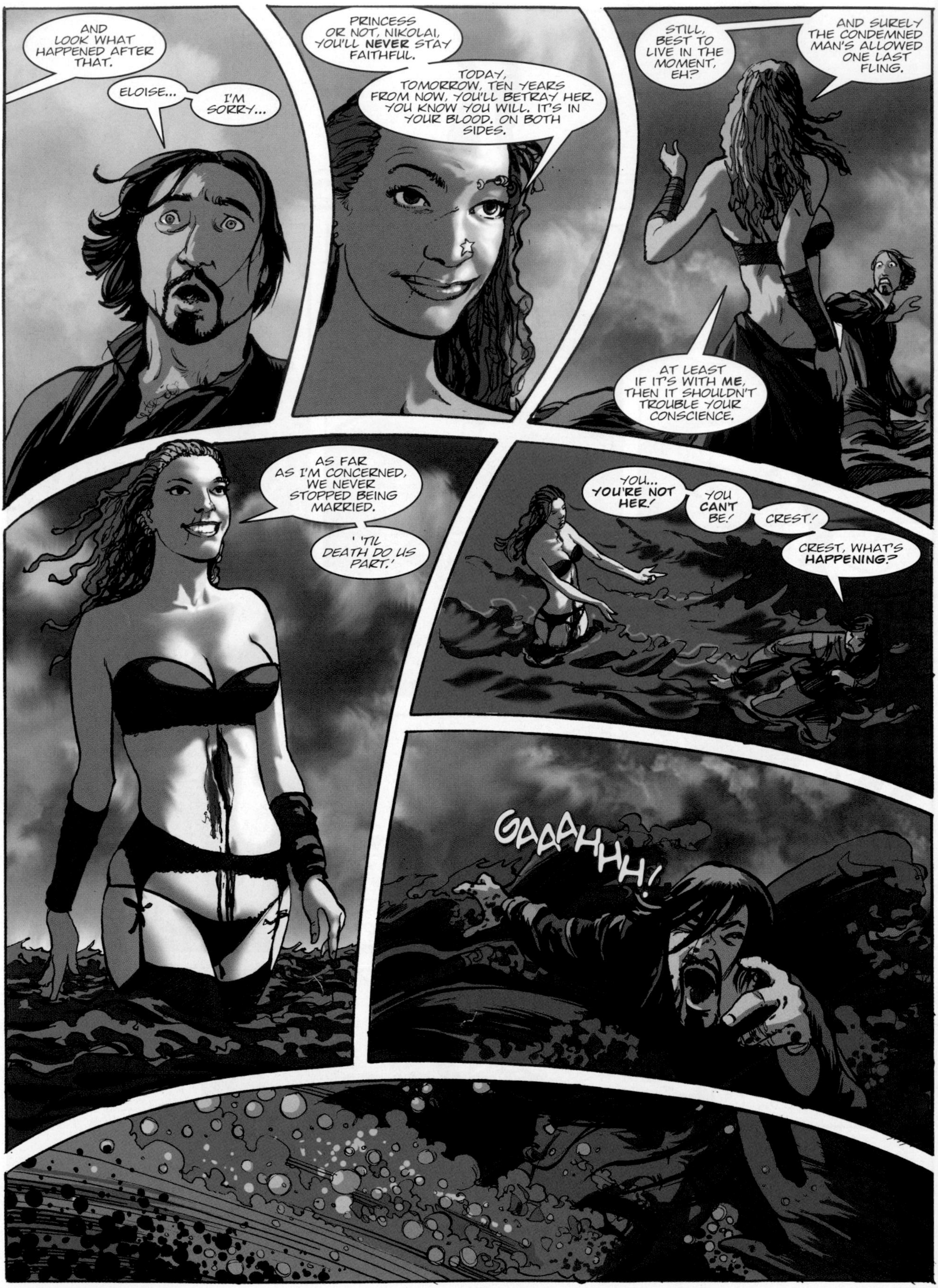
AND LOOK WHAT HAPPENED AFTER THAT.
ELOISE...
I'M SORRY...
PRINCESS OR NOT, NIKOLAI, YOU'LL **NEVER** STAY FAITHFUL.
TODAY, TOMORROW, TEN YEARS FROM NOW, YOU'LL BETRAY HER. YOU KNOW YOU WILL. IT'S IN YOUR BLOOD. ON BOTH SIDES.
STILL, BEST TO LIVE IN THE MOMENT, EH?
AND SURELY THE CONDEMNED MAN'S ALLOWED ONE LAST FLING.
AT LEAST IF IT'S WITH **ME**, THEN IT SHOULDN'T TROUBLE YOUR CONSCIENCE.
AS FAR AS I'M CONCERNED, WE NEVER STOPPED BEING MARRIED.
''TIL DEATH DO US PART.'
YOU... **YOU'RE NOT HER!**
YOU **CAN'T** BE!
CREST!
CREST, WHAT'S **HAPPENING?**
GAAAHHH!

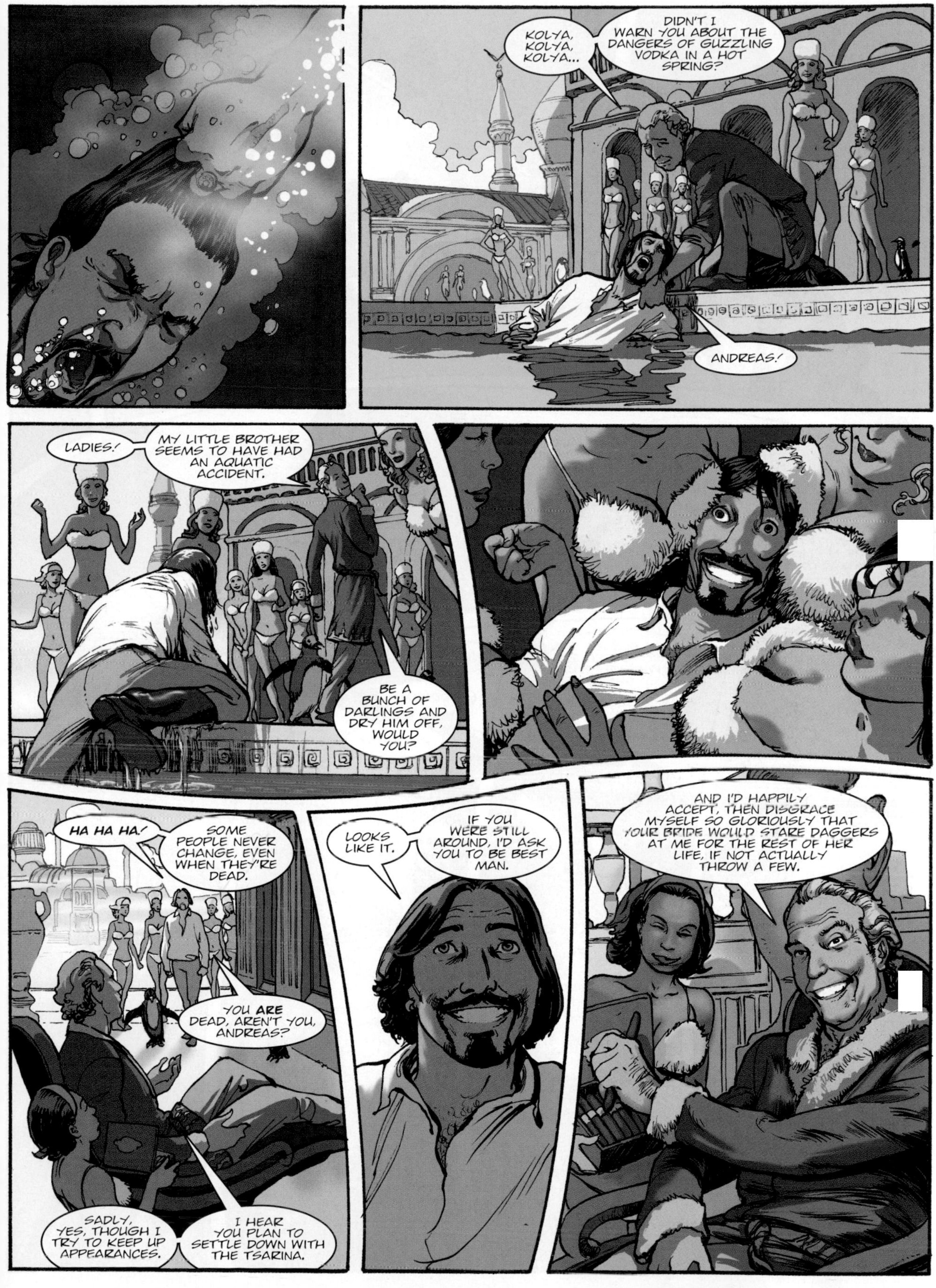
KOLYA, KOLYA, KOLYA...
DIDN'T I WARN YOU ABOUT THE DANGERS OF GUZZLING VODKA IN A HOT SPRING?
ANDREAS!
LADIES!
MY LITTLE BROTHER SEEMS TO HAVE HAD AN AQUATIC ACCIDENT.
BE A BUNCH OF DARLINGS AND DRY HIM OFF, WOULD YOU?
HA HA HA!
SOME PEOPLE NEVER CHANGE, EVEN WHEN THEY'RE DEAD.
YOU ARE DEAD, AREN'T YOU, ANDREAS?
SADLY, YES, THOUGH I TRY TO KEEP UP APPEARANCES.
I HEAR YOU PLAN TO SETTLE DOWN WITH THE TSARINA.
LOOKS LIKE IT.
IF YOU WERE STILL AROUND, I'D ASK YOU TO BE BEST MAN.
AND I'D HAPPILY ACCEPT, THEN DISGRACE MYSELF SO GLORIOUSLY THAT YOUR BRIDE WOULD STARE DAGGERS AT ME FOR THE REST OF HER LIFE, IF NOT ACTUALLY THROW A FEW.

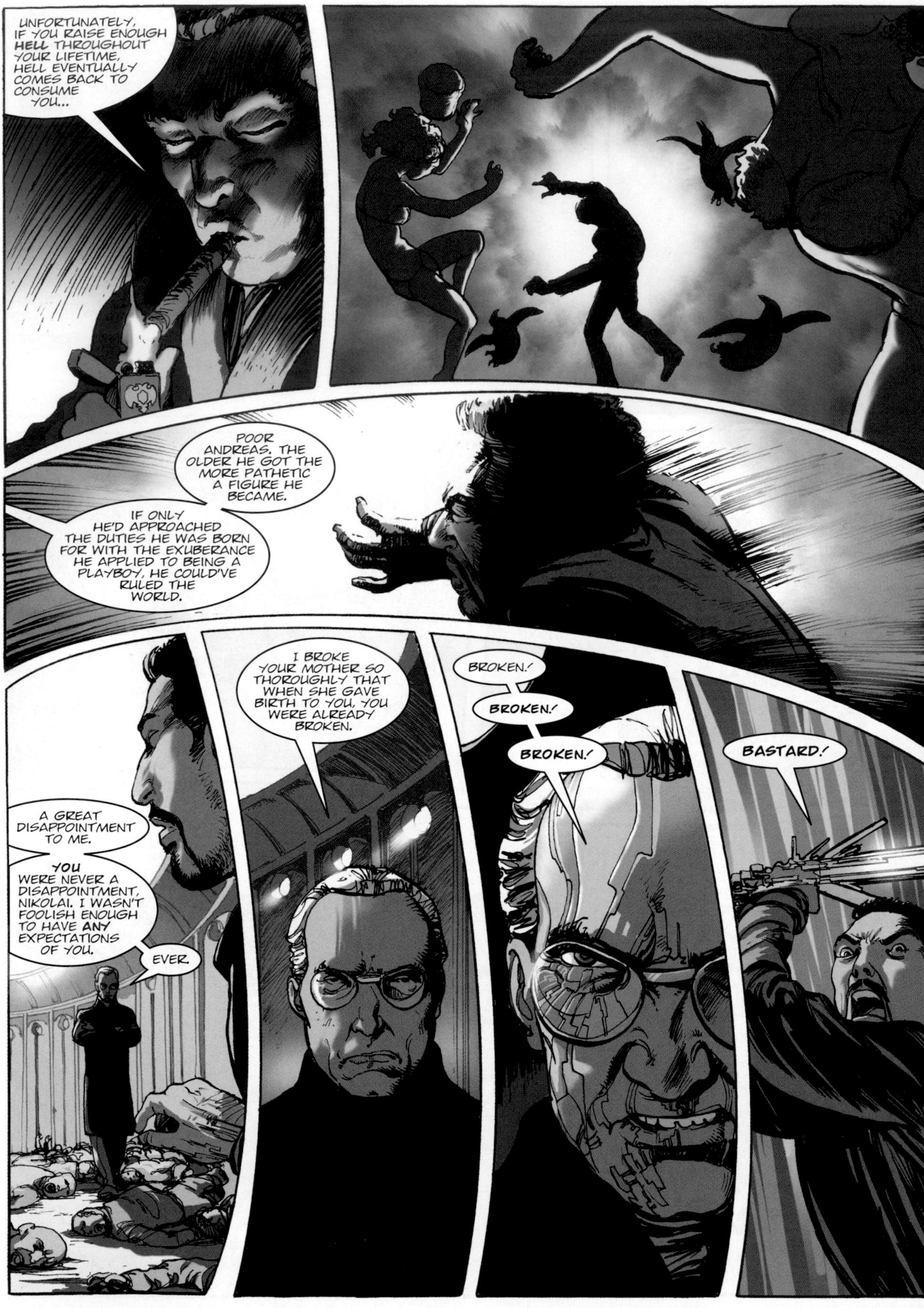
UNFORTUNATELY, IF YOU RAISE ENOUGH HELL THROUGHOUT YOUR LIFETIME, HELL EVENTUALLY COMES BACK TO CONSUME YOU...
POOR ANDREAS. THE OLDER HE GOT THE MORE PATHETIC A FIGURE HE BECAME.
IF ONLY HE'D APPROACHED THE DUTIES HE WAS BORN FOR WITH THE EXUBERANCE HE APPLIED TO BEING A PLAYBOY, HE COULD'VE RULED THE WORLD.
A GREAT DISAPPOINTMENT TO ME.
YOU WERE NEVER A DISAPPOINTMENT, NIKOLAI. I WASN'T FOOLISH ENOUGH TO HAVE ANY EXPECTATIONS OF YOU.
EVER.
I BROKE YOUR MOTHER SO THOROUGHLY THAT WHEN SHE GAVE BIRTH TO YOU, YOU WERE ALREADY BROKEN.
BROKEN!
BROKEN!
BROKEN!
BASTARD!

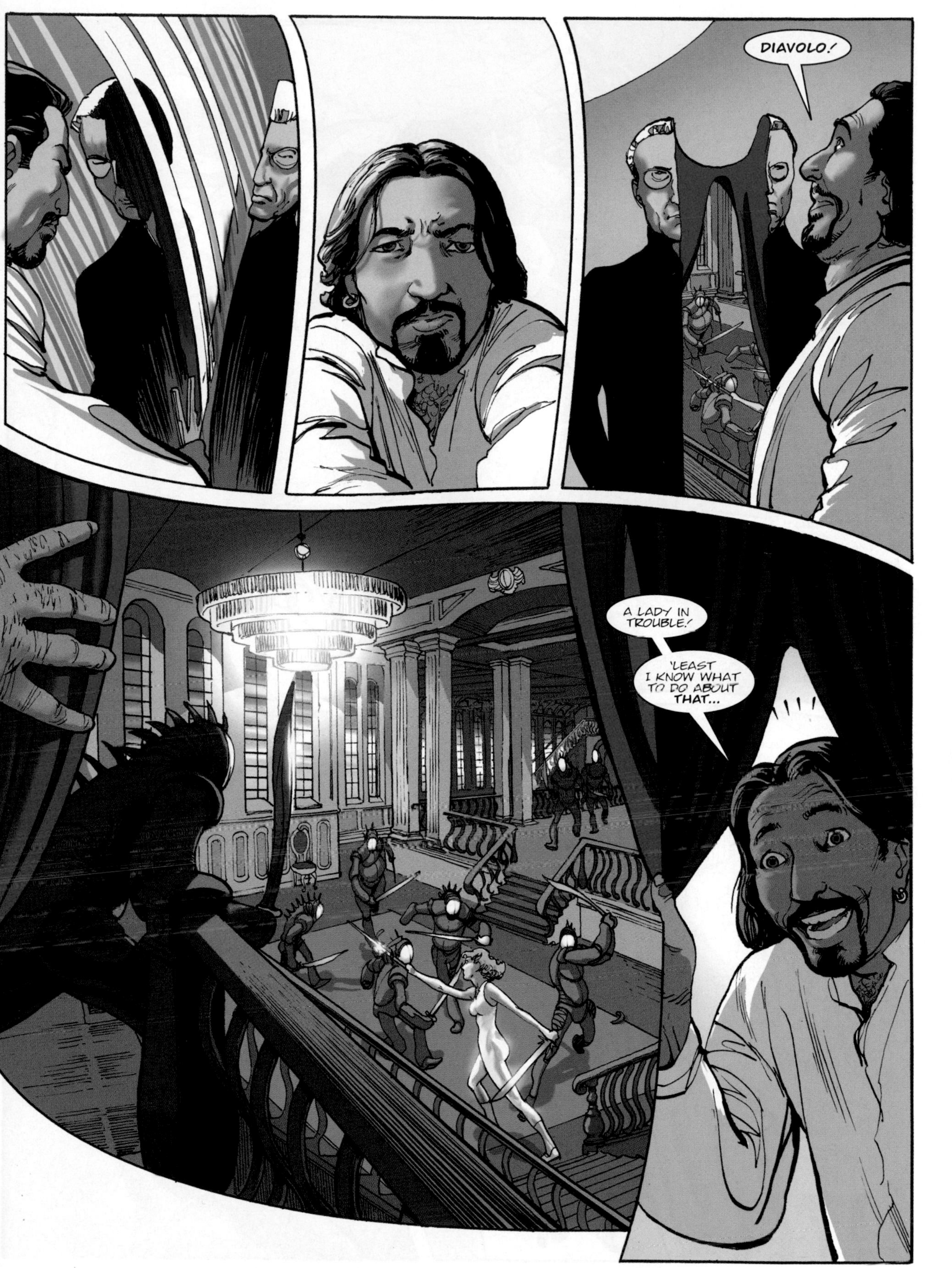
DIAVOLO!
A LADY IN TROUBLE!
'LEAST I KNOW WHAT TO DO ABOUT THAT...

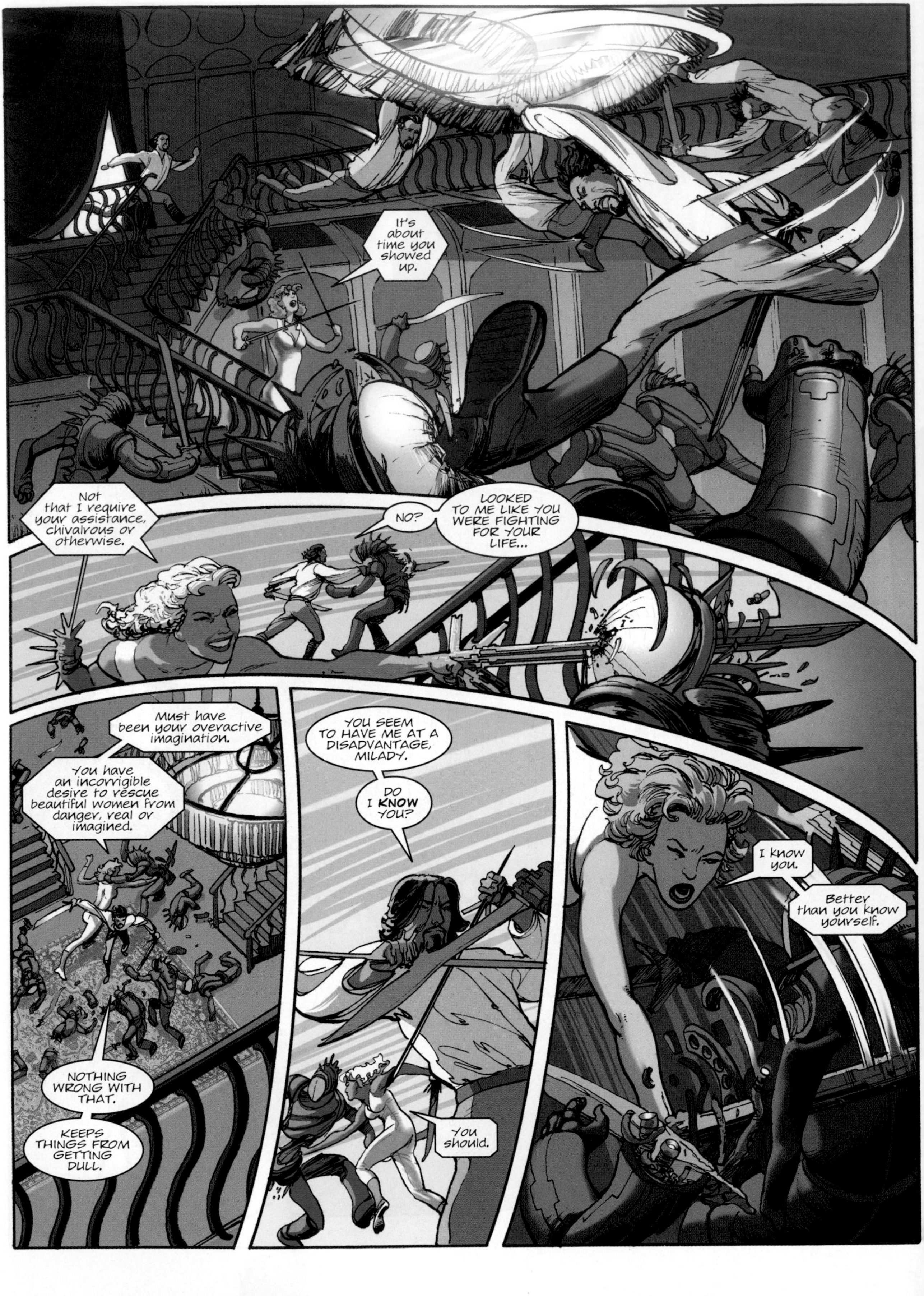
It's about time you showed up.
Not that I require your assistance, chivalrous or otherwise.
NO?
LOOKED TO ME LIKE YOU WERE FIGHTING FOR YOUR LIFE...
Must have been your overactive imagination.
You have an incorrigible desire to rescue beautiful women from danger, real or imagined.
NOTHING WRONG WITH THAT.
KEEPS THINGS FROM GETTING DULL.
YOU SEEM TO HAVE ME AT A DISADVANTAGE, MILADY.
DO I KNOW YOU?
You should.
I know you.
Better than you know yourself.

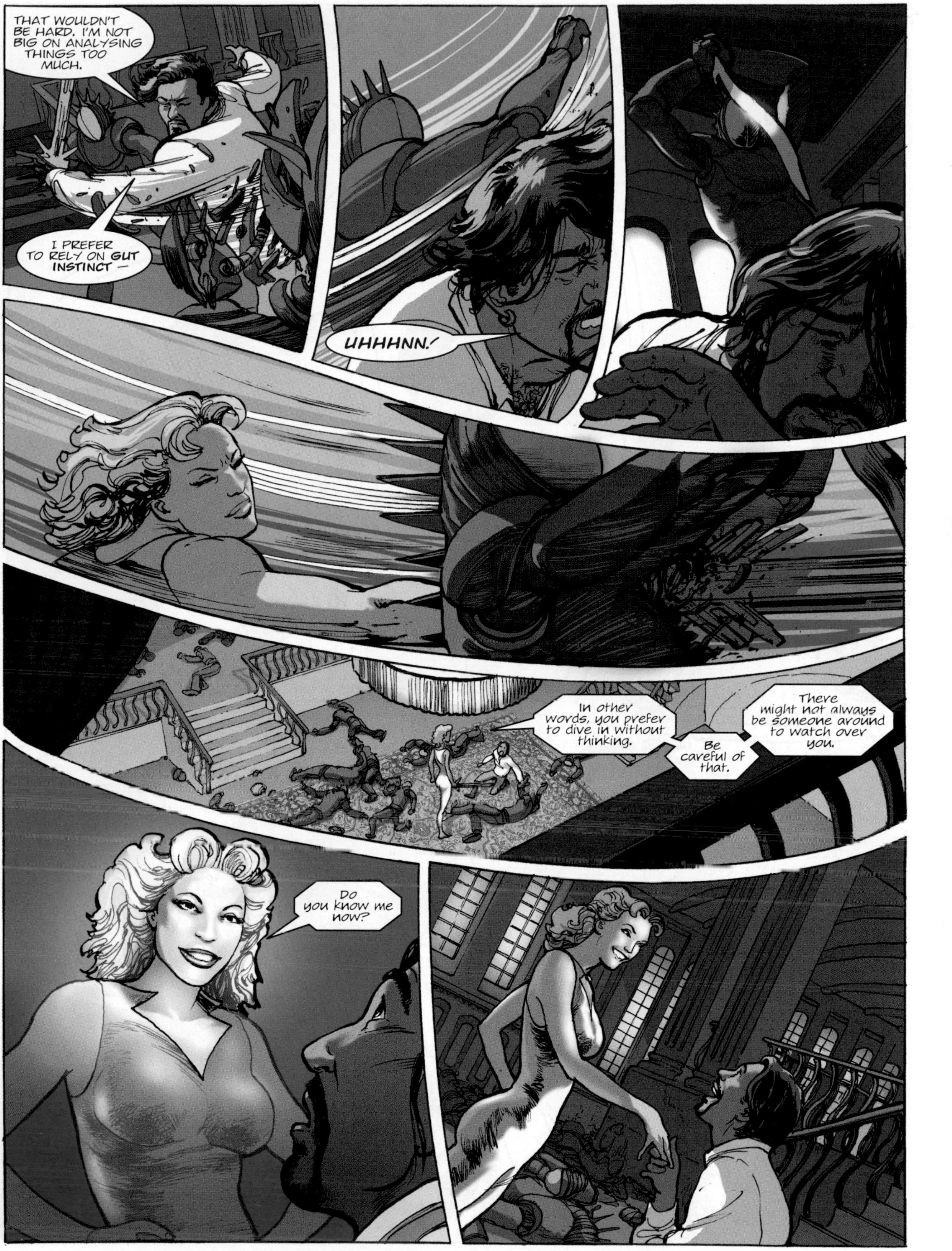
THAT WOULDN'T BE HARD. I'M NOT BIG ON ANALYSING THINGS TOO MUCH.
I PREFER TO RELY ON **GUT INSTINCT** —
UHHHNN!
In other words, you prefer to dive in without thinking.
Be careful of that.
There might not always be someone around to watch over you.
Do you know me now?

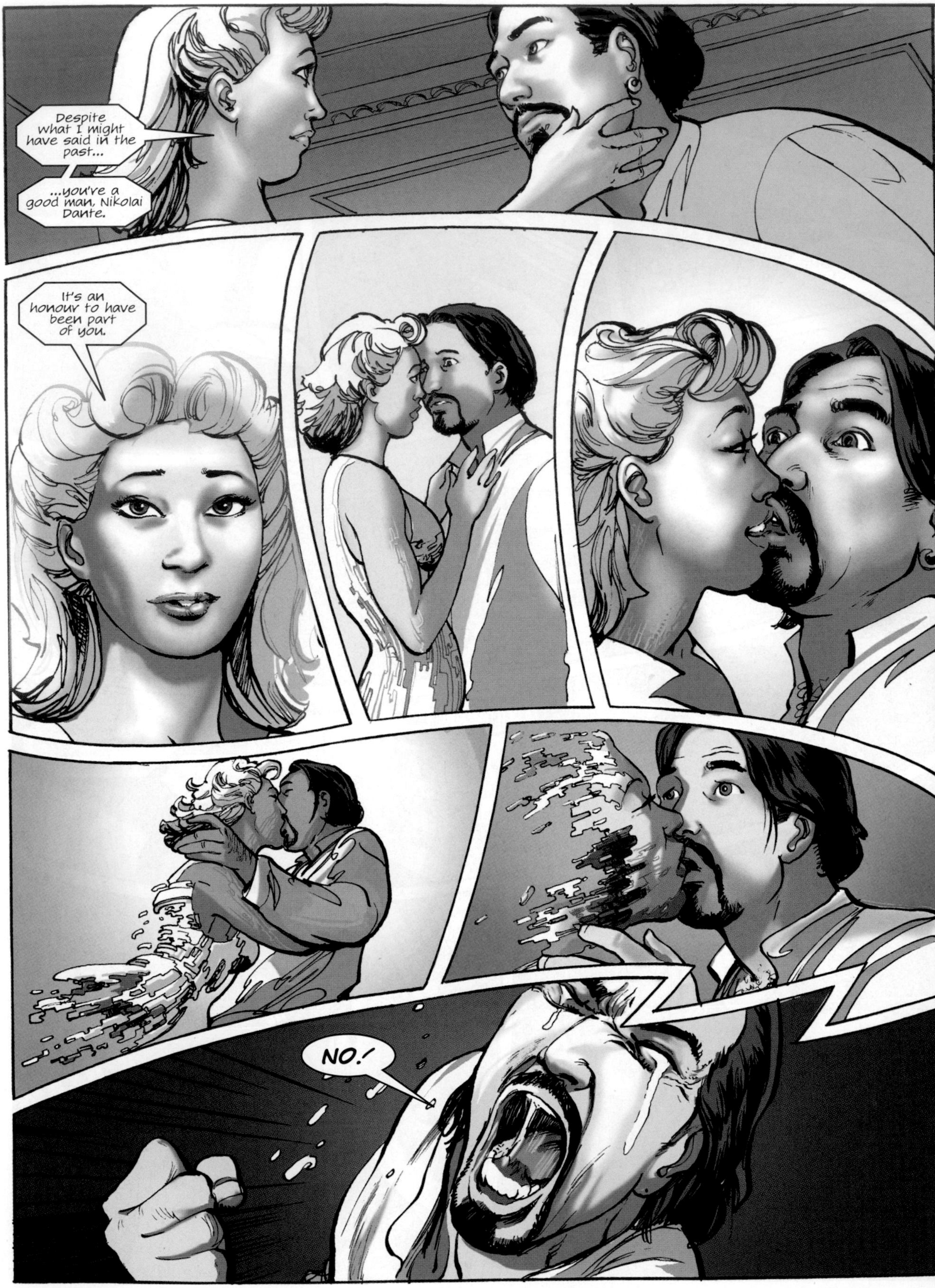
Despite what I might have said in the past...
...you're a good man, Nikolai Dante.
It's an honour to have been part of you.
NO.!

NO.!
ELENA...
CREST...?
CREST.!

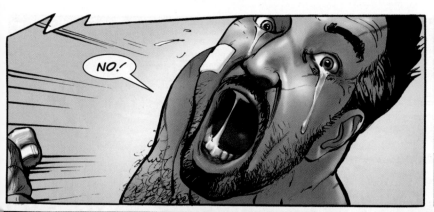

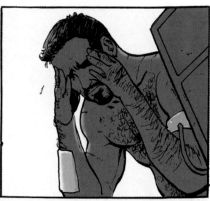

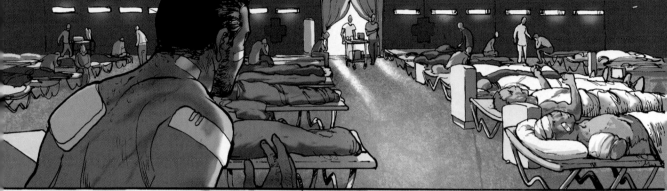

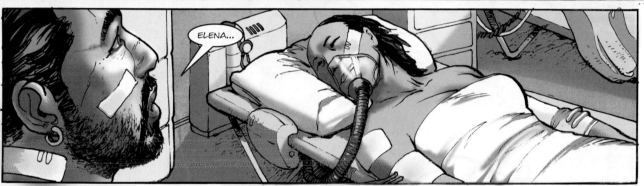

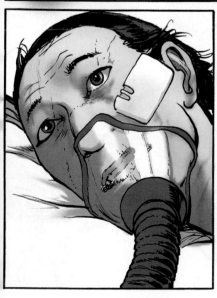

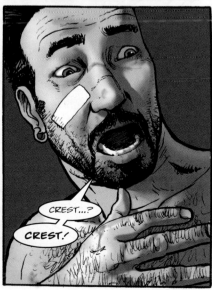

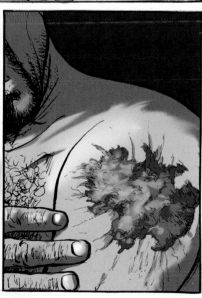

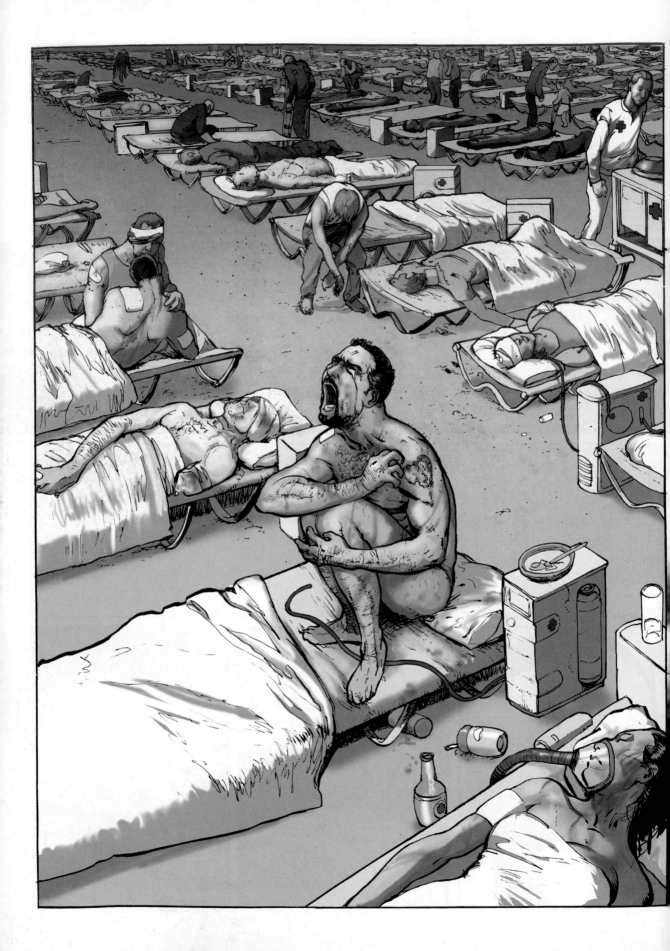

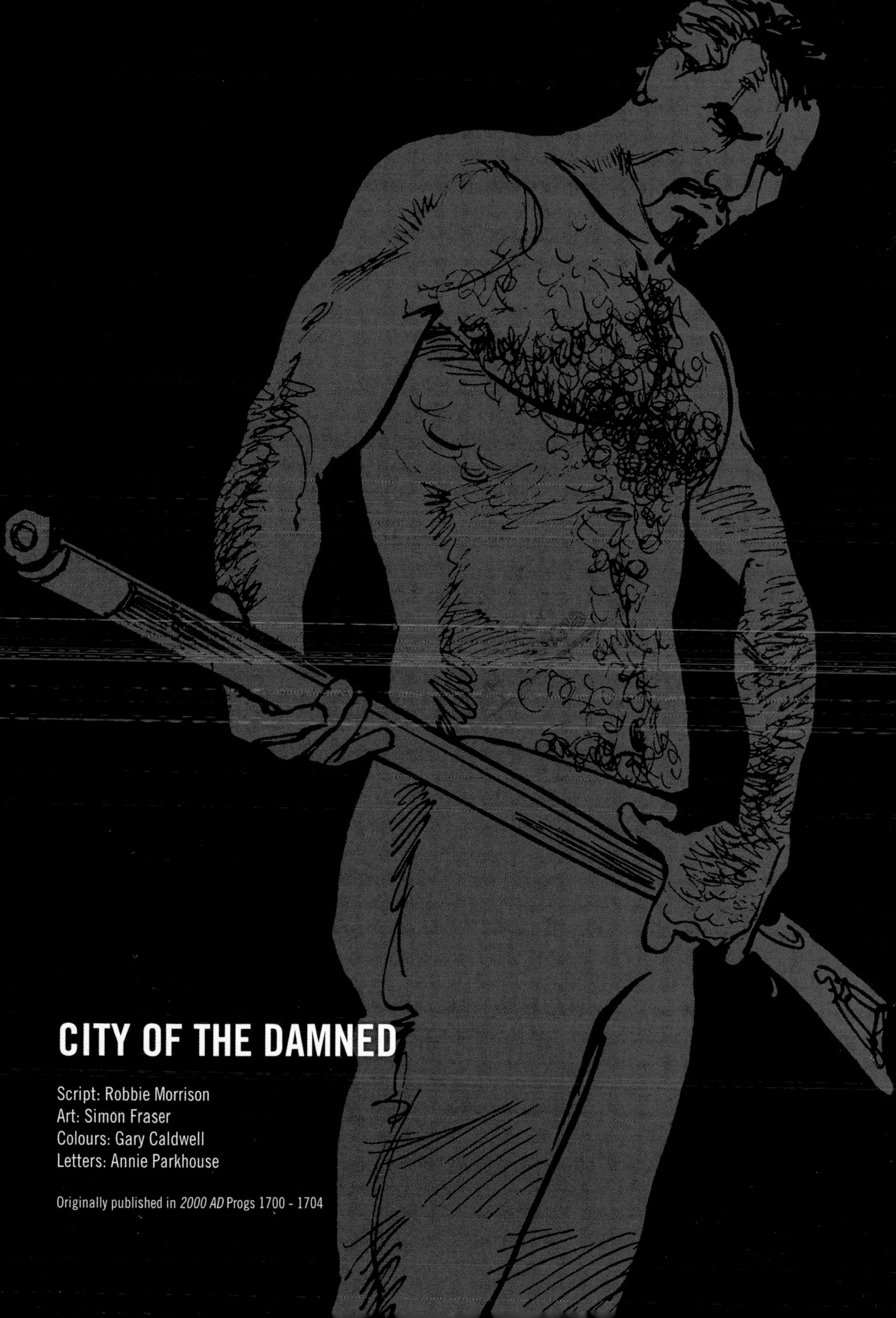

CITY OF THE DAMNED

Script: Robbie Morrison
Art: Simon Fraser
Colours: Gary Caldwell
Letters: Annie Parkhouse

Originally published in *2000 AD* Progs 1700 - 1704

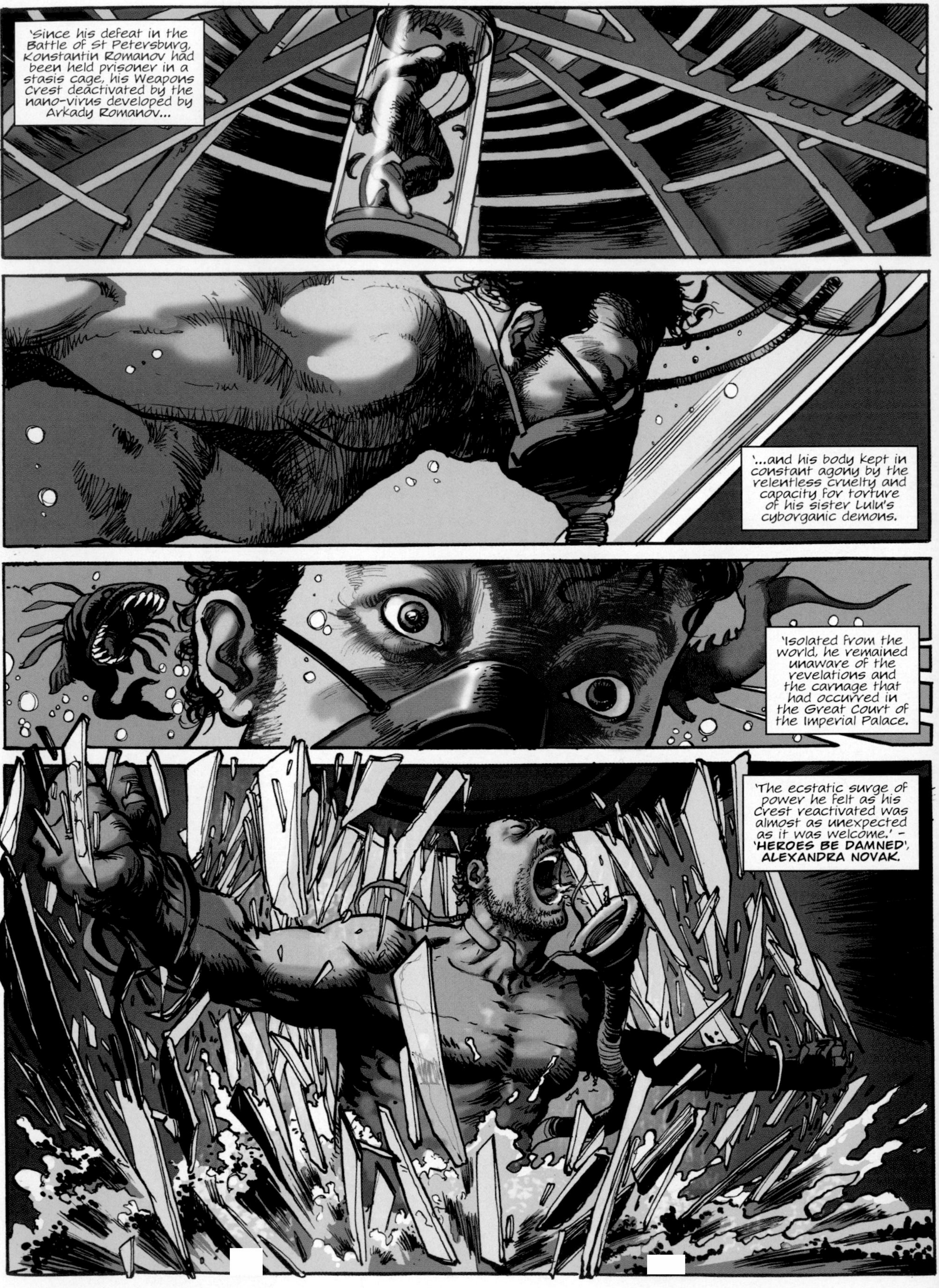
'Since his defeat in the Battle of St Petersburg, Konstantin Romanov had been held prisoner in a stasis cage, his Weapons Crest deactivated by the nano-virus developed by Arkady Romanov...
'...and his body kept in constant agony by the relentless cruelty and capacity for torture of his sister Lulu's cyborganic demons.
'Isolated from the world, he remained unaware of the revelations and the carnage that had occurred in the Great Court of the Imperial Palace.
'The ecstatic surge of power he felt as his Crest reactivated was almost as unexpected as it was welcome.' – 'HEROES BE DAMNED', ALEXANDRA NOVAK.

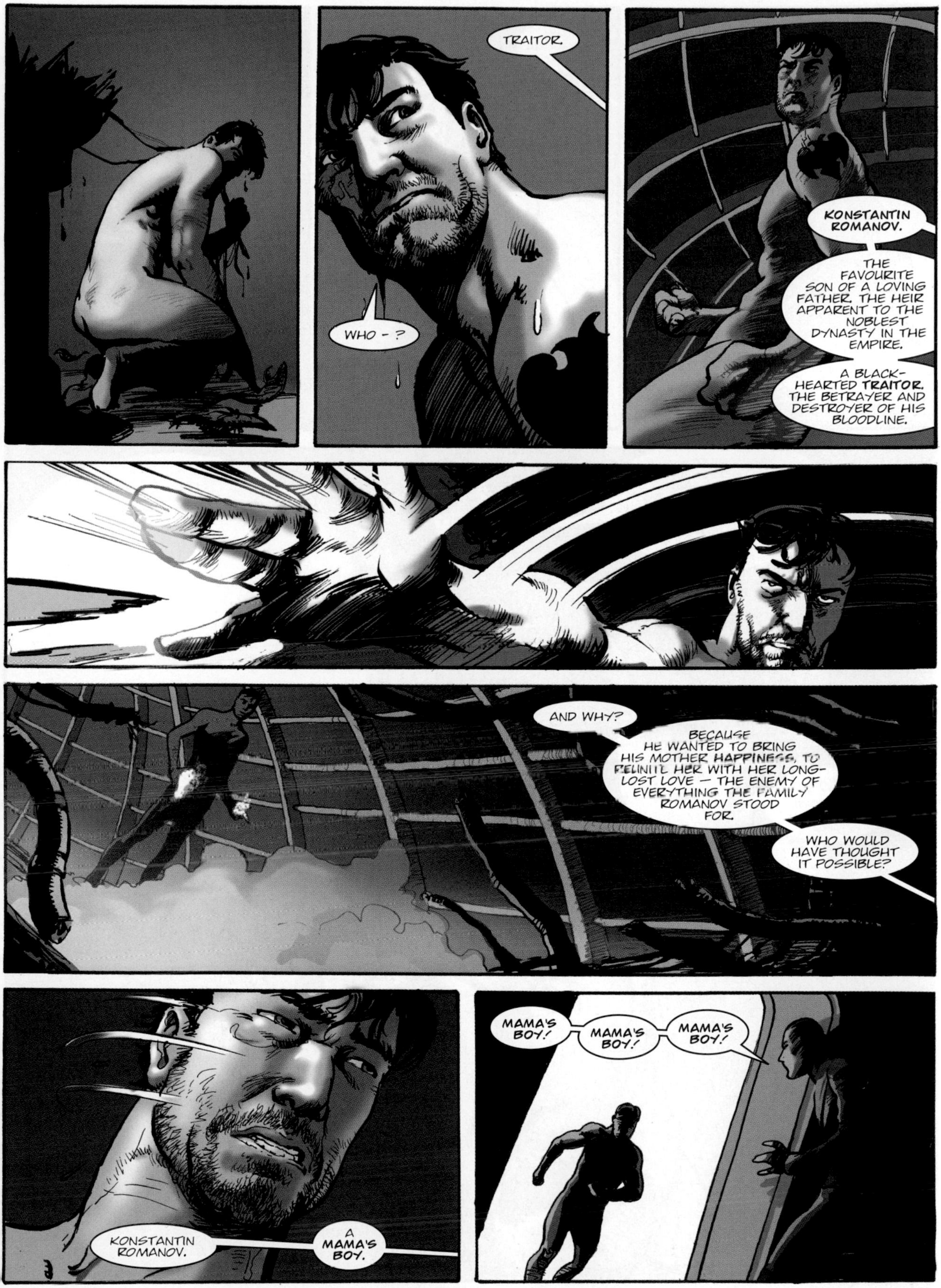
TRAITOR.
WHO - ?
KONSTANTIN ROMANOV.
THE FAVOURITE SON OF A LOVING FATHER. THE HEIR APPARENT TO THE NOBLEST DYNASTY IN THE EMPIRE.
A BLACK-HEARTED TRAITOR. THE BETRAYER AND DESTROYER OF HIS BLOODLINE.
AND WHY?
BECAUSE HE WANTED TO BRING HIS MOTHER HAPPINESS, TO REUNITE HER WITH HER LONG-LOST LOVE — THE ENEMY OF EVERYTHING THE FAMILY ROMANOV STOOD FOR.
WHO WOULD HAVE THOUGHT IT POSSIBLE?
KONSTANTIN ROMANOV.
A MAMA'S BOY.
MAMA'S BOY!
MAMA'S BOY!
MAMA'S BOY!

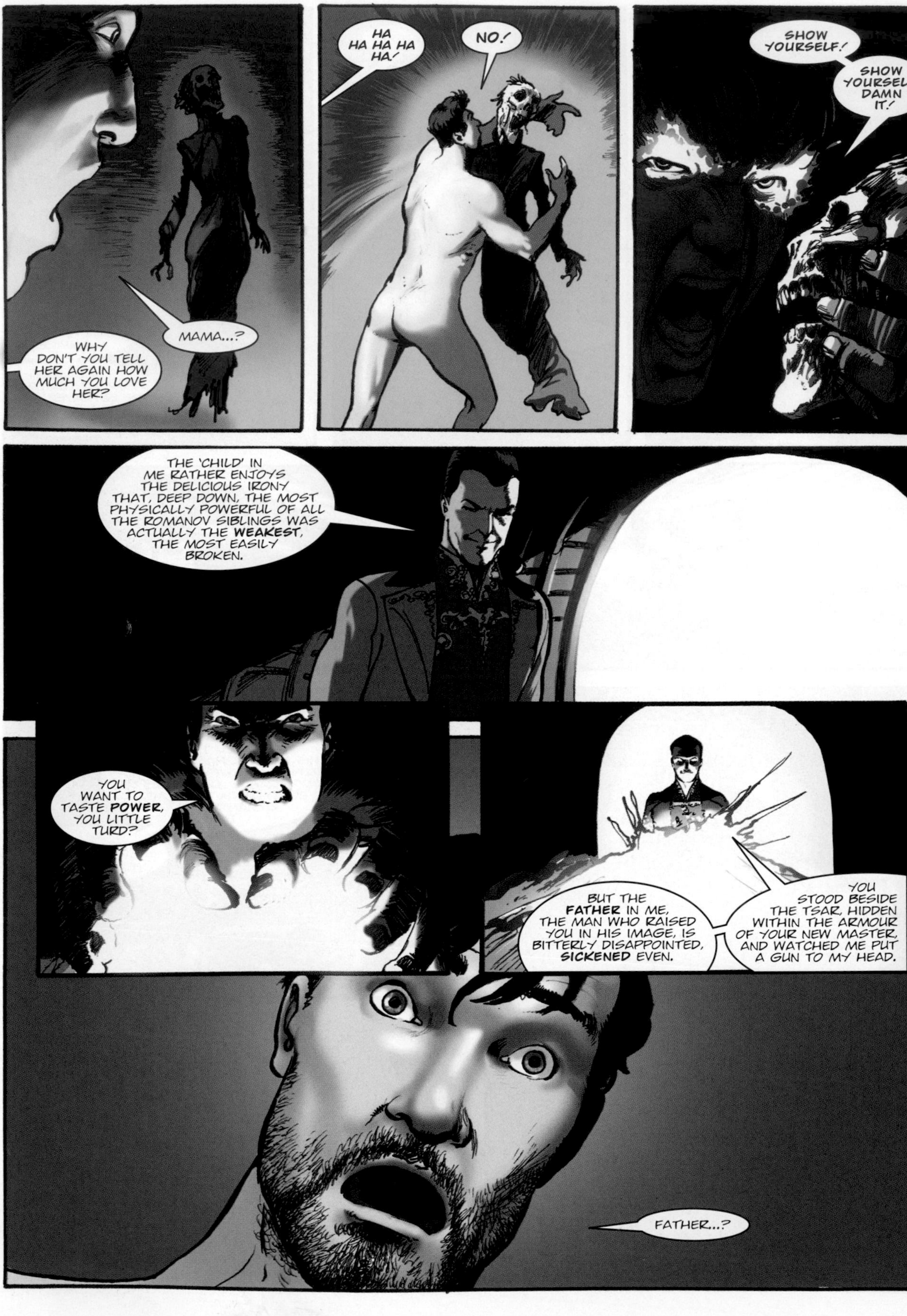
WHY DON'T YOU TELL HER AGAIN HOW MUCH YOU LOVE HER?
MAMA...?
HA HA HA HA HA!
NO!
SHOW YOURSELF!
SHOW YOURSELF, DAMN IT!
THE 'CHILD' IN ME RATHER ENJOYS THE DELICIOUS IRONY THAT, DEEP DOWN, THE MOST PHYSICALLY POWERFUL OF ALL THE ROMANOV SIBLINGS WAS ACTUALLY THE WEAKEST, THE MOST EASILY BROKEN.
YOU WANT TO TASTE POWER, YOU LITTLE TURD?
YOU STOOD BESIDE THE TSAR, HIDDEN WITHIN THE ARMOUR OF YOUR NEW MASTER, AND WATCHED ME PUT A GUN TO MY HEAD.
BUT THE FATHER IN ME, THE MAN WHO RAISED YOU IN HIS IMAGE, IS BITTERLY DISAPPOINTED, SICKENED EVEN.
FATHER...?

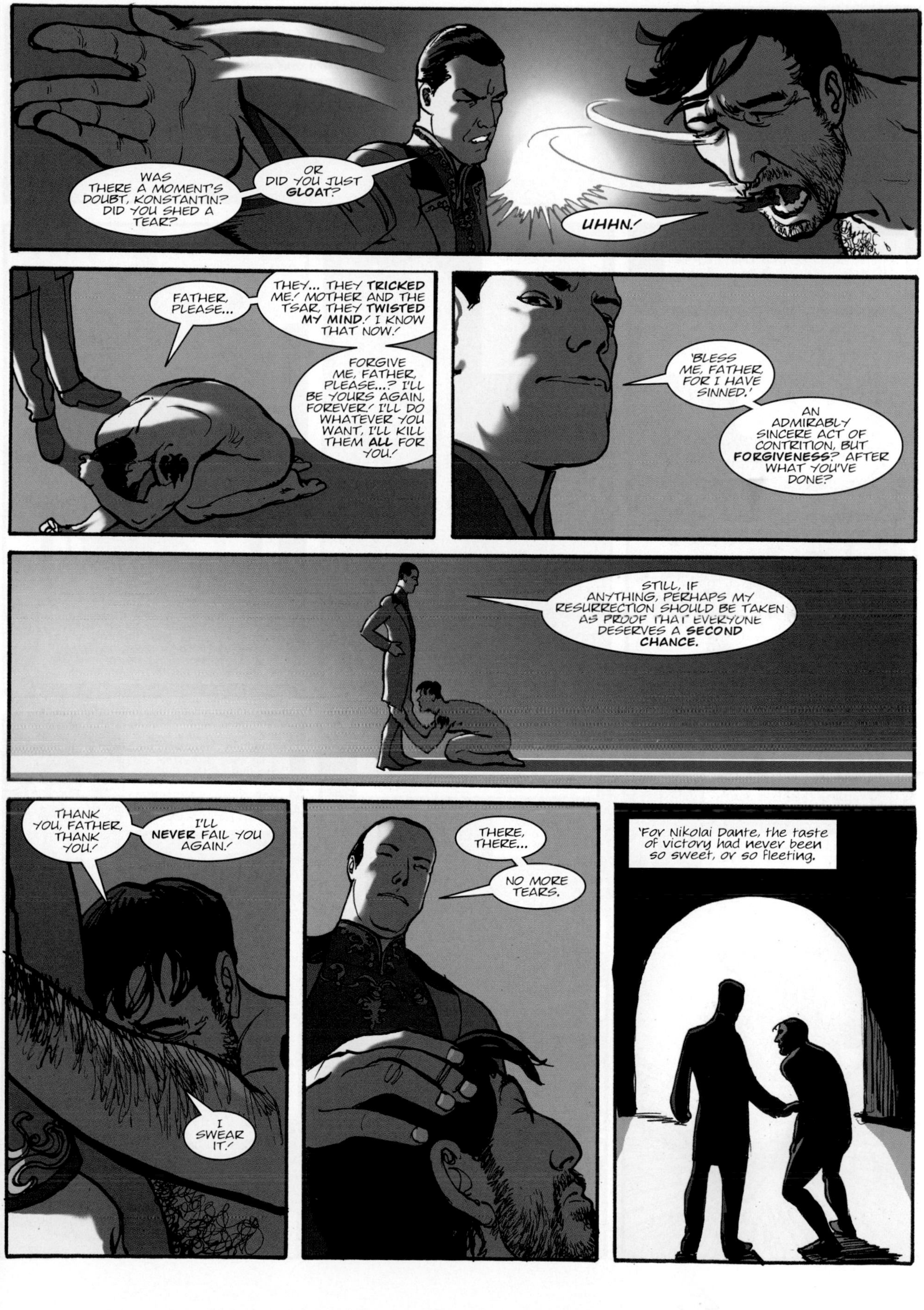
WAS THERE A MOMENT'S DOUBT, KONSTANTIN? DID YOU SHED A TEAR?
OR DID YOU JUST GLOAT?
UHHN!
FATHER, PLEASE...
THEY... THEY TRICKED ME! MOTHER AND THE TSAR, THEY TWISTED MY MIND! I KNOW THAT NOW!
FORGIVE ME, FATHER, PLEASE...? I'LL BE YOURS AGAIN, FOREVER! I'LL DO WHATEVER YOU WANT, I'LL KILL THEM ALL FOR YOU!
'BLESS ME, FATHER, FOR I HAVE SINNED.'
AN ADMIRABLY SINCERE ACT OF CONTRITION, BUT FORGIVENESS? AFTER WHAT YOU'VE DONE?
STILL, IF ANYTHING, PERHAPS MY RESURRECTION SHOULD BE TAKEN AS PROOF THAT EVERYONE DESERVES A SECOND CHANCE.
THANK YOU, FATHER, THANK YOU!
I'LL NEVER FAIL YOU AGAIN!
I SWEAR IT!
THERE, THERE...
NO MORE TEARS.
'For Nikolai Dante, the taste of victory had never been so sweet, or so fleeting.

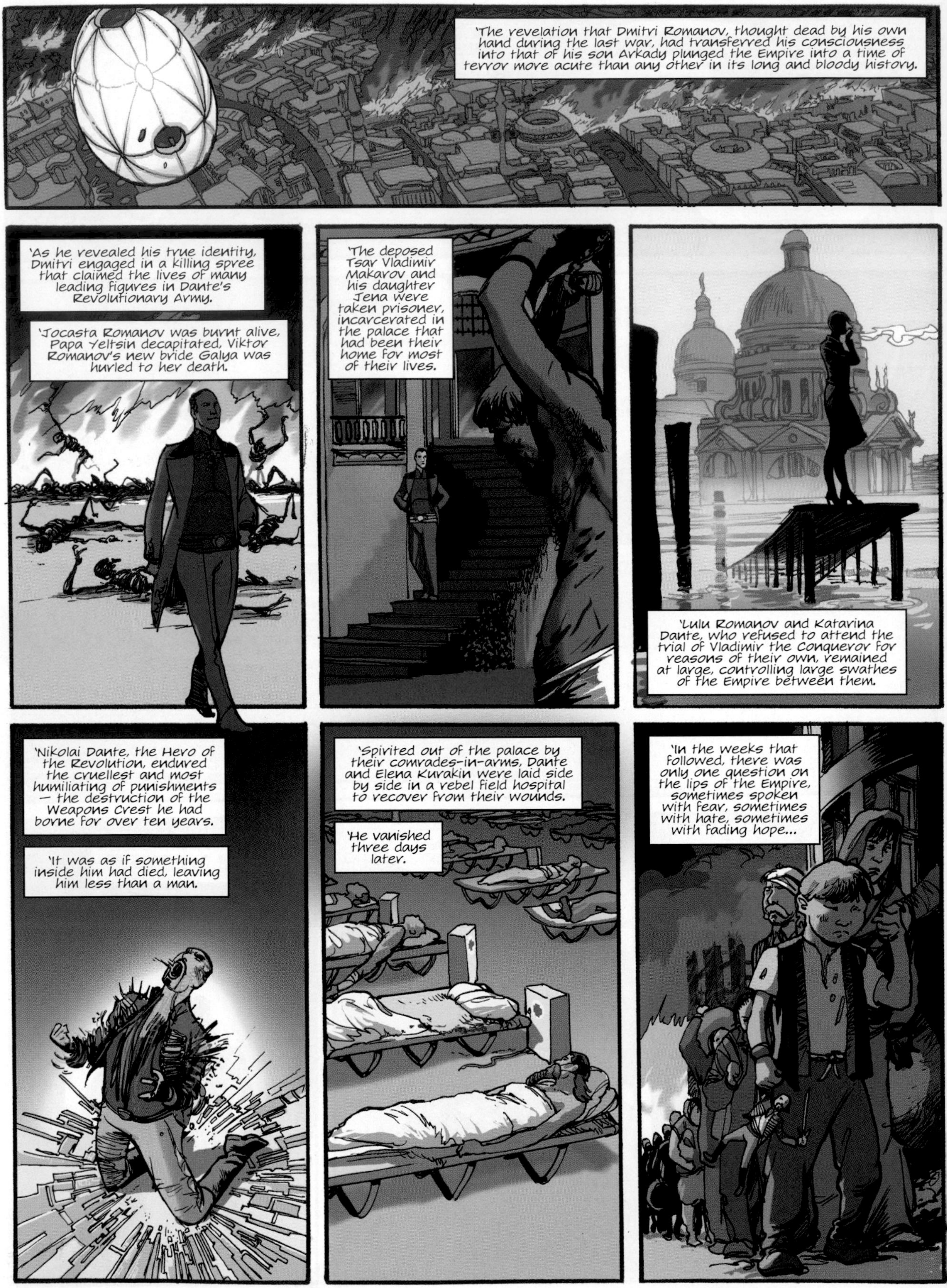
'The revelation that Dmitri Romanov, thought dead by his own hand during the last war, had transferred his consciousness into that of his son Arkady plunged the Empire into a time of terror more acute than any other in its long and bloody history.
'As he revealed his true identity, Dmitri engaged in a killing spree that claimed the lives of many leading figures in Dante's Revolutionary Army.
'Jocasta Romanov was burnt alive, Papa Yeltsin decapitated, Viktor Romanov's new bride Galya was hurled to her death.
'The deposed Tsar Vladimir Makarov and his daughter Jena were taken prisoner, incarcerated in the palace that had been their home for most of their lives.
'Lulu Romanov and Katarina Dante, who refused to attend the trial of Vladimir the Conqueror for reasons of their own, remained at large, controlling large swathes of the Empire between them.
'Nikolai Dante, the Hero of the Revolution, endured the cruellest and most humiliating of punishments — the destruction of the Weapons Crest he had borne for over ten years.
'It was as if something inside him had died, leaving him less than a man.
'Spirited out of the palace by their comrades-in-arms, Dante and Elena Kurakin were laid side by side in a rebel field hospital to recover from their wounds.
'He vanished three days later.
'In the weeks that followed, there was only one question on the lips of the Empire, sometimes spoken with fear, sometimes with hate, sometimes with fading hope...

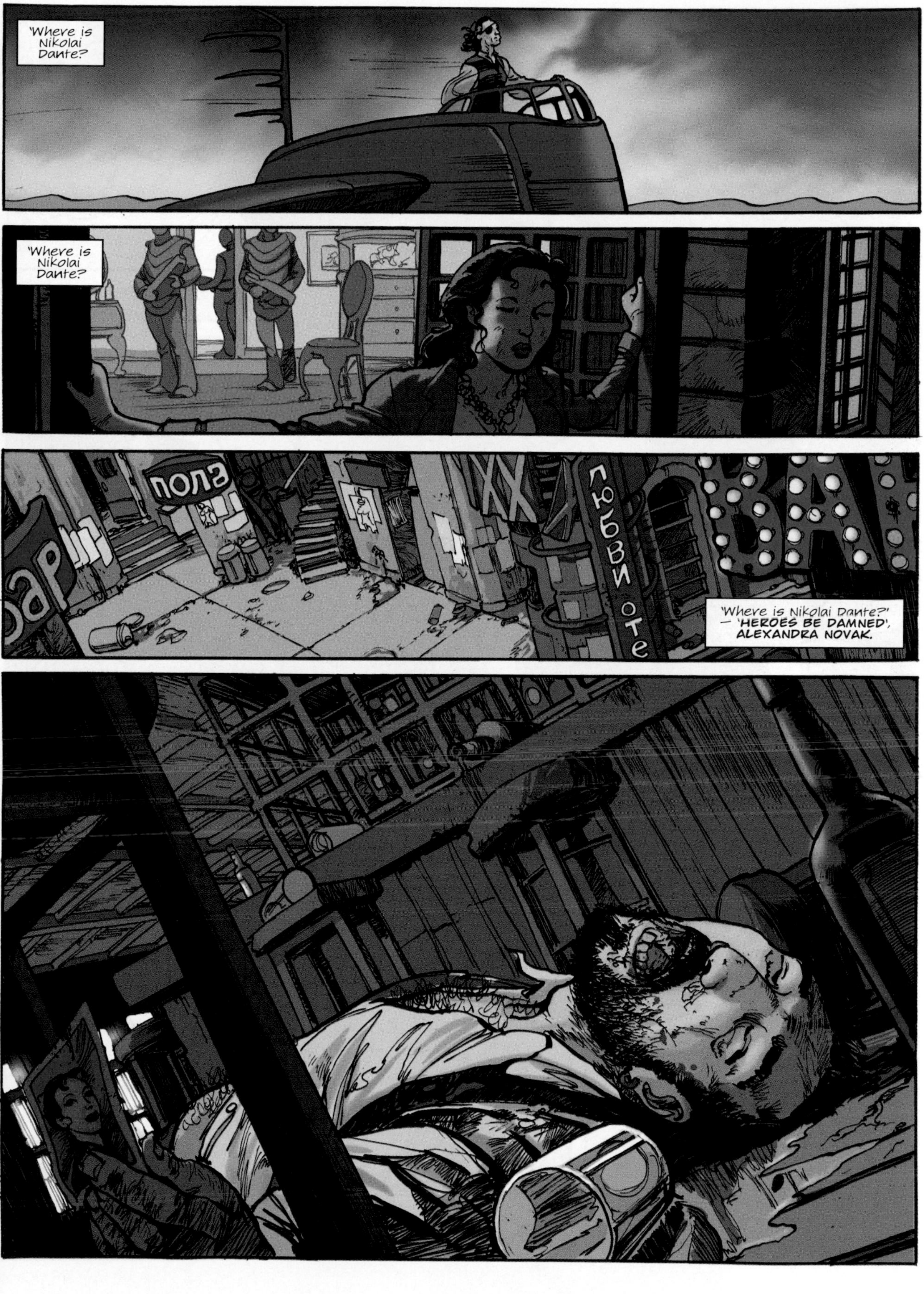
'Where is Nikolai Dante?
'Where is Nikolai Dante?
пола
любви оте
'Where is Nikolai Dante?' — 'HEROES BE DAMNED', ALEXANDRA NOVAK.

WHOA! KOFF KOFF!

WHAT...? WHO....?

NIKOLAI DANTE.

THE HERO OF THE REVOLUTION.

HOW THE MIGHTY HAVE FALLEN.

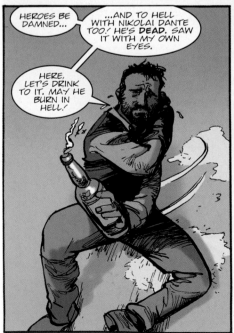

HEROES BE DAMNED...

...AND TO HELL WITH NIKOLAI DANTE TOO! HE'S DEAD. SAW IT WITH MY OWN EYES.

HERE, LET'S DRINK TO IT. MAY HE BURN IN HELL!

OH, YOU'LL BURN, YOU BASTARD! I'LL SEE TO THAT. YOU'LL BURN, YOU'LL BLEED, YOU'LL BEG...

WHAT? YOU DON'T RECOGNISE ME? YOU DON'T SEE THE FAMILY RESEMBLANCE?

THE NAME'S ARBATOV. MAJOR ANDREI ARBATOV.

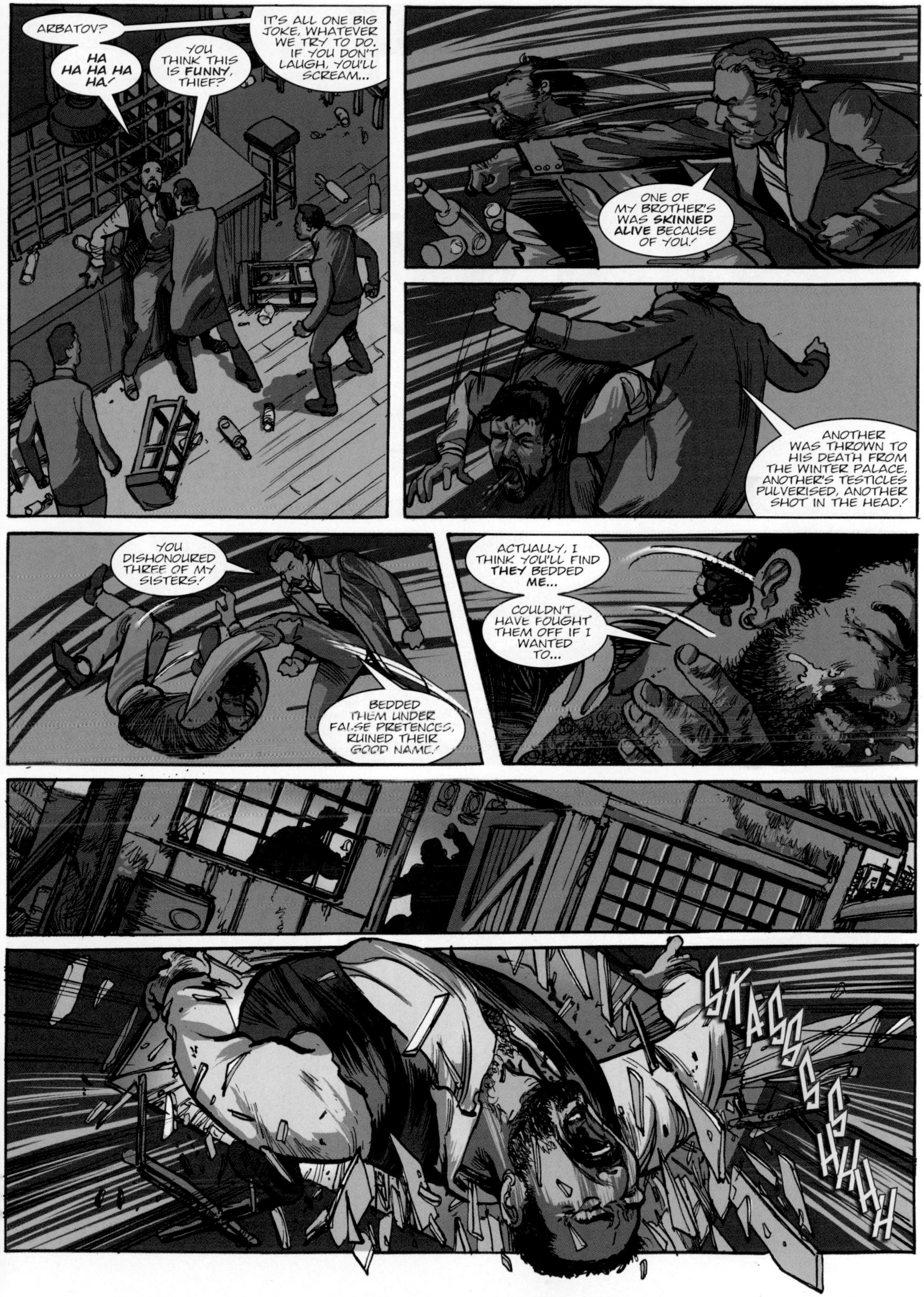
ARBATOV?
HA HA HA HA HA!
YOU THINK THIS IS FUNNY, THIEF?
IT'S ALL ONE BIG JOKE, WHATEVER WE TRY TO DO. IF YOU DON'T LAUGH, YOU'LL SCREAM...
ONE OF MY BROTHER'S WAS SKINNED ALIVE BECAUSE OF YOU!
ANOTHER WAS THROWN TO HIS DEATH FROM THE WINTER PALACE, ANOTHER'S TESTICLES PULVERISED, ANOTHER SHOT IN THE HEAD!
YOU DISHONOURED THREE OF MY SISTERS!
BEDDED THEM UNDER FALSE PRETENCES, RUINED THEIR GOOD NAME!
ACTUALLY, I THINK YOU'LL FIND THEY BEDDED ME...
COULDN'T HAVE FOUGHT THEM OFF IF I WANTED TO...
SKASSSSHHHH

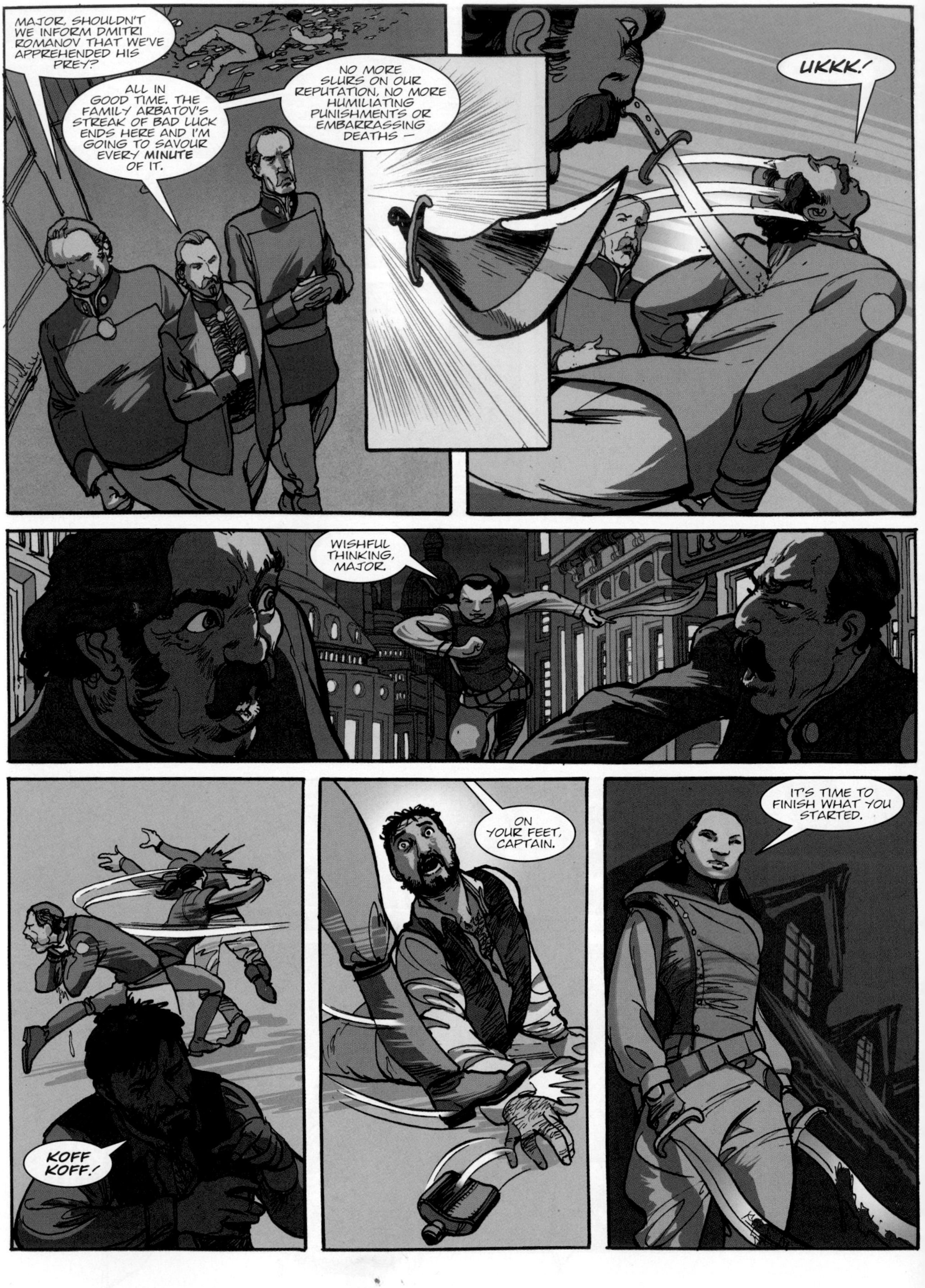
MAJOR, SHOULDN'T WE INFORM DMITRI ROMANOV THAT WE'VE APPREHENDED HIS PREY?
ALL IN GOOD TIME. THE FAMILY ARBATOV'S STREAK OF BAD LUCK ENDS HERE AND I'M GOING TO SAVOUR EVERY **MINUTE** OF IT.
NO MORE SLURS ON OUR REPUTATION, NO MORE HUMILIATING PUNISHMENTS OR EMBARRASSING DEATHS —
UKKK!
WISHFUL THINKING, MAJOR.
KOFF KOFF!
ON YOUR FEET, CAPTAIN.
IT'S TIME TO FINISH WHAT YOU STARTED.

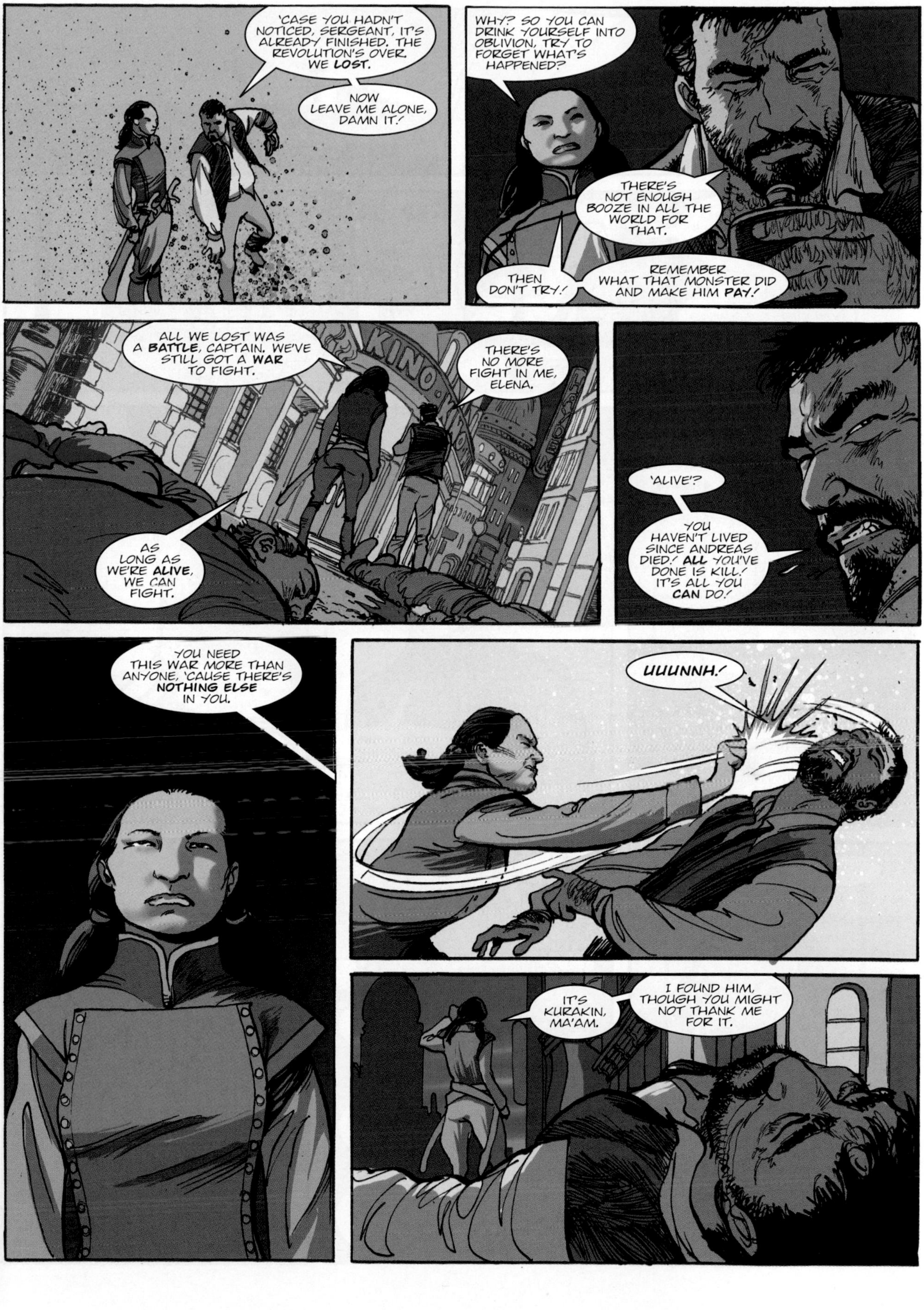
'CASE YOU HADN'T NOTICED, SERGEANT, IT'S ALREADY FINISHED. THE REVOLUTION'S OVER. WE **LOST.**
NOW LEAVE ME ALONE, DAMN IT!
WHY? SO YOU CAN DRINK YOURSELF INTO OBLIVION, TRY TO FORGET WHAT'S HAPPENED?
THERE'S NOT ENOUGH BOOZE IN ALL THE WORLD FOR THAT.
THEN DON'T TRY!
REMEMBER WHAT THAT MONSTER DID AND MAKE HIM **PAY!**
KINO
ALL WE LOST WAS A **BATTLE**, CAPTAIN. WE'VE STILL GOT A **WAR** TO FIGHT.
THERE'S NO MORE FIGHT IN ME, ELENA.
AS LONG AS WE'RE **ALIVE**, WE CAN FIGHT.
'ALIVE'?
YOU HAVEN'T LIVED SINCE ANDREAS DIED! **ALL** YOU'VE DONE IS KILL! IT'S ALL YOU **CAN** DO!
YOU NEED THIS WAR MORE THAN ANYONE, 'CAUSE THERE'S **NOTHING ELSE** IN YOU.
UUUNNH!
IT'S KURAKIN, MA'AM.
I FOUND HIM, THOUGH YOU MIGHT NOT THANK ME FOR IT.

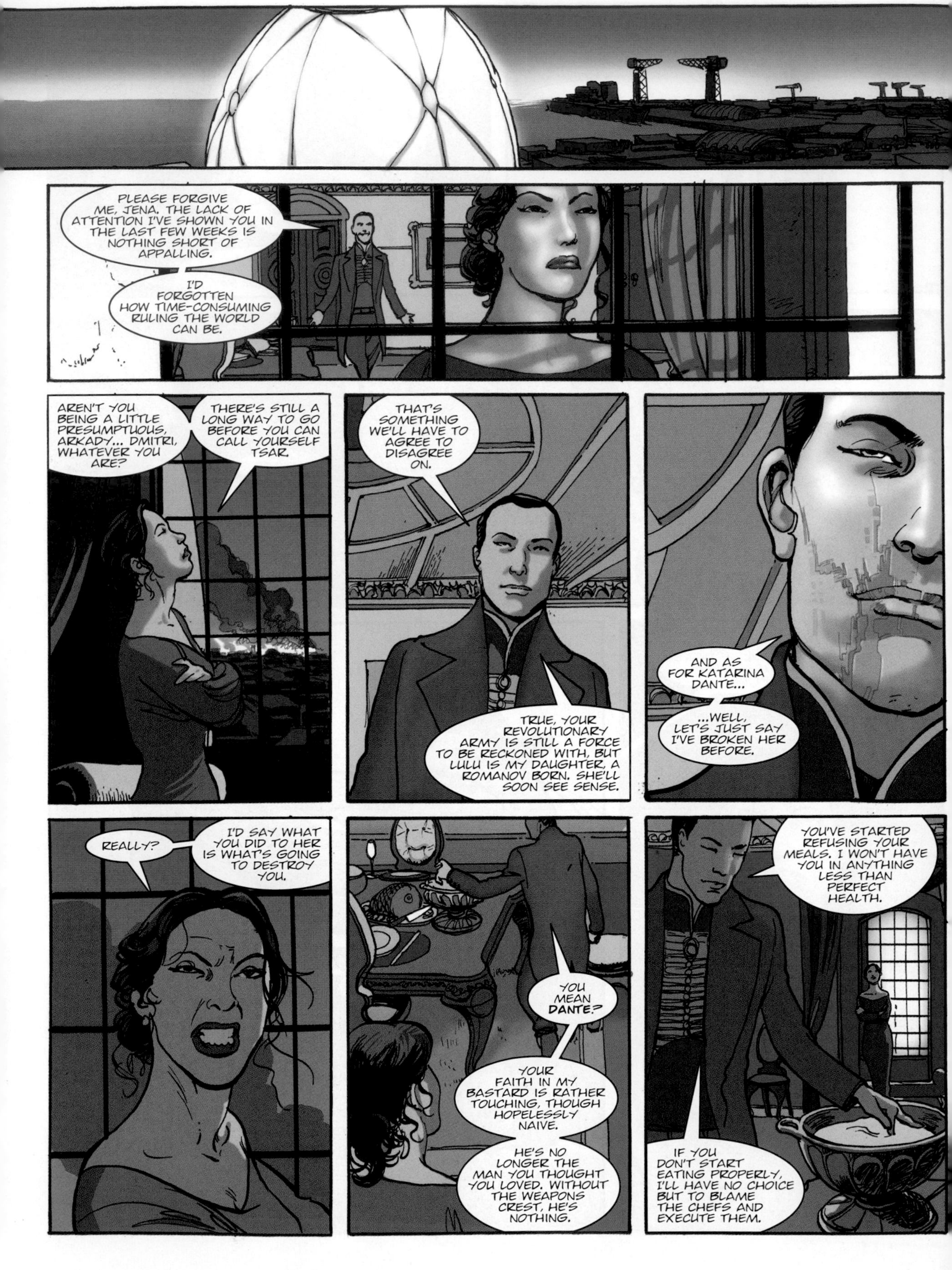
PLEASE FORGIVE ME, JENA. THE LACK OF ATTENTION I'VE SHOWN YOU IN THE LAST FEW WEEKS IS NOTHING SHORT OF APPALLING.
I'D FORGOTTEN HOW TIME-CONSUMING RULING THE WORLD CAN BE.
AREN'T YOU BEING A LITTLE PRESUMPTUOUS, ARKADY... DMITRI, WHATEVER YOU ARE?
THERE'S STILL A LONG WAY TO GO BEFORE YOU CAN CALL YOURSELF TSAR.
THAT'S SOMETHING WE'LL HAVE TO AGREE TO DISAGREE ON.
TRUE, YOUR REVOLUTIONARY ARMY IS STILL A FORCE TO BE RECKONED WITH, BUT LULU IS MY DAUGHTER, A ROMANOV BORN. SHE'LL SOON SEE SENSE.
AND AS FOR KATARINA DANTE...
...WELL, LET'S JUST SAY I'VE BROKEN HER BEFORE.
REALLY?
I'D SAY WHAT YOU DID TO HER IS WHAT'S GOING TO DESTROY YOU.
YOU MEAN DANTE?
YOUR FAITH IN MY BASTARD IS RATHER TOUCHING, THOUGH HOPELESSLY NAIVE.
HE'S NO LONGER THE MAN YOU THOUGHT YOU LOVED. WITHOUT THE WEAPONS CREST, HE'S NOTHING.
YOU'VE STARTED REFUSING YOUR MEALS. I WON'T HAVE YOU IN ANYTHING LESS THAN PERFECT HEALTH.
IF YOU DON'T START EATING PROPERLY, I'LL HAVE NO CHOICE BUT TO BLAME THE CHEFS AND EXECUTE THEM.

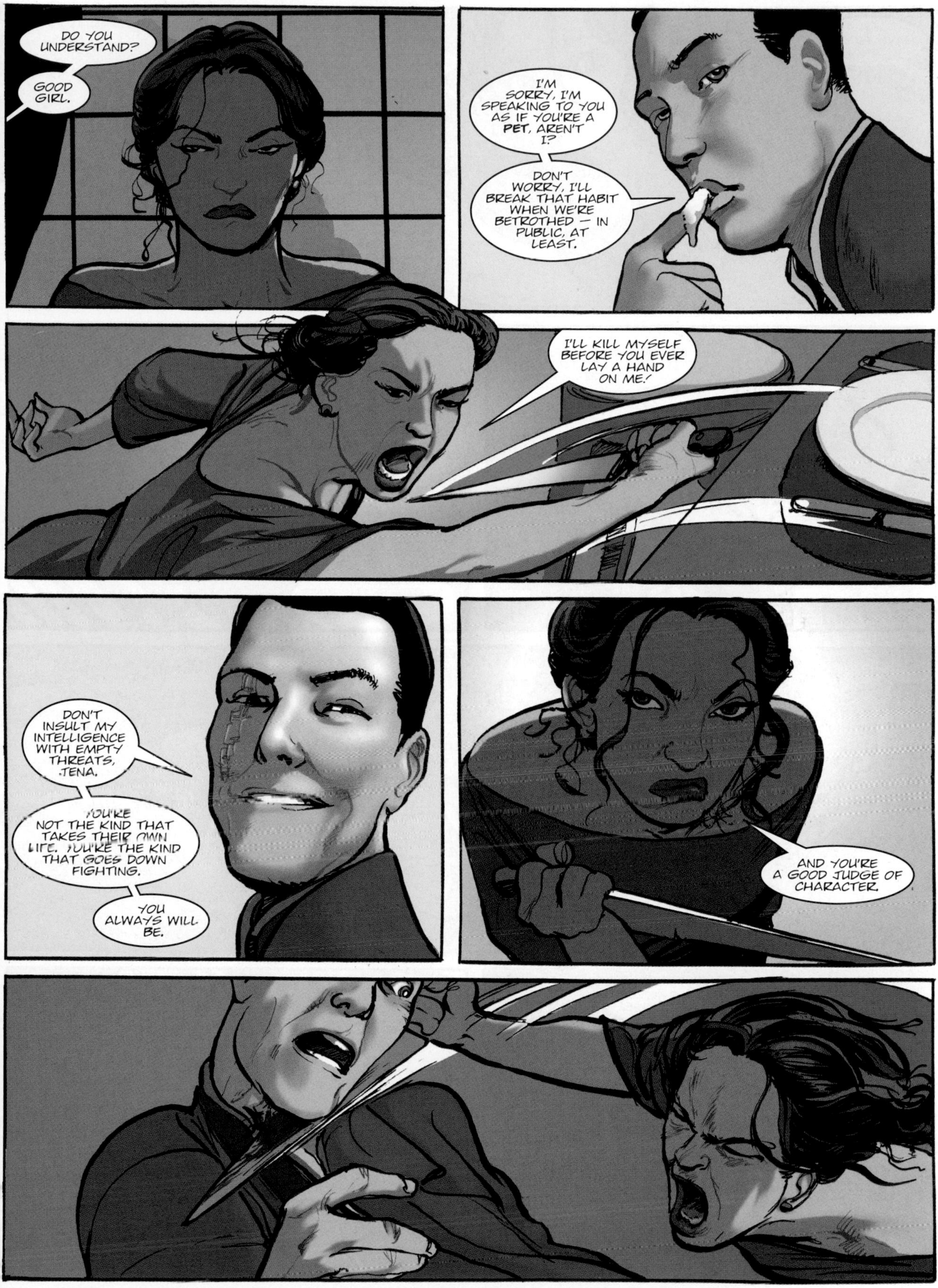
DO YOU UNDERSTAND?
GOOD GIRL.
I'M SORRY, I'M SPEAKING TO YOU AS IF YOU'RE A PET, AREN'T I?
DON'T WORRY, I'LL BREAK THAT HABIT WHEN WE'RE BETROTHED — IN PUBLIC, AT LEAST.
I'LL KILL MYSELF BEFORE YOU EVER LAY A HAND ON ME!
DON'T INSULT MY INTELLIGENCE WITH EMPTY THREATS, TENA.
YOU'RE NOT THE KIND THAT TAKES THEIR OWN LIFE. YOU'RE THE KIND THAT GOES DOWN FIGHTING.
YOU ALWAYS WILL BE.
AND YOU'RE A GOOD JUDGE OF CHARACTER.

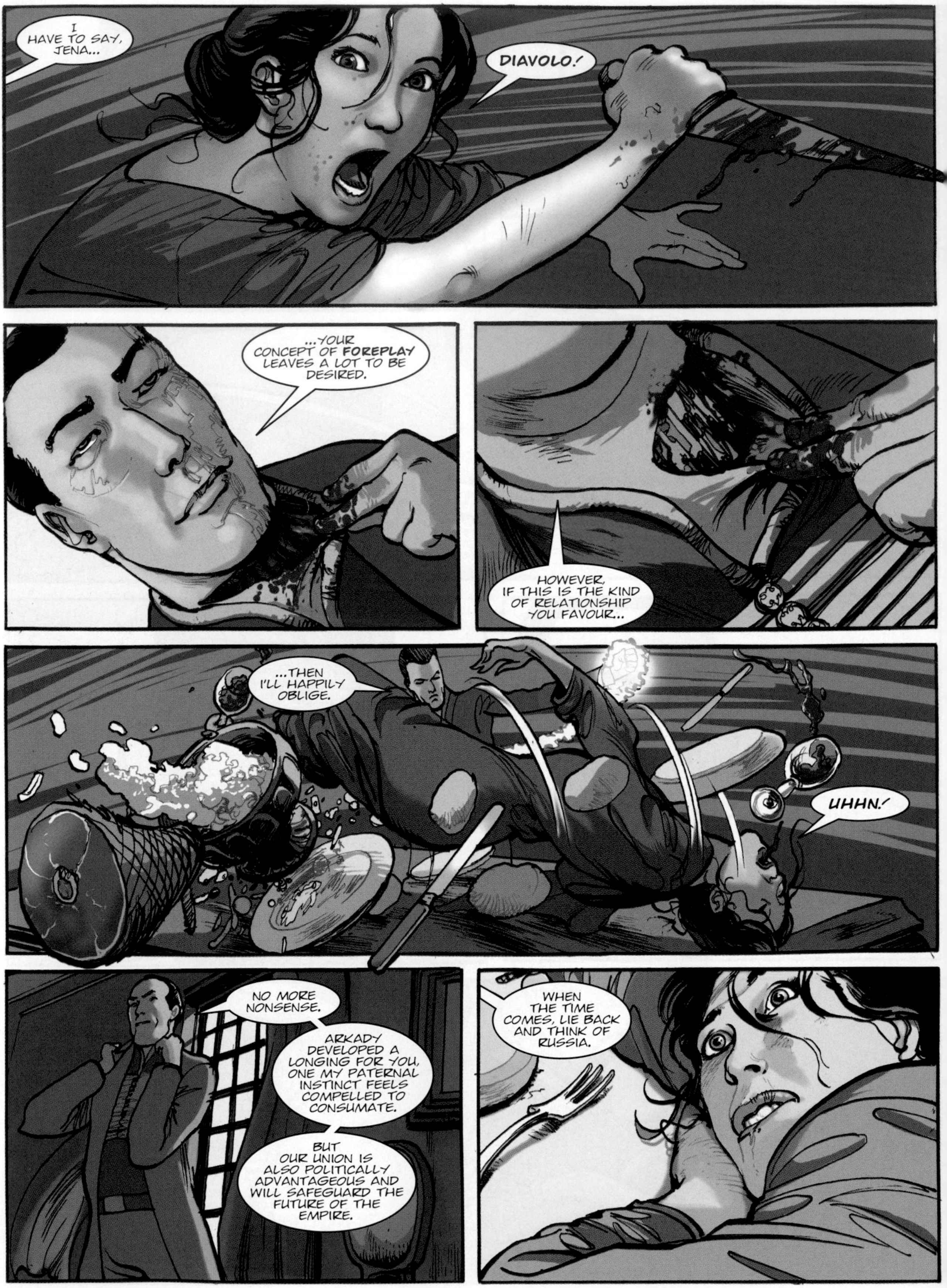

I HAVE TO SAY, JENA...
DIAVOLO.!
...YOUR CONCEPT OF FOREPLAY LEAVES A LOT TO BE DESIRED.
HOWEVER, IF THIS IS THE KIND OF RELATIONSHIP YOU FAVOUR...
...THEN I'LL HAPPILY OBLIGE.
UHHN.!
NO MORE NONSENSE.
ARKADY DEVELOPED A LONGING FOR YOU, ONE MY PATERNAL INSTINCT FEELS COMPELLED TO CONSUMATE.
BUT OUR UNION IS ALSO POLITICALLY ADVANTAGEOUS AND WILL SAFEGUARD THE FUTURE OF THE EMPIRE.
WHEN THE TIME COMES, LIE BACK AND THINK OF RUSSIA.

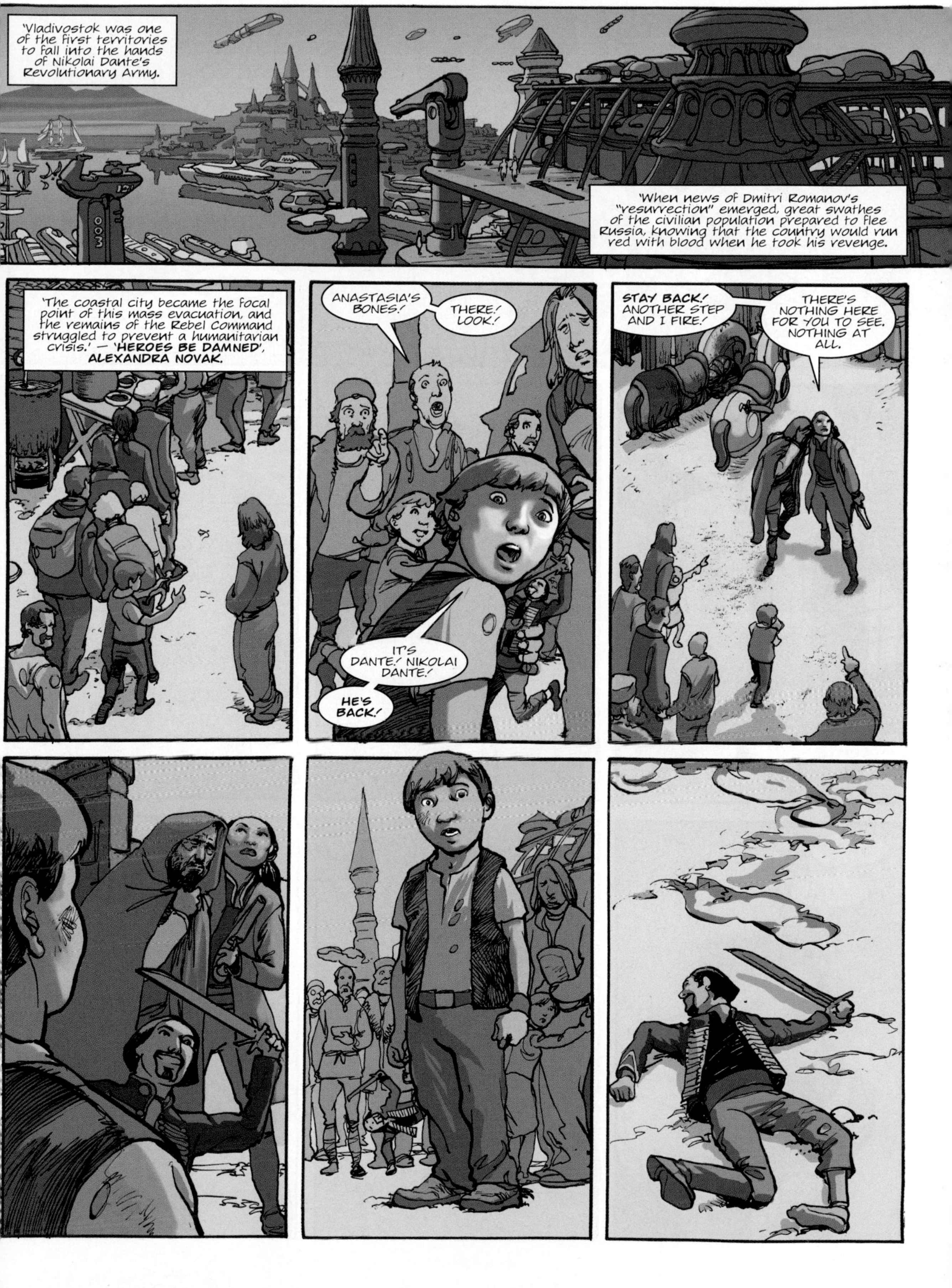
'Vladivostok was one of the first territories to fall into the hands of Nikolai Dante's Revolutionary Army.
'When news of Dmitri Romanov's "resurrection" emerged, great swathes of the civilian population prepared to flee Russia, knowing that the country would run red with blood when he took his revenge.
'The coastal city became the focal point of this mass evacuation, and the remains of the Rebel Command struggled to prevent a humanitarian crisis.' — '**HEROES BE DAMNED**', **ALEXANDRA NOVAK.**
ANASTASIA'S BONES!
THERE! LOOK!
IT'S DANTE! NIKOLAI DANTE!
HE'S BACK!
STAY BACK! ANOTHER STEP AND I FIRE!
THERE'S NOTHING HERE FOR YOU TO SEE. NOTHING AT ALL.

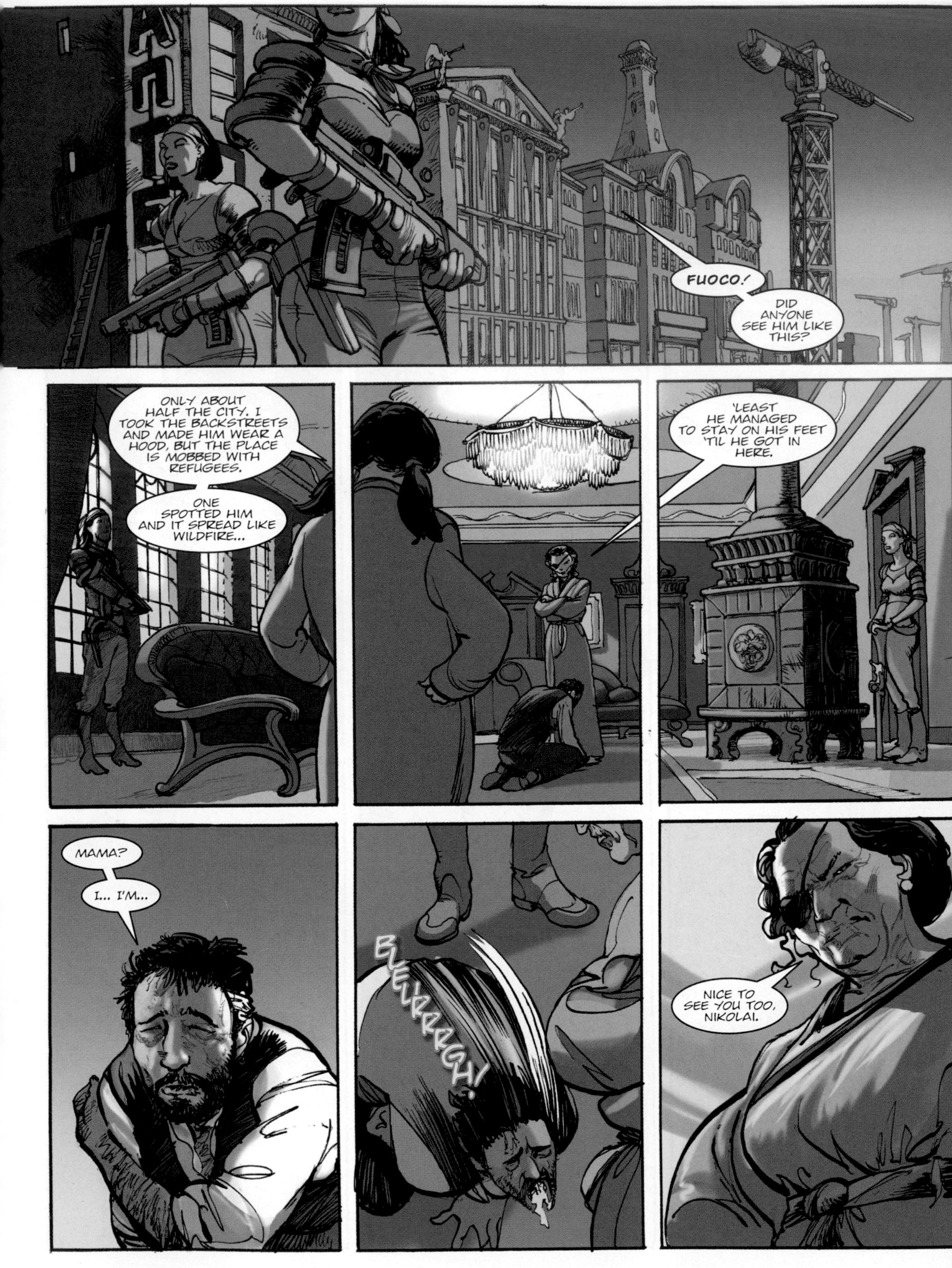
FUOCO!
DID ANYONE SEE HIM LIKE THIS?
ONLY ABOUT HALF THE CITY. I TOOK THE BACKSTREETS AND MADE HIM WEAR A HOOD, BUT THE PLACE IS MOBBED WITH REFUGEES.
ONE SPOTTED HIM AND IT SPREAD LIKE WILDFIRE...
'LEAST HE MANAGED TO STAY ON HIS FEET 'TIL HE GOT IN HERE.
MAMA?
I... I'M...
BLEURRRGH!
NICE TO SEE YOU TOO, NIKOLAI.

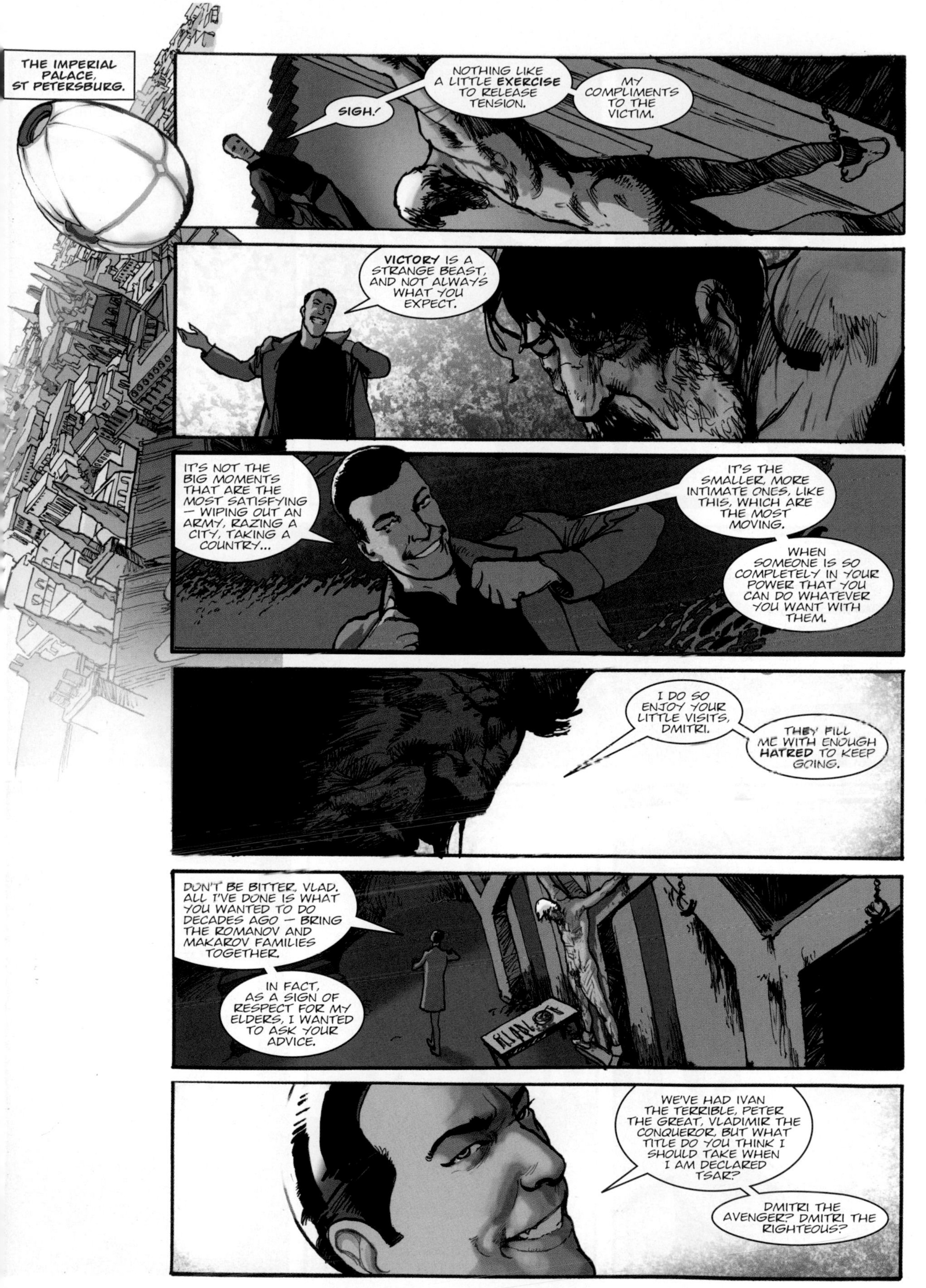

THE IMPERIAL PALACE, ST PETERSBURG.
SIGH!
NOTHING LIKE A LITTLE **EXERCISE** TO RELEASE TENSION.
MY COMPLIMENTS TO THE VICTIM.
VICTORY IS A STRANGE BEAST, AND NOT ALWAYS WHAT YOU EXPECT.
IT'S NOT THE BIG MOMENTS THAT ARE THE MOST SATISFYING — WIPING OUT AN ARMY, RAZING A CITY, TAKING A COUNTRY...
IT'S THE SMALLER, MORE INTIMATE ONES, LIKE THIS, WHICH ARE THE MOST MOVING.
WHEN SOMEONE IS SO COMPLETELY IN YOUR POWER THAT YOU CAN DO WHATEVER YOU WANT WITH THEM.
I DO SO ENJOY YOUR LITTLE VISITS, DMITRI.
THEY FILL ME WITH ENOUGH **HATRED** TO KEEP GOING.
DON'T BE BITTER, VLAD. ALL I'VE DONE IS WHAT YOU WANTED TO DO DECADES AGO — BRING THE ROMANOV AND MAKAROV FAMILIES TOGETHER.
IN FACT, AS A SIGN OF RESPECT FOR MY ELDERS, I WANTED TO ASK YOUR ADVICE.
WE'VE HAD IVAN THE TERRIBLE, PETER THE GREAT, VLADIMIR THE CONQUEROR, BUT WHAT TITLE DO YOU THINK I SHOULD TAKE WHEN I AM DECLARED TSAR?
DMITRI THE AVENGER? DMITRI THE RIGHTEOUS?

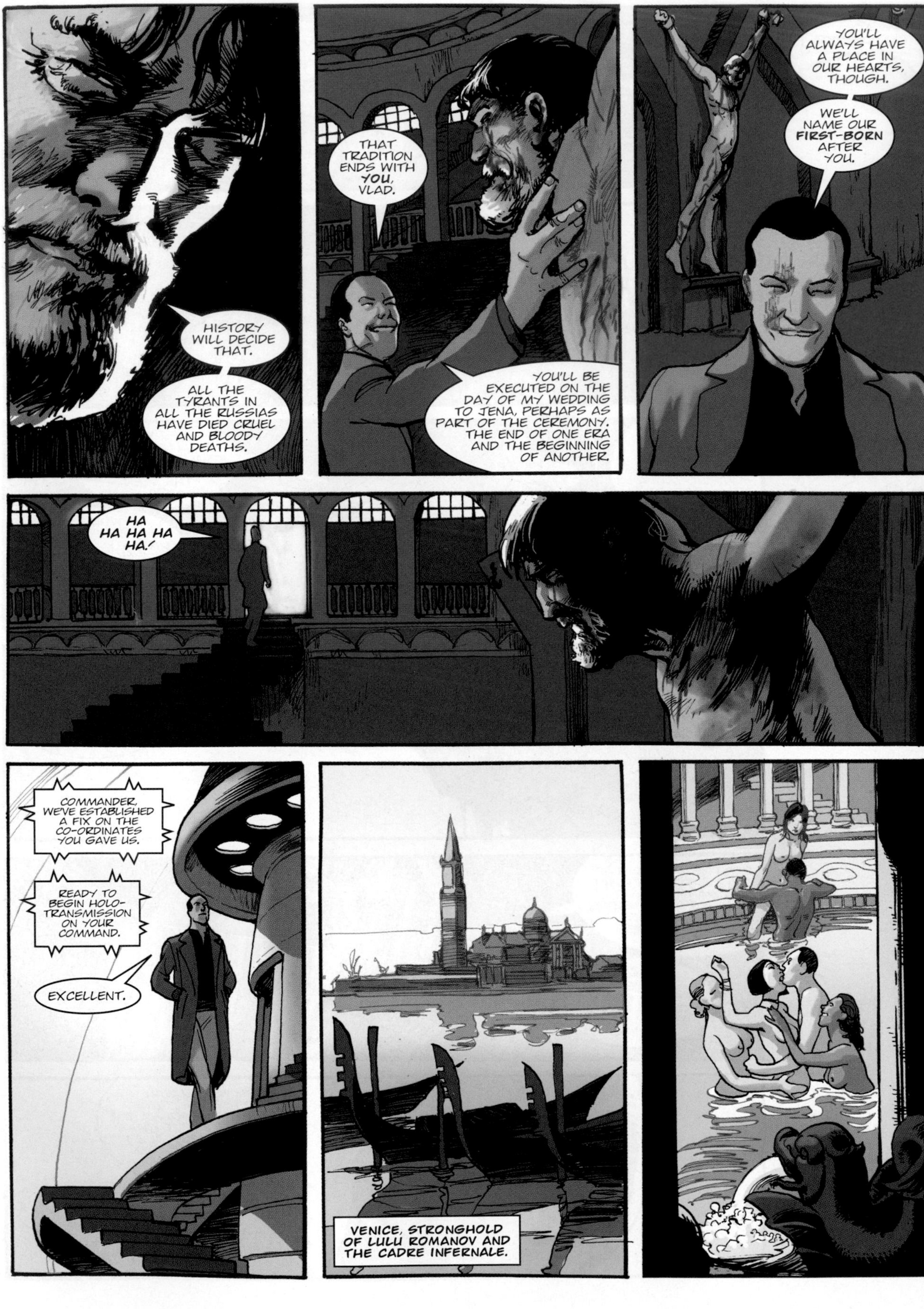
HISTORY WILL DECIDE THAT.
ALL THE TYRANTS IN ALL THE RUSSIAS HAVE DIED CRUEL AND BLOODY DEATHS.
THAT TRADITION ENDS WITH YOU, VLAD.
YOU'LL BE EXECUTED ON THE DAY OF MY WEDDING TO JENA, PERHAPS AS PART OF THE CEREMONY. THE END OF ONE ERA AND THE BEGINNING OF ANOTHER.
YOU'LL ALWAYS HAVE A PLACE IN OUR HEARTS, THOUGH.
WE'LL NAME OUR FIRST-BORN AFTER YOU.
HA HA HA HA HA!
COMMANDER. WE'VE ESTABLISHED A FIX ON THE CO-ORDINATES YOU GAVE US.
READY TO BEGIN HOLO-TRANSMISSION ON YOUR COMMAND.
EXCELLENT.
VENICE, STRONGHOLD OF LULU ROMANOV AND THE CADRE INFERNALE.

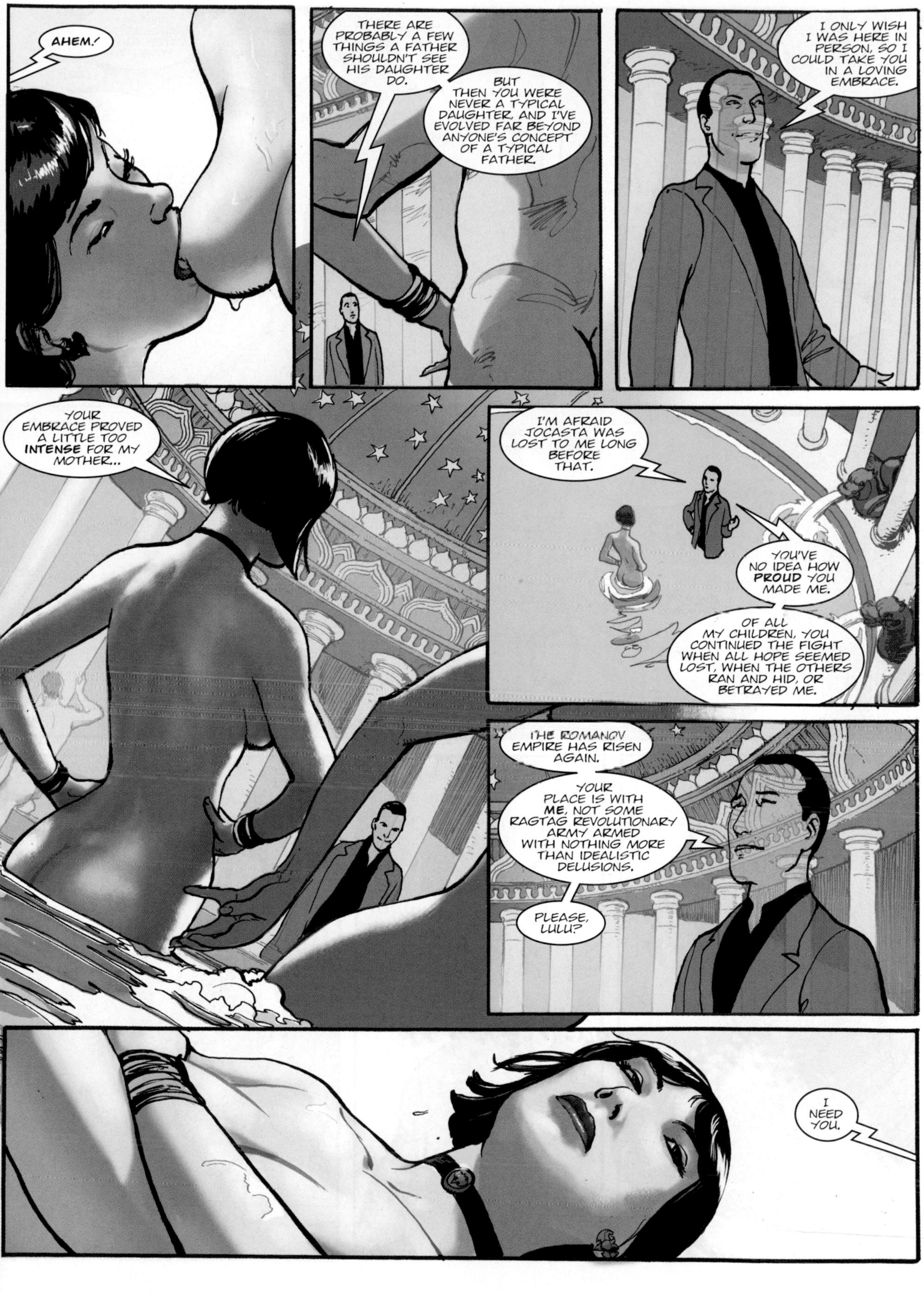
AHEM!
THERE ARE PROBABLY A FEW THINGS A FATHER SHOULDN'T SEE HIS DAUGHTER DO.
BUT THEN YOU WERE NEVER A TYPICAL DAUGHTER, AND I'VE EVOLVED FAR BEYOND ANYONE'S CONCEPT OF A TYPICAL FATHER.
I ONLY WISH I WAS HERE IN PERSON, SO I COULD TAKE YOU IN A LOVING EMBRACE.
YOUR EMBRACE PROVED A LITTLE TOO INTENSE FOR MY MOTHER...
I'M AFRAID JOCASTA WAS LOST TO ME LONG BEFORE THAT.
YOU'VE NO IDEA HOW PROUD YOU MADE ME.
OF ALL MY CHILDREN, YOU CONTINUED THE FIGHT WHEN ALL HOPE SEEMED LOST, WHEN THE OTHERS RAN AND HID, OR BETRAYED ME.
THE ROMANOV EMPIRE HAS RISEN AGAIN.
YOUR PLACE IS WITH ME, NOT SOME RAGTAG REVOLUTIONARY ARMY ARMED WITH NOTHING MORE THAN IDEALISTIC DELUSIONS.
PLEASE, LULU?
I NEED YOU.

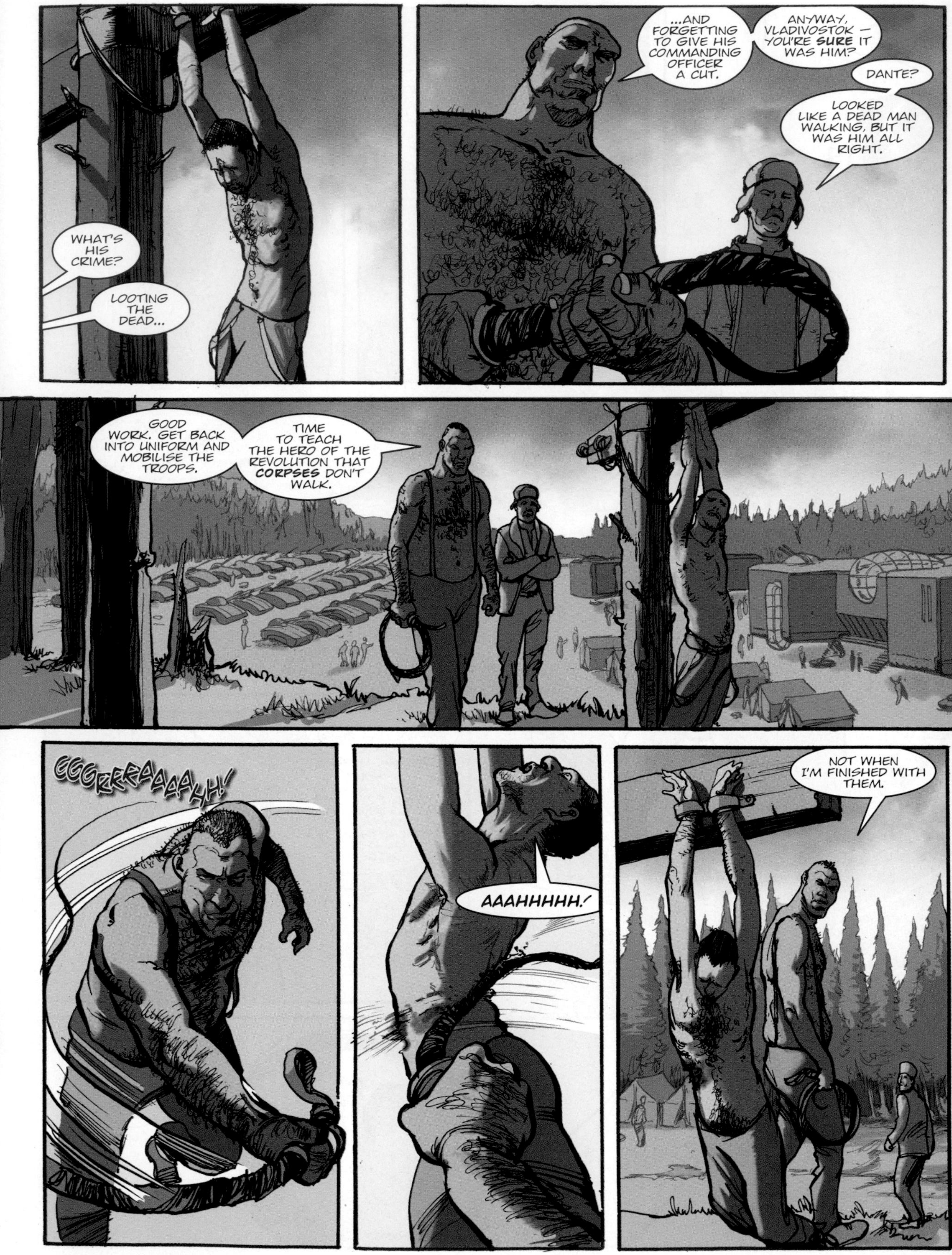
WHAT'S HIS CRIME?
LOOTING THE DEAD...
...AND FORGETTING TO GIVE HIS COMMANDING OFFICER A CUT.
ANYWAY, VLADIVOSTOK — YOU'RE SURE IT WAS HIM?
DANTE?
LOOKED LIKE A DEAD MAN WALKING, BUT IT WAS HIM ALL RIGHT.
GOOD WORK. GET BACK INTO UNIFORM AND MOBILISE THE TROOPS.
TIME TO TEACH THE HERO OF THE REVOLUTION THAT CORPSES DON'T WALK.
EEGRRRAAAAHH!
AAAHHHHH!
NOT WHEN I'M FINISHED WITH THEM.

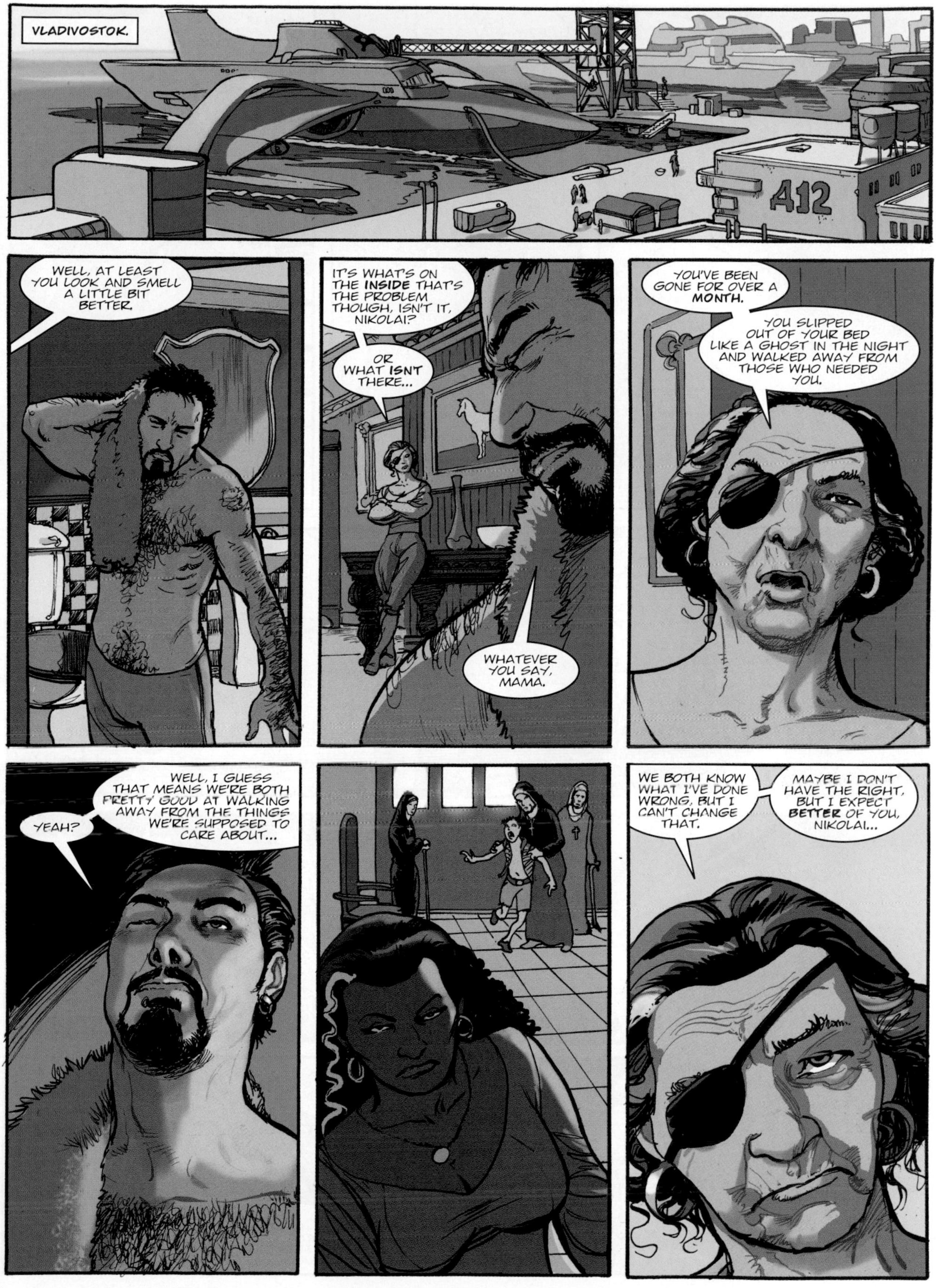
VLADIVOSTOK.
A12
WELL, AT LEAST YOU LOOK AND SMELL A LITTLE BIT BETTER.
IT'S WHAT'S ON THE **INSIDE** THAT'S THE PROBLEM THOUGH, ISN'T IT, NIKOLAI?
OR WHAT **ISN'T** THERE...
WHATEVER YOU SAY, MAMA.
YOU'VE BEEN GONE FOR OVER A **MONTH**.
YOU SLIPPED OUT OF YOUR BED LIKE A GHOST IN THE NIGHT AND WALKED AWAY FROM THOSE WHO NEEDED YOU.
YEAH?
WELL, I GUESS THAT MEANS WE'RE BOTH PRETTY GOOD AT WALKING AWAY FROM THE THINGS WE'RE SUPPOSED TO CARE ABOUT...
WE BOTH KNOW WHAT I'VE DONE WRONG, BUT I CAN'T CHANGE THAT.
MAYBE I DON'T HAVE THE RIGHT, BUT I EXPECT **BETTER** OF YOU, NIKOLAI...

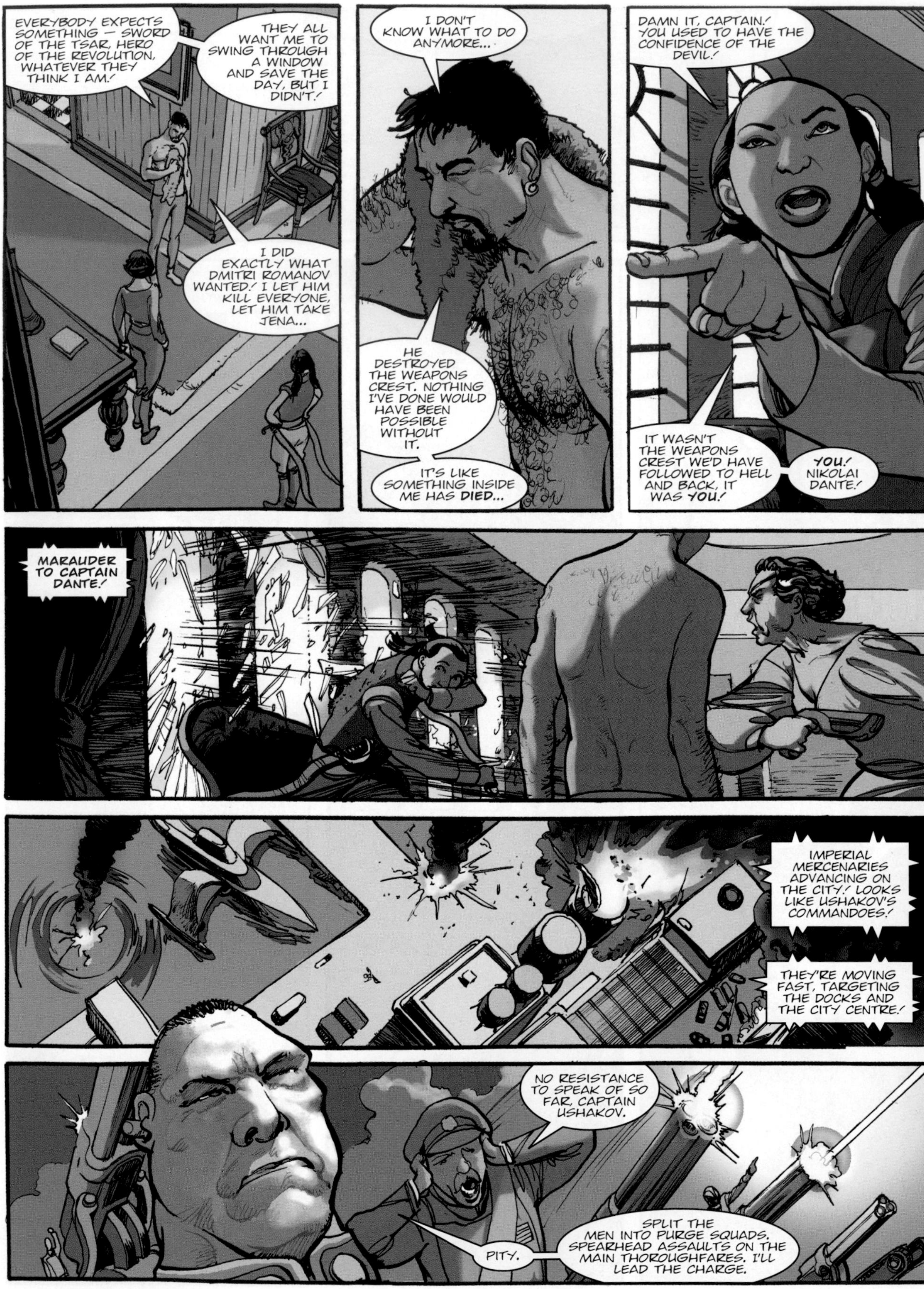
EVERYBODY EXPECTS SOMETHING — SWORD OF THE TSAR, HERO OF THE REVOLUTION, WHATEVER THEY THINK I AM!
THEY ALL WANT ME TO SWING THROUGH A WINDOW AND SAVE THE DAY, BUT I DIDN'T!
I DID EXACTLY WHAT DMITRI ROMANOV WANTED! I LET HIM KILL EVERYONE, LET HIM TAKE JENA...
I DON'T KNOW WHAT TO DO ANYMORE...
HE DESTROYED THE WEAPONS CREST. NOTHING I'VE DONE WOULD HAVE BEEN POSSIBLE WITHOUT IT.
IT'S LIKE SOMETHING INSIDE ME HAS DIED...
DAMN IT, CAPTAIN! YOU USED TO HAVE THE CONFIDENCE OF THE DEVIL!
IT WASN'T THE WEAPONS CREST WE'D HAVE FOLLOWED TO HELL AND BACK, IT WAS YOU!
YOU! NIKOLAI DANTE!
MARAUDER TO CAPTAIN DANTE!
IMPERIAL MERCENARIES ADVANCING ON THE CITY! LOOKS LIKE USHAKOV'S COMMANDOES!
THEY'RE MOVING FAST, TARGETING THE DOCKS AND THE CITY CENTRE!
NO RESISTANCE TO SPEAK OF SO FAR, CAPTAIN USHAKOV.
PITY.
SPLIT THE MEN INTO PURGE SQUADS. SPEARHEAD ASSAULTS ON THE MAIN THOROUGHFARES. I'LL LEAD THE CHARGE.

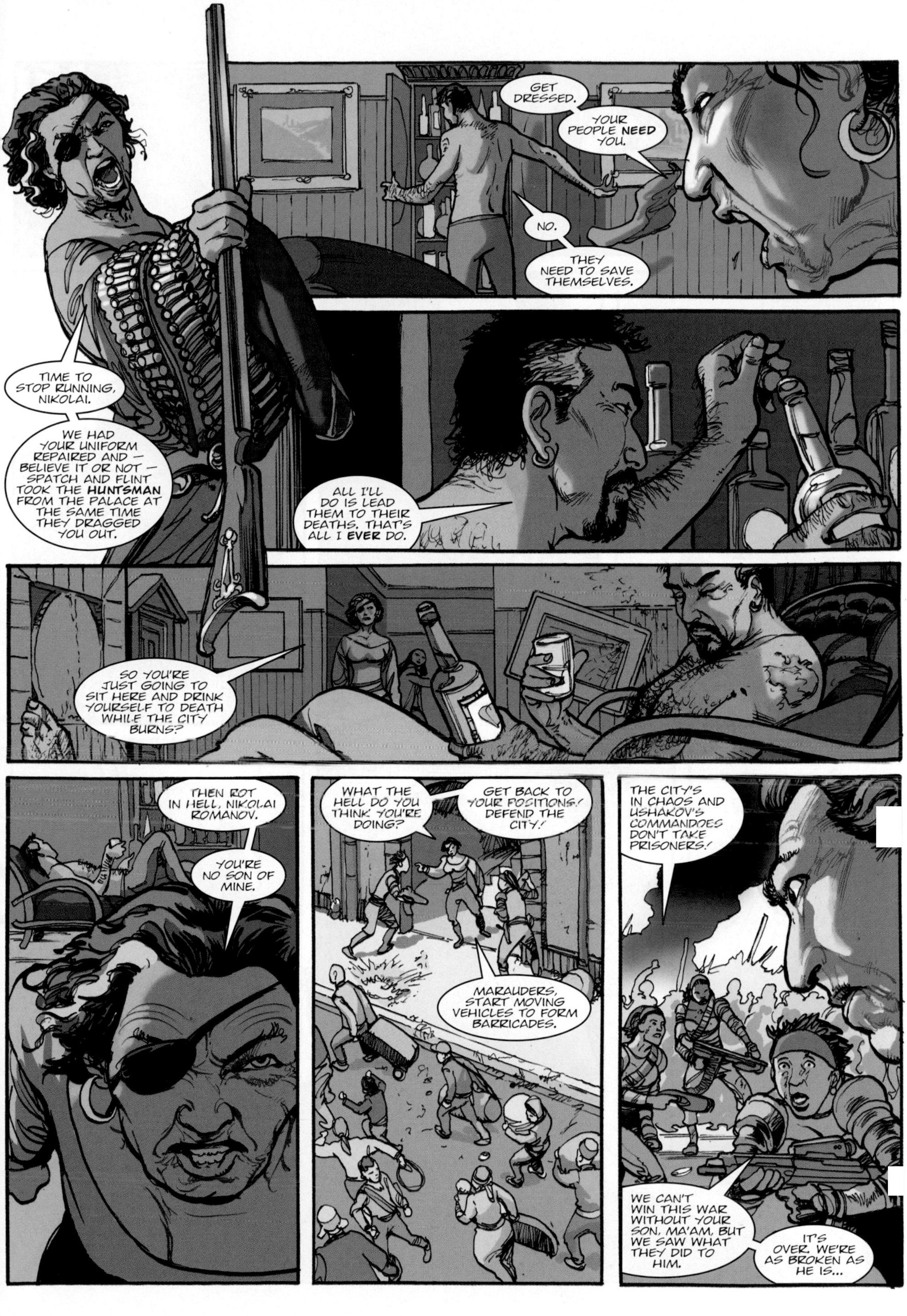
GET DRESSED.
YOUR PEOPLE NEED YOU.
NO.
THEY NEED TO SAVE THEMSELVES.
TIME TO STOP RUNNING, NIKOLAI.
WE HAD YOUR UNIFORM REPAIRED AND — BELIEVE IT OR NOT — SPATCH AND FLINT TOOK THE HUNTSMAN FROM THE PALACE AT THE SAME TIME THEY DRAGGED YOU OUT.
ALL I'LL DO IS LEAD THEM TO THEIR DEATHS. THAT'S ALL I EVER DO.
SO YOU'RE JUST GOING TO SIT HERE AND DRINK YOURSELF TO DEATH WHILE THE CITY BURNS?
THEN ROT IN HELL, NIKOLAI ROMANOV.
YOU'RE NO SON OF MINE.
WHAT THE HELL DO YOU THINK YOU'RE DOING?
GET BACK TO YOUR POSITIONS! DEFEND THE CITY!
MARAUDERS, START MOVING VEHICLES TO FORM BARRICADES.
THE CITY'S IN CHAOS AND USHAKOV'S COMMANDOES DON'T TAKE PRISONERS!
WE CAN'T WIN THIS WAR WITHOUT YOUR SON, MA'AM, BUT WE SAW WHAT THEY DID TO HIM.
IT'S OVER. WE'RE AS BROKEN AS HE IS...

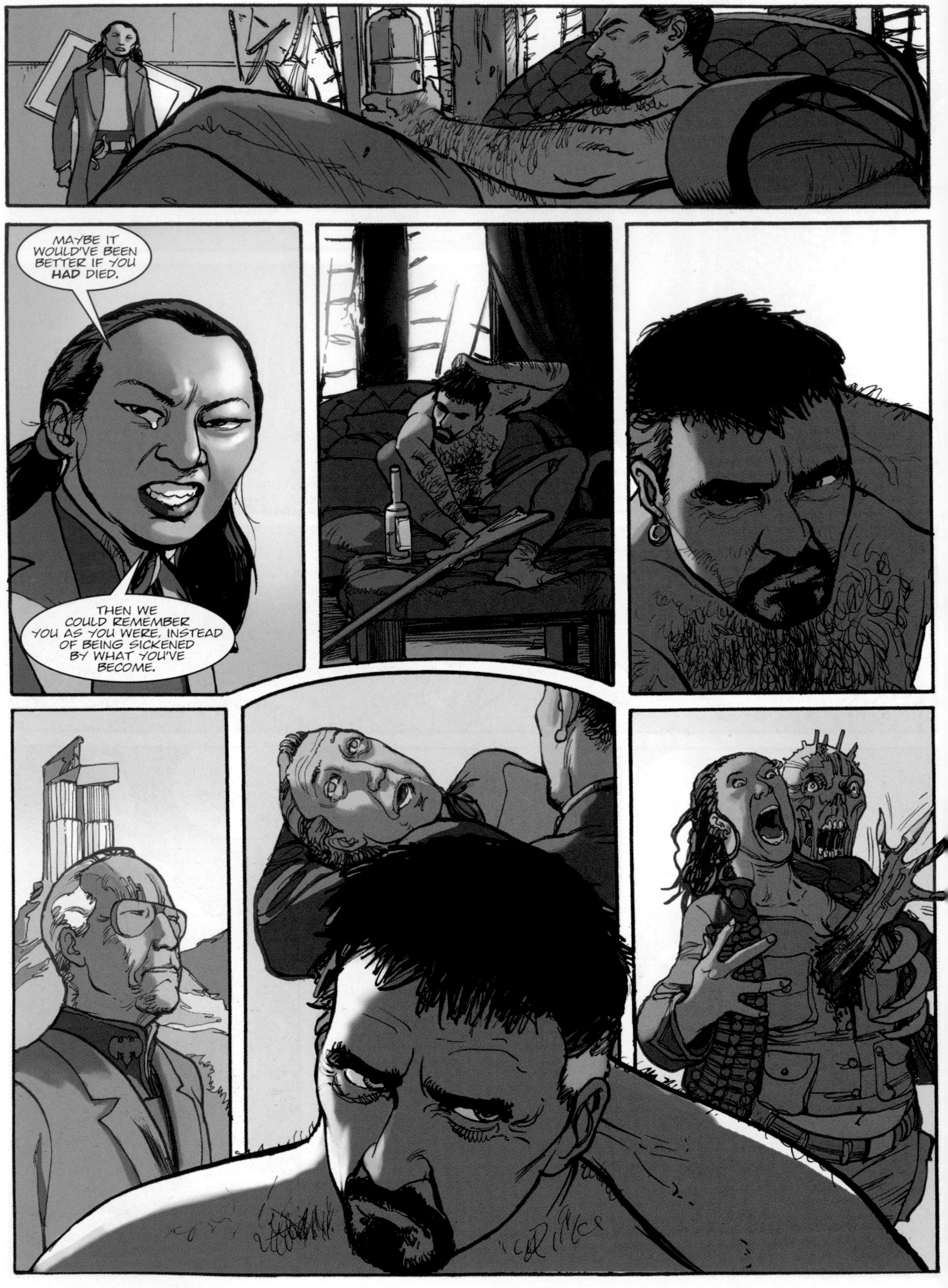
MAYBE IT WOULD'VE BEEN BETTER IF YOU **HAD** DIED.
THEN WE COULD REMEMBER YOU AS YOU WERE, INSTEAD OF BEING SICKENED BY WHAT YOU'VE BECOME.

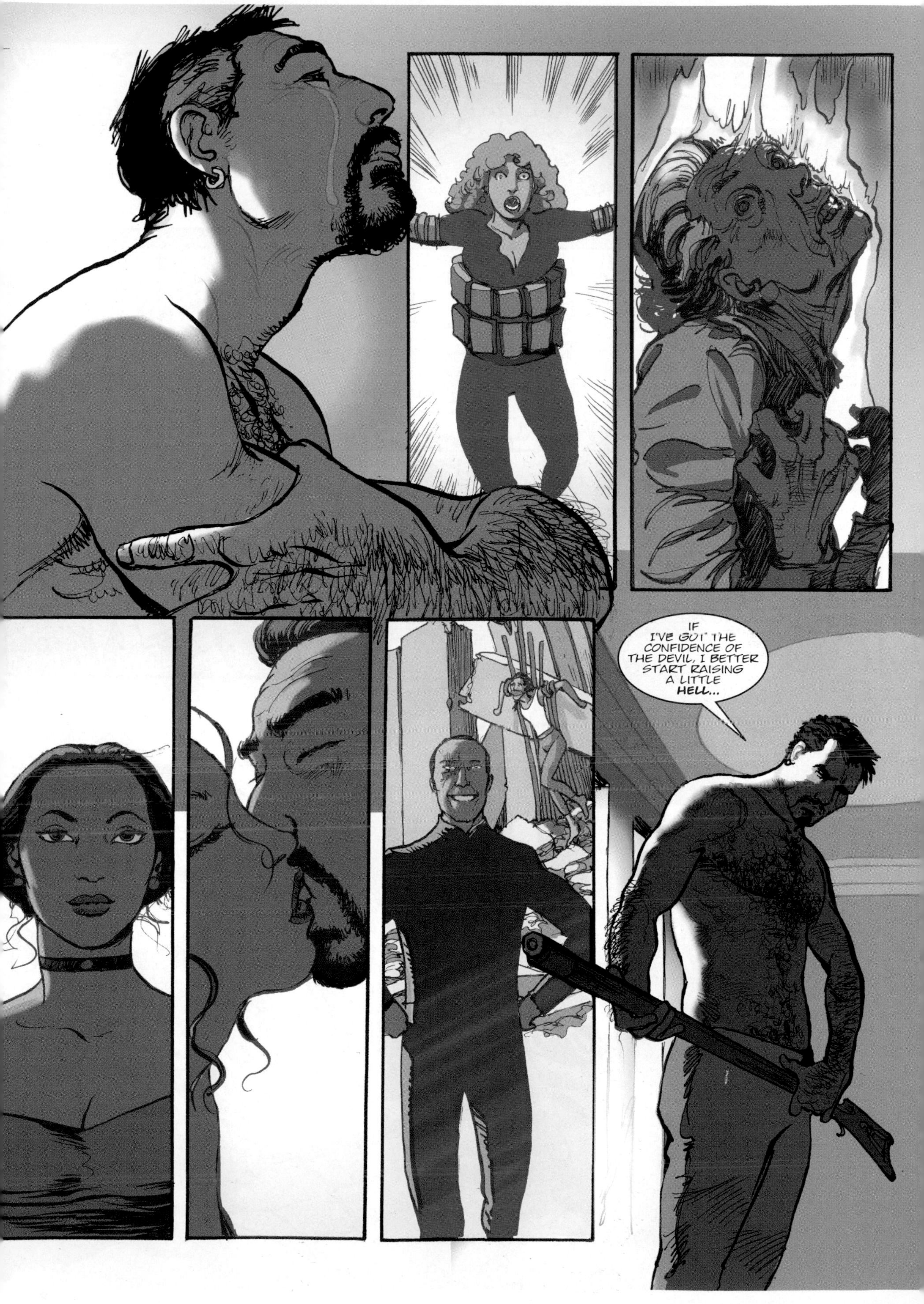
IF I'VE GOT THE CONFIDENCE OF THE DEVIL, I BETTER START RAISING A LITTLE **HELL...**

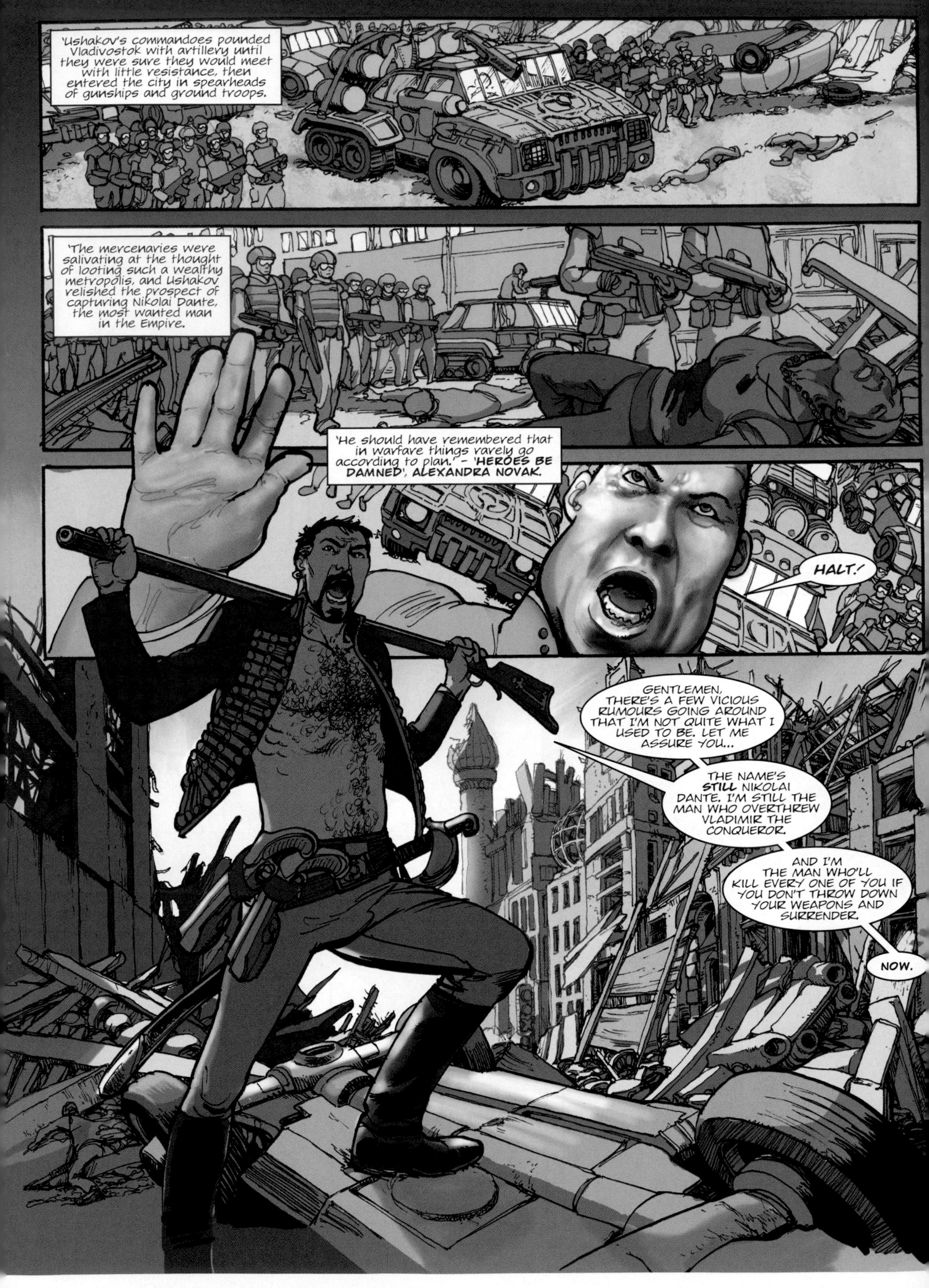
'Ushakov's commandoes pounded Vladivostok with artillery until they were sure they would meet with little resistance, then entered the city in spearheads of gunships and ground troops.
'The mercenaries were salivating at the thought of looting such a wealthy metropolis, and Ushakov relished the prospect of capturing Nikolai Dante, the most wanted man in the Empire.
'He should have remembered that in warfare things rarely go according to plan.' – 'HEROES BE DAMNED', ALEXANDRA NOVAK.
HALT!
GENTLEMEN, THERE'S A FEW VICIOUS RUMOURS GOING AROUND THAT I'M NOT QUITE WHAT I USED TO BE. LET ME ASSURE YOU...
THE NAME'S STILL NIKOLAI DANTE. I'M STILL THE MAN WHO OVERTHREW VLADIMIR THE CONQUEROR.
AND I'M THE MAN WHO'LL KILL EVERY ONE OF YOU IF YOU DON'T THROW DOWN YOUR WEAPONS AND SURRENDER.
NOW.

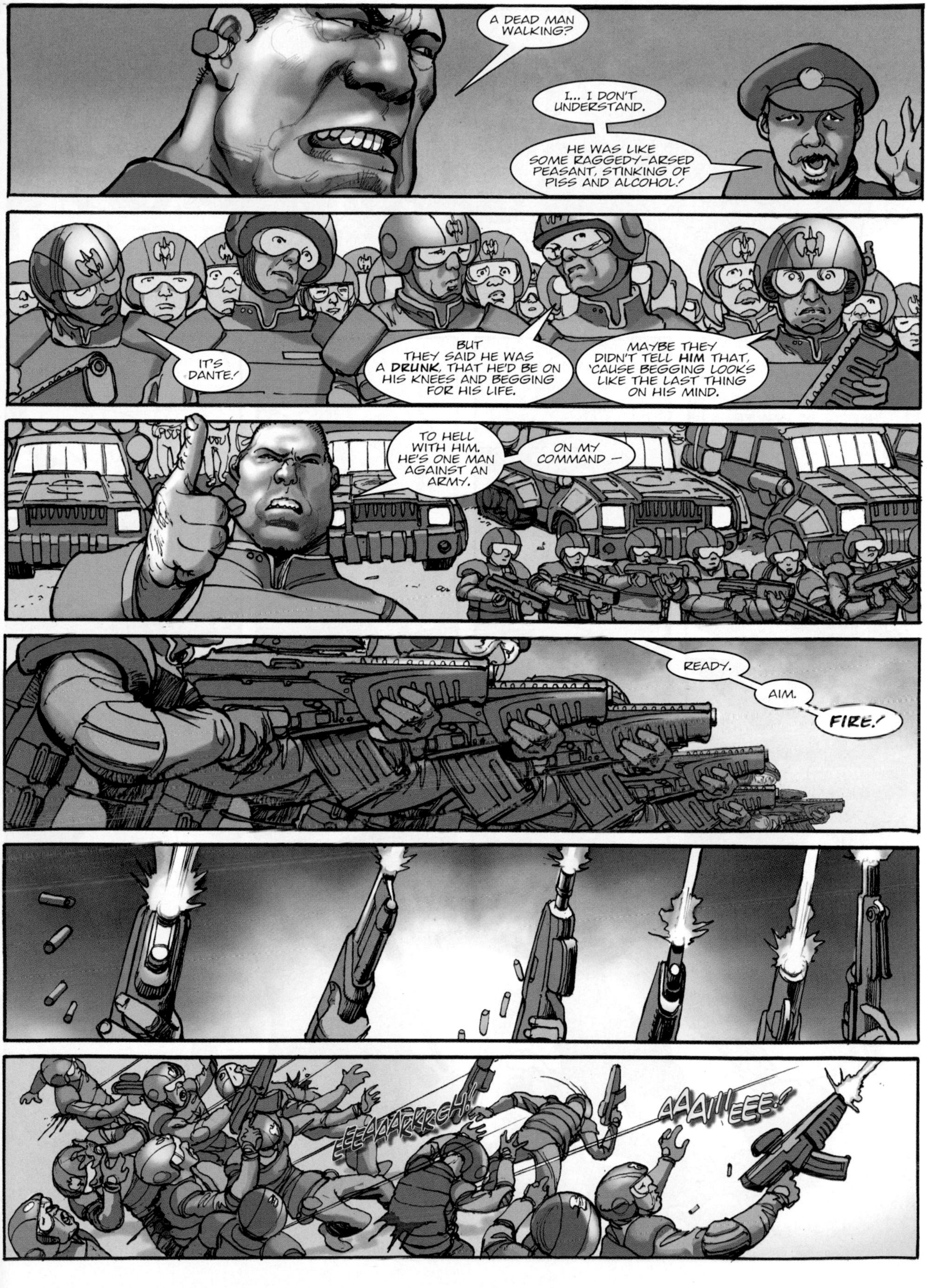
A DEAD MAN WALKING?
I... I DON'T UNDERSTAND.
HE WAS LIKE SOME RAGGEDY-ARSED PEASANT, STINKING OF PISS AND ALCOHOL!
IT'S DANTE!
BUT THEY SAID HE WAS A DRUNK, THAT HE'D BE ON HIS KNEES AND BEGGING FOR HIS LIFE.
MAYBE THEY DIDN'T TELL HIM THAT, 'CAUSE BEGGING LOOKS LIKE THE LAST THING ON HIS MIND.
TO HELL WITH HIM. HE'S ONE MAN AGAINST AN ARMY.
ON MY COMMAND —
READY.
AIM.
FIRE!
EEEAAARRRGH!
AAAIIIEEE!

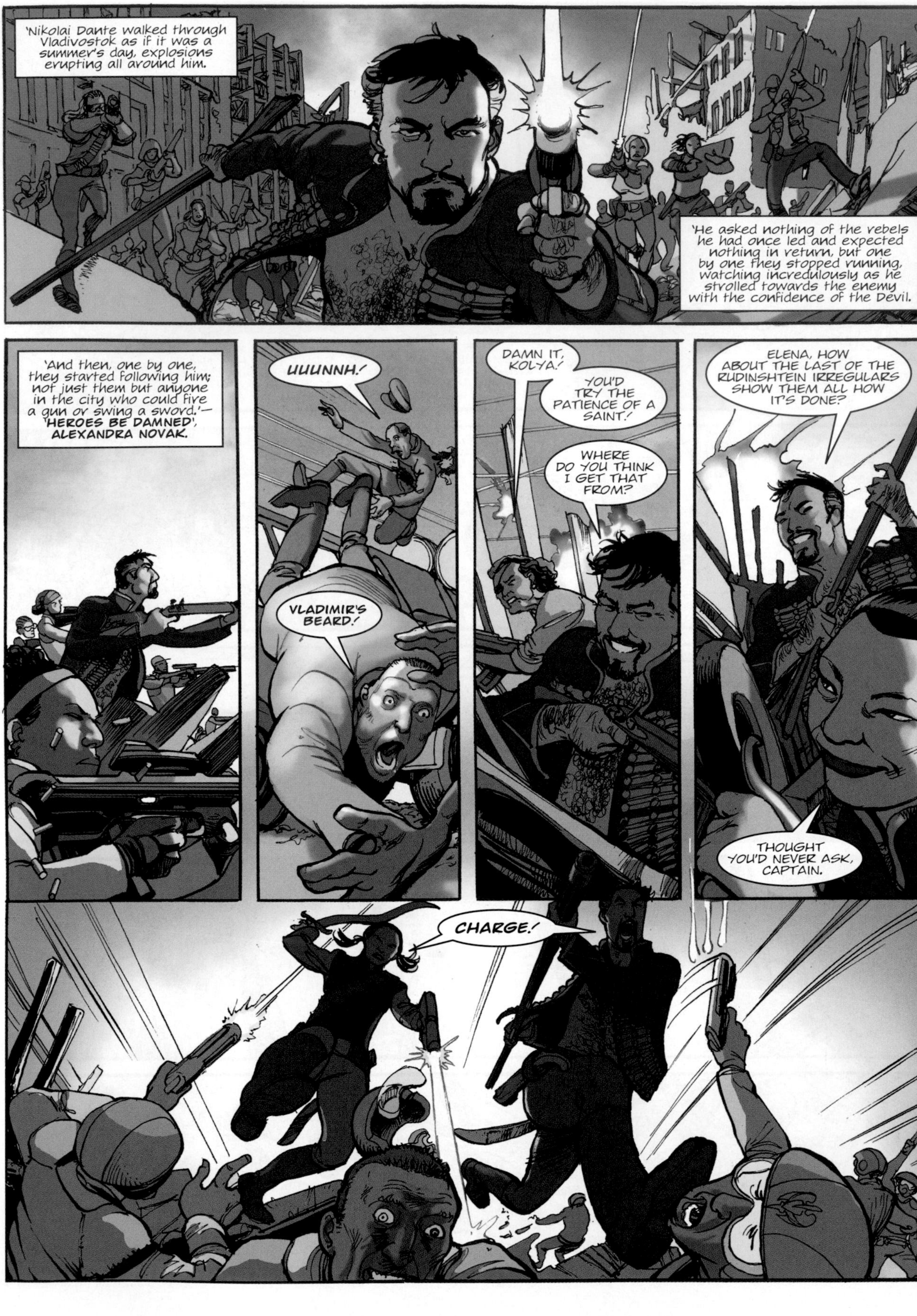
'Nikolai Dante walked through Vladivostok as if it was a summer's day, explosions erupting all around him.
'He asked nothing of the rebels he had once led and expected nothing in return, but one by one they stopped running, watching incredulously as he strolled towards the enemy with the confidence of the Devil.
'And then, one by one, they started following him; not just them but anyone in the city who could fire a gun or swing a sword.'— 'HEROES BE DAMNED', ALEXANDRA NOVAK.
UUUNNH!
VLADIMIR'S BEARD!
DAMN IT, KOLYA!
YOU'D TRY THE PATIENCE OF A SAINT!
WHERE DO YOU THINK I GET THAT FROM?
ELENA, HOW ABOUT THE LAST OF THE RUDINSHTEIN IRREGULARS SHOW THEM ALL HOW IT'S DONE?
THOUGHT YOU'D NEVER ASK, CAPTAIN.
CHARGE!

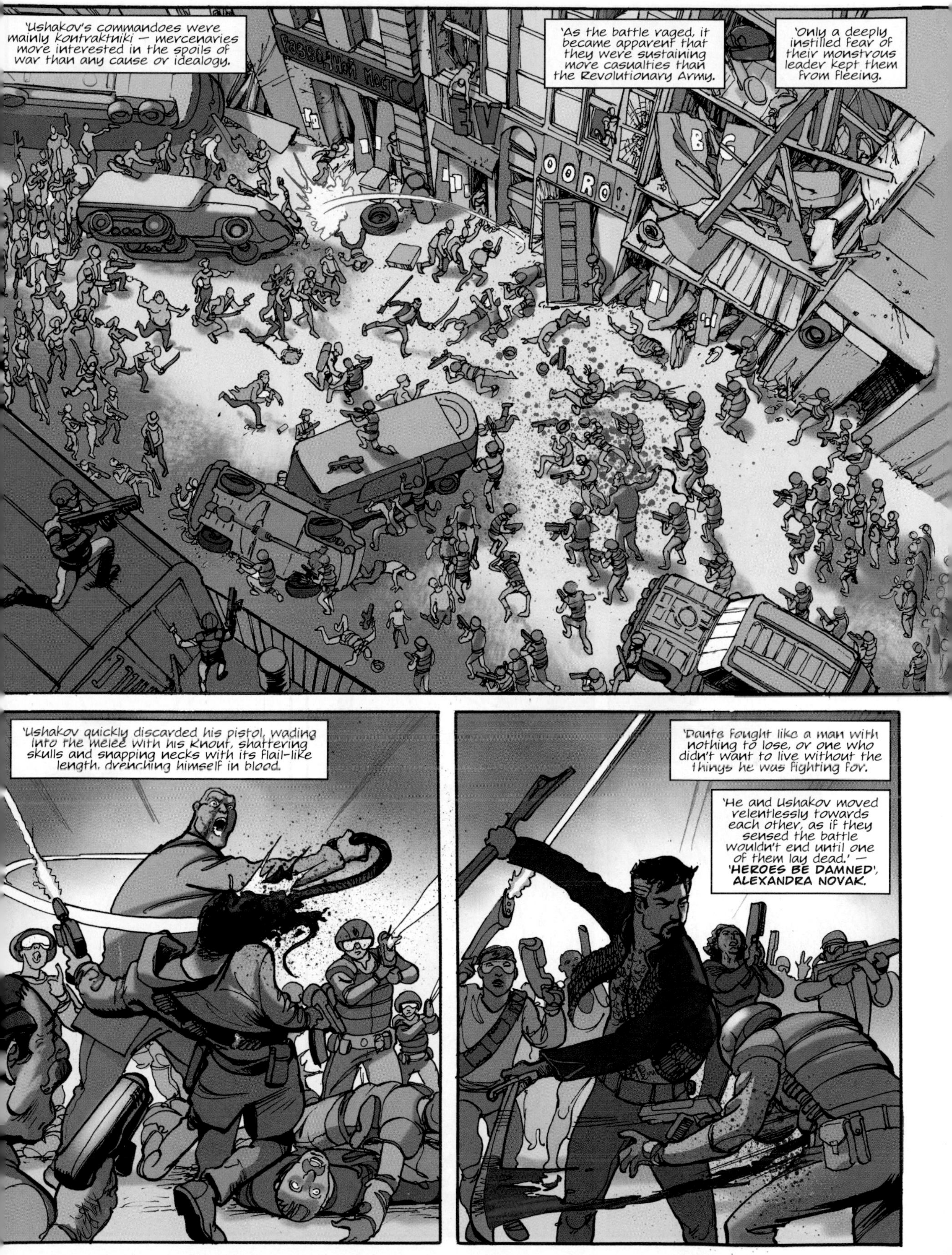
'Ushakov's commandoes were mainly kontraktniki — mercenaries more interested in the spoils of war than any cause or idealogy.
'As the battle raged, it became apparent that they were sustaining more casualties than the Revolutionary Army.
'Only a deeply instilled fear of their monstrous leader kept them from fleeing.
'Ushakov quickly discarded his pistol, wading into the melee with his knout, shattering skulls and snapping necks with its flail-like length, drenching himself in blood.
'Dante fought like a man with nothing to lose, or one who didn't want to live without the things he was fighting for.
'He and Ushakov moved relentlessly towards each other, as if they sensed the battle wouldn't end until one of them lay dead.' — 'HEROES BE DAMNED', ALEXANDRA NOVAK.

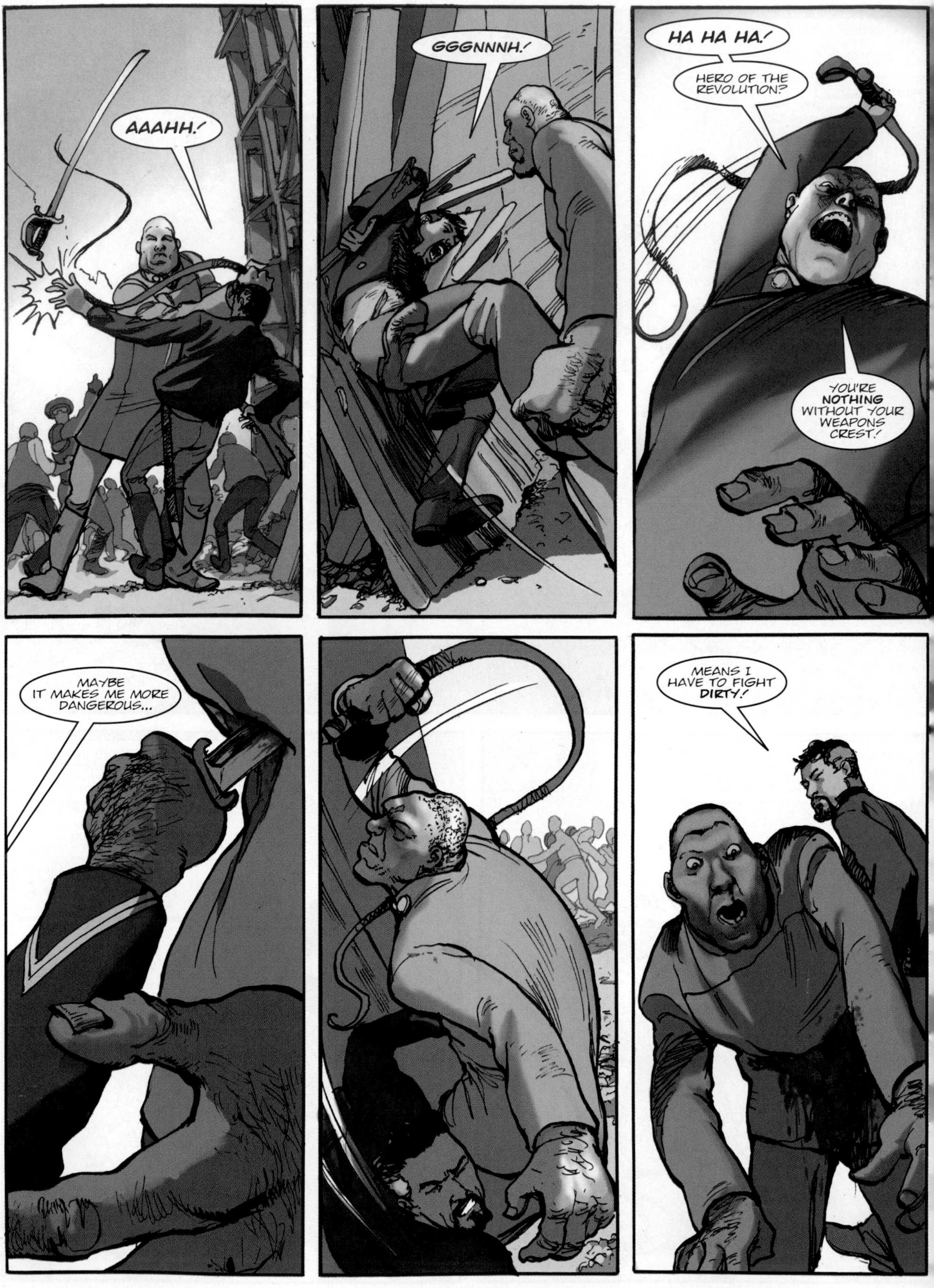
AAAHH!
GGGNNNH!
HA HA HA!
HERO OF THE REVOLUTION?
YOU'RE **NOTHING** WITHOUT YOUR WEAPONS CREST!
MAYBE IT MAKES ME MORE DANGEROUS...
MEANS I HAVE TO FIGHT **DIRTY**!

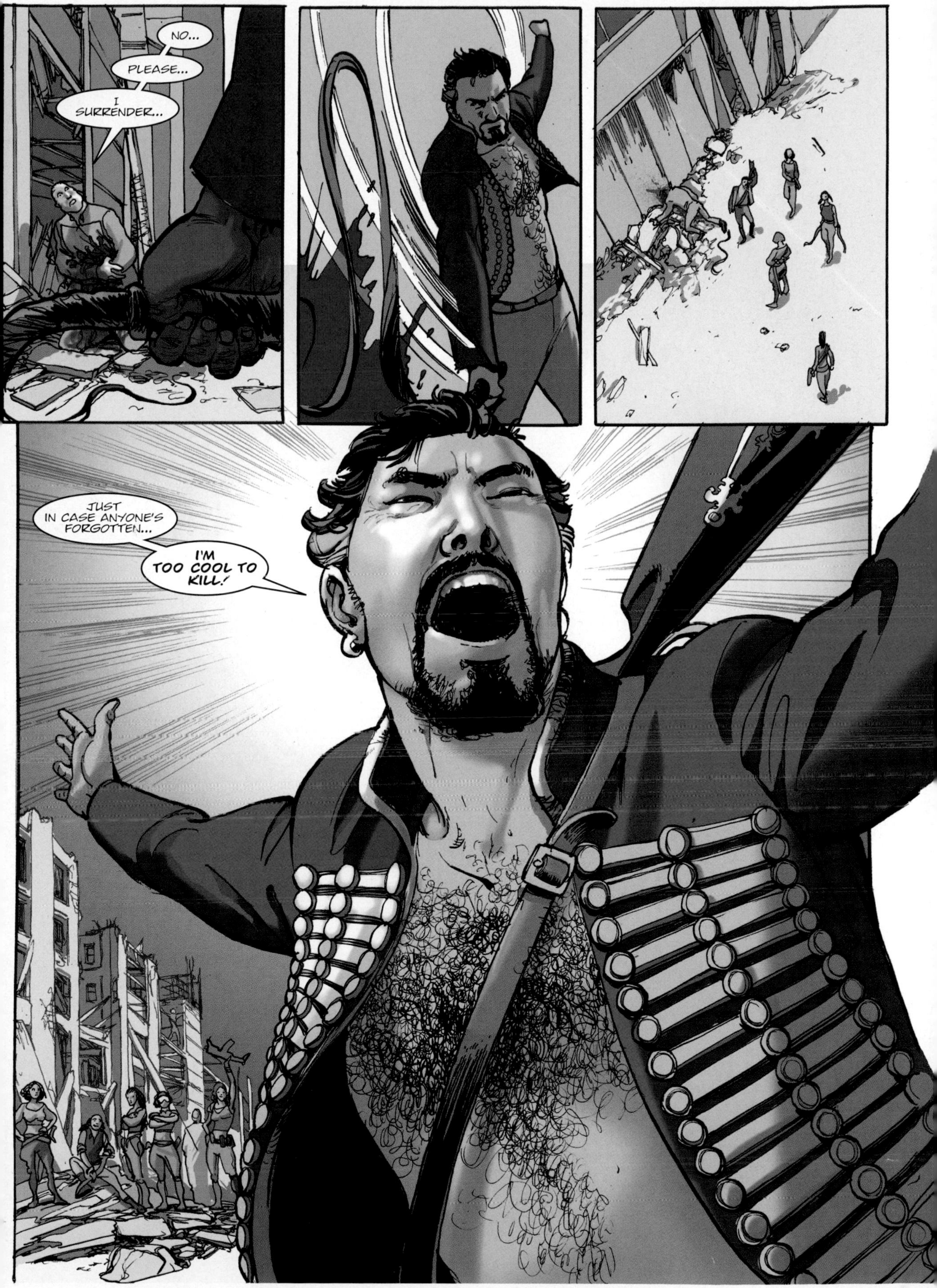
NO...
PLEASE...
I SURRENDER...
JUST IN CASE ANYONE'S FORGOTTEN...
I'M TOO COOL TO KILL!

THE MASTER OF KRONSTADT

Script: Robbie Morrison
Art: John Burns
Letters: Annie Parkhouse

Originally published in *2000 AD* Progs 1705 - 1708

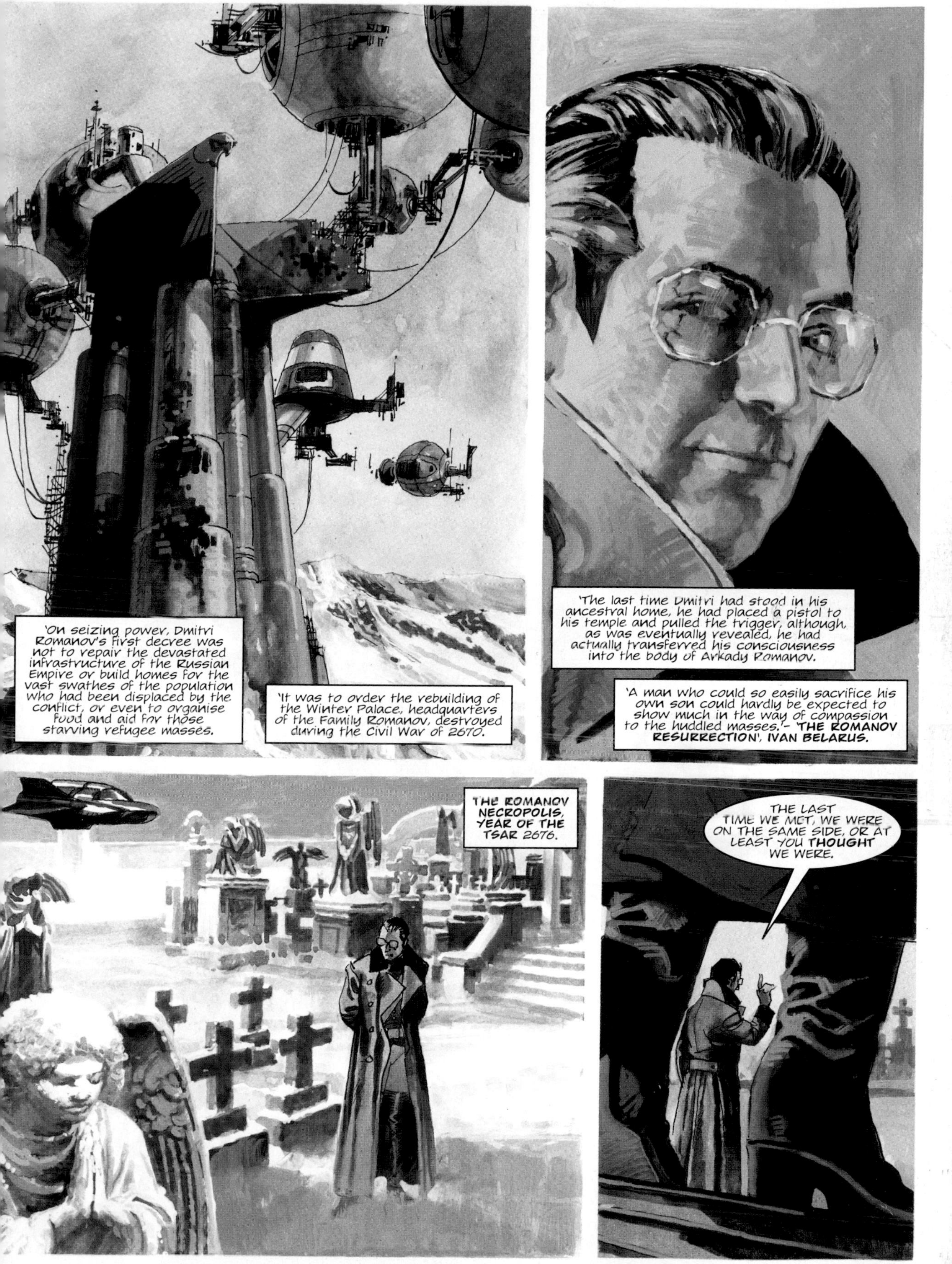
'On seizing power, Dmitri Romanov's first decree was not to repair the devastated infrastructure of the Russian Empire or build homes for the vast swathes of the population who had been displaced by the conflict, or even to organise food and aid for those starving refugee masses.
'It was to order the rebuilding of the Winter Palace, headquarters of the Family Romanov, destroyed during the Civil War of 2670.
'The last time Dmitri had stood in his ancestral home, he had placed a pistol to his temple and pulled the trigger, although, as was eventually revealed, he had actually transferred his consciousness into the body of Arkady Romanov.
'A man who could so easily sacrifice his own son could hardly be expected to show much in the way of compassion to the huddled masses.'– **'THE ROMANOV RESURRECTION', IVAN BELARUS.**
THE ROMANOV NECROPOLIS, YEAR OF THE TSAR 2676.
THE LAST TIME WE MET, WE WERE ON THE SAME SIDE, OR AT LEAST YOU **THOUGHT** WE WERE.

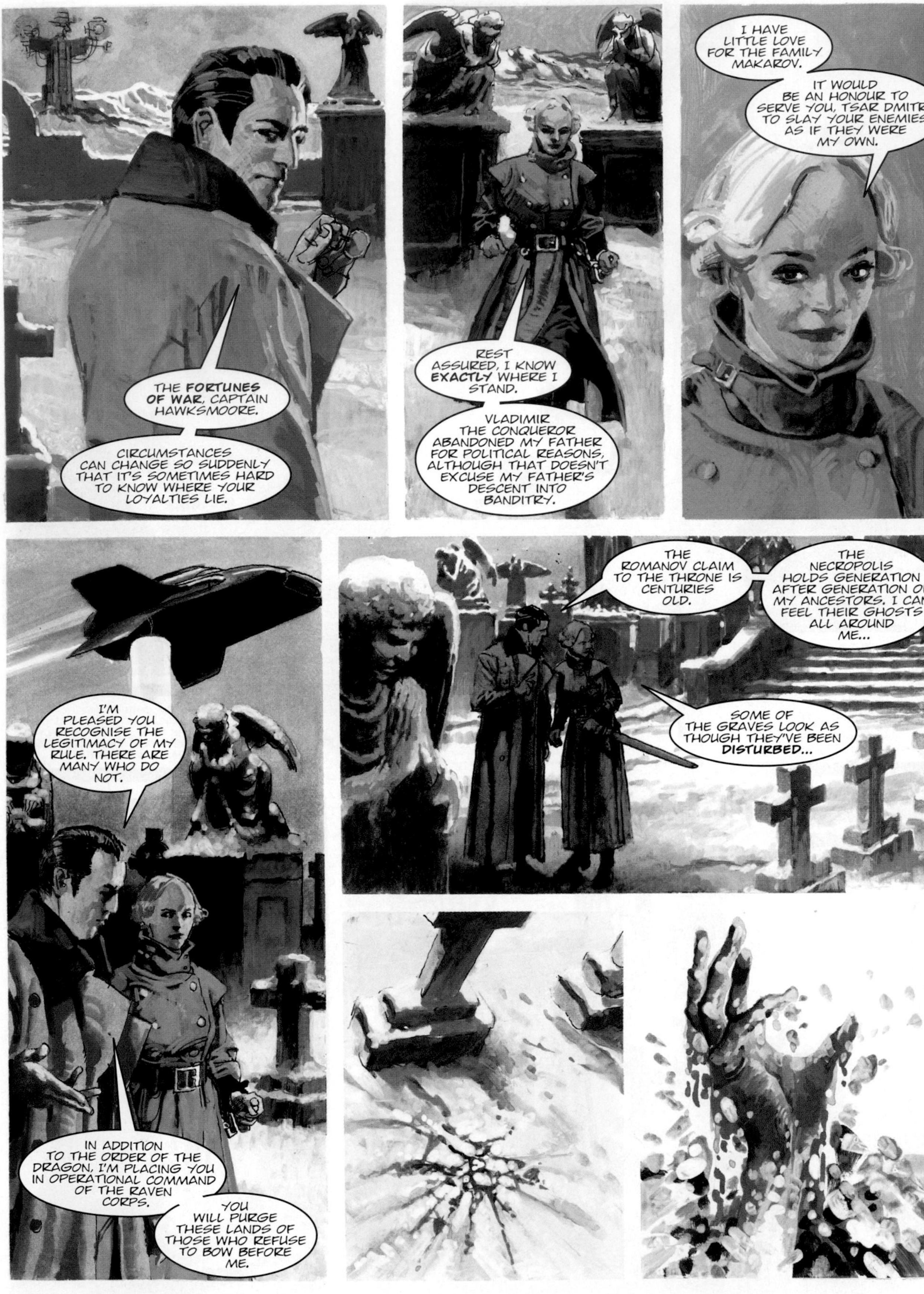

THE FORTUNES OF WAR, CAPTAIN HAWKSMOORE.
CIRCUMSTANCES CAN CHANGE SO SUDDENLY THAT IT'S SOMETIMES HARD TO KNOW WHERE YOUR LOYALTIES LIE.
REST ASSURED, I KNOW EXACTLY WHERE I STAND.
VLADIMIR THE CONQUEROR ABANDONED MY FATHER FOR POLITICAL REASONS, ALTHOUGH THAT DOESN'T EXCUSE MY FATHER'S DESCENT INTO BANDITRY.
I HAVE LITTLE LOVE FOR THE FAMILY MAKAROV.
IT WOULD BE AN HONOUR TO SERVE YOU, TSAR DMITRI, TO SLAY YOUR ENEMIES AS IF THEY WERE MY OWN.
I'M PLEASED YOU RECOGNISE THE LEGITIMACY OF MY RULE. THERE ARE MANY WHO DO NOT.
IN ADDITION TO THE ORDER OF THE DRAGON, I'M PLACING YOU IN OPERATIONAL COMMAND OF THE RAVEN CORPS.
YOU WILL PURGE THESE LANDS OF THOSE WHO REFUSE TO BOW BEFORE ME.
THE ROMANOV CLAIM TO THE THRONE IS CENTURIES OLD.
THE NECROPOLIS HOLDS GENERATION AFTER GENERATION OF MY ANCESTORS. I CAN FEEL THEIR GHOSTS ALL AROUND ME...
SOME OF THE GRAVES LOOK AS THOUGH THEY'VE BEEN DISTURBED...

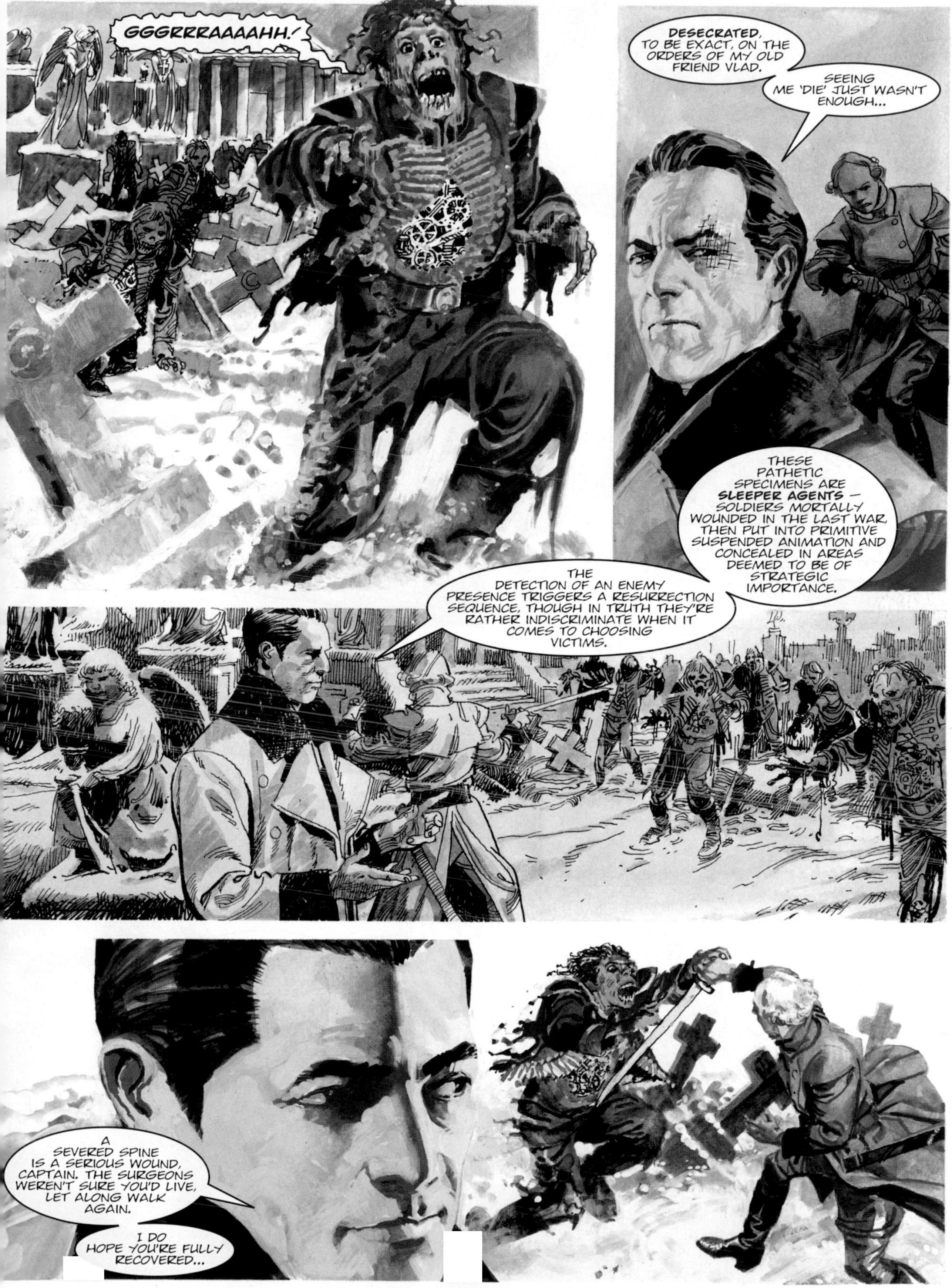
GGGRRRAAAAHH!
DESECRATED, TO BE EXACT, ON THE ORDERS OF MY OLD FRIEND VLAD.
SEEING ME 'DIE' JUST WASN'T ENOUGH...
THESE PATHETIC SPECIMENS ARE SLEEPER AGENTS — SOLDIERS MORTALLY WOUNDED IN THE LAST WAR, THEN PUT INTO PRIMITIVE SUSPENDED ANIMATION AND CONCEALED IN AREAS DEEMED TO BE OF STRATEGIC IMPORTANCE.
THE DETECTION OF AN ENEMY PRESENCE TRIGGERS A RESURRECTION SEQUENCE, THOUGH IN TRUTH THEY'RE RATHER INDISCRIMINATE WHEN IT COMES TO CHOOSING VICTIMS.
A SEVERED SPINE IS A SERIOUS WOUND, CAPTAIN. THE SURGEONS WEREN'T SURE YOU'D LIVE, LET ALONG WALK AGAIN.
I DO HOPE YOU'RE FULLY RECOVERED...

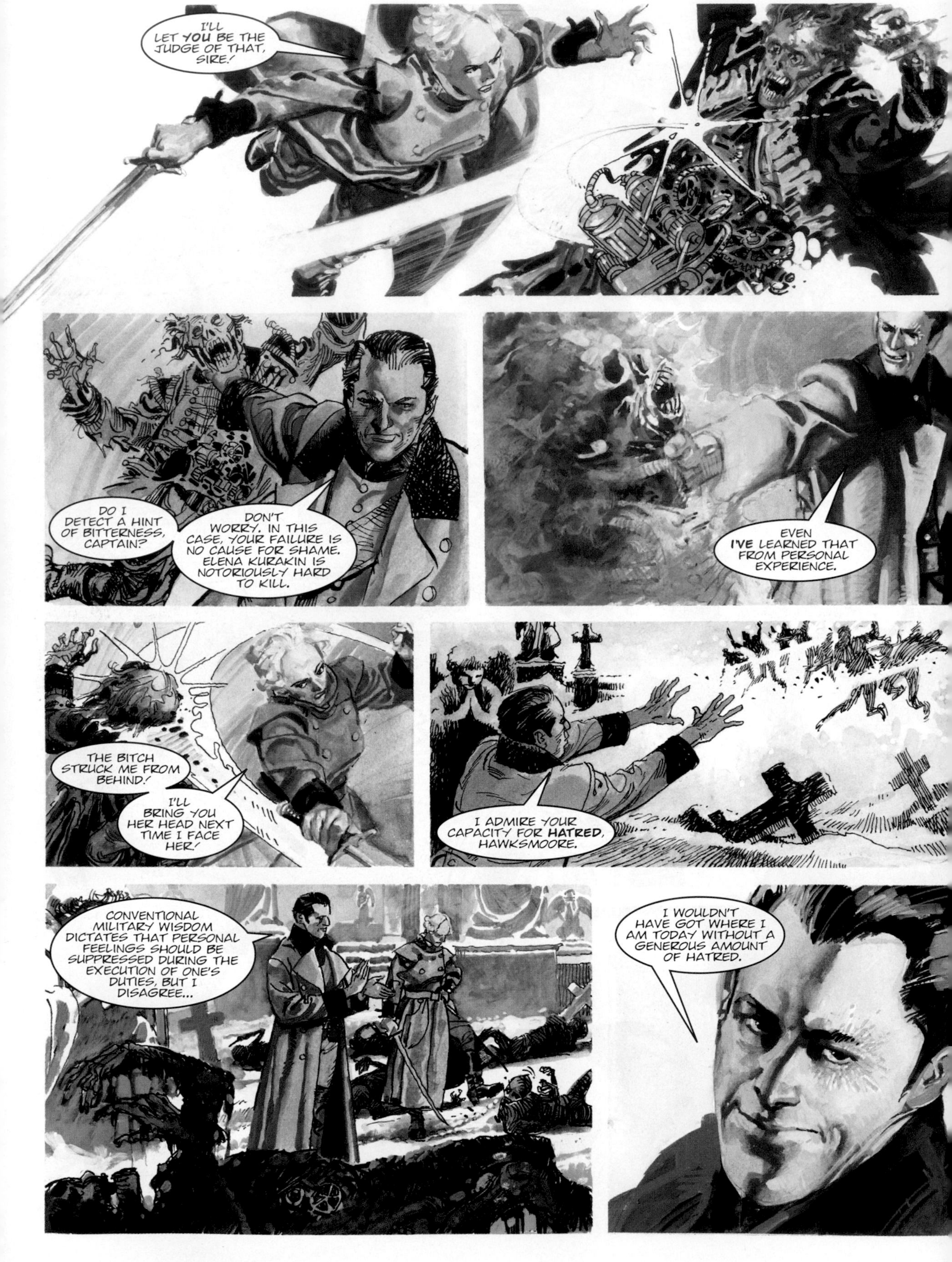
I'LL LET YOU BE THE JUDGE OF THAT, SIRE!
DO I DETECT A HINT OF BITTERNESS, CAPTAIN?
DON'T WORRY. IN THIS CASE, YOUR FAILURE IS NO CAUSE FOR SHAME. ELENA KURAKIN IS NOTORIOUSLY HARD TO KILL.
EVEN I'VE LEARNED THAT FROM PERSONAL EXPERIENCE.
THE BITCH STRUCK ME FROM BEHIND!
I'LL BRING YOU HER HEAD NEXT TIME I FACE HER!
I ADMIRE YOUR CAPACITY FOR HATRED, HAWKSMOORE.
CONVENTIONAL MILITARY WISDOM DICTATES THAT PERSONAL FEELINGS SHOULD BE SUPPRESSED DURING THE EXECUTION OF ONE'S DUTIES, BUT I DISAGREE...
I WOULDN'T HAVE GOT WHERE I AM TODAY WITHOUT A GENEROUS AMOUNT OF HATRED.

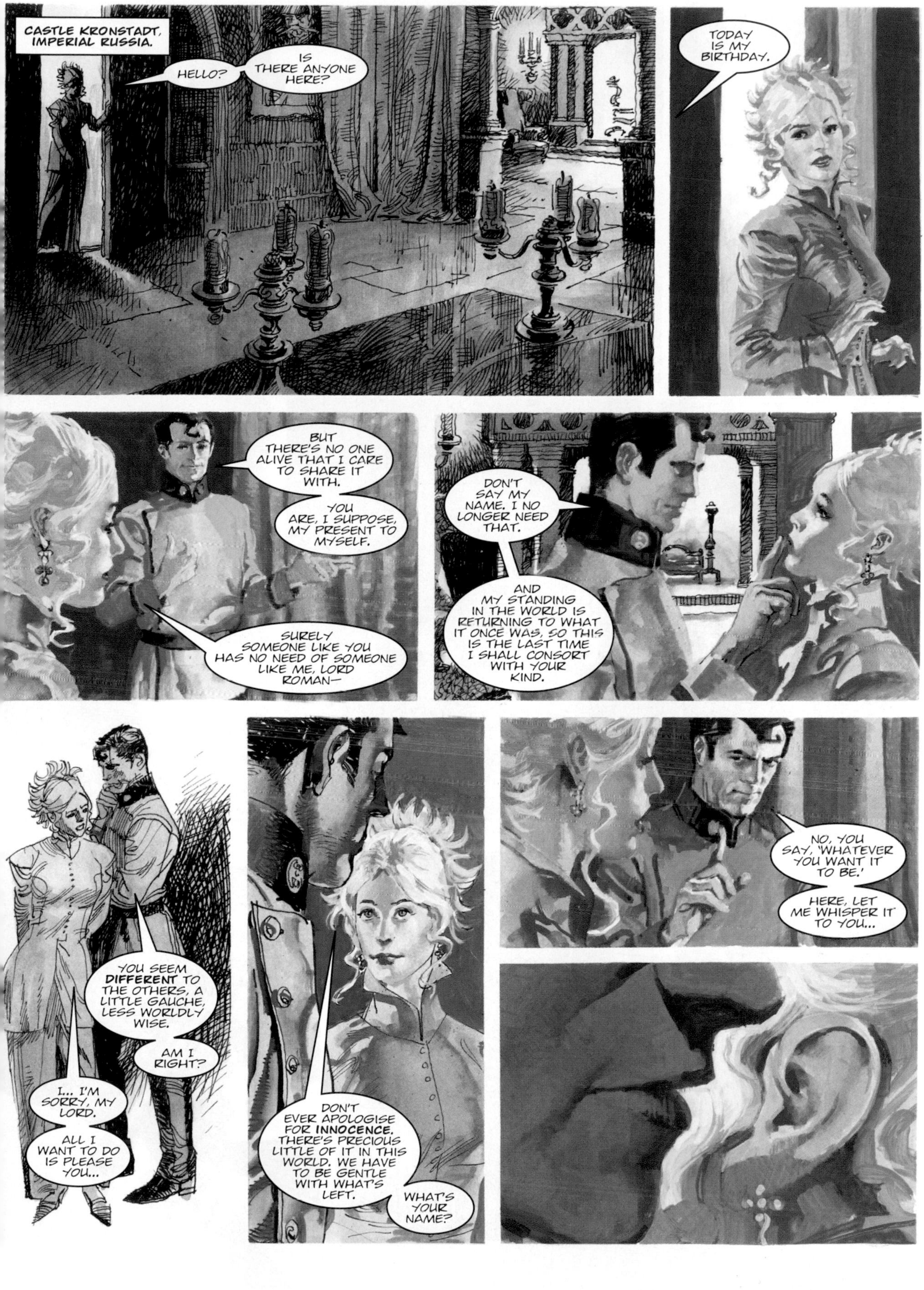
CASTLE KRONSTADT, IMPERIAL RUSSIA.
HELLO?
IS THERE ANYONE HERE?
TODAY IS MY BIRTHDAY.
BUT THERE'S NO ONE ALIVE THAT I CARE TO SHARE IT WITH.
YOU ARE, I SUPPOSE, MY PRESENT TO MYSELF.
SURELY SOMEONE LIKE YOU HAS NO NEED OF SOMEONE LIKE ME, LORD ROMAN—
DON'T SAY MY NAME. I NO LONGER NEED THAT.
AND MY STANDING IN THE WORLD IS RETURNING TO WHAT IT ONCE WAS, SO THIS IS THE LAST TIME I SHALL CONSORT WITH YOUR KIND.
YOU SEEM **DIFFERENT** TO THE OTHERS, A LITTLE GAUCHE, LESS WORLDLY WISE.
AM I RIGHT?
I... I'M SORRY, MY LORD.
ALL I WANT TO DO IS PLEASE YOU...
DON'T EVER APOLOGISE FOR **INNOCENCE**. THERE'S PRECIOUS LITTLE OF IT IN THIS WORLD. WE HAVE TO BE GENTLE WITH WHAT'S LEFT.
WHAT'S YOUR NAME?
NO, YOU SAY, 'WHATEVER YOU WANT IT TO BE.'
HERE, LET ME WHISPER IT TO YOU...

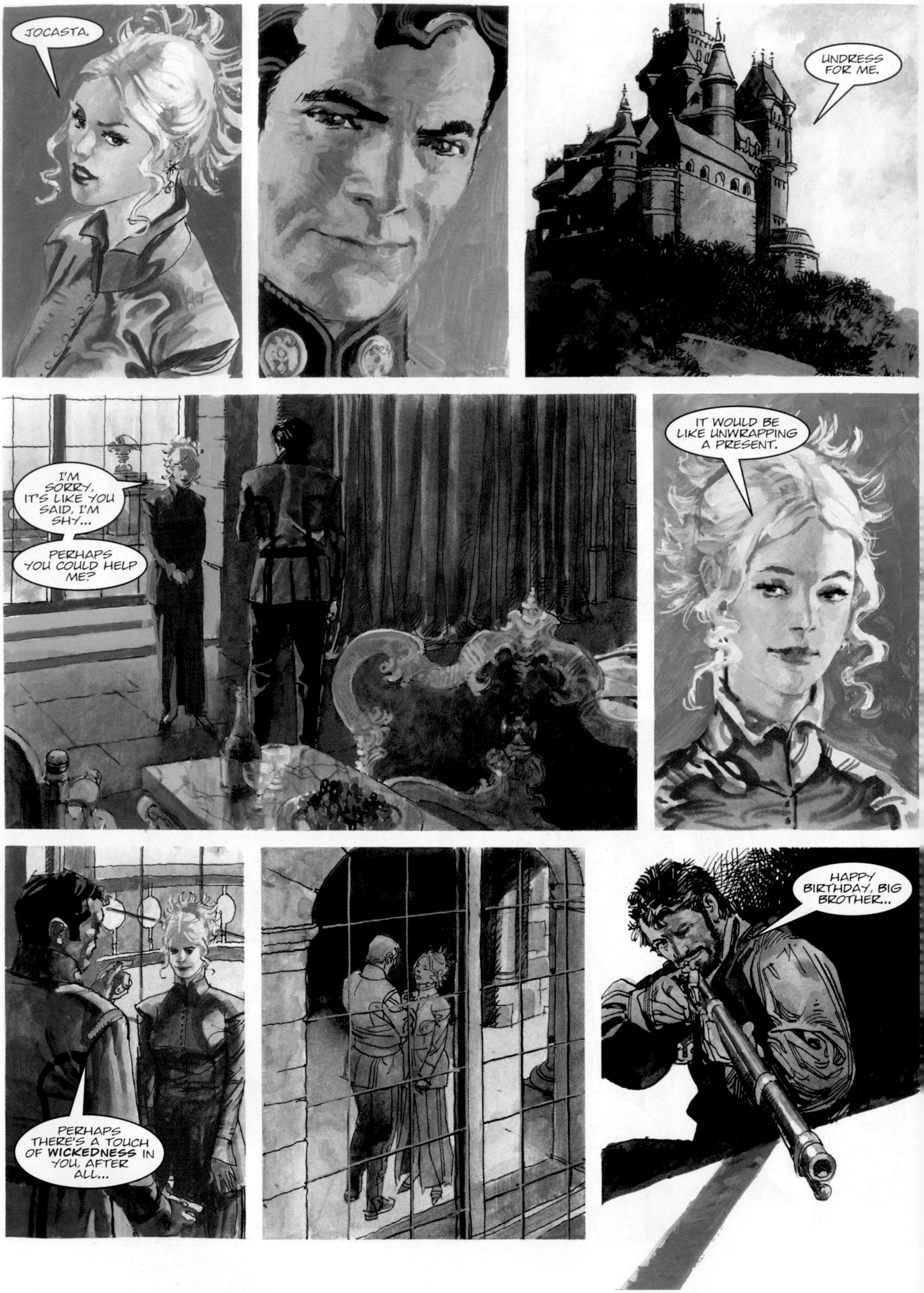
JOCASTA.
UNDRESS FOR ME.
I'M SORRY, IT'S LIKE YOU SAID, I'M SHY...
PERHAPS YOU COULD HELP ME?
IT WOULD BE LIKE UNWRAPPING A PRESENT.
PERHAPS THERE'S A TOUCH OF **WICKEDNESS** IN YOU, AFTER ALL...
HAPPY BIRTHDAY, BIG BROTHER...

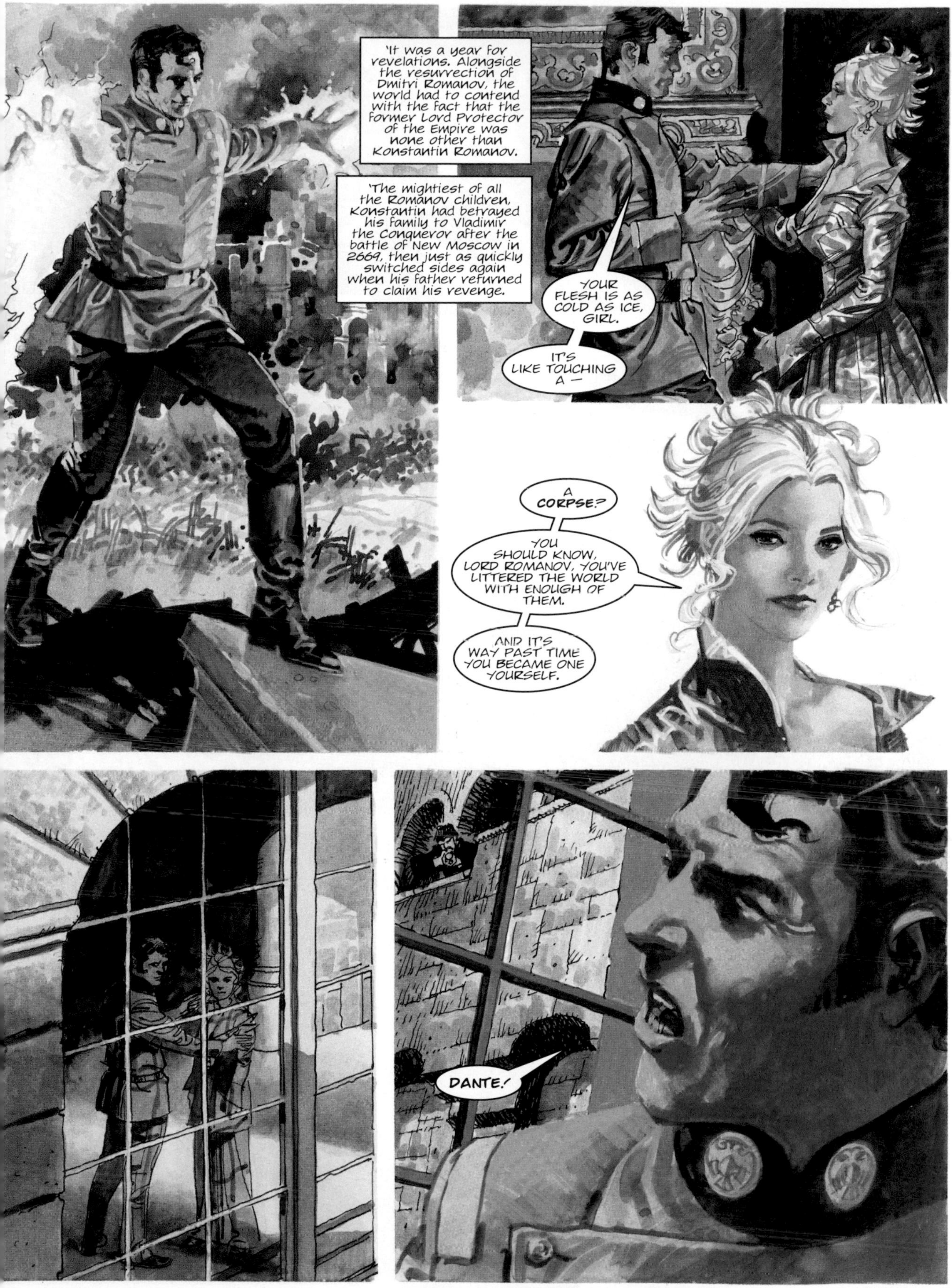
'It was a year for revelations. Alongside the resurrection of Dmitri Romanov, the world had to contend with the fact that the former Lord Protector of the Empire was none other than Konstantin Romanov.
'The mightiest of all the Romanov children, Konstantin had betrayed his family to Vladimir the Conqueror after the battle of New Moscow in 2669, then just as quickly switched sides again when his father returned to claim his revenge.
YOUR FLESH IS AS COLD AS ICE, GIRL.
IT'S LIKE TOUCHING A —
A CORPSE?
YOU SHOULD KNOW, LORD ROMANOV, YOU'VE LITTERED THE WORLD WITH ENOUGH OF THEM.
AND IT'S WAY PAST TIME YOU BECAME ONE YOURSELF.
DANTE!

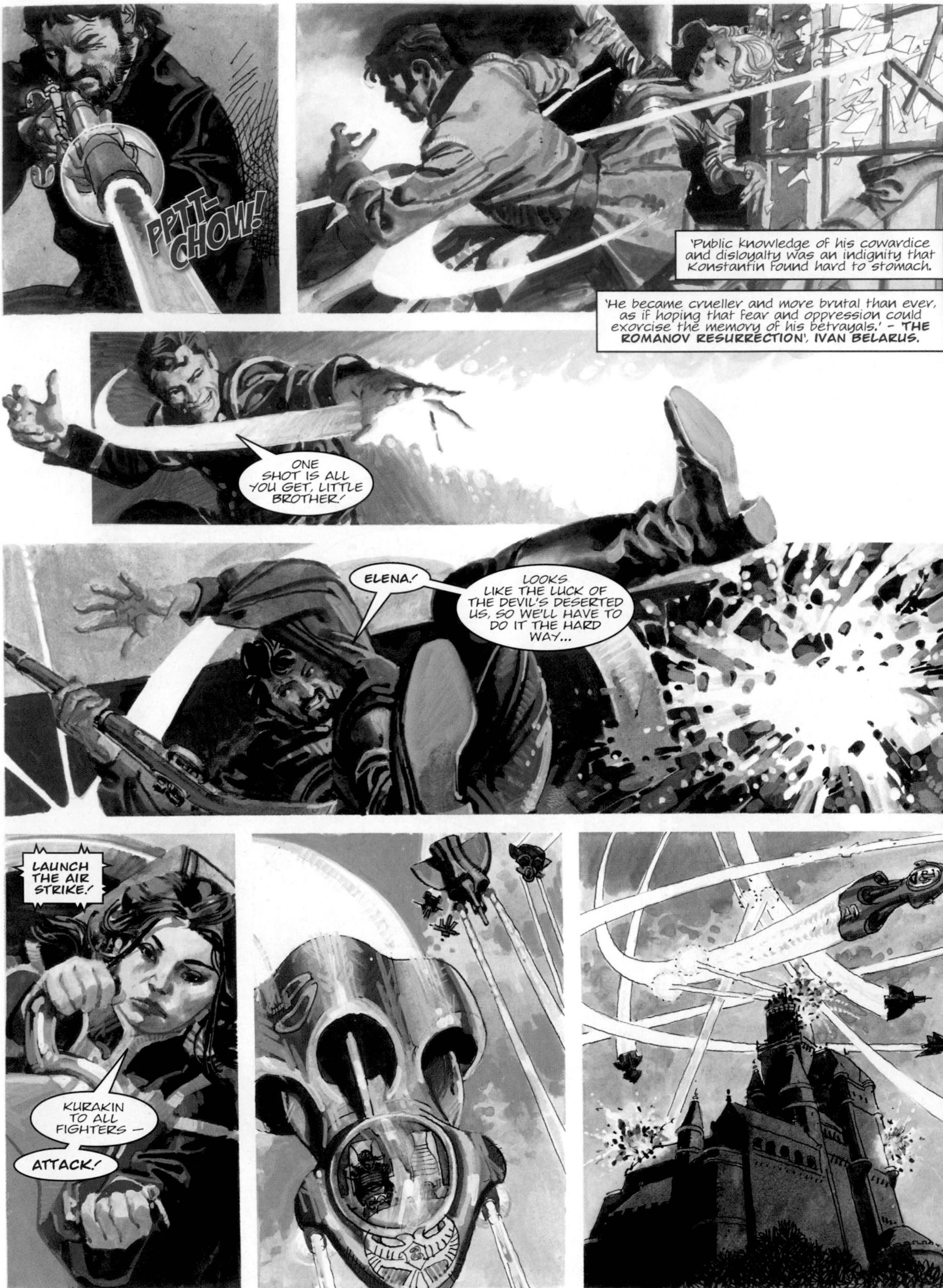

PPTT-CHOW!
'Public knowledge of his cowardice and disloyalty was an indignity that Konstantin found hard to stomach.
'He became crueller and more brutal than ever, as if hoping that fear and oppression could exorcise the memory of his betrayals.' – 'THE ROMANOV RESURRECTION', IVAN BELARUS.
ONE SHOT IS ALL YOU GET, LITTLE BROTHER!
ELENA!
LOOKS LIKE THE LUCK OF THE DEVIL'S DESERTED US, SO WE'LL HAVE TO DO IT THE HARD WAY...
LAUNCH THE AIR STRIKE!
KURAKIN TO ALL FIGHTERS –
ATTACK!

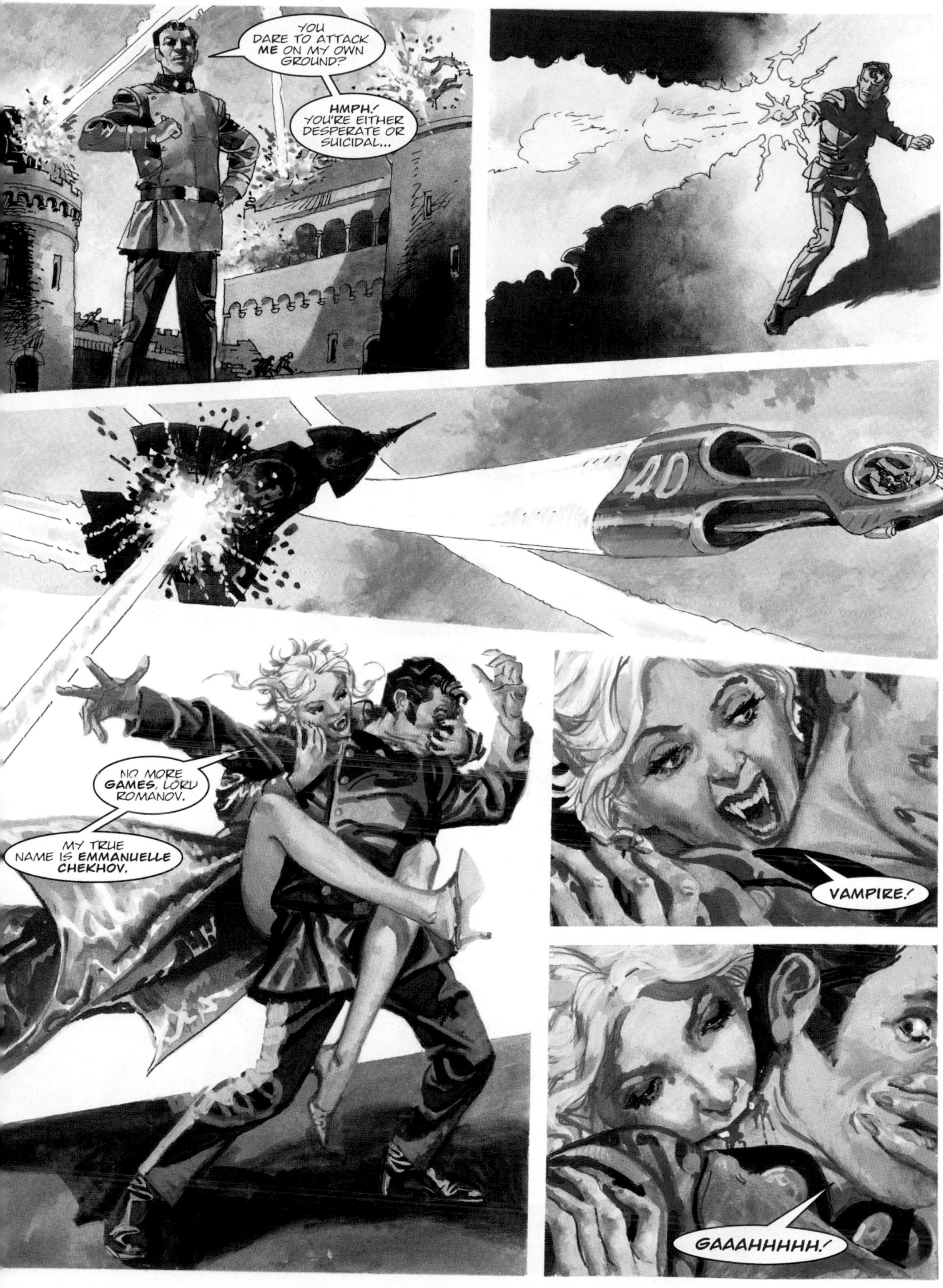
YOU DARE TO ATTACK ME ON MY OWN GROUND?
HMPH! YOU'RE EITHER DESPERATE OR SUICIDAL...
40
NO MORE GAMES, LORD ROMANOV.
MY TRUE NAME IS EMMANUELLE CHEKHOV.
VAMPIRE!
GAAAHHHHH!

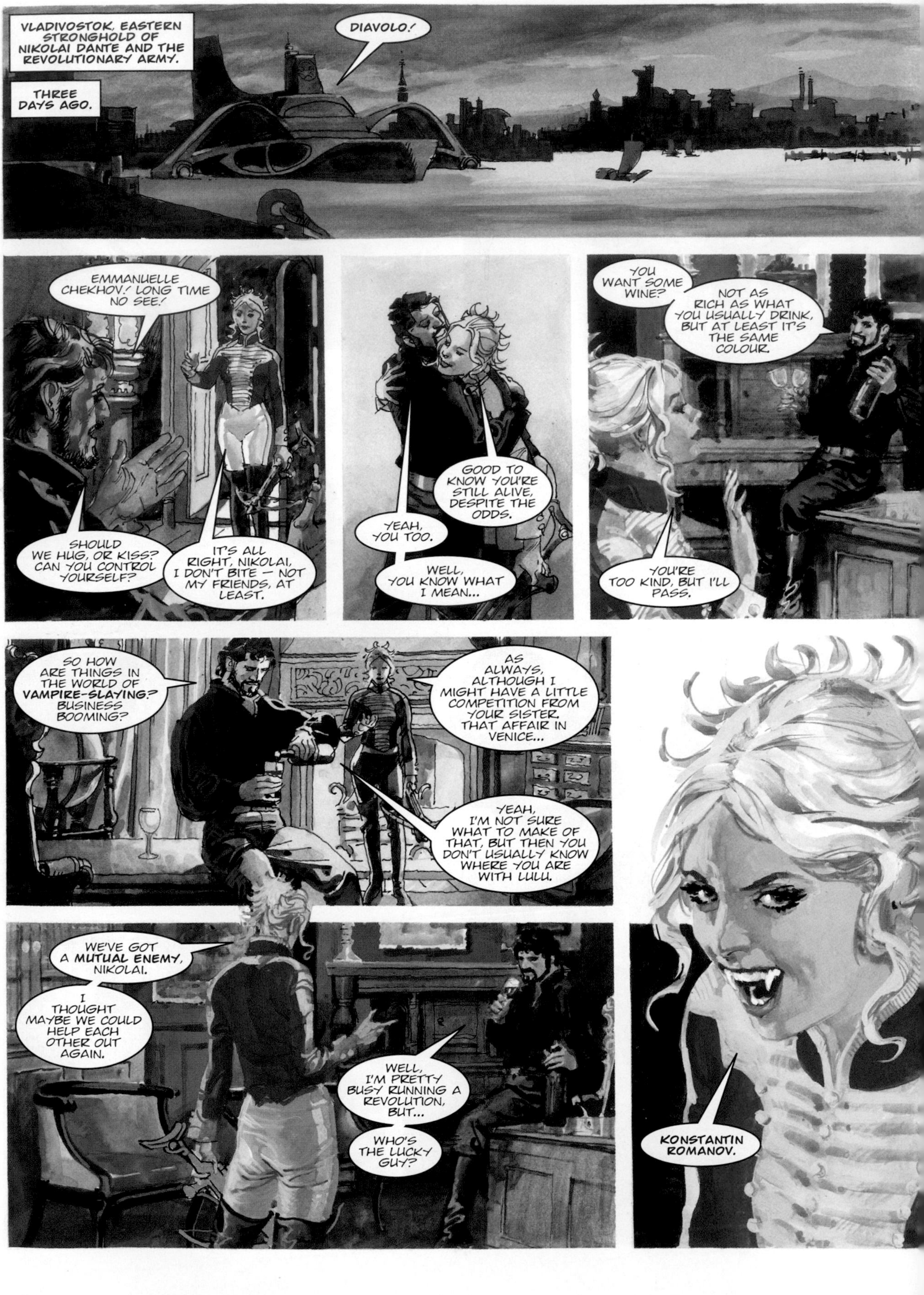
VLADIVOSTOK, EASTERN STRONGHOLD OF NIKOLAI DANTE AND THE REVOLUTIONARY ARMY.
THREE DAYS AGO.
DIAVOLO!
EMMANUELLE CHEKHOV! LONG TIME NO SEE!
SHOULD WE HUG, OR KISS? CAN YOU CONTROL YOURSELF?
IT'S ALL RIGHT, NIKOLAI, I DON'T BITE — NOT MY FRIENDS, AT LEAST.
GOOD TO KNOW YOU'RE STILL ALIVE, DESPITE THE ODDS.
YEAH, YOU TOO.
WELL, YOU KNOW WHAT I MEAN...
YOU WANT SOME WINE?
NOT AS RICH AS WHAT YOU USUALLY DRINK, BUT AT LEAST IT'S THE SAME COLOUR.
YOU'RE TOO KIND, BUT I'LL PASS.
SO HOW ARE THINGS IN THE WORLD OF VAMPIRE-SLAYING? BUSINESS BOOMING?
AS ALWAYS, ALTHOUGH I MIGHT HAVE A LITTLE COMPETITION FROM YOUR SISTER. THAT AFFAIR IN VENICE...
YEAH, I'M NOT SURE WHAT TO MAKE OF THAT, BUT THEN YOU DON'T USUALLY KNOW WHERE YOU ARE WITH LULU.
WE'VE GOT A MUTUAL ENEMY, NIKOLAI.
I THOUGHT MAYBE WE COULD HELP EACH OTHER OUT AGAIN.
WELL, I'M PRETTY BUSY RUNNING A REVOLUTION, BUT...
WHO'S THE LUCKY GUY?
KONSTANTIN ROMANOV.

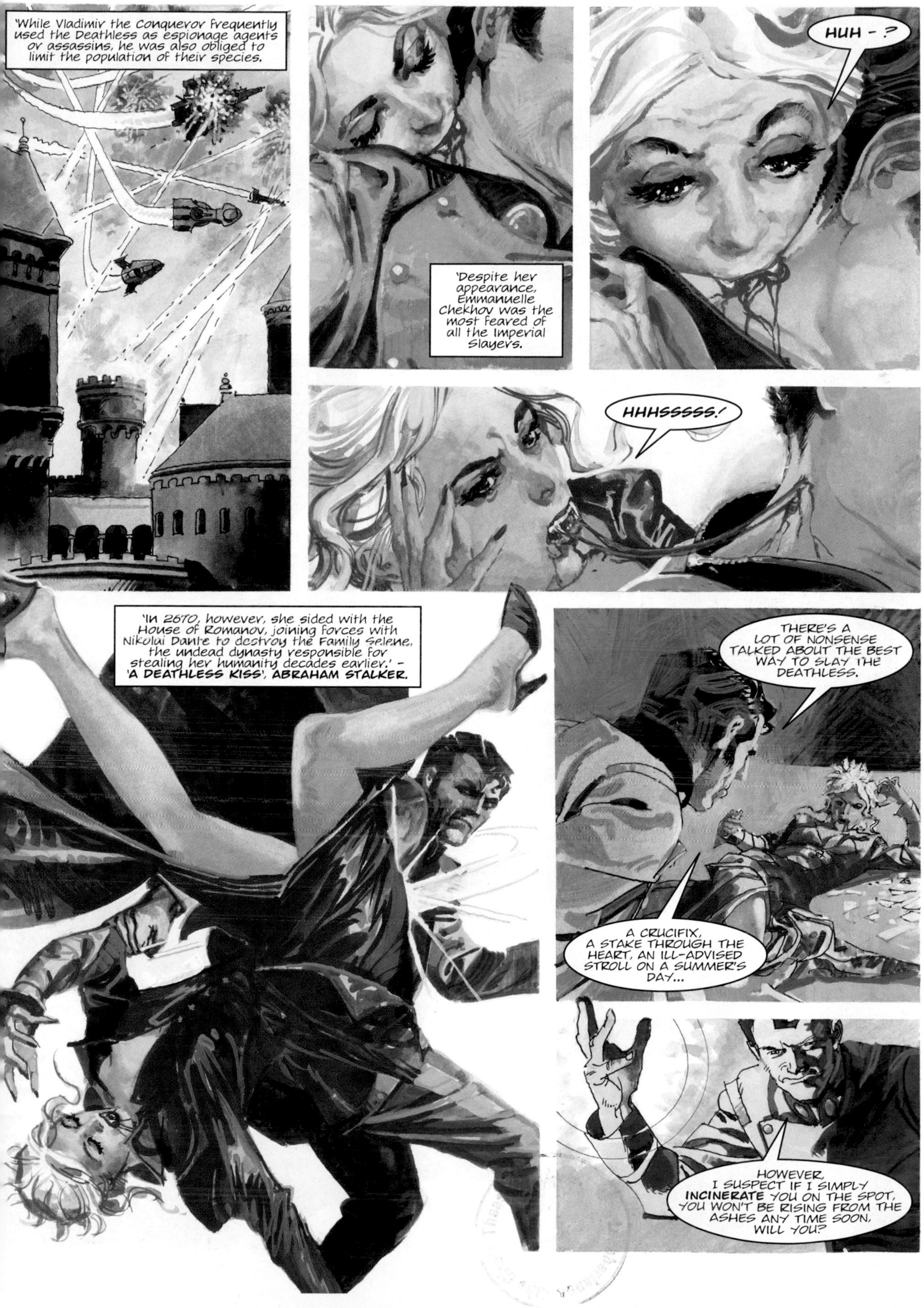
'While Vladimir the Conqueror frequently used the Deathless as espionage agents or assassins, he was also obliged to limit the population of their species.
'Despite her appearance, Emmanuelle Chekhov was the most feared of all the Imperial Slayers.
HUH - ?
HHHSSSSS!
'In 2670, however, she sided with the House of Romanov, joining forces with Nikolai Dante to destroy the Family Selene, the undead dynasty responsible for stealing her humanity decades earlier.' - 'A DEATHLESS KISS', ABRAHAM STALKER.
THERE'S A LOT OF NONSENSE TALKED ABOUT THE BEST WAY TO SLAY THE DEATHLESS.
A CRUCIFIX, A STAKE THROUGH THE HEART, AN ILL-ADVISED STROLL ON A SUMMER'S DAY...
HOWEVER, I SUSPECT IF I SIMPLY INCINERATE YOU ON THE SPOT, YOU WON'T BE RISING FROM THE ASHES ANY TIME SOON, WILL YOU?

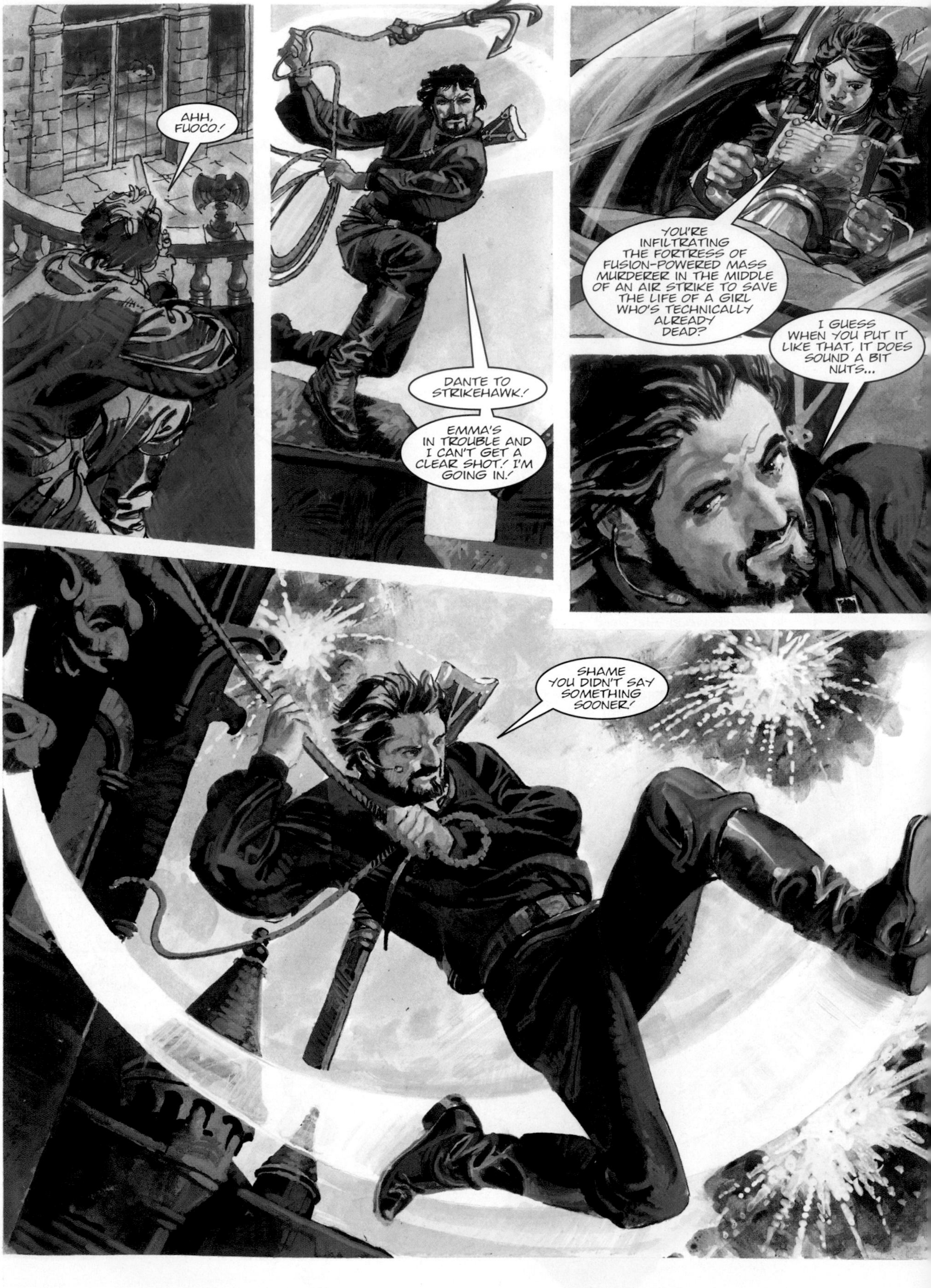
AHH, FUOCO!
DANTE TO STRIKEHAWK!
EMMA'S IN TROUBLE AND I CAN'T GET A CLEAR SHOT! I'M GOING IN!
YOU'RE INFILTRATING THE FORTRESS OF FUSION-POWERED MASS MURDERER IN THE MIDDLE OF AN AIR STRIKE TO SAVE THE LIFE OF A GIRL WHO'S TECHNICALLY ALREADY DEAD?
I GUESS WHEN YOU PUT IT LIKE THAT, IT DOES SOUND A BIT NUTS...
SHAME YOU DIDN'T SAY SOMETHING SOONER!

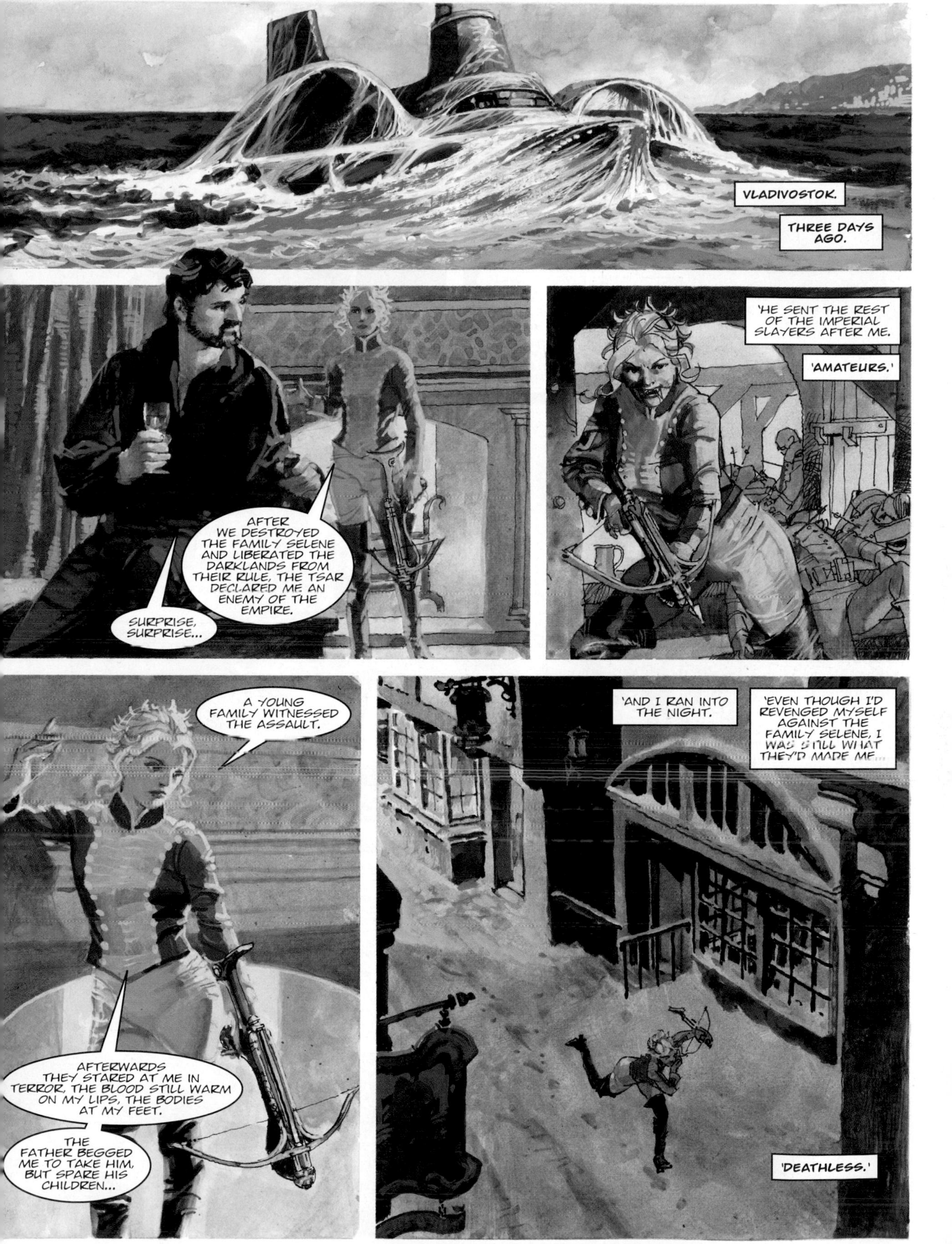

VLADIVOSTOK.
THREE DAYS AGO.
AFTER WE DESTROYED THE FAMILY SELENE AND LIBERATED THE DARKLANDS FROM THEIR RULE, THE TSAR DECLARED ME AN ENEMY OF THE EMPIRE.
SURPRISE, SURPRISE...
'HE SENT THE REST OF THE IMPERIAL SLAYERS AFTER ME.
'AMATEURS.'
A YOUNG FAMILY WITNESSED THE ASSAULT.
AFTERWARDS THEY STARED AT ME IN TERROR, THE BLOOD STILL WARM ON MY LIPS, THE BODIES AT MY FEET.
THE FATHER BEGGED ME TO TAKE HIM, BUT SPARE HIS CHILDREN...
'AND I RAN INTO THE NIGHT.
'EVEN THOUGH I'D REVENGED MYSELF AGAINST THE FAMILY SELENE, I WAS STILL WHAT THEY'D MADE ME...
'DEATHLESS.'

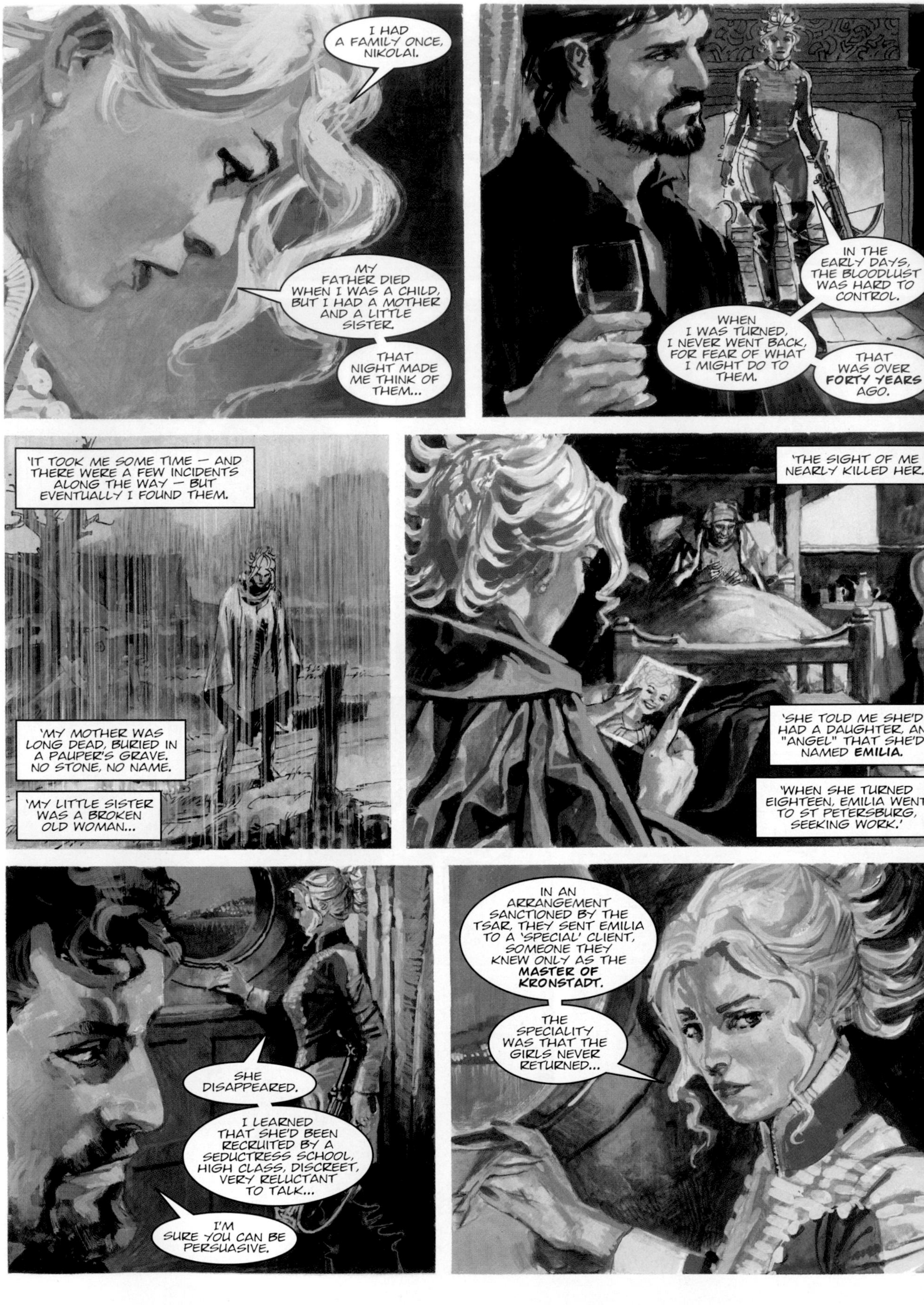
I HAD A FAMILY ONCE, NIKOLAI.
MY FATHER DIED WHEN I WAS A CHILD, BUT I HAD A MOTHER AND A LITTLE SISTER.
THAT NIGHT MADE ME THINK OF THEM...
IN THE EARLY DAYS, THE BLOODLUST WAS HARD TO CONTROL.
WHEN I WAS TURNED, I NEVER WENT BACK, FOR FEAR OF WHAT I MIGHT DO TO THEM.
THAT WAS OVER FORTY YEARS AGO.
'IT TOOK ME SOME TIME — AND THERE WERE A FEW INCIDENTS ALONG THE WAY — BUT EVENTUALLY I FOUND THEM.
'MY MOTHER WAS LONG DEAD, BURIED IN A PAUPER'S GRAVE. NO STONE, NO NAME.
'MY LITTLE SISTER WAS A BROKEN OLD WOMAN...
'THE SIGHT OF ME NEARLY KILLED HER.
'SHE TOLD ME SHE'D HAD A DAUGHTER, AN "ANGEL" THAT SHE'D NAMED EMILIA.
'WHEN SHE TURNED EIGHTEEN, EMILIA WENT TO ST PETERSBURG, SEEKING WORK.'
SHE DISAPPEARED.
I LEARNED THAT SHE'D BEEN RECRUITED BY A SEDUCTRESS SCHOOL, HIGH CLASS, DISCREET, VERY RELUCTANT TO TALK...
I'M SURE YOU CAN BE PERSUASIVE.
IN AN ARRANGEMENT SANCTIONED BY THE TSAR, THEY SENT EMILIA TO A 'SPECIAL' CLIENT, SOMEONE THEY KNEW ONLY AS THE MASTER OF KRONSTADT.
THE SPECIALITY WAS THAT THE GIRLS NEVER RETURNED...

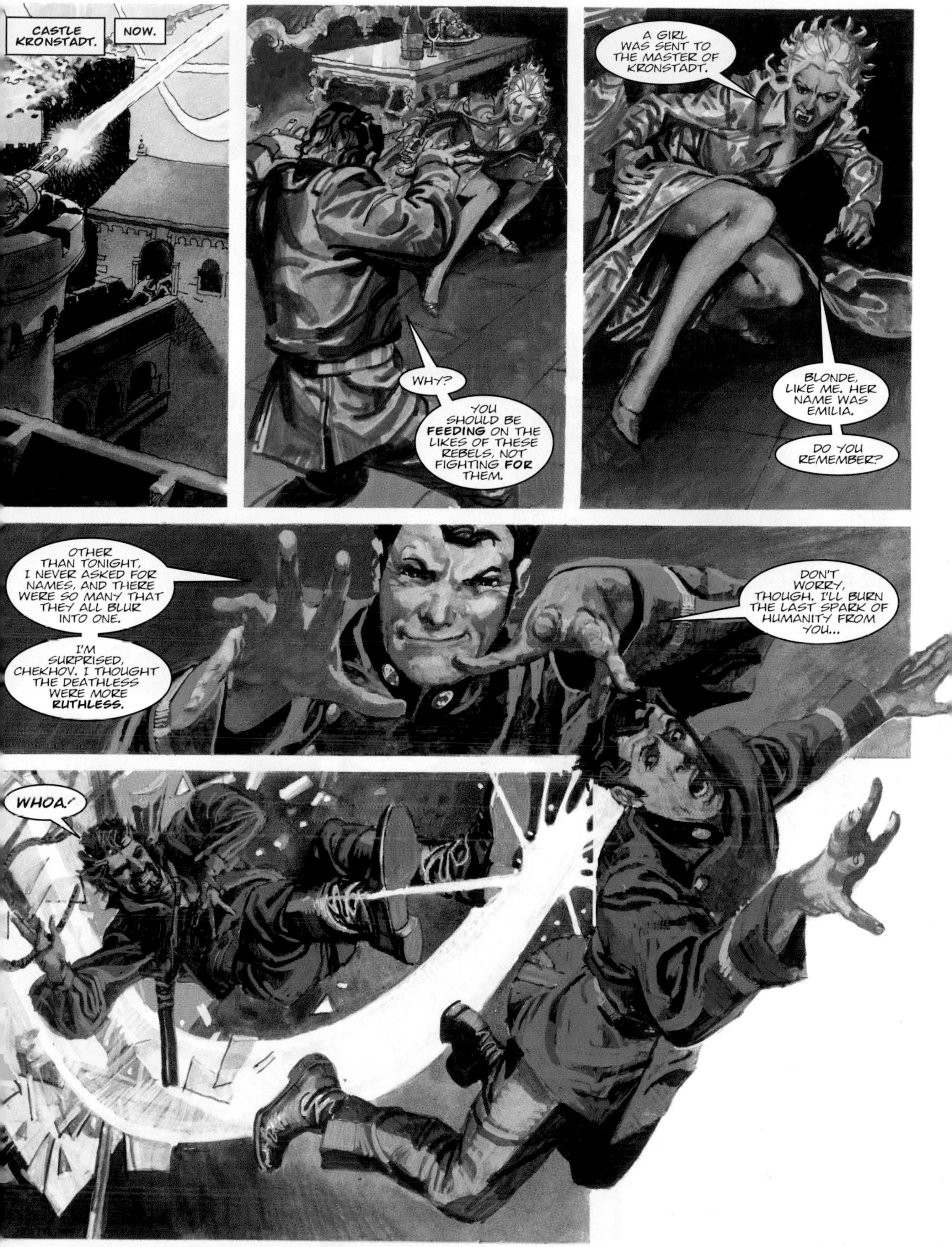
CASTLE KRONSTADT.
NOW.
WHY?
YOU SHOULD BE **FEEDING** ON THE LIKES OF THESE REBELS, NOT FIGHTING **FOR** THEM.
A GIRL WAS SENT TO THE MASTER OF KRONSTADT.
BLONDE, LIKE ME. HER NAME WAS EMILIA.
DO YOU REMEMBER?
OTHER THAN TONIGHT, I NEVER ASKED FOR NAMES, AND THERE WERE SO MANY THAT THEY ALL BLUR INTO ONE.
I'M SURPRISED, CHEKHOV. I THOUGHT THE DEATHLESS WERE MORE **RUTHLESS.**
DON'T WORRY, THOUGH. I'LL BURN THE LAST SPARK OF HUMANITY FROM YOU...
WHOA!

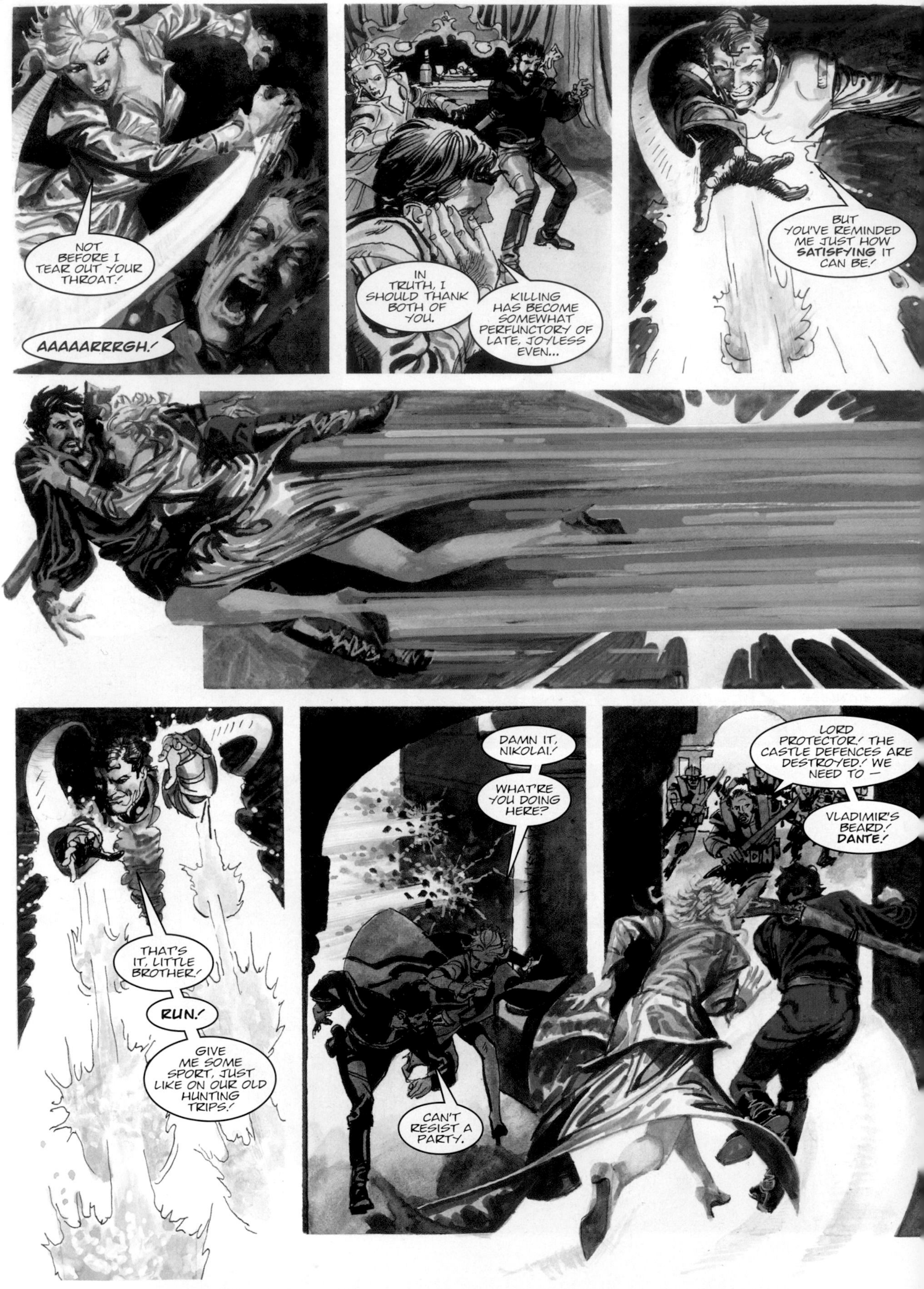
NOT BEFORE I TEAR OUT YOUR THROAT!
AAAAARRRGH!
IN TRUTH, I SHOULD THANK BOTH OF YOU.
KILLING HAS BECOME SOMEWHAT PERFUNCTORY OF LATE, JOYLESS EVEN...
BUT YOU'VE REMINDED ME JUST HOW SATISFYING IT CAN BE!
THAT'S IT, LITTLE BROTHER!
RUN!
GIVE ME SOME SPORT, JUST LIKE ON OUR OLD HUNTING TRIPS!
DAMN IT, NIKOLAI!
WHAT'RE YOU DOING HERE?
CAN'T RESIST A PARTY.
LORD PROTECTOR! THE CASTLE DEFENCES ARE DESTROYED! WE NEED TO —
VLADIMIR'S BEARD! DANTE!

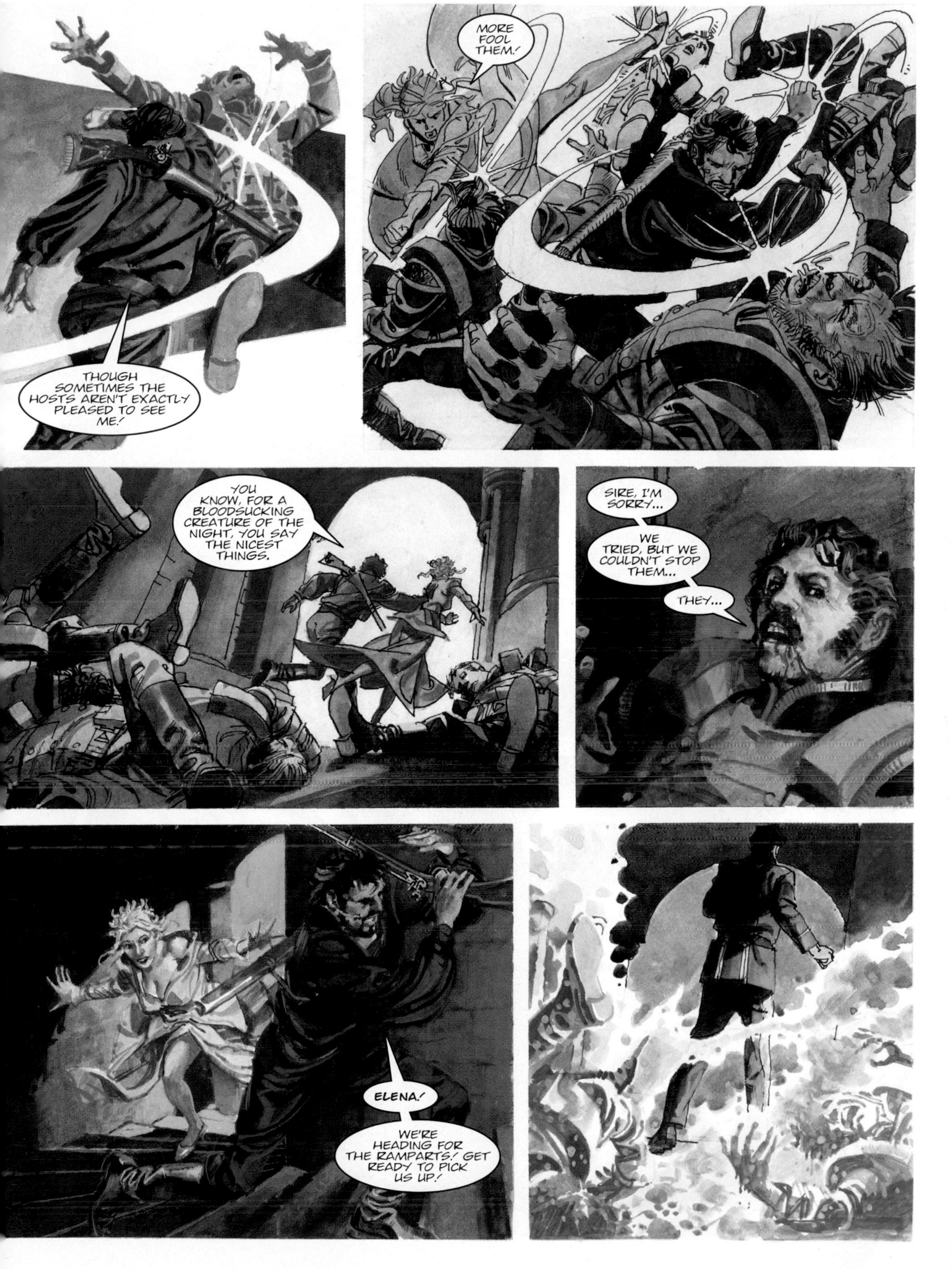
THOUGH SOMETIMES THE HOSTS AREN'T EXACTLY PLEASED TO SEE ME!
MORE FOOL THEM!
YOU KNOW, FOR A BLOODSUCKING CREATURE OF THE NIGHT, YOU SAY THE NICEST THINGS.
SIRE, I'M SORRY...
WE TRIED, BUT WE COULDN'T STOP THEM...
THEY...
ELENA!
WE'RE HEADING FOR THE RAMPARTS! GET READY TO PICK US UP!

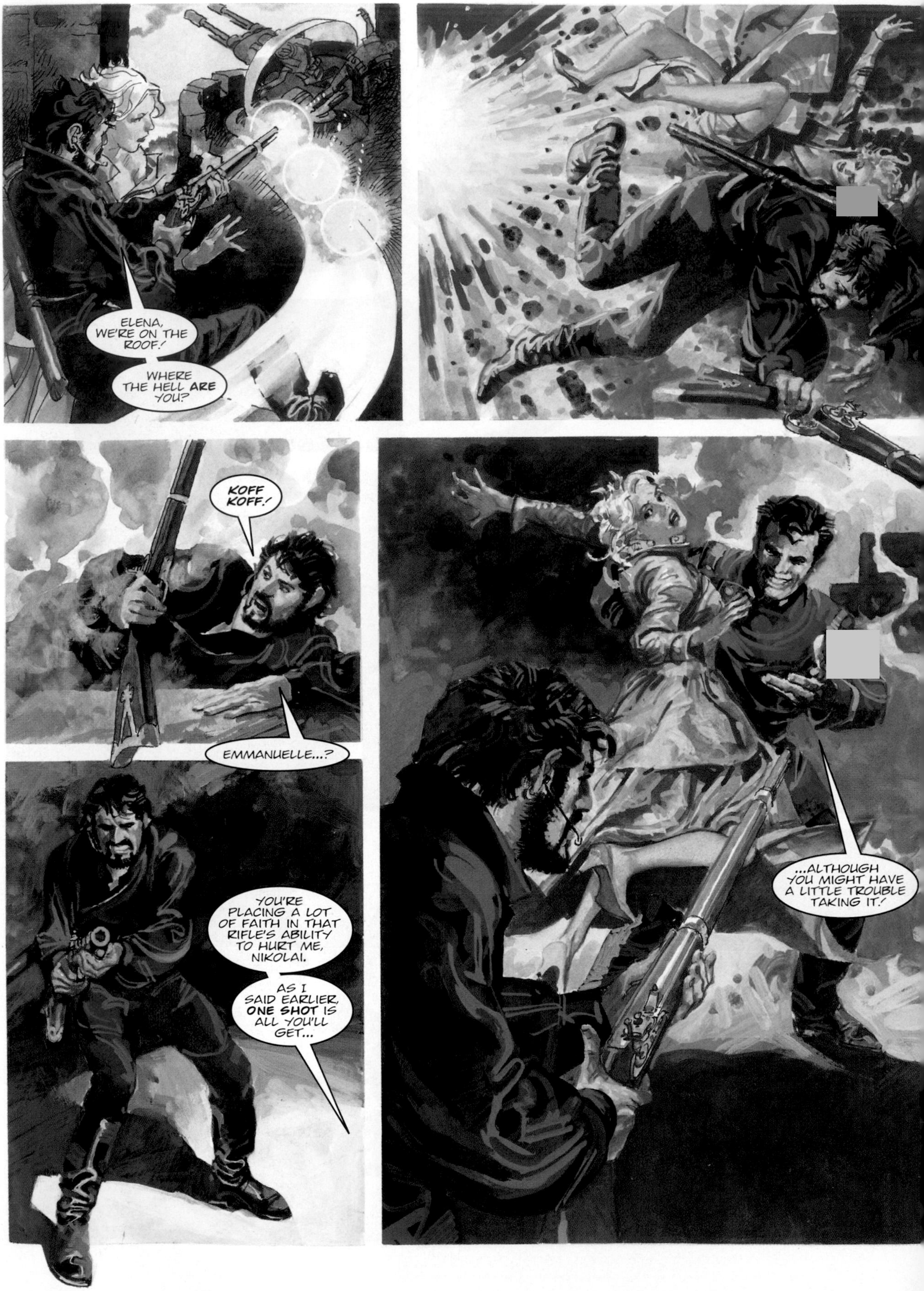
ELENA, WE'RE ON THE ROOF!
WHERE THE HELL ARE YOU?
KOFF KOFF!
EMMANUELLE...?
YOU'RE PLACING A LOT OF FAITH IN THAT RIFLE'S ABILITY TO HURT ME, NIKOLAI.
AS I SAID EARLIER, ONE SHOT IS ALL YOU'LL GET...
...ALTHOUGH YOU MIGHT HAVE A LITTLE TROUBLE TAKING IT!

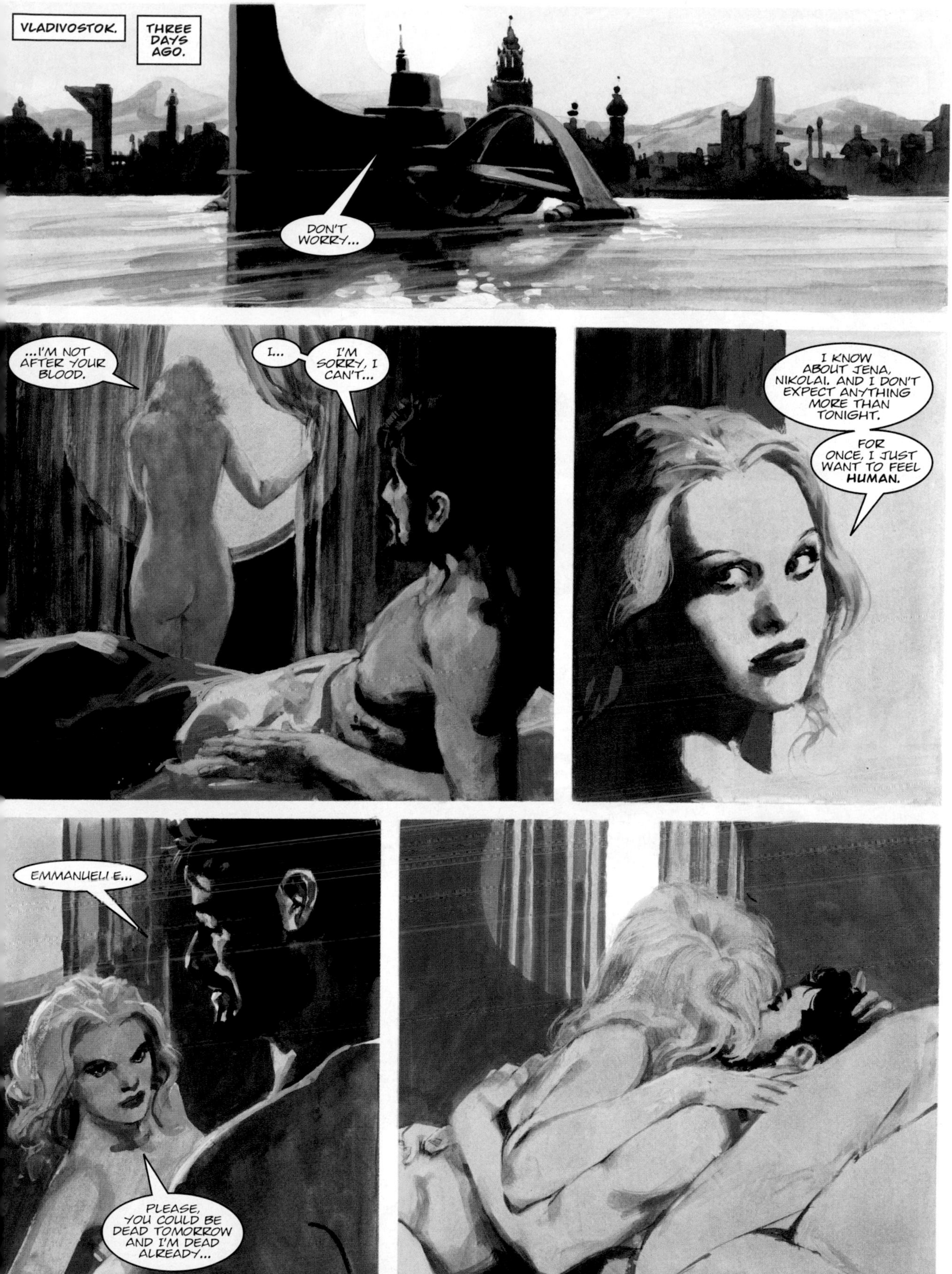
VLADIVOSTOK.
THREE DAYS AGO.
DON'T WORRY...
...I'M NOT AFTER YOUR BLOOD.
I...
I'M SORRY, I CAN'T...
I KNOW ABOUT JENA, NIKOLAI. AND I DON'T EXPECT ANYTHING MORE THAN TONIGHT.
FOR ONCE, I JUST WANT TO FEEL **HUMAN.**
EMMANUELLE...
PLEASE, YOU COULD BE DEAD TOMORROW AND I'M DEAD ALREADY...

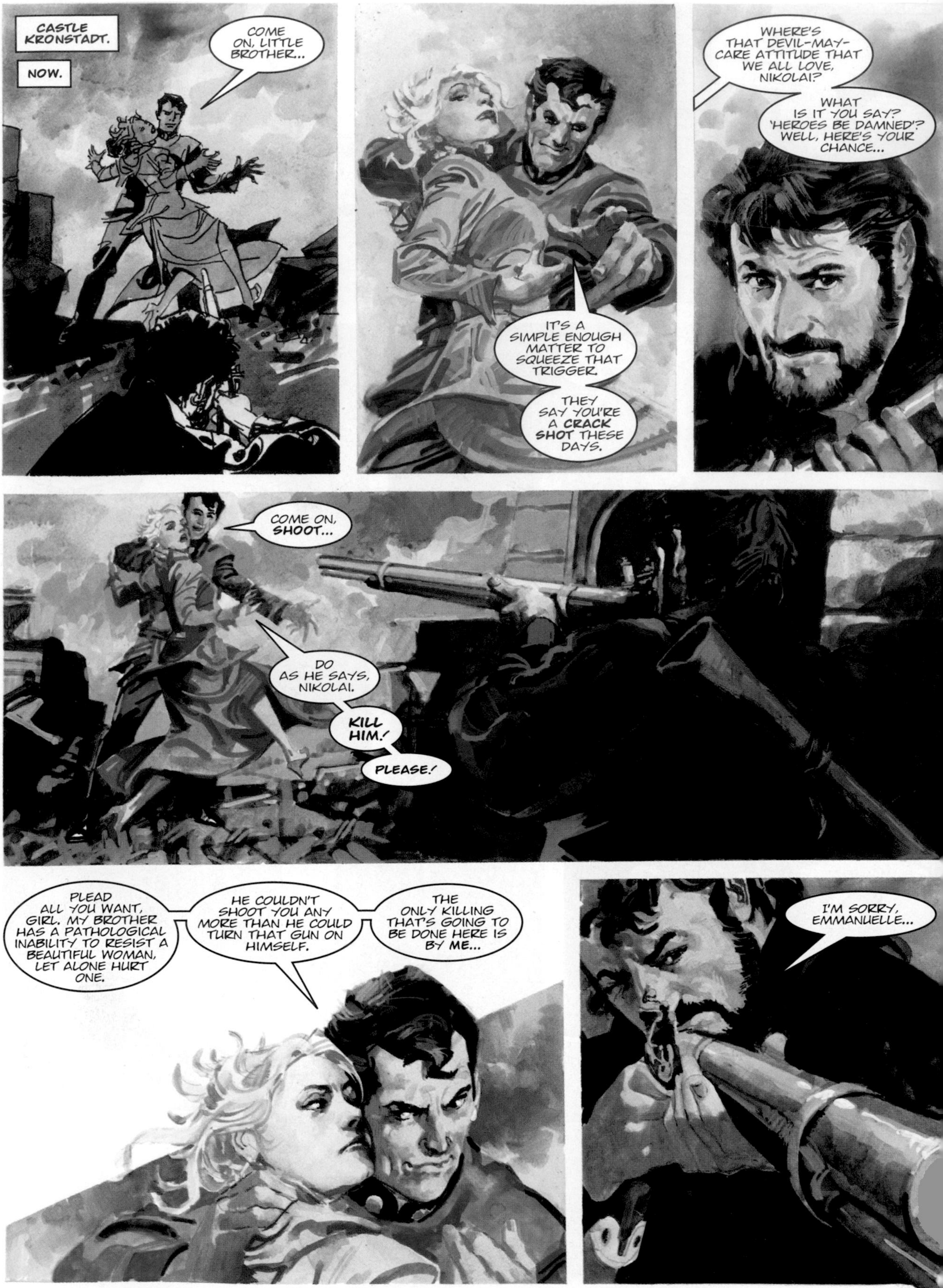
CASTLE KRONSTADT.
NOW.
COME ON, LITTLE BROTHER...
IT'S A SIMPLE ENOUGH MATTER TO SQUEEZE THAT TRIGGER.
THEY SAY YOU'RE A CRACK SHOT THESE DAYS.
WHERE'S THAT DEVIL-MAY-CARE ATTITUDE THAT WE ALL LOVE, NIKOLAI?
WHAT IS IT YOU SAY? 'HEROES BE DAMNED'? WELL, HERE'S YOUR CHANCE...
COME ON, SHOOT...
DO AS HE SAYS, NIKOLAI.
KILL HIM!
PLEASE!
PLEAD ALL YOU WANT, GIRL. MY BROTHER HAS A PATHOLOGICAL INABILITY TO RESIST A BEAUTIFUL WOMAN, LET ALONE HURT ONE.
HE COULDN'T SHOOT YOU ANY MORE THAN HE COULD TURN THAT GUN ON HIMSELF.
THE ONLY KILLING THAT'S GOING TO BE DONE HERE IS BY ME...
I'M SORRY, EMMANUELLE...

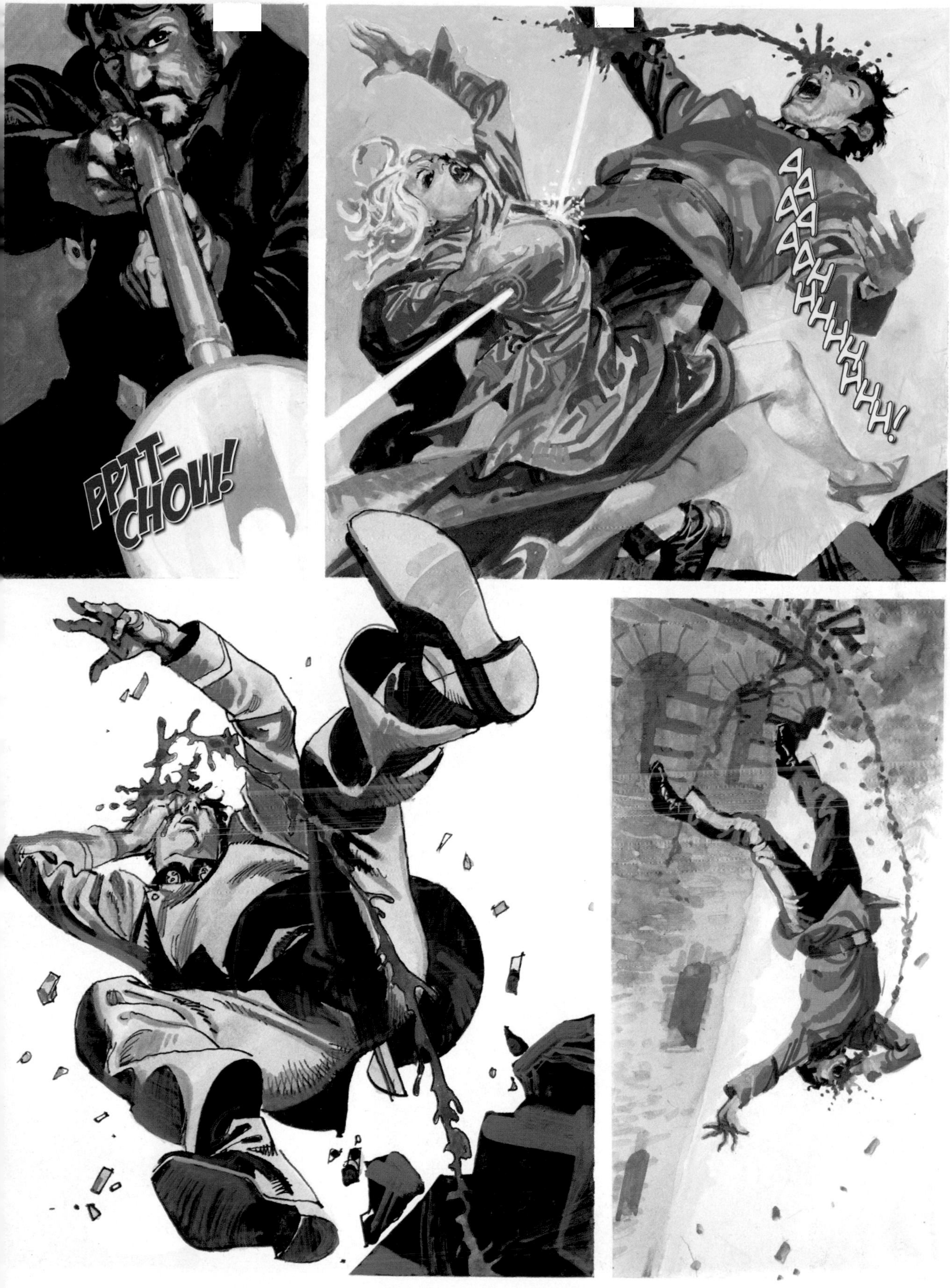
PPTT-CHOW!
AAAAAAHHHHHHHHH!

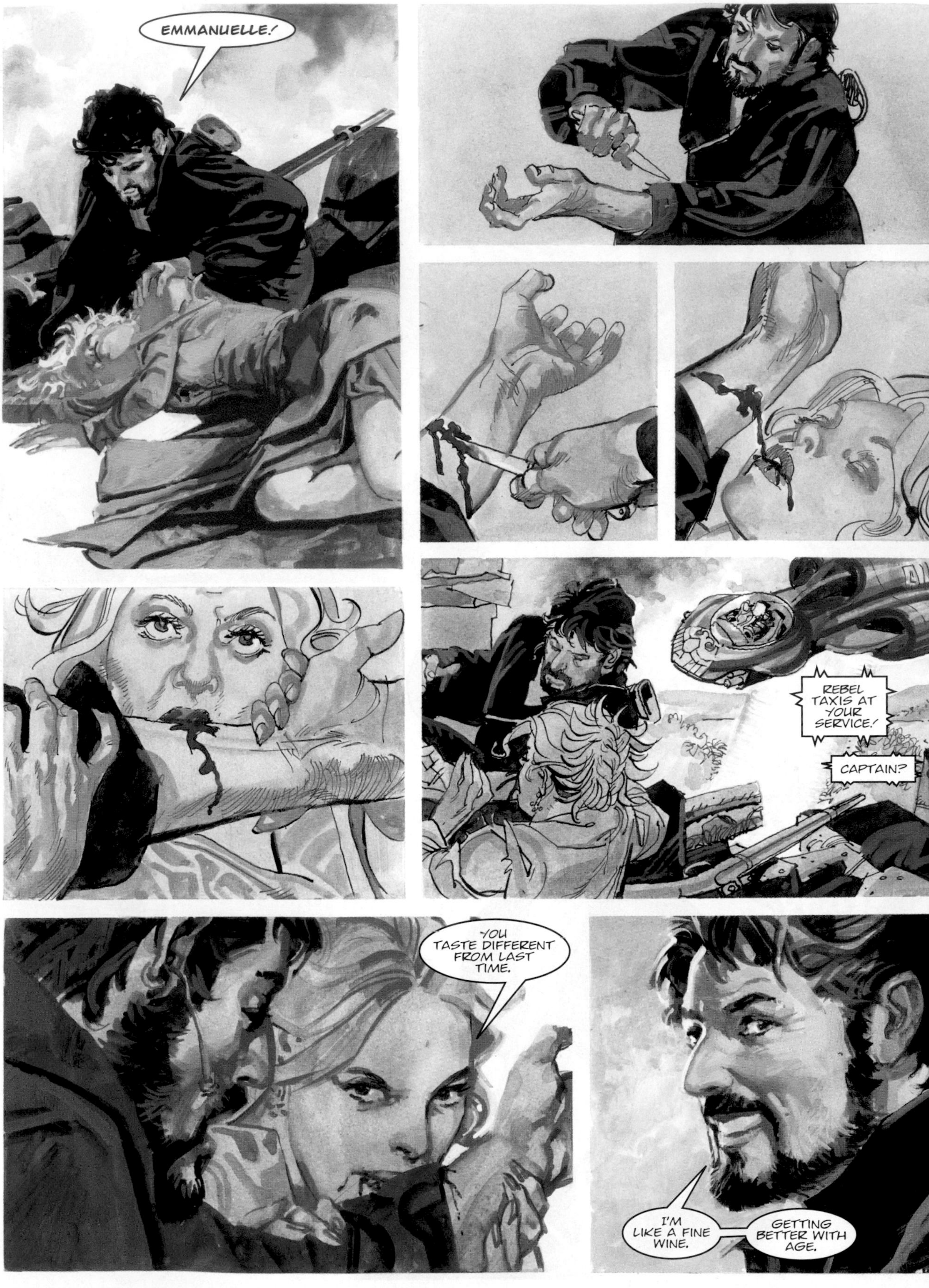
EMMANUELLE!
REBEL TAXIS AT YOUR SERVICE!
CAPTAIN?
YOU TASTE DIFFERENT FROM LAST TIME.
I'M LIKE A FINE WINE.
GETTING BETTER WITH AGE.

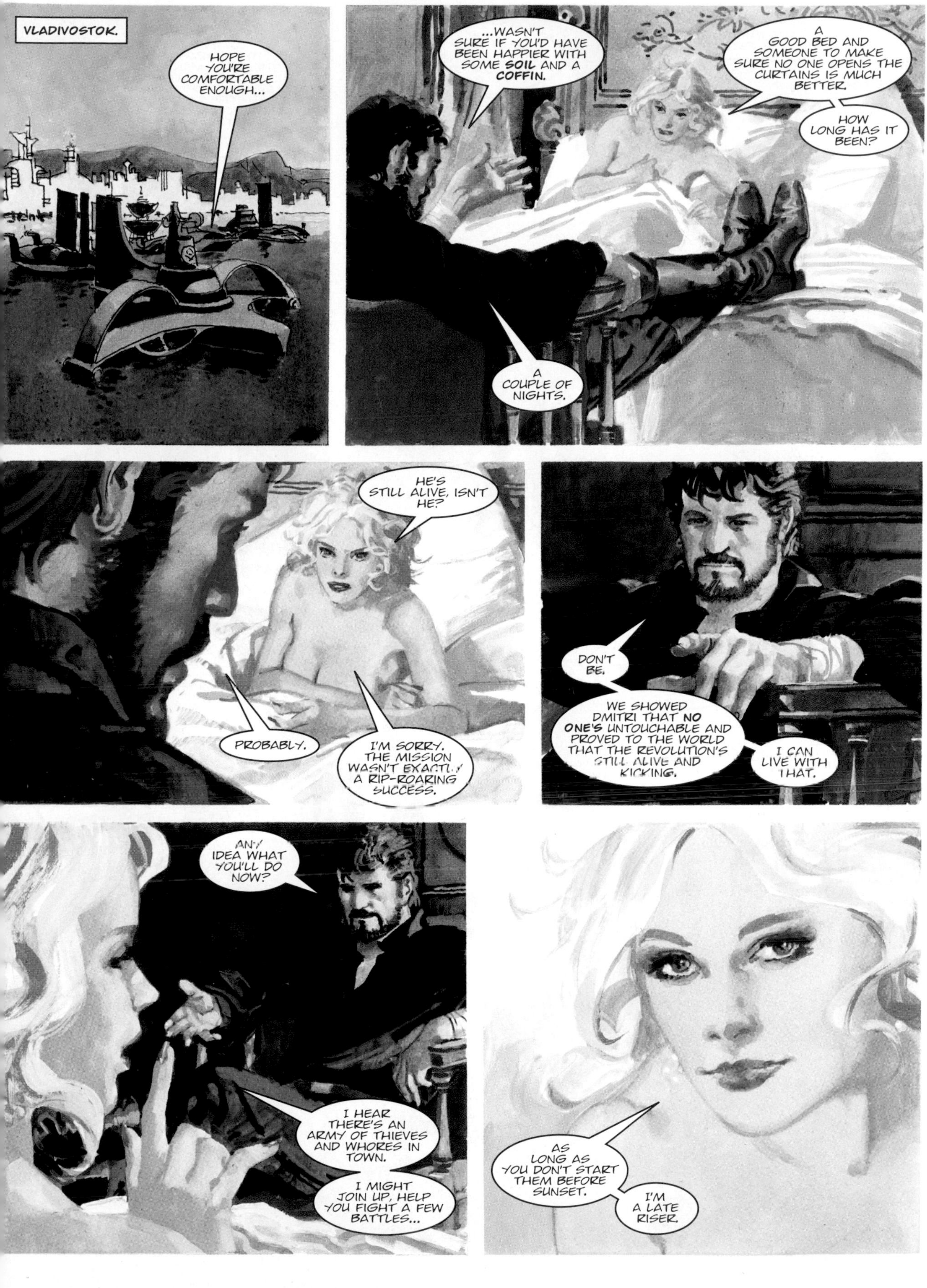
VLADIVOSTOK.
HOPE YOU'RE COMFORTABLE ENOUGH...
...WASN'T SURE IF YOU'D HAVE BEEN HAPPIER WITH SOME **SOIL** AND A **COFFIN.**
A GOOD BED AND SOMEONE TO MAKE SURE NO ONE OPENS THE CURTAINS IS MUCH BETTER.
HOW LONG HAS IT BEEN?
A COUPLE OF NIGHTS.
HE'S STILL ALIVE, ISN'T HE?
PROBABLY.
I'M SORRY. THE MISSION WASN'T EXACTLY A RIP-ROARING SUCCESS.
DON'T BE.
WE SHOWED DMITRI THAT **NO ONE'S** UNTOUCHABLE AND PROVED TO THE WORLD THAT THE REVOLUTION'S STILL ALIVE AND KICKING.
I CAN LIVE WITH THAT.
ANY IDEA WHAT YOU'LL DO NOW?
I HEAR THERE'S AN ARMY OF THIEVES AND WHORES IN TOWN.
I MIGHT JOIN UP, HELP YOU FIGHT A FEW BATTLES...
AS LONG AS YOU DON'T START THEM BEFORE SUNSET.
I'M A LATE RISER.

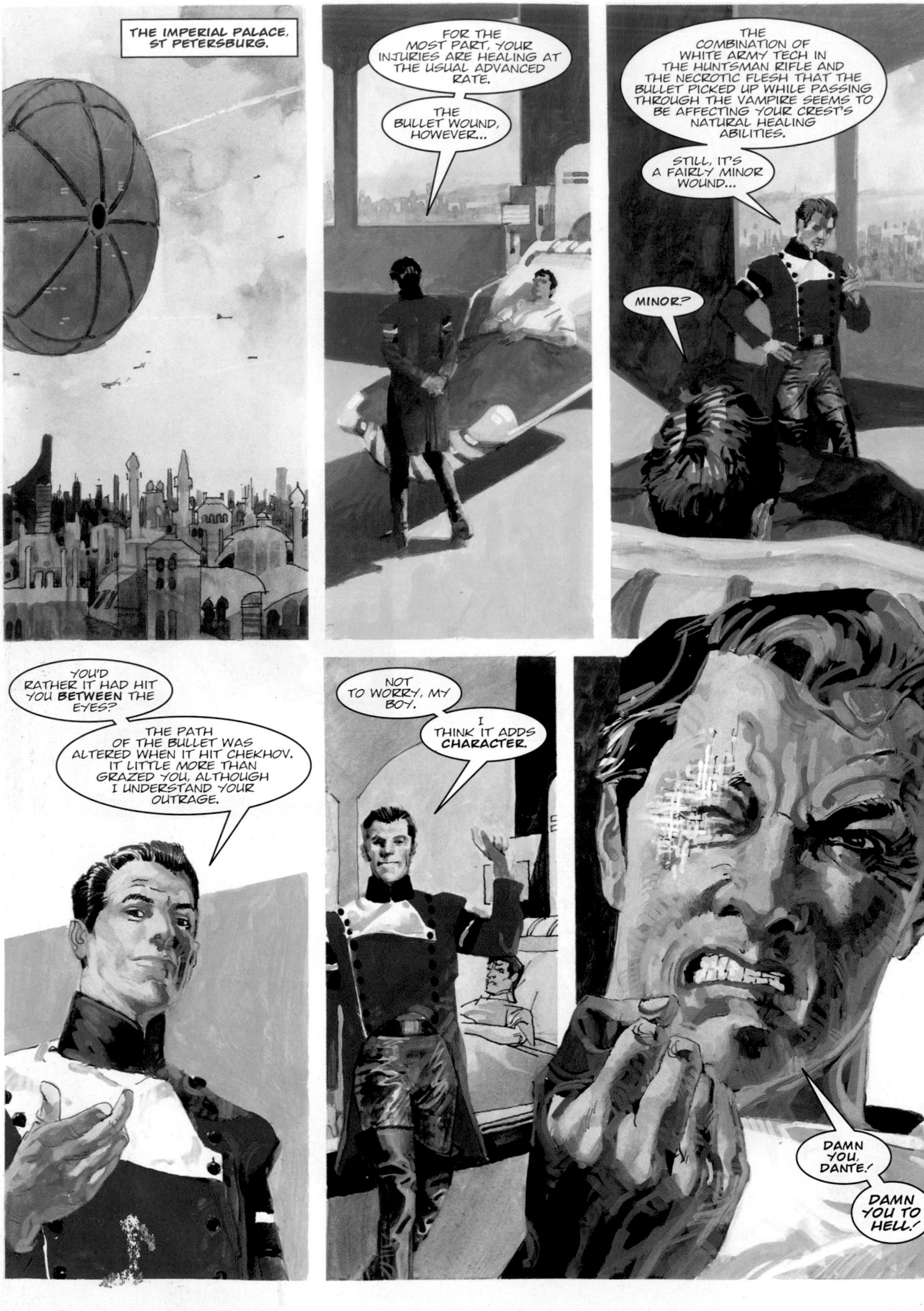

THE IMPERIAL PALACE, ST PETERSBURG.
FOR THE MOST PART, YOUR INJURIES ARE HEALING AT THE USUAL ADVANCED RATE.
THE BULLET WOUND, HOWEVER...
THE COMBINATION OF WHITE ARMY TECH IN THE HUNTSMAN RIFLE AND THE NECROTIC FLESH THAT THE BULLET PICKED UP WHILE PASSING THROUGH THE VAMPIRE SEEMS TO BE AFFECTING YOUR CREST'S NATURAL HEALING ABILITIES.
STILL, IT'S A FAIRLY MINOR WOUND...
MINOR?
YOU'D RATHER IT HAD HIT YOU **BETWEEN** THE EYES?
THE PATH OF THE BULLET WAS ALTERED WHEN IT HIT CHEKHOV. IT LITTLE MORE THAN GRAZED YOU, ALTHOUGH I UNDERSTAND YOUR OUTRAGE.
NOT TO WORRY, MY BOY.
I THINK IT ADDS **CHARACTER**.
DAMN YOU, DANTE!
DAMN YOU TO HELL!

COVERS GALLERY

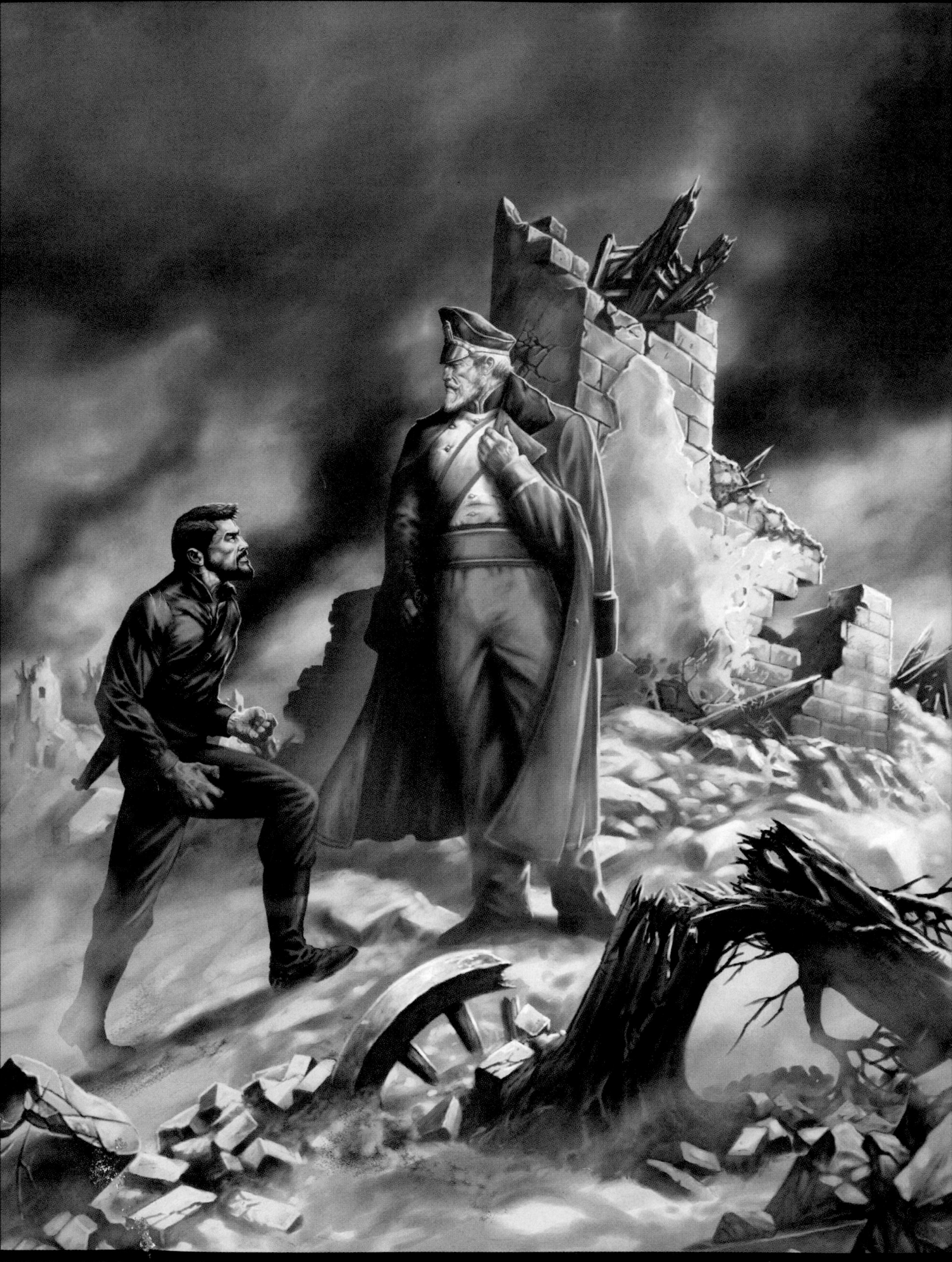

2000 AD Prog 1668: Cover by **Karl Richardson**

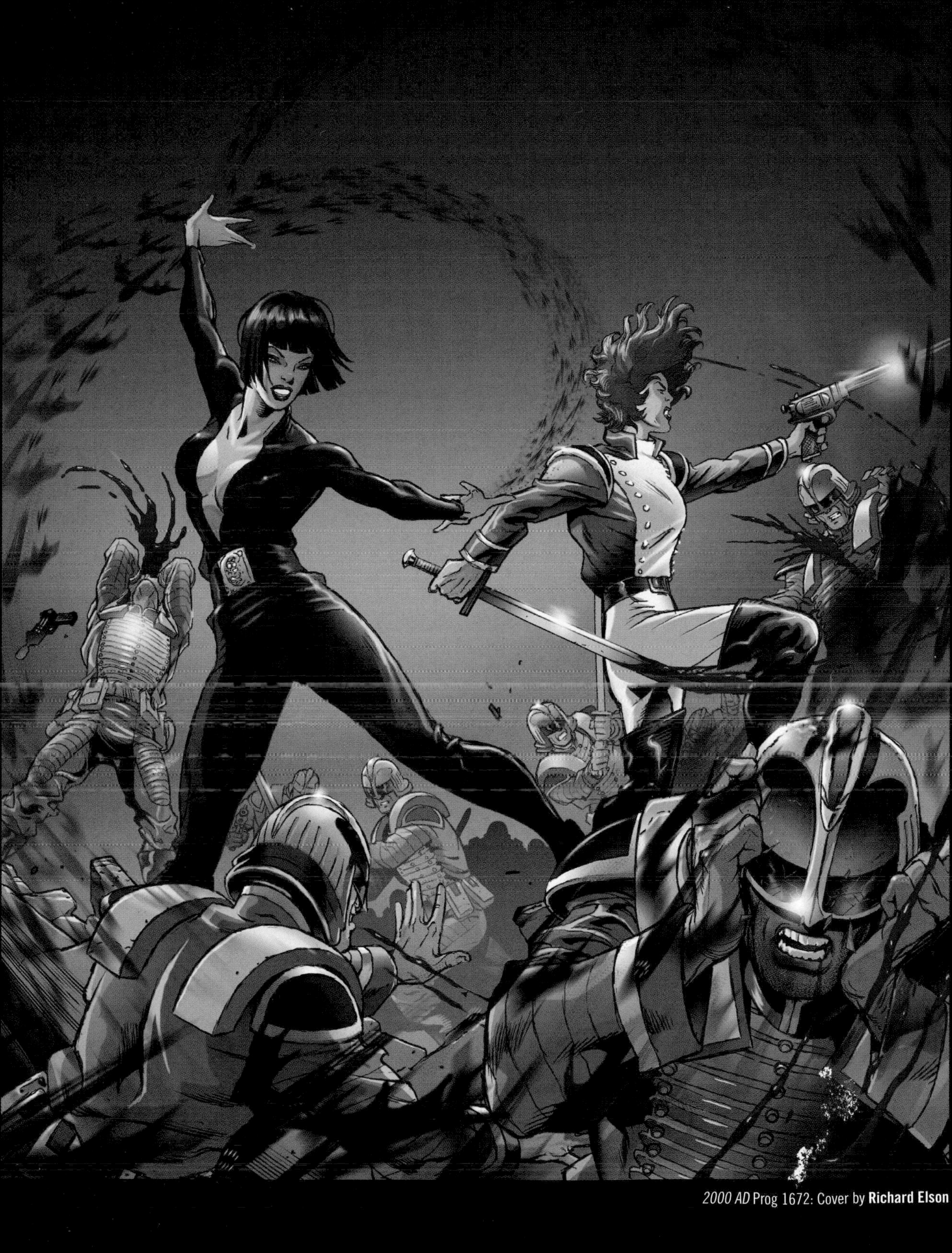

2000 AD Prog 1672: Cover by **Richard Elson**

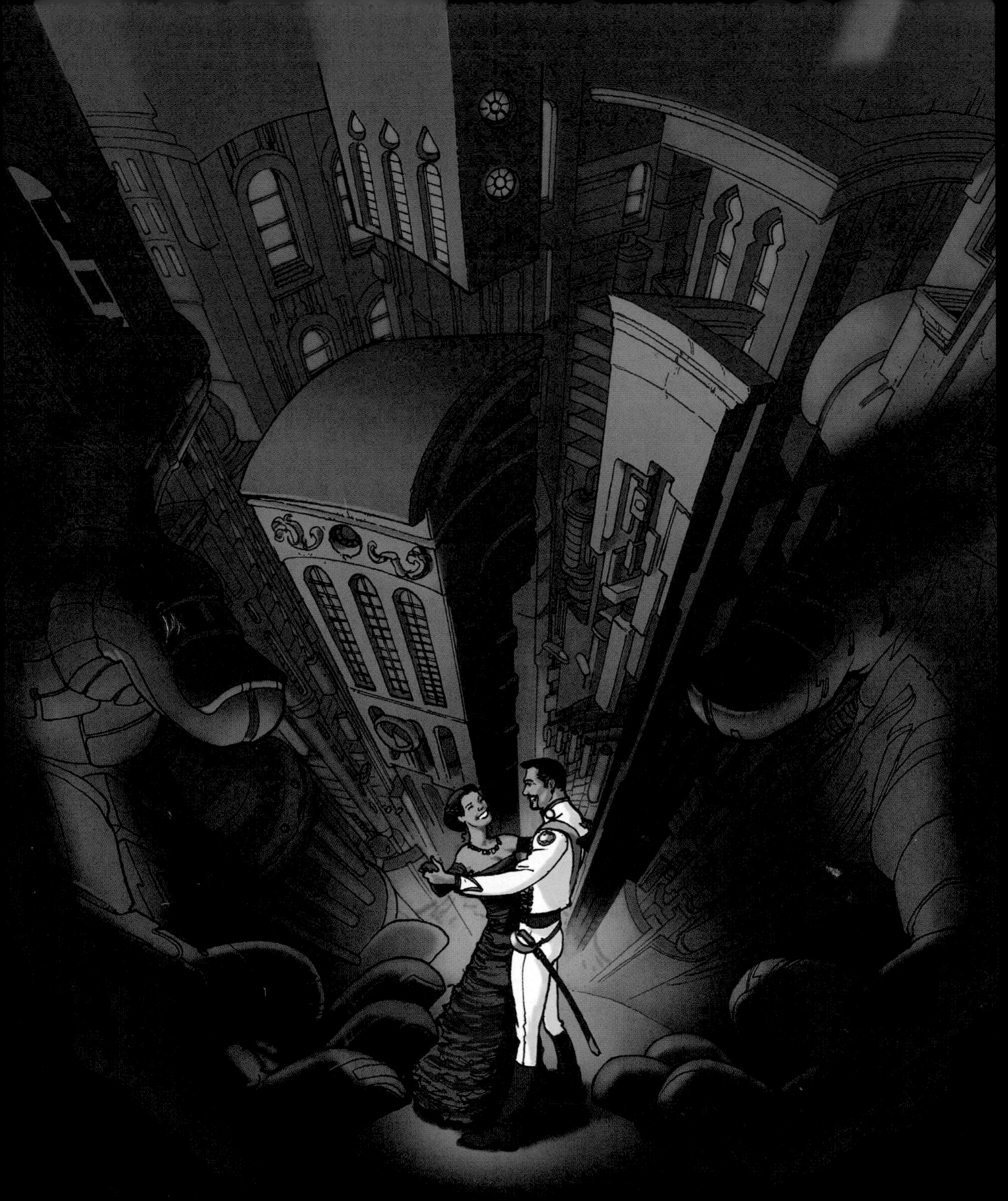

2000 AD Prog 1679: Cover by **Simon Fraser**

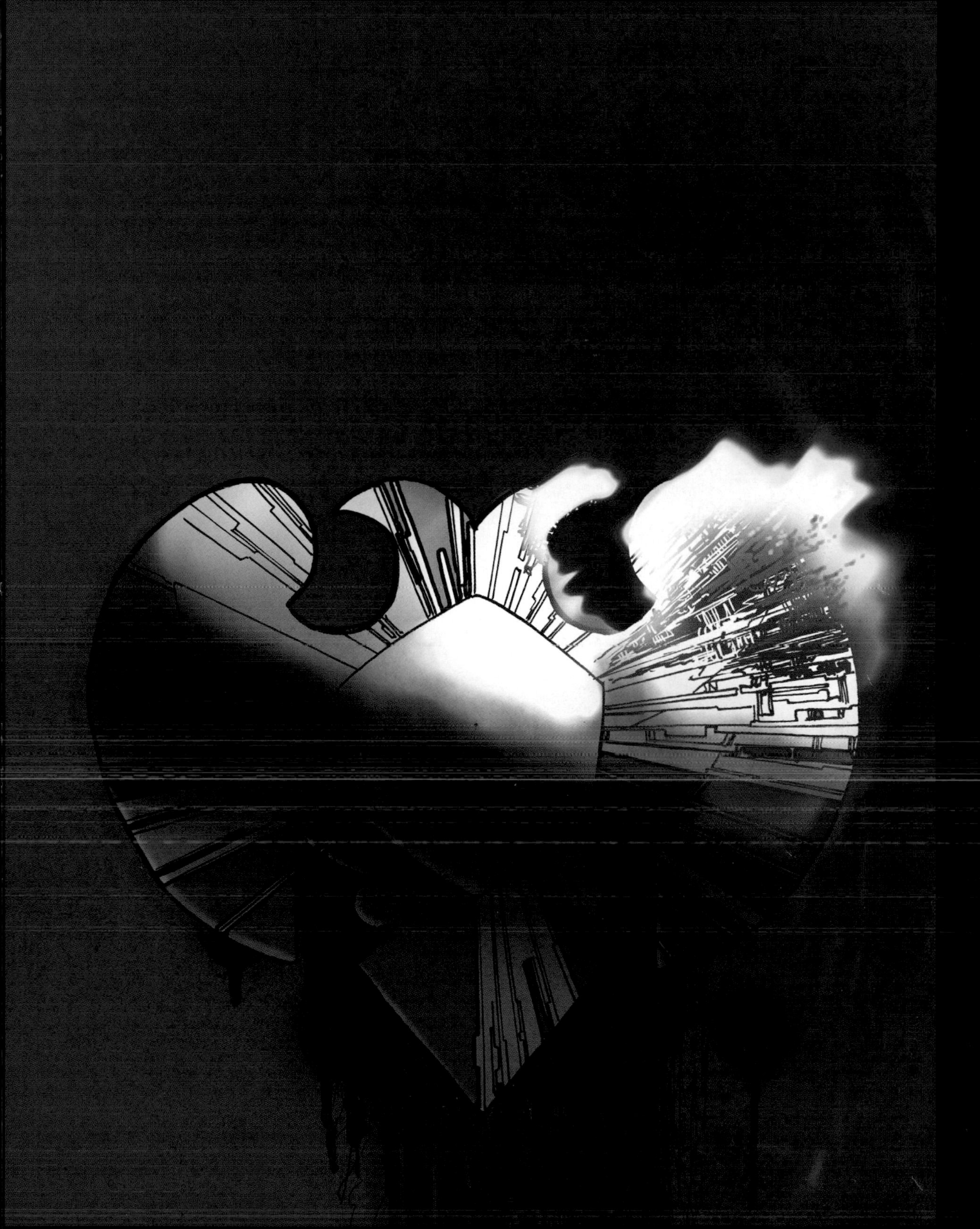

2000 AD Prog 1685: Cover by **Simon Fraser**

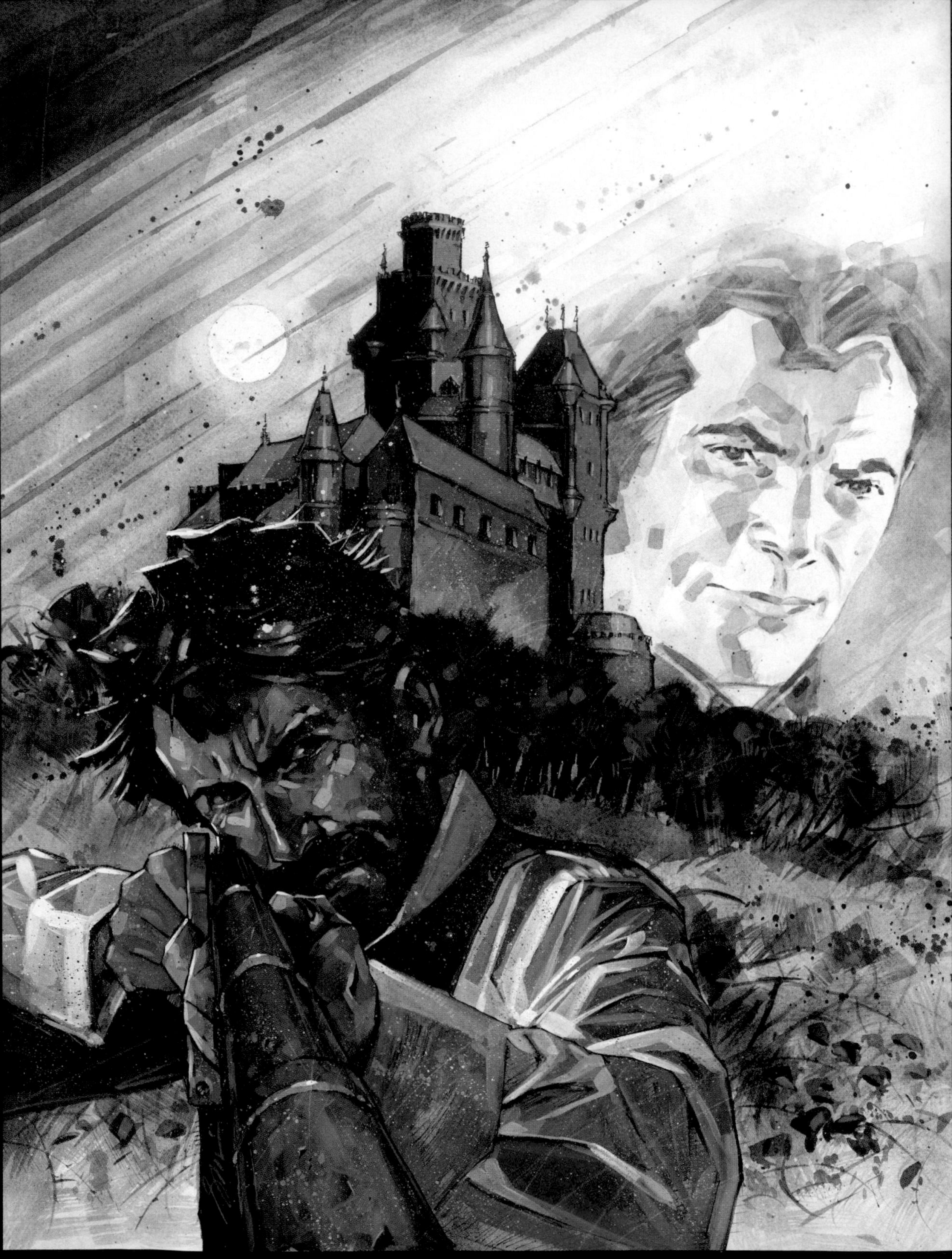

2000 AD Prog 1706: Cover by **Simon Davis**

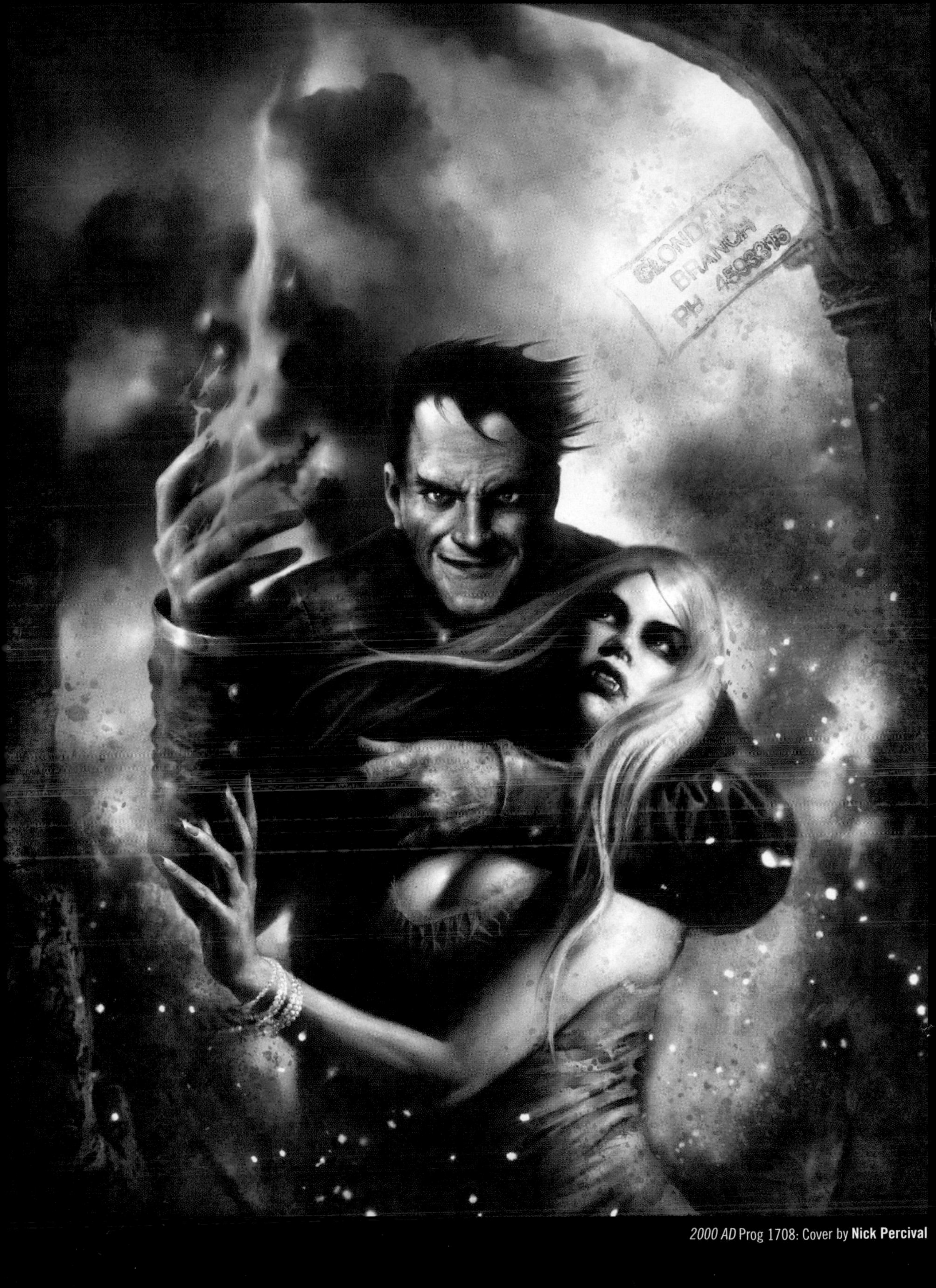

2000 AD Prog 1708: Cover by **Nick Percival**

ROBBIE MORRISON

Robbie Morrison is one of *2000 AD's* most popular writers, having co-created *The Bendatti Vendetta*, *Shakara*, *Shimura* and *Vanguard*, and has chronicled the adventures of *Judge Dredd* in *2000 AD* and the *Judge Dredd Megazine*. He is also co-creator of fan-favourite Russian rogue *Nikolai Dante*, which won an Eagle award for 'Best UK Character', beating *Judge Dredd* to this accolade for the first time in almost twenty years. In the US, he has written Spider-Man's *Tangled Web* for Marvel and *The Authority* for DC/WildStorm. His and artist Charlie Adlard's critically acclaimed graphic novel *White Death* has also been hugely successful in both Europe and the US.

JOHN BURNS

John Burns' painted art has graced several *2000 AD* series, notably *Judge Dredd* and *Nikolai Dante*, as well in as his own co-creation, *The Bendatti Vendetta*. He has also contributed to *Black Light, Doctor Sin, The Scarlet Apocrypha, Vector 13* and *Witchworld*. Outside the Galaxy's Greatest Comic, he has pencilled Eclipse's *ESPers* and the James Bond miniseries, *A Silent Armageddon*.

SIMON FRASER

Simon Fraser is best known to *2000 AD* fans as the co-creator of Russian rogue *Nikolai Dante*, whose adventures have been a staple of the comic since his debut in 1997. Fraser is also the co-creator of *Family* in the *Judge Dredd Megazine*, and has drawn *Judge Dredd* and *Shimura*.
His best-known non-*2000 AD* work is *Lux & Alby: Sign On and Save the Universe*, a collaboration with Scottish post-punk author Martin Millar. Fraser's creator-owned project *Lilly MacKenzie and the Mines of Charbydis* has recently seen print in the *Judge Dredd Megazine*. His website is www.simonfraser.net.